教育
お育

ORDINARY PEOPLE, EXTRAORDINARY LIVES

Political and Economic Change in a Tōhoku Village

Jackson H. Bailey

University of Hawaii Press
Honolulu

Library of Congress Cataloging-in-Publication Data

Bailey, Jackson H.
　　Ordinary people, extraordinary lives : political and economic
　change in a Tōhoku village / Jackson H. Bailey.
　　　　p.　　cm.
　　Includes bibliographical references and index.
　　ISBN 0–8248–1299–9
　　1. Tanohata-mura (Japan)—History.　I. Title.
DS897.T635B35　1991
　　952'.11—dc20　　　　　　　　　　　　　　　　　　91–15781
　　　　　　　　　　　　　　　　　　　　　　　　　　　　CIP

Text design by Alexandru Preiss
Kennedy & Preiss Design

Frontispiece: *Kyōiku Risson* (A Village Built on Education).
Calligraphy by Hayano Senpei, mayor of Tanohata.

CONTENTS

CONTENTS

INTRODUCTION

The resiliency and vitality of Japanese rural society and culture have long fascinated all those interested in comparative social change. Whether one examines social structure, basic values, economic development, or the phenomenon of urbanization, one is impressed by that resiliency and vitality. Sitting in the home of a fishing-farming family on the Rikuchū coast of Iwate Prefecture late one night in March 1983, my wife and I were again struck by this fact. We were there because the family's eldest son and his wife had rescued us from a blinding snowstorm that had clogged the roads and reduced visibility to zero. On the spur of the moment, they had invited us to spend the night in their home. Here were humble folk. The eldest son ran heavy road equipment in the off-season when his father (sixty-five and still an active fisherman) didn't need him in the fishing and farming operation. He and his bride of a few weeks, returning from their first official visit to her parents since their marriage, had found us about to be stranded for the night. He had a junior high school education and had been abroad once on the Iwate Prefecture–sponsored ship *Seinen no Fune,* which travels on a goodwill mission to Southeast Asia each year. None of the rest of his family had ever met a foreigner directly, however, to say nothing of hosting two overnight. They soon recovered from their initial awe of having both a foreigner *and* a professor in their midst, and we spent a delightful evening around the fire talking till well past midnight while the storm howled outside. They were impressive people, unsophisticated but wise, generous, and kind. They represent a tremendous strength in a society that is being battered ever more fiercely by the worldwide storms of social and economic change.

Although these people and many others we met in our year in Tano-hata have the same solid, sensible humanity that we find in the people farming the cornfields of Indiana and the soybean and wheat fields of Illinois, Iowa, and Nebraska, the common strands of humanity that bind us fall far short of telling the whole story. There are fundamental cultural differences between Americans and Japanese, which are produced and reinforced by differences in historical experience. For instance, the home of some of our closest friends in Tanohata, a dairy farm family, was built before 1730. It has a traditional thatched roof *(kayabuki)*, and the original beams, blackened with age and smoke, still show here and there in the main rooms. Two hundred fifty years of family tradition in one spot make the life experience of this family very different from that of an Indiana farm family, with less than half that history on the same land.

Equally important to recognize is the variety of rural culture that exists within Japan itself. Differences of climate—from the subtropical conditions of southern Kyūshū to the short growing season of northeast Honshū and Hokkaidō, from the snow country on the Japan Sea side of Honshū, to the temperate Inland Sea and the harsh northeast Pacific coast —have provided dramatically different physical environments for the development of variations on the basic patterns of mainstream Japanese culture. The researcher and student of Japanese culture must take these regional differences into account and be careful not to overgeneralize from one set of research data.

Studies of Japanese villages and rural life abound in Japanese scholarly literature, and there are a significant number of them in English as well. The first important study by a Westerner, John Embree's *Suye Mura: A Japanese Village,* has been supplemented in recent years by the publication of his wife's research on the role of women in the life of the village (Robert J. Smith and Ella Lury Wiswell, *The Women of Suye Mura*). Basic rural social structure (the so-called *dozoku* system) was studied by John Bennett and his Japanese colleagues in the early 1950s. At the end of that decade, Richard Beardsley and the University of Michigan Center for Japanese Studies published a baseline book, *Village Japan.* More specialized studies followed in the 1960s and 1970s, and a number of significant monographs appeared: Edward Norbeck's study of Takashima, which includes a follow-up some fifteen years later *(Takashima: A Japanese Fishing Community),* and Smith's study, *Kurusu: The Price of Progress in a Japanese Village, 1951–1975,* are particularly important for the longitudinal depth they give to social science research. Theodore Bestor's recent book *Neighborhood Tokyo* brings a fine counterpoint to studies of rural Japan, and Ronald Dore's *Shinohata* sets new standards for scholarly research and writing. L. Keith Brown's translation of the village records of Shinjō in Iwate Prefecture just as the village was being absorbed in a municipal consolidation gives insight into Japanese views of themselves as they confront social and economic change.

Also important to this study has been the growing body of literature on regional politics and economic development. The work of Ronald

Aqua, Richard Samuels, and Steven Reed, in particular, provides significant new ways of examining the structure and working of Japanese society at the regional and local level. (See, e.g., T. MacDougall, ed., *Political Leadership in Contemporary Japan.*) Additionally, I have drawn heavily on regional publications in Japanese from such organizations as the *Iwate Keizai Kenkyū-sho* (Iwate Economic Research Institute) and official documents from the prefectures, towns, and villages of the Tōhoku region.

These studies and others like them in English and Japanese provide a relatively full and broad-ranging view of the nature of Japanese society, its values, and the worldview of rural and small town Japanese. As the pace of social and economic change has quickened in Japan over the last thirty years, Japanese sociologists and social critics have hastened to point out the tensions and dislocations that have resulted. They have also examined the basic shift in national government policy for agriculture that occurred in the early 1960s. A new national policy was put in place by the Basic Agricultural Law of 1961. This law established two fundamental policy objectives: (1) rationalization of land-holdings (i.e., bringing together a family's various holdings to make all of them contiguous) to increase the scale of production and (2) mechanization of the agricultural production process.

These policies accelerated the pace of change and dramatically stimulated the shift of population from rural to urban areas. In 1955, 39 percent of the working population was in agriculture; in 1980, only 9 percent. In 1955, 18 percent of GNP was generated by agriculture; by 1980 only 2.5 percent came from that sector. These changes have produced vectors of force in Japanese life that are still at work. They have been disruptive and disorienting for many, but at the same time the material benefits and the rise in the overall standard of living in rural Japan has been dramatic. Ironically, the crisis in Japanese agriculture in the early 1990s, precipitated by massive surpluses of subsidized home-grown rice and deepened by rising trade friction with the United States, is, in one sense, the result of the success of that 1961 policy shift.

The study of political development and economic change takes on added meaning when it is placed against the background of national trends, especially since it complements the studies of other regions of Japan done over the past three decades. The accompanying map of Japan, which show's the locations of these studies, brings this point into clear focus. Tanohata, situated as it is on the northeast coast, away from the main rice-growing areas, represents a very different part of Japan. Yet its differences, significant as they are, can be seen in proper perspective only as part of the larger picture of national trends of development and change.

Since Tanohata, though rural, is not a rice-producing area, it has, until recently, been outside the pale of mainstream developments in Japanese agricultural life. Then in the 1970s, with its fledgling dairy business,

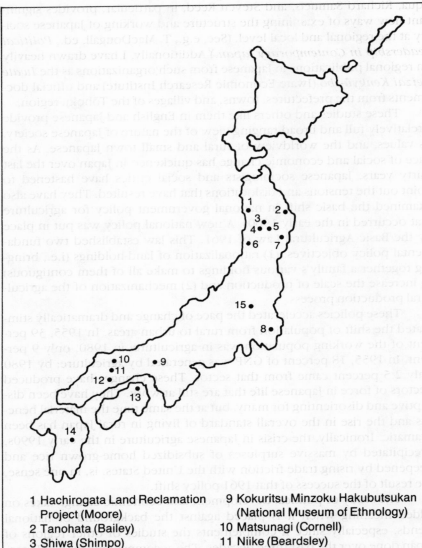

1 Hachirogata Land Reclamation
   Project (Moore)
2 Tanohata (Bailey)
3 Shiwa (Shimpo)
4 Shinjo (Brown)
5 Tono (Kato & Yoneyama)
6 Toyohara
7 Nakada (Moore)
8 Miyamoto-cho (Bestor)
   Mamachi (Vogel)
   Shitayama-cho (Dore)

9 Kokuritsu Minzoku Hakubutsukan
   (National Museum of Ethnology)
10 Matsunagi (Cornell)
11 Niike (Beardsley)
12 Takashima (Norbeck)
13 Kurusu (Smith)
14 Suye Mura
   (John & Ella Embree)
15 Shinohata (Dore)

Village studies and ethnographic research areas.

and in the 1980s, with its developing contract vegetable production and tourism industries, it has moved into the mainstream. Just where Tanohata will fit in the stage of rural development that results from the present crisis, however, remains to be seen.

Although in socio-political and even in more general economic terms Tanohata is now fully involved in the mainstream of Japanese life, its entry is so recent and the pace of change has been so rapid that one can, by studying this microcosm, highlight some of the key issues now being confronted throughout Japanese society at both the regional and the national level.

The question remains: Why this village? Why this study? First, Tanohata is different in important ways from the typical Japanese rural village. These differences arise from its geography and climate, which both, in turn, have a bearing on its history. Though the village is not especially large (155.64 square kilometers) compared to many in the Tōhoku, it contains not only coastal fishing hamlets but also upland farms and mountain forests. Its climate is significantly different from that of the surrounding villages. In this sense Tanohata represents the variety and diversity of Japanese culture.

Second, Tanohata shares with the whole Tōhoku region (and other outlying parts of Japan such as Kyūshū) certain fundamental socioeconomic problems of the postwar era. The high-growth decade of the 1960s masked these problems but exacerbated them as well. Chief among them are the related phenomena of *dekasegi* (seasonal employment of males outside the home village) and urbanization. Resulting from these phenomena are two other problems: finding males to succeed to the farms *(atotsugi mondai)* and finding wives for these young males *(hanayome mondai)*. In this day and age, who would want to marry a young farmer, and who would want to be under the thumb of a demanding mother-in-law?

Third, Tanohata has a gorgeous coastline, and the hills and mountains of the interior frame farms and hamlets dramatically. But in addition to its beauty, it is a village engaged in discovering itself and building a new life, individually and collectively, in a bootstrap operation, with all the problems, successes, and failures that that implies. Its people are attempting to define the future and make it happen. And, having observed this process unfolding in the decade of the 1970s and participated in it vicariously through several generations of undergraduate students and graduate teachers, I only naturally wanted to understand what was happening more fully and to chronicle it.

In that village, and on the Rikuchū coast, more generally, we can trace the same process that took place in the central areas of Japan over four decades occurring in only two. The very compression of this process highlights what has happened. Since the changes have happened so fast and so recently, people are still poignantly aware of them and the "what" and the "why" can be documented and analyzed more clearly than at the national level. Because Tanohata is small and remote, we can identify and isolate the key factors and plot the course of events with more surety. Tanohata is not typical, perhaps, but it is illustrative. Its story commands attention both on its own terms and as a means to a larger understanding of Japan in the late twentieth century.

Few stories have a clear beginning point, but Tanohata of the 1950s was light-years away from Tanohata of the 1970s. The 1953 law regarding consolidation of towns and villages *(Shichōson gappei-ho)* created an environment nationally into which Tanohata would be dragged, against its will; that law literally changed the landscape and the lives of the people there. In broadest terms, historically, we can see that law as the original agent of change in Tanohata. The law and its results by 1957 had generated forces that impinged directly on Tanohata, as they did on hundreds of other towns and villages in the Tōhoku and thoughout the country. Tanohata's response was unusual and traumatic in the extreme. The village resisted and in the end refused to accept the prefectural consolidation plan, precipitating a political crisis within the village and in Tanohata's relationship with its neighbors and the prefectural government (see Chapter 2 for a detailed discussion of this crisis).

In the 1950s, when Tanohata was an isolated village, life there was so miserable that those who could do so moved away. Many of those who remained saw no hope for themselves. By the 1980s, however, Tanohata had joined mainstream Japanese life; it had a national, even an international, reputation and aspirations. Further, in certain respects it was in the forefront of the vital experiments in hybrid public-private enterprise aimed at regional development in Japan. How this came about is a dramatic story of political leadership and of bootstrap efforts by ordinary people.

In recounting the story of Tanohata, I will make every attempt to relate it to larger entities and larger trends in Japan; it is not just a quaint tale from a strange far-off place. The issues faced by the people of Tanohata are much the same as those faced in other parts of Japan, and in many remote rural areas of the United States as well. When the village's mayor visited the United States in 1984, he found much to interest him and common problems to discuss with people in the hills and valleys of Vermont, where tourism and economic development are "bread and butter" issues as they are for him and his colleagues on the Rikuchū coast. The sense of kinship that Mayor Hayano felt underscored the fact that Tanohata had become part of a modern industrial society.

Tanohata is a village with little history. What documents remain are scattered and fragmented. The village is compiling a *son-shi* (village history) but it is really a *mura no kokorozashi* (reminiscences of the village), a kind of memoir, rather than a real history. The materials are just not available to write the latter. The records of the oldest families in the village go back to the middle or even the early part of the Edo period (1603–1868), but no family, so far as I have been able to determine, claims to be able to trace its history in any detail beyond that. There is ample evidence of human life in this region all the way back to Jōmon times (c. 5000–300 B.C.). Some magnificent Jōmon artifacts have been unearthed in the village; many are kept as uncatalogued family heirlooms. On an afternoon walk in the fall of 1982, my wife and I were invited into a farmhouse for tea and proudly shown some lovely Jōmon pieces that had been unearthed when the house was rebuilt ten years before. Most accounts of regional history (e.g., the *Tanohata fudōki*) speak of the early settlements in the village by mainstream Japanese as going back seven or eight hundred years.

Records are spotty even for nineteenth-century history, and one is forced to depend on scanty documentary evidence to reconstruct the story of Tanohata all the way down to the 1950s. A few brief charts of statistics on population, occupational distribution, crops, and transportation are available for the first half of the twentieth century. These sketchy materials, when combined with a few family records and interviews with older people, make it possible to develop at least an outline of village history over the last century. The situation is in part the result of the fact that Tanohata as a *mura* or village is an artificial creation of the Meiji-period Town and Village Consolidation Law of 1889, when three old constituent *mura* were combined to establish the present Tanohata. A document tracing the history of one of the primary schools for a century in Tanohata also provides helpful material.

Fortunately for the period from 1952 to 1966 a few major documents and studies of the village and the region are available. Such materials provide the basis for corroborating oral reports and information obtained through interviews with a variety of people in the village. These documents include two Iwate Prefecture-sponsored studies (in 1953 and 1955), one on education and one done as part of the implementation of the 1953 national Town and Village Consolidation Law. There are also a 1964 village publication entitled *Tanohata sonsei yōran* (A survey of conditions in Tanohata) and a special study done in 1964 of Tanohata as a village in a "backward and remote region" *(hekichi)* by a research group from Senshū University in Tokyo. These four documents give a poignant —and dismal—picture of just how backward Tanohata remained in the two postwar decades.

From 1966 on, there is ample documentation of conditions and of the process of change in Tanohata. One of the most important sources are the transcripts of the annual State of the Village addresses given by the mayor to the Village Assembly in March *(Sonchō shisei enjutsu).*[1] In addition, planning documents, reports, and other editions of the *Sonsei yōran* help to fill in the picture. By the mid-1970s, carefully kept statistics

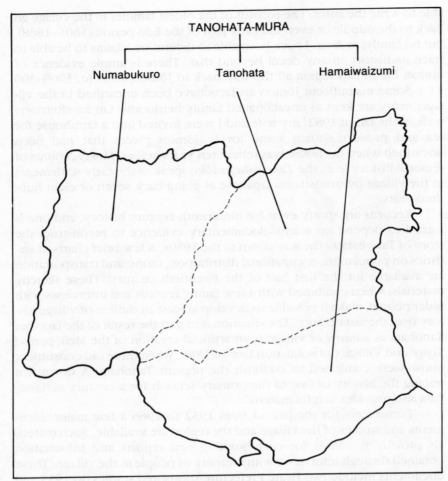

The three constituent mura which were merged in 1889.
Source: Tanohata-mura, *Nōson sōgō seibi Keikaku-sho,* 1982, p. 4.

and comparative charts and data were being used extensively in making reports and developing planning documents. By the 1980s there seemed to be some danger that the village would become overly bureaucratized and inundated by reports and planning documents.

The other major sources of information and documentation for this study have been interviews and photographs. I have recorded the way of life and documented the coexistence and interaction of new and old in the daily round of people's activities. My wife and I have also interviewed a wide range of people including village elders, those responsible for education, for construction, and for general village administration in Tanohata, and ordinary people in many walks of life. We have been careful to select a reasonable cross-section of people representing the geographic, economic, and age distribution of the village. We have included in our interviews probing questions on problems and setbacks as well as accomplishments and progress, and we have interviewed both supporters and critics of the present village administration.

The story of Tanohata raises many questions. Two, in particular, seem relevant here. First, there is the issue of local autonomy and initiative versus central policy and leadership, and, second, the issue of the role and nature of political leadership itself at the local level. A third issue lurks in the background as well—the nature of the whole process of rural development. What is the message of the Tanohata experience in this regard? My conclusion will address each of these issues in turn. First, however, let us examine where Tanohata fits in this larger context.

That the pace of change has been so rapid—two decades for Tanohata instead of four—is what makes the story so compelling. The intensity of change that engulfed these people is almost palpable. Moreover, Tanohata's story has the potential to draw a larger meaning that will enhance our understanding of Japan and its place in the contemporary world, as well as shed light on the whole process of social and economic development. Why is this so?

First, we have the data to trace what actually happened in Tanohata between 1955 and 1985. As a result we then can attempt to explain why it happened with some hope of success. Development came to Tanohata for the following reasons: (1) conditions had become so bad in the first half of the 1960s that people were willing to accept new leadership and new ways; (2) national trends and conditions that were creating tremendous growth all over Japan in the 1960s had created an opportunity for change and made available the material resources for Tanohata to "plug into" this process and become part of it; (3) dynamic leadership emerged and gave direction, cohesion, and thrust to the development efforts; (4) as the process gathered momentum in the 1970s, opportunities were seized by the leaders for Tanohata to step forth as a recognized regional force in both economic development and in international education. The success of these efforts in turn fed the development process itself.

Conventional wisdom about Japan has said that political leadership for social and economic change comes from the top down and is characterized by what is called vertical insularity; that is, local units take their lead and focus their efforts on their relationships to central authority (at the prefectural or national level) and have relatively less contact horizontally with other units.

Recent work by political scientists challenges this assumption. My research data support this challenge. In fact, even though Tanohata benefited tremendously from prefectural and national government policies and received from above massive infusions of capital and other economic aid in the period 1965–1985, the village has overtaken and become a leader of a peer group of local units that started with better resources and better locations, units that had at least equal structural access to higher-echelon help and resources. Tanohata, through local initiative, sometimes even in spite of higher-echelon opposition, did things that have given it a distinctive place in the contemporary scene. At the same time Tanohata is not just one of a kind, a strange "botanical sport." Other local units as far away as Oita Prefecture in northern Kyūshū or even Kagoshima in southern Kyūshū have carved out for themselves special roles and have been recognized in similar ways. This phenomenon of local development is particularly useful to study as a counterweight to superficial analyses of Japanese societal structure that overemphasize "top-down" political and economic initiative.

Having delineated what actually happened, inevitably one must raise the second issue. How and why did it happen? The answer in the case of Tanohata is clearly because of dynamic, even charismatic, political leadership. Hayano Senpei was elected to his first term as mayor of Tanohata in August 1965. He was re-elected to a fifth term, running unopposed, in 1981; thus, as he completed that fifth term in 1985, he had presided over twenty years of phenomenal social and economic change. Four aspects of his work, each in a different way, confirm the significance of his role in this process.

1. In the years after the 1961 consolidation fiasco, it was Hayano, then at the beginning of his first term as mayor, who articulated effectively the call to create a real Tanohata. His clear and steady vision of that goal and his commitment to vigorous action to attain it inspired the citizens of Tanohata to transcend hamlet loyalties for the greater good of the whole.
2. He recognized early that long-term growth and prosperity required a fundamental commitment to education. He made that commitment, articulated it, sought the economic resources to implement the policy and made that policy the cornerstone of his administration. His slogan, *Kyōiku risson* (A village built on education), has been a watchword in Tanohata for twenty years.
3. Hayano has been signally successful in getting development funds from higher echelons of government for local projects, not only for education but for a variety of economic development initiatives. He has used the system as political reality required but without being the "handmaiden" of central government policy implementation, as critics occasionally charged. In addition to tapping outside funding sources successfully, he has also built a larger local tax base. During his tenure, Tanohata's budgetary dependence on outside sources has gone down from 94.5 percent to about 87 percent.
4. His vision of the future led him to define Tanohata's larger world not just in national but in international terms. In the mid-1970s, he articu-

lated and implemented a policy of initiatives in international education that has become a model for all of Iwate Prefecture and has been recognized nationally as a contribution to Japan's emerging need to internationalize. By 1985, twenty other towns and villages in Iwate Prefecture were following Tanohata's (i.e., Hayano's) lead by supporting activities in international education with a substantial commitment of local funds.

The larger issue of the meaning of the Tanohata experience for rural development does not lend itself to easy generalizations. Yet as distinctive, perhaps even exceptional, as Tanohata is, some tentative conclusions can be drawn in the areas of political leadership and structural interaction between central and regional or local bodies engaged in the development process. Political vision and charismatic leadership can make a difference. (Some might say, "even in Japan.") On the structural side, for development to be successful a delicate balance must be created between central authority and initiative and local autonomy. Local entities that lack initiative and drive almost surely will continue to languish, and the failure or unwillingness to "play ball" within the ground rules and under the leadership of higher authority may doom local initiative from the start. Tanohata seems to have balanced those requisites with relative effectiveness.

Getting to Know Tanohata

Today's visitor to Tanohata enjoys the luxury of paved roads and regular train service and finds the facilities and amenities Japanese and Westerners have come to expect when they travel. It is difficult to imagine the dramatic changes that have taken place in the preceding thirty years as the people of Tanohata have come to participate in mainstream culture and economic life in Japan. The reminiscences of old-timers in the village, however, vividly, convey the look and feel of Tanohata of the late 1940s and 1950s. Iwami Hisako, who moved to the village in 1948, has been an articulate and astute participant in and observer of village life for more than forty years. Her words give life and a poignant sense of drama to the way Tanohata looked and felt in those days when she first arrived. After her first husband, and her first child, died, she received a letter from her brother-in-law in Iwate, asking her to come to Tanohata.

BEYOND THE MOUNTAIN ROAD

"At that time I was living in my parents' home in Ōsaka Prefecture. My husband's and child's graves were in Yagi, in the town of Taneichi in Kunohe-*gun* (county), Iwate. I went there first, and the next morning set out for Tanohata-*mura*. I took the train to the end of the

Hachinohe Line in Kuji, and then took a bus from there to Fudai-*mura*. It was a difficult two-hour journey over an incredibly rough road. My luggage was tossed about. It was afternoon when I got off at Fudai, at the end of the line. There I was met by my deceased husband's half-brother, who was to take me over a short-cut mountain road to Tanohata.

> Jagged rocks wet by the Tani River
> You offered me your soft hand to help me cross

"We sat on the rocks and ate our *nigiri* (kneaded rice balls). In the distance we could hear the sounds of approaching evening, the temple *taiko* drums drifted to us—a pastoral song. . . .

"Here was a world unto itself. The sky, the clouds, the mountains, the streams, the sea, the people who lived here, too. They all lived and moved in a kind of purified atmosphere. I became completely enraptured by Tanohata."[3]

Over the next year and a half, Mrs. Iwami was confirmed in her love of Tanohata and came to regard it as her real home. In March 1950, she was appointed public health nurse at Tanohata middle school; soon afterward, she married her brother-in-law, who was the priest at Tanohata's only temple.

"Tanohata then had a population of 6,400 but no doctor, and only in the coastal hamlets was there even one midwife. Right near the temple there was the barracks-like, ramshackle middle school, and I was responsible for it and for the five branch middle schools. The principal said 'Think of yourself as a doctor and be ready to consult about anything,' and he introduced me to the children. I thought: 'I've really gotten myself into something.' No matter what I was supposed to be, instead of being a public health teacher I turned out to be the person whom students' families consulted about any kind of illness.

"In the village office there were first aid clinic supplies, and I found myself using them. A man who had gashed his foot with a sickle came with a gaping wound, and I sewed him up without any proper sutures. Most of those who came with stomach ailments had worms and were cured with small doses of santonin, but there were people who had tapeworms, which had to be treated [outside the village]. The neighboring town, Iwaizumi, had a dentist, but you had to walk all day to get there, so people really couldn't get dental care. Since most people let such things as cavities go, when people caught cold and the colds spread, the number of people with toothaches and other tooth trouble increased because the cold congested the sinuses around the teeth and made those with cavities ache. I got the dentist (in Iwaizumi) to teach me how to give quick treatment, and I got hold of a simple instrument to clean out cavities. You can't imagine how even this one small instrument could help the villagers. Children—

and adults, too—would come to me crying and holding their cheeks where they hurt. Once their pain subsided, they'd go away smiling and overjoyed.

"Treatment for pregnancy and childbirth was my responsibility. Women in the village in general gave birth with the help of their mother, an elderly neighbor-woman, their mother-in-law, or even sometimes their husband. There were even startling tales of brave women who, having given birth, would wash the baby themselves. They would ask for help from me only when birth itself was difficult or the placenta didn't clean out properly. Usually when I went to help, I would be able to take care of things fairly easily.

"In the autumn of 1956, I was asked by the village office to become the officially designated 'Pioneer Health Worker' in the village and I accepted. In 1953 my second son had been born, so I now had two children at home. Though by 1956 I had already been in the village for more than six years, even so I didn't know where the pioneer land in the village was, or what life was like there. . . .[2]

"The Magisawa pioneer settlement of thirty-three households had been enveloped by a mountain fire fed by a strong wind in April 1956, and twenty-two houses, which had only recently been built, along with their contents, had been consumed. The people suffered through the winter cold in temporary shacks, but come spring, they set to with a will to rebuild their homes. The head of the local co-op in Magisawa told me that after the disaster people made up their minds to pull together and go into dairying, and in the end they were better off. . . .

"In 1965, Magisawa Bridge linking Tanohata to areas to the south opened. It was 105 meters high and 240 meters long, and because it joined National Road 45 from Jishoku-zaka and Matsumae-zawa, buses could now travel that route into the village. In addition, a new clinic was completed in the center of the village. It included facilities for simple hospital care.

"Since then, twenty or more years have passed and the village has developed tremendously. . . . At the same time, I think we must recognize and not overlook the negative factors that came with all of this fast-paced change.

"There is the reality that a certain percentage of the rise in income is from *dekasegi* [seasonal work for men outside the village; see Chapter 5]. Many of the wives working in small local businesses that have sprung up have come to depend on "instant" foods to feed the children, and since the children go home from school to watch television, it is rare now to see kids and hear the noise of kids playing outside.

". . . The sea is more and more polluted, and the catch of *uni* [sea urchins] and *awabi* [abalone] diminishes year by year. That ocean that so fascinated me when I first came no longer exists. In a world of economic growth, the gulls and cormorants are no longer there to catch fish. Instead, they gather to grab the bread thrown to them by passengers on the sightseeing boats.

"A few years ago this village was designated by the prefecture as a prime location for an atomic generating plant. Those of us in the women's group organized a campaign against it. Fortunately, the prefectural plan was not realized, and we heaved a great sigh of relief.

"In a daily life now filled with conveniences, we need to resist being caught up in the stream of economic materialism. I believe we need to consider the joy of living here, rethink how we can preserve the most important things, and bend every effort to that end.

Let only the good things from the city cross Shii Ōhashi (Shii Bridge)
And be preserved in this world of Tanohata."

Iwami Hisako's description and her comments underscore both the stark beauty and the humanity of the village. Her assessment of what life was like was confirmed time and again in other interviews, and these personal stories give human substance to the statistics and analysis that later chapters will present.

My own introduction to Tanohata came after the process of development and change was well under way. In early December of 1972, I boarded an express train with Waseda Professor Oda Yasuichi for the eight-hour trip up the bumpy Tōhoku main line bound for Morioka. We arrived in mid-afternoon at the crowded Morioka station. The scars of World War II remained in that part of the city; the area around the station, which had been bombed, was still frowsy and ramshackle. A formal audience with Governor Chida that afternoon renewed the connection I had established some years before and revealed a fascinating glimpse of a man I would come to know and admire over the next few years. As a young man just out of college, Chida, a Waseda University graduate, had gone abroad to the United States. He ended up in Ohio and enrolled in Heidelberg College, where he completed a second undergraduate degree. He returned to Japan and plunged into a career in politics. He became one of the most important postwar political figures in the Tōhoku region, serving in the House of Councilors in the 1950s and then, in 1963, becoming governor of Iwate Prefecture. He served four terms, and was an inspiring leader of Iwate's bootstrap effort toward creating a better life for its people. Education was the centerpiece of his vision, and he had a long-term commitment to it as a fundamental strategy for development. This explained why officials of the Iwate Board of Education had sought me out in Tokyo four years before and invited me to Iwate to launch the English Teachers Program. Chida's vision included international education, which he saw as another way to enhance Iwate's educational programs.

With Professor Oda I spent the night at a traditional Japanese inn in Morioka, for the trip to Tanohata would take much of the next day. Getting to Tanohata was something of an endurance test. In fact, even in the

1970s people from Morioka dreaded having to go out to the coast on business. Public officials from Morioka talked of a minimum of three days needed to do any business out there—one day to get there, a day to get anything done, and a third day to return to Morioka. The burden of this is underscored when one remembers that in 1972 the Shinkansen Bullet Train had been running between Tokyo and Ōsaka for nearly a decade, allowing officials and businessmen to cover four times the distance from Morioka to the coast, do a day's work, and return home by mid-evening of the same day!

Professor Oda was to take me to Tanohata, put me in the hands of his associate who represented him there, do his own work, and then return to Tokyo, leaving me to fend for myself. The night at the inn and the train ride to the coast the next day proved invaluable opportunities to absorb some of Professor Oda's philosophy and objectives for the Waseda Program in Tanohata. Much later, I learned that he had spent several years in Los Angeles teaching English to Japanese students and immigrants, but on our trip to Iwate, Japanese was our only medium of communication and he gave no hint that he even understood English. No doubt I was being both tested and indoctrinated. The thrust of his approach in Tanohata was austere self-help, combined with respect for local sensibilities and traditional Japanese cultural values. After supper at the inn he brought out a brush, ink stone, and ink and set about recording impressions and ideas from the day in a journal. Then he turned to me, produced a copy of the history of Shii no Mori, the self-help reforestation center in Tanohata, published two years before, and proceeded to inscribe it to me. On the page following his personal inscription is the dedication of the book, which begins: "For our universe, let there be one world and one desire: a passionate commitment to life. This is what it means to be human." What a combination this man was—scholar, teacher, artist, patriot, practical doer, and quiet, sensitive listener! He made it clear to me that we were not going to some backwoods, poverty-stricken village far removed from civilization. Rather he was taking me to meet his colleagues and friends, who were providing important educational opportunities for him and his students. How fortunate I was to have this kind of an introduction to Tanohata!

We got off the train from Morioka in Miyako after a three-hour ride and were met by Professor Oda's associate, Date Katsumi, who came to pick us up in a rugged four–wheel drive station wagon. The drive to Tanohata would take another two hours on National Highway 45, much of which was still unpaved.

Date was an energetic man in his early thirties, who moved with a confidence that belied his youth and relative inexperience. To me he was an old-timer. He obviously knew and was well-known in Tanohata. He paid Professor Oda the kind of respect and deference due one's senior. Only later did I discover that he was Oda's prize pupil and *deshi* (disciple); in fact, Oda and his wife had served as formal go-betweens for Date's marriage. Date had grown up in the neighboring town of Iwaizumi and gone to Waseda. Oda had brought Date with him to Tanohata in the mid-sixties, introduced him to the mayor and thereby unwittingly launched him on what would become a spectacular career of leadership in regional development. I was handed over to Date and placed in his care for the next few days. By the next morning Professor Oda had disappeared and I was on my own with Date.

He packed me into the jeep belonging to the village office, a 1950s-type vehicle being produced by Mitsubishi Motors under a licensing agreement with American Motors, to accompany him on his round of visits to farms in the village. I was astonished at the sight of silos and dairy cattle. This was not the Japanese countryside I was familiar with. There was no rice paddy and no terracing; cows were grazing here and there. At one stop, after introducing me to the farmer, Date immediately got down to business, inspecting some of his fall vegetables and showing him samples of seed. Evidently they were talking about next year's plans. There were no formalities, no tea drinking, just direct discussion of the business at hand, with no undue deference on either side. Clearly it was a discussion based on mutual respect, and I was accepted as part of a total context without need for much ceremony or explanation.

By late afternoon we had made our way across one major ravine and over a mountain pass to the far side of the village, to a hamlet called Tashiro. Date explained that we would visit the Kumagais, an old, established family. Its members now made their living by dairy farming, but in the Edo period (1603–1868) they had raised horses to supply the samurai of the Nambu fief. There we would spend the night and discuss plans for the Earlham group's arrival next summer.

The Kumagais' house, on a bluff above the narrow valley in which Tashiro was located, was a large, stately thatched-roof building, flanked on one side by the white stucco *kura* (family storehouse) that bespoke means, status, and continuity and on the other by a large shop, a silo, and the dairy barn. A red International tractor stood by the shop, highlighting the contrast of old and new.

Four generations were housed here. Daily operation of the farm was being turned over to the family patriarch's grandson, Ryūkō, and Ryūkō's wife, Sachiko, young people in their thirties, he a university graduate in agricultural economics. They had one child, with another on the way. Grandpa Kumajirō, the patriarch, then in his late seventies, was still vigorous of mind and able to be about and observe operations. His wife had died some years before. Ryūkō's mother, Tsuya, was one of five daughters born to Kumajirō. Since there had been no sons in that generation, Ryūkō's father, Shōzō, had been brought into the family to marry Tsuya and carry on the family line and name.[4] Here was the traditional Tōhoku family structure alive and vigorously in evidence. This family was the *honke* (main family); I learned later that there were several *bunke* (branch families) living in Tashiro. At New Year's and Obon, the summer festival honoring the spirits of the dead, representatives of the *bunke* climb the hill to bring gifts and pay their respects before the ancestral tablets of the *honke.*

After milking, chores, and supper with the men around the *kotatsu* (a charcoal fire set into the floor and covered with a table, with a blanket over our laps to hold in the heat), tea and fruit were brought and Date explained our request to Kumajirō. We had come to ask Kumagais to host an American faculty family for two weeks while the Earlham students worked in the reforestation project. The discussion approached the matter indirectly, with long pauses and explanations of who I was and why Americans would want to come to Tanohata. One tense moment climaxed in a discussion of World War II and the Occupation of Japan. Shōzō had been a soldier in Manchuria; the family's only other direct contact with the war and with Americans had been during the Occupation. Those contacts had not been pleasant. I explained that as a Quaker conscientious objector I had served in the U.S. Army Medical Corps for a year in Japan in 1945–46, and then returned to Japan with my wife in 1951 to spend three years doing relief work with the American Friends Service Committee. The conversation ended inconclusively, and I retired for the night, wondering what might come of that conversation.

Several days later, Date received word that the Kumagais had agreed to let Professor Smith and his wife and three children stay with them for two weeks the next summer. Years later, Date explained what had happened in his book on Tanohata:

> Professor Oda introduced us to Kumagai Kumajirō of Tashiro. Kumajirō (now deceased) was head of the Wayama-ke (the *ie,* or household, name of the Kumagai family), a very old *ie* but one with a long history of commitment to education. We went and asked the Kumagais to take the Smiths for two weeks. Their house was large, but I could hardly imagine that it would be possible for them to take in another family of five people, Americans who could speak hardly any Japanese! However, for all my worry, the conversation between Kumajirō and Professor Bailey went smoothly.
>
> ### BRIDGE ACROSS THE PACIFIC
>
> The Pacific War was still a recent event in people's minds, since many from this village had lost their lives in it. Inevitably the conversation turned to the Japanese-American conflict. Far into the night Bailey and Kumagai talked, and Kumajirō must have been moved and understood what Bailey was saying. Bailey stressed that Earlham was a Quaker college, noting that the college had, because of that, a connection with Nitobe Inazo (a native of Iwate Prefecture). As the talk turned to the war, I thought, "Oh my, what will happen?" but amaz-

ingly, it took a good turn. Grandpa Kumagai turned to me and said, "I detest America, but Professor Bailey seems to be different. I will do all I can to cooperate with you." When he said that, I heaved a sigh of relief.

Even so, I was still worried. For him to say yes was one thing, but unless the women of the house agreed, things would not go well. Sometime later I heard the story. There must have been a lot of discussion of pros and cons, but in the end they all agreed to do it. Even now, the courage of the Wayama-ke in taking this on fills me with admiration. What happened was truly a historical breakthrough for that place, by people of great courage.[5]

The next day, hopeful but still unsure of the outcome of our negotiations, we left the Kumagais and headed for the village office, where Date had arranged for me to meet Mayor Hayano. Hayano had met him through the reforestation project when Date was still an undergraduate student at Waseda University, and he was one of the mayor's key appointments in his second term of office. At a party at Waseda in Date's junior year, Hayano had said to him in a seemingly casual way, "Why don't you come to Tanohata and work with me to realize the dream of regional development?"[6]

Date never forgot that remark. After a year of graduate work in regional development, and in spite of a tentative agreement to accept a job with a national road-building corporation, he accepted Hayano's offer of a job. Though an outsider to Tanohata, he was from the neighboring town of Iwaizumi, so he knew the region well. Hired in 1971, he had plunged with enthusiasm into the development work in Tanohata. By the time I met him a year and a half later, he was well on his way to becoming Hayano's right-hand man, despite his youth and his outsider status.

Hayano and Date had already agreed on the plan to have Tanohata host the Earlham Program the following summer, so this meeting was arranged in order to establish the formal relationship between the village and the college. Hayano was young, vigorous, personable, and ready to hammer out the details of the plan. There was little of the fuss and formality of most such meetings when foreign guests are brought for ceremonial introductions. I learned over the years that Hayano, though relatively unlettered and unsophisticated (he had gone only partway through middle school under the prewar education system when he was forced to return home to work in the family business), was clear-headed, quick to grasp the essence of the issue at hand, and decisive in his administrative and leadership roles. The formalities of the meeting were covered as we drank piping hot Tanohata milk, and we moved immediately to the business at hand. Our meeting was unhurried but intense as we focused on the details of the plan for the program. At the end, over traditional tea, there was small talk but also some probing as to the college's long-term plans and intentions as well as to reconfirm that our motives in coming to the village were centered in education *for both sides.*

On my return to Tokyo a few days later, a phone call from Date brought the good news that the Kumagais had agreed to take in the Smith family. Now, with the plan in place, I could return to the United States assured that the next summer's program could be implemented.

I returned to visit Tanohata each year to discuss program development and to make plans for the next group of students. In 1976 Hayano and Date approached me with the request for a full-time resident American teacher, and the long-term continuity of the program was assured. Unusual as their idea was, it made sense in their overall plan that was gradually unfolding.

In the summer of 1977, I took a TV camera crew to Tanohata to film material for a lengthy series of programs on Japanese culture and history. Thanks to Date's careful behind-the-scenes negotiations, we were able to get excellent footage on local politics as well as a fine sequence on the Kumagai family farm. Then, just when success seemed assured, we ran aground on the shoals of cultural misunderstanding. For a time it even looked as if there might be a major international incident. One day we were filming the annual field day exercises of the Tanohata Volunteer Firemen's Association. Some of the firemen casually said to the TV producer and cameraman through an interpreter, "We're having a party tonight. Why don't you come?" My colleagues were overjoyed and rushed to tell me. I checked with Date, who blanched. He said we shouldn't go, but gave no explanation. My colleagues were furious and, surrounded by village officials and firemen, we had a shouting match over this. I scurried around to see what could be done, and finally Date was able to arrange for us to go to the party. Later he told me why he had resisted. The head of the Firemen's Association was a former Japanese Navy commander whose submarine had been sunk in the war. Because he was notoriously anti-American, Date had feared that at the party he might make an anti-American diatribe, causing a serious incident. In the end, all went well, however, to everyone's relief and satisfaction, and the series contains some fine footage of the party. The episode was etched in my memory as an illustration of the unpredictable hazards of international cultural interaction.

Thirty years before we arrived, the village was quite a different place. Let us return briefly to Iwami Hisako's account of her early life and work in Tanohata, which contrasts starkly with my wife's and my experience and helps us to visualize the changes that occurred in those three decades. She relates:

SONG OF THE VILLAGE

"When I first took up my duties, the barrier of dialect made me uneasy, until I got to know the village people and began to see familiar faces. Then I began to get along all right. In late April and early May plum, peach, and cherry trees flowered all at once. The gray-purple of winter began to give way to the light green of the new leaves on the mountain sides, and day by day the green spread. The wind rustled in the azaleas that lined the streams in the foothills. Then came the long spring rainy season, and in every house the big kitchen hearths poured forth thick white smoke from water-logged fuel. The massive old houses stood with their straight lines of roofs of chestnut or cryptomeria, each of them filled with a multigenerational group of old folks, couples, and children. Against the deep green of the mountainsides, flocks of black birds sang, and forty flocks of sparrows flew up from the woods, twittering as they went. . . .

"With its full growth of leaves and under the warming rays of the sun, spring turned into summer. The sound of bullfrogs and streams filled the days; in the evenings came the call of the night hawk to his mate; in the night sky, so cloudy that one could hardly see the stars, the lonely cry of the screech owl could be heard.

> The silent trees and grass, the dead of night
> I feel the loneliness of the Buddhist monk."

The round of the seasons continues, and summer turns to autumn. Again, Mrs. Iwami turns to poetry to express her thoughts and feelings.

> "The luxuriant growth of summer
> Is it a blessing or a parting regret?
> The mountains are on fire with red

"Autumn in the north country is short. The mushrooms and chestnuts are gathered, and the colors of autumn leaves pass away. The golden leaves on the great silver apricots outside the garden come swirling down overnight, and winter approaches quickly. The December cold settles in with snow flurries, and unrelenting cold pervades. In my kitchen, water that ran freely at night had turned to ice by morning. By year's end our entryway was piled high with bags of charcoal, the precious result of people's labor. Fourteen bags were brought to me by village people in gratitude for my help in sick care.

"In January my eldest son was born, so I had to give up my post at the middle school. Even though I was now at home, more and more people came to me for help. They included old ladies who wanted *shiatsu* or *katamomi* (traditional East Asian medical treatments using finger pressure and massage). There were so many that, at times, the temple became the gathering place for all kinds of people to talk and socialize.

". . . One snowy night I made my way the four kilometers to a mountain household to help with a birth. Heavy snow had caused the electric lights to go out, so the birth was by candlelight. It was 2:00 A.M. by the time the birthing and bathing were finished. The husband was to take me back to my home. By the time we started, the snow had stopped and the moon was shining in the clear sky. The moon glistened on the mountainsides, turning the dead leaves to silver, shimmering in the light. As we traversed this silver world I saw myself in a separate universe; I was a princess in a mythical country transported into a world of dreams. My duty completed, my spirit lightened of its burdens, I felt the mountain had been turned into a great imperial palace made of snow now transformed by the moon.

"In the spring of 1952 a small clinic was completed in the center of the village, and a doctor named Komatsu, just turned fifty, came to work there. Though the doctor, trained in Manchuria, loved to drink, he could do anything and was easy to get along with. You can imagine how grateful village people were; till then when someone had a sudden or serious illness, a doctor would have to be brought from the neighboring village by horse or truck. It meant also that things could be handled without my having to do the medical treatment."[7]

In the late summer of 1982, when my wife and I arrived in Tanohata to take up residence for a year, the journey from Morioka was a pleasant two and a half hour ride by car over paved roads right to the door of our small apartment in a public housing development. We were able to settle into a comfortable routine of everyday living with ease, thanks to the careful preparations that had been made and the warm welcome we received. And one of the first people we met in the village was the newly arrived Dr. Shōgimen, who, with his family, had moved to Tanohata in the spring to become the first resident doctor in many years. The desire and desperate need of decades had been fulfilled!

Ohayō gozaimasu (Good morning)! *Konnichi wa* (Hello)! This is how we were greeted in the days and weeks after our arrival. Any foreigner who has traveled or lived extensively in Japan will immediately be struck by these friendly responses. Typically, the foreigner almost anywhere outside of Tokyo and the major metropolitan centers (and sometimes even in such places as well) is met with stares, embarrassed smiles, giggles, or, from children, perhaps a stammered "Haro" (hello). All too often, the attempts of foreigners to converse in Japanese will be met with blank looks and embarrassment because the listener, seeing a foreign face, assumes that communication will be impossible, since, by definition, foreigners can't speak Japanese. People in Tanohata, young and old, greeted us cordially and even rather casually, however, as if they were used to having foreigners among them—and, in fact, they were.

And what a contrast it was to my first visit to Tanohata in 1972! Then the trip from Morioka, the prefectural capital, had taken more than half a day. First there was a three-hour train ride to Miyako up through the Kuzakai Pass and down the narrow Heii River valley, through tunnel after tunnel. (This section of the Yamada Line has more tunnels per kilometer than any other in Japan.) Then came a two-hour jeep ride over bumpy gravel roads, around hairpin curves, and along steep switchbacks. Finally, in the early afternoon, we arrived at the village office. Ten years later, this trip had become an easy, pleasant morning's journey. Some of the switchbacks remained, but tunnels had replaced many of them. The trip was no longer the ordeal it had been just ten years before.

As we drove up National Route 45 from Miyako and entered Tanohata from the south, the sight of new houses dramatically demonstrated the quickening pace of change. Everywhere we could see the effects of new jobs and rising income. There were stores, a restaurant, and a sign for a new coffee shop now on the highway near the consolidated middle school, an architectural showpiece that was completed in 1974. The blue corrugated roofs of new houses dotting the countryside testified to Tanohata's emerging prosperity.

The first weeks of our stay were spent exploring the village, camera and map in hand, wandering down side roads, going back into the mountains and along the coast. Seldom were we treated as mere curiosities. More often we were welcomed for tea and talk, as we struggled to understand the heavy Iwate coastal dialect of the elderly and the rapid-fire colloquialisms of children and young people. Old friends of a decade took us in hand to explain local customs and introduce us to local people; new friends eagerly sought to help with information and suggestions. Knowing I was a historian, some produced Jōmon pots, proudly preserved family treasures. Others took us to the Nagamine Farm, the village-run highland barn and pasture complex, with its great silos, its sturdy pasture fences, and its young Holstein dairy stock.

Come December, we would see piles of salmon on the harbor dock, then see them smoked and hung from racks in storefronts. (Our friends in Tokyo reported the New Year's salmon we sent them to be the best they had ever eaten.) And *wakame* (dried seaweed, a staple in *miso* soup), Tanohata's own, packaged and sold under its name. Formal introductions for a first-time visitor at the village office would usually be preceded or followed not by tea, but by fresh, warm Tanohata milk (which is pasteurized and bottled for local consumption at the village-run dairy). We were proudly told that Tanohata milk is shipped and sold as far away as Tokyo.

Everywhere we went there was construction—new houses being built (in both the settled parts of the village and on back road farms), road work, roadside erosion control. There were also new harbor facilities, with their giant concrete tetrahedrons being lifted into place like jack straws to reinforce breakwaters and protect the fishing boats. Asparagus beds were being dug to expand vegetable production, and a portable sawmill was ripping logs for boards. Tanohata was on the move.

As the year went by, we were included in more and more village activities. There was Culture Day in the fall. New Year's rituals, such as the *kagura* dances to cleanse houses, brought a troupe of amateur musicians and dancers young and old, who moved their performance from home to home during the first ten days of January. The great snows of late February and March were succeeded by hints of spring in April and the cherry blossoms and local spring shrine festivals of May. Our neighborhood celebration included amateur dramatic performances, singing, and story-telling, as well as a sumptuous picnic with copious supplies of sake for the adults and soft drinks for the children.

As our year in Tanohata unfolded, the story of what had happened in the village consolidation fiasco was revealed to us by the son of one of the principal actors in the drama. This story, along with scores of other less significant but equally fascinating stories, were shared with us by various of our friends and neighbors in the village. Statistics we could get from the village office, the prefectural government, the *Iwate Keizai Kenkyū-sho* and elsewhere, but these personal, human-interest dimensions of the recent history of Tanohata were a privilege that came to us only because we were living there and sharing in the life of this remote community.

As our year drew to a close, we felt at home in this place and accepted as part of the community. And as we reviewed our time there and marveled at the village's generous and open spirit, we realized how far Tanohata had come just in the decade we had known it. The stories we had heard and the documents we had read filled out the picture of a place in a headlong process of change with staggering implications for the future. These people had come so far in so short a time, it was no wonder that at times they seemed tired and breathless, unable to savor fully the changes they had witnessed and participated in.

I have attempted to chronicle these changes and to analyze what caused them. For Tanohata, the past twenty years had been a wrenching, almost unnerving process. There had been resistance and failure as well as cooperation and success. The chapters that follow analyze this process and relate it to larger regional and national issues of development in Japan.

Chapter 1 provides background information on the physical and human setting in Tanohata as well as a brief overview of its history. Through the use of the Kumagai family records as well as lengthy interviews with various members of the family, it is possible to piece together a historical perspective on the village in spite of the relative paucity of formal historical documents.

Chapter 2 presents an overview of the whole developmental process from 1955 to 1982, setting the stage for a detailed analysis of the political and educational scene, which follows in Chapters 3 and 4. Chapter 5 then examines the key issue in regional development, the desperate search for jobs at the local level. Without viable employment opportunities in the village, there is no way to stem the outflow of young people, especially males. The problems of *dekasegi* (outside seasonal employment) and *ato-tsugi* (succession to the family headship) are really two sides of this coin; everyone recognizes jobs as the key to healthy long-term economic growth. One way to address the need is through the development of an infrastructure that will sustain economic life in the region. A promising approach being tried on the northeast coast of Iwate is the creation of "Third Sector" *(dai san sekutaa)* companies or hybrid enterprises to mobilize public and private resources to create the necessary local developmental mechanisms in transportation and marketing needed to support new jobs in the private sector. Chapter 6 examines this phenomenon through two brief case studies.

The conclusion, Chapter 7, looks at the problems of the village and the region that remain, for all the progress of the twenty years from 1965 to 1985. Tanohata shares with Japan at large a continuing malaise in the structure and the implementation of education at all levels, but especially at the lower and upper secondary levels. And when it comes to jobs, it is not at all clear that either the village or the region can sustain the developmental process and provide sufficient jobs to attract and hold its young people. As they look back, adults in Tanohata can take great satisfaction in how far the village has come since 1965, but as they look ahead they have no assurance that the road is clear.

I have tried to convey a sense of the range of people in Tanohata, young and old, male and female, forward-looking and conservative, in order to establish the humanity of the place. Tanohata is not just a stark beauty spot; nor is it merely development-related statistics of population decline or income growth. It is people, with their hopes and fears, their joys and sorrows. That truth is often tossed off in clichés or ignored in social science analysis.

There is really no conclusion to the Tanohata story. Life goes on, as it does everywhere. However, 1985 did signal a punctuation mark in the process. In 1985 Mayor Hayano entered the last year of his fifth four-year term, having largely completed the initial task he had laid out for himself —to create a sense of community in the village among people who had belonged only to scattered hamlets separated by mountains and ravines. He had breathed life into that village and, for good or ill, led it into the mainstream of life in Japan, in the process even defining something of a leadership role for himself and the village in Iwate Prefecture. What happens next will be of a different order.

At the same time, we can make some tentative generalizations from these two decades of development experience in Tanohata. One set of generalizations relates to the developmental process itself; the other to the role of local political leadership. How much influence or power lies with a local mayor? What leverage and latitude does he have to assert charismatic leadership? With Mayor Hayano, it seems clear that he had significant latitude. These issues will also be explored in the concluding chapter.

Now, let us get on with the story.

The Tanohata coastline with Hotel Ragasō and the Raga hamlet harbor in the background, 1990. Photo by the author.

View from Nagamine Experimental Farm to Numabukuro, 1990.
Photo by the author.

Close-up of serried uplift plateau in Nishiwano hamlet, 1990.
Photo by the author.

Late winter blizzard isolates Tanohata, 1964.
Photo from *Tanohata 101*.

Road linking upland and Hiraiga coast, 1990.
Photo by the author.

A grandmother at a traditional hearth in Kitayama hamlet, n.d.
Photo from *Tanohata 101*.

Date Katsumi, 1990.
Photo from Tanohata
village office files.

Ōmiya Shrine Festival in Raga hamlet harbor, c. 1963.
Photo from *Tanohata 101*.

Kumagai Ryūkō, Yoshizuka Toshiko, and Kimio, 1990.
Photo by the author.

L–R: Mayor Hayano, Superintendent Chiba, and Mr. Kumagai in the mayor's
office, 1990. Photo by the author.

初めて歌を作ったうれしさに
感想聞けば子らは逃げてゆく　節子

My first poem—the joy of it!
　　　Ask the children their impression?
They'd just run off.

Maze Setsuko

Hajimete uta o tsukutta ureshisa ni
Kansō kikeba kora wa nigete yuku

Setsuko

TANOHATA
EMERGES

In the 1950s, the *mura* (village) called Tanohata was still an artificial creation of national and prefectural officials who, in the middle Meiji years, had struggled to shape a rational, effective structure for local government in Japan. Tanohata-*mura* could be found on a map and seen listed on tax rolls and in government publications. The people who lived there, however, had little sense of belonging to an entity of local government. How could they? Spread thinly over a large area, separated by high mountains and deep ravines, they belonged to a hamlet, not to a village, and certainly not to the administrative figment created in Morioka and Tokyo in 1889 by which three Edo period villages (Hamaiwaizumi, Tanohata, and Numabukuro) were merged to establish the new unit to be called Tano-hata-*mura*.

History seemed to be repeating itself when, in 1953, the national government passed another law aimed at streamlining local government. The Law for the Consolidation of Cities, Towns, and Villages *(Shichōson gappei-hō)* pushed further the process begun by the law of 1889 that had created Tanohata in the first place. This time, the central government planners put pressure on Tanohata to consolidate with its neighbor to the north, Fudai, a coastal village smaller in size and population than Tanohata, and headed by a mayor with strong ties to the prefectural government in Morioka.

As I began my study of Tanohata, I followed the trail of documents that chronicle the five-year effort to force the completion of this union. In meeting after meeting, eager prefectural officials had shepherded the principals through the necessary steps. The process was slow—so slow that an early 1960 memorandum from Tokyo officials asks if the Morioka people wanted Tokyo to take a direct hand. The reply from the prefectural offices pled with national officials not to interfere, assuring them that the process was nearly complete and asking for their patience. A final joint meeting of representatives of the prefecture and the two villages was scheduled in May 1960 to consummate the union. Documents had been drawn up for the official announcement and an official congratulatory telegram was sent from the prefectural offices: "In full accord with your merger plan. Convey our heartfelt satisfaction with its adoption. Iwate Prefecture."[1] Then, suddenly, the trail of documents slows to a trickle, and a year later it stops. The record does not indicate what happened. Knowing that consolidation had indeed not taken place, I found my curiosity aroused. The documents suggest that it had been an all but foregone conclusion. What had happened?

I had talked to various people in the village, and finally one day I asked the proprietor of a local gasoline and heating oil company about it. "Oh!" he said, "my father was mayor back then. The prefecture pushed consolidation so hard that even though people here didn't want it, they couldn't resist in any formal way. It looked as if it would go through. At the formal meeting scheduled to complete the process and celebrate the establishment of the new village, he got drunk; he insulted everyone in sight and broke things up so we didn't have to go through with it."[2] No wonder the documents didn't provide the answer! No one would put that story in writing. (See Chapter Two for a full discussion of these negotiations.)

The mayor's desperate act of rejection was, it turned out, the catalyst that opened the way for new leadership in Tanohata. It triggered the process of village-building, creating a Tanohata where none had existed before. Over the next five years the forces at work nationally converged with prefecture-wide efforts and were brought to bear in Tanohata. These forces would bring it into the mainstream of Japanese national and regional life. But first, however, conditions in Tanohata went from bad to worse, as the same national trends that were lifting the national standard of living as a whole destroyed the major local source of cash income (charcoal), leaving the people of Tanohata in desperate straits.

In August 1965, Hayano Senpei was elected mayor of Tanohata in a hard-fought election. He won by a good margin but not by a landslide. Change for the better in the village clearly dates from this time, though in retrospect we can identify important developments outside the village that predated his election and contributed to the process of change. Since that time, the pace of change in Tanohata has quickened year by year. In March 1966, after Hayano had been in office for six months, he gave his first annual State of the Village speech to the village assembly. At that time he said: "For a long time this village has been known as a remote and backward place. We must first of all review carefully those circumstances that have created this situation and hindered regional development and the improvement of our lives."[3] A year later, he had this to say: "Recently we have become known not just as a backward village but also as a region that has great potential for development."[4]

Village people and outsiders as well had long viewed Tanohata as "the end of the line," which it literally was. This has been as true for bus transportation in recent times as it was for samurai defeated in battle in older times. Hayano Senpei saw the tremendous challenge that this represented and vowed to do something about it. In a conversation in 1982 reviewing his administration, he told me: "The problem was to get people to see that our very backwardness meant that this was a village with a future. That was our first task."[5] In his State of the Village speech on March 7, 1983, he said, "Tanohata and other rural villages as well are just like Tokyo—caught by the winds of affluence. Our challenge is to commit ourselves as an entire community to build for ourselves, through our own efforts, the kind of culture and community we want."

Yet for all of its isolation, even in the 1950s Tanohata was part of a larger history and culture. To understand the enormity of the changes that have come to it and to the region, as well as the continuities that remain, we need to examine the physical and cultural setting that are the context within which these ordinary people have played out their extraordinary lives.

The Setting and Historical Background

The popular images of the Tōhoku region of northern Honshū are stark. In early times it was the frontier, the land of the *Ezo* (barbarians, i.e., the Ainu), against whom there was constant warfare. As the Ainu were pushed northward, mainstream Japanese culture came to dominate Honshū. By late Heian times (twelfth century), the region had to some extent been absorbed into that culture but was still considered somewhat remote and mysterious. The establishment of the Fujiwara stronghold at Hiraizumi in southern Iwate and the flowering of culture there added romance to the mystery, particularly as legends surrounding the last days of the Minamoto hero, Yoshitsune, took root. Further north, Morioka, the present capital of Iwate, became a castle town and the center of political control for the northeast district.

Historically, Japanese culture has traveled northward up the river valleys and up the west coast of Honshū on the Japan Sea side. The central valley in northern Honshū leading from Miyagi Prefecture to Morioka in Iwate contains the Kitakami River, a broad and rich rice-producing area even today. Mainstream culture moved northward early with the establishment of the cultural center at Hiraizumi, but what came to be known as Kitakami *sanchi* (the Kitakami mountain district) on the east coast of Honshū was cut off from this early development by the mountains. In the middle ages, and even as late as the nineteenth century, this region served

Iwate-ken

Iwate Prefecture in relation to the main islands of Japan
Source: Tōhoku Regional Construction Bureau, Ministry of Construction, Japan.

as both a repository of older culture and a refuge for those either defeated in battle or else so disaffected or independent in spirit that they sought escape from mainstream culture.

Since premodern times, the northern part of the Kitakami Valley has been dominated by the Nambu fiefdom or clan *(han)*. Because the Nambu lords traced their origins back to the Sewa Genji line, ancestors of the Minamoto, they had close connections with the centers of power in Kyōto and Kamakura. The fief was established in Morioka in the late twelfth century, and Nambu lords ruled the region from then until the Meiji Restoration in 1868. This political power made Morioka a rich cultural and economic center for the Tōhoku region, whose cultural tradi-

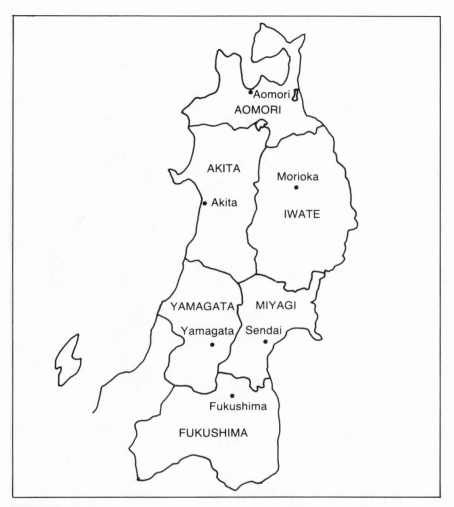

Tōhoku region
Source: Tōhoku Regional Construction Bureau, Ministry of Construction, Japan.

tion remains alive today. The best-known artifact of this tradition is Nambu ironware, which is recognized internationally as an expression of fine traditional Japanese craftsmanship.

Morioka's dominance made the areas to the east and west pale in cultural and political significance. Even today, Morioka acts as a magnet, drawing people, ideas, and activity to itself from all over Iwate as the central force in northern Tōhoku life. Although people in Akita (on the Japan Sea) and Aomori (to the north) aspire to leadership roles in the region, clearly Morioka sets the pace culturally and economically.

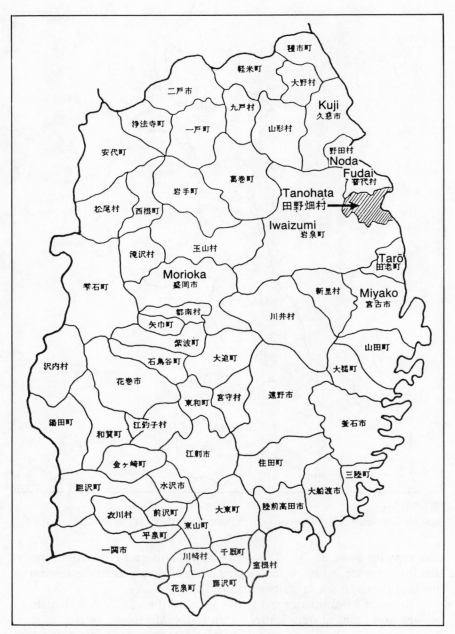

Cities, towns, and villages of Iwate Prefecture.
Source: Tanohata-mura, *Komyunitei karejji kōsō,* 1979.

Politically Morioka (and Iwate as a whole) has a proud tradition of contributing to Japanese national life. A recently published book entitled *Iwate saishō-ron* (A treatise on Iwate prime ministers) deals with Iwate Prefecture as the birthplace of national political figures such as Hara Kei.[6] In all, the prefecture has produced five prime ministers—Hara Kei, Saitō Makoto, Yonai Mitsumasa, Tōjō Hideki, and Suzuki Zenkō—and a disproportionate number of other leaders in national public life. However, these have been the exceptions that prove the rule that Iwate as a whole is remote and backward. The butt of jokes about "country hicks," it is seen as a place not to brag about. One young man who had returned to live and work in Tanohata described to me how, when he went to Tokyo to college, he hid the fact that he was from Iwate Prefecture for fear of being ridiculed. (He also said that people from Tanohata often did the same when they went to Morioka!)

Iwate is Japan's largest prefecture, with an area almost as large as the whole island of Shikoku and encompassing a great variety of terrains. The Kitakami Valley dominates Iwate life and culture; the Rikuchū coast, by its very remoteness, presents an intriguing contrast. Its stark, spectacular beauty makes it one of the most scenic spots in all of Japan. The coastline, from Kesennuma on the Miyagi Prefecture border in the south to the northern edge of Shimohei-*gun* (four-fifths of the entire Iwate coast), was set aside as a national park in 1961, and vigorous efforts are being made to develop the coast's tourist industry. The land formations are unusual for Japan. This region was created by a massive uplift of sedimentary rock from the ocean floor that formed a high plateau sloping gently from rugged mountains on the west (the Kitakami Sankei) to the ocean and then plunging in sheer cliffs a hundred meters or more high straight to the sea. Since the area is formed from sedimentary rather than volcanic material, the rocks are relatively soft and easily weathered. Two geological features result from this. First, the uplifted plain is serrated by deep and precipitous ravines, which have prevented easy access to and travel through the area. Second, much of the northern part of the region is soft limestone, which has led to the formation of beautiful dissolution caves. These caves served as hiding places for political refugees in early times, and some of them have been developed as tourist attractions.

The topography and climate of the Rikuchū coast comes to a dramatic climax in the village of Tanohata. Here the ravines are deepest, the coastal fishing villages the most isolated. Here winter comes earliest and lasts the longest, the snow from the spring coastal storms is heaviest and piles up on the plateau and in the ravines the deepest. Before bridges, tunnels, and modern road-building equipment came to the region, the hamlets of Tanohata were not only isolated from the rest of the coastal villages, where American whalers had been driven ashore in the early nineteenth century, but even cut off from each other.

The Tanohata shore is enclosed by the stark beauty of Unosudangai (lit. Cormorant's Nest Cliff) on the south and Kitayamasaki (Kitayama Promontory) on the north. In between are three small fishing villages, with houses backed up to the cliffs and extending up into the ravines, and pitifully vulnerable to the coastal storms and tidal waves (tsunami) that periodically ravage the coast. (The last great wave, in 1933, caused by an undersea quake, sent a great wall of water twenty-two meters high crashing against the coast, destroying half of the coastal homes and in one hamlet killing half the people.) The uplands of Tanohata provide flat, reasonably fertile land for farming, but the ravines that cut into the plateau long prevented effective use of this land; until the 1960s, there was no way to get agricultural produce to market. Because the land is fragile and the soil thin, without extreme care environmental degradation easily takes place. The people must expend great time and energy to prevent erosion and landslides, and even so, they are constantly having to repair what they have been unable to prevent.

The physical isolation produced by the topography of the region is highlighted by two place names and the local lore attached to them. Access to Tanohata from the south is guarded by a steep ravine and hill called Shianzaka (Contemplation Hill). Local legend has it that public officials sent to Tanohata by the Nambu Han would, on arriving at the base of the hill, sit down to contemplate the climb that lay ahead. Then, having climbed Shianzaka and gone on north, they were confronted by Jishokuzaka (Resignation Hill), where they are said to have stopped and even resigned their commissions rather than attempt the climb.

Stark beauty and isolation are the watchwords in Tanohata, and the weather reinforces this reality. In late winter the east winds from the ocean called *okiage* bring heavy snow. In the summer the same east winds, hitting the plateau and mountains behind, produce fog and light rain *(yamase),* sometimes for days on end, robbing the crops of badly needed sunshine.

Pockets of settled agriculture, fishing, and communal life have long existed in Tanohata. People on the coast forged intermittent links with each other by boat. Some struggled up the steep ravines to make charcoal that they hauled on their backs to the coast, but the upland area was sparsely settled until the last two decades. Community and cultural life revolved around the local Shinto shrines. Each major hamlet had a large community shrine, with smaller family shrines dotting most of the heights of land and hilltops throughout the village. There was no Buddhist temple in Tanohata until the 1930s. In the wake of the terrible tsunami of 1933, people felt a desperate need for one and a Zen temple was established. It was built only after a rather unseemly struggle over where it should be located was resolved by putting it up on the plateau, more or less in the geographic center of the village.

Early History

The presence of Jōmon (c. 5000–300 B.C.) artifacts in Tanohata indicates that it shared that historical experience with much of the rest of the Japanese archipelago. Some of the Jōmon pieces are beautiful and have been carefully preserved. Yayoi artifacts (300 B.C.–A.D. 300) also abound in the Tanohata digs, but the gap from Yayoi to historical times is a long one. There are no tomb remains, and mainstream Japanese culture from the Nara period did not penetrate this far north and east until late. It appears that Tanohata was a place of refuge for the Ainu as mainstream culture advanced north in Heian times, just as it was later for warriors and political refugees fleeing from the central political and military authorities. This tradition of being a place of refuge and a repository emerged early and remained strong until late in the nineteenth century.

The first documents that give insight into the nature of life in the region date from the Sengoku period (c. 1470–1570). They confirm the picture of the region as a remote place of refuge.[7]

Not until the Edo period can the activities of individuals and families in Tanohata itself clearly be traced. Even those families which have records confess that they are scant and incomplete. The ravages of time and the ever-present threat of fire in wood-frame, thatched-roof farmhouses have militated against their preservation. Perhaps equally important has been a lack of a sense of the value of historical records among people living in Tanohata. Their lives seemed to them to have no larger significance beyond the daily routine. Since life was so bleak, conditions so harsh, and literacy so rare, it is not surprising that few records were kept, fewer were preserved. There were exceptions, however. One branch of the Hatakeyama family (one of the most important families in Tanohata) traces its ancestry to the late Sengoku period and the battles that led eventually to the reunification of Japan under Tokugawa Ieyasu. Four generations later (in the late seventeenth century), the eldest son in the line fled to Hiraiga (a Tanohata fishing hamlet) and later moved to the plateau. By the mid-eighteenth century, when the present family's records begin, this branch of the Hatakeyama family was a well-established *ie* (patrilineal household) in Tanohata. The Hatakeyama family was obviously ambitious and prosperous. They have among their family records a journal of a religious pilgrimage made in the 1840s to the Ise shrines and Mount Kōya by a family member who walked the whole distance, a springtime journey of some three months.

Another representative of the long-time residents of Tanohata, mentioned earlier, is the Kumagai family.[8] During the 1970s, I visited the Kumagais frequently, and in 1982 and 1983 my wife and daughter and I spent many days working on the farm and soaking up the history of the family. Kumajirō, the old patriarch, is now dead, but Shōzō, Tsuya, and

Ryūkō (who is the fourteenth recorded eldest son to carry the family name) vigorously uphold the responsibilities that go with the status the household has in the village.

Our lengthy conversations about the family and village affairs and explanations of the contents of the family records revealed much about the Kumagai family today, its history, and the background of life in Tanohata. An examination of the family itself, its structure, and its values as they are actualized in practice gives us insight into contemporary Japanese social practices. The Kumagais as a family are by no means typical, even in a relatively conservative village like Tanohata. They are well-to-do and they have preserved traditional Tōhoku family structure and practice to a surprising degree. However, they represent stability, continuity, and continuing vitality in the village, while at the same time providing leadership for evolutionary development and change.

Before Grandfather Kumajirō died he saw to it that all of his five grandchildren (three of them women) received higher education. His grandson Ryūkō went to a major university in Tokyo to study agriculture. There he met Sachiko and convinced her to marry him and come to Tanohata to live. On the farm Ryūkō has pioneered new dairying methods, and he is recognized as one of the rising leaders in the village. His contemporary role is revealing of the nature of the political process in the village. (See Chapter 3 for a discussion of his political stance.)

The pioneering spirit that is seen in generation after generation of this family complements the family's commitment to the old *honke/ bunke ie* pattern, which scholars have identified in studies of traditional Japanese village culture.[9] A review of Kumagai family history over the more than 250 years for which they have records confirms this combination of the conservative and innovative strands in Japanese culture.

The Kumagais' ancestors came to the region under much the same circumstances as the Hatakeyamas. Defeated in battle in the late sixteenth century, one Kumagai warrior fled to Ōtomo (on the Omoto River in Iwaizumi just south of Tanohata), where he settled. His descendant, after a family dispute, sought new land to the north on which to settle, and moved his whole family to Tashiro in the northwestern part of present-day Tanohata. The document that records this move lists the people, animals, and goods that were resettled. A total of fourteen people, nine cows, and seven horses made the trek (some 35 kilometers) in the late fall of 1719, the year of the wild boar in Japanese reckoning. The family included three generations, the patriarch Sukeimon (then seventy-nine years old), his second wife (fifty), his eldest son, Sukenoto (thirty-seven), and his son's eldest son, Yoshinosuke (fourteen), plus six other kin and four *kenin* (workers unrelated by blood).

The family survived in primitive accommodations the first year, suffering the destruction of home and property by fire. Then, by dint of hard work and astute management, they acquired extensive land and a relatively prosperous position in an area where climate and natural environment make farming an arduous and risky business. Within a few years, the present farmhouse was constructed. One can still see some of the original posts and beams, now blackened with age and centuries of smoke, which constitute the frame of this ancient and honored thatch-roofed building. It stands on a promontory overlooking the Tashiro Valley.

Over the next two centuries, the family grew and prospered through a combination of subsistence farming and vigorous entrepreneurship, evidence of the same pioneering spirit that had brought them to the valley in the first place. Farming provided food, and their forest land produced fuel (wood for building material and heat as well as charcoal for cooking). In that remote and inhospitable place, what to do for cash income was an even bigger challenge. The family evolved a combination that stood them in good stead for two centuries. Wood from the trees on the steep mountainsides was either made into charcoal or sold directly to people on the coast. There it was burned under the kettles used to make salt, the single most important source of cash for people on the seashore. Some of the salt was transported overland to Morioka, where there was a good market for it. The Kumagais would run pack-trains across the mountains to Morioka, carrying salt and sometimes fish on the trip over and rice and other necessities on the return trip. Tashiro (and Numabukuro) were on the best route from this part of the Rikuchū coast to Morioka, and there was good access to the more prosperous, open areas to the north through the Fudai River Valley. At times, the Kumagais sold surplus horses at the Numabukuro market. They continued to raise horses well into the twentieth century, using them and oxen for heavy farm work and for hauling wood and charcoal out of the hills.

Professor Hashimoto provides interesting background on the Kumagai family's role and status in the area in his introduction to his interview of Kumagai Tsuya.

> On the upper reaches of the Fudai River is the Numabukuro area of Tanohata. One of the central hamlets is Tashiro. You can count 45 households there. Before the war there were 21, of which about half were *nago* (households unrelated by blood, who worked for the *honke* family in subordinate positions). *Nago* houses had two main rooms: a kitchen and a living room. The main line *(dana)* houses had three, they say. The continuation of the household lineage did not rely only on succession through a male child of the household. When it came to the twelfth generation, Tsuya's husband, Shōzō, like others before him, married into the household. Tsuya's father, Kumajirō, was full of the entrepreneurial spirit. In Shōwa 3 (1928), when there were no roads a car could travel on, he purchased a Ford truck and made a road to Fudai, in order to haul ash wood for baseball bats to fulfill a contract with the Mizuno Sporting Goods Co. He cut railroad

ties and delivered them to the Mitsuno River inlet. He organized the forestry cooperative, and took an active interest in a road construction company. From silkworm droppings he made methane gas to light gas lamps. In Shōwa 15, at Shōzō and Tsuya's wedding celebration, he surprised the assembled guests with electric lights. Seven years later, electricity reached the village. The people of the Kumagai household are not very talkative, even when you include Ryūkō's wife, who comes from Ibaragi Prefecture, but they have a gentle character. The strength of that spirit wraps you in its warmth. On this fall day, one has a sweeping view from the thatched-roof house. Set on a high plain, it looks out over the deep autumn colors of Tashiro. In the living area, below the large Buddhist altar and god-shelf, Tsuya quietly reminisces. The morning dawns with brilliant, clear color.[10]

Then Tsuya, relating memories of her youth and household traditions, gives a vivid sense of that way of life and its hold on the Kumagai family. She says:

"Ha. I was the oldest of 5 girls . . . born in Taishō 9 (1920). There was a boy born at the very end, but because of the great disparity in age, they made me the inheritor of the house, and bought my brother land in Fudai to start a branch house. My husband came in Shōwa 15 (1940).

"What was generally women's work? Well, first, sewing. Also, we had to do all the proper courtesies connected with household duties. In addition, we'd help others cut grass or pick mulberry leaves. I heard tales of the past and received training in how things should be done from my parents.

"Doing the washing was really something. Water left over from the bath was recycled. First, you had to get water from the stream. In this area only two or three houses had wells. We got washing machines in Shōwa 30 (1955) or so. We were the first ones [to have one] in the area, but even so my father said we didn't need that kind of thing, I should just keep washing stuff myself, he said. . . . But it made mending things a lot easier. When the children went to school, their pants, everything, they gave to me to mend. No matter how messed up the garment was, we couldn't throw it out, so I'd launder it, then cut out the good parts to use again. We even did that with the soles of shoes. Today that would be considered more effort than it's worth.

"About clothes? Hmm. My mother's generation wove their own on looms. Yes, they did it all. (No one had others do it.) When you wanted something good, you asked the store to make it. Also dyers and tailors from Fudai and Iwaizumi would make their rounds through Tashiro. They'd take the plain white woven cloth and dye it for us. Because our house had silkworms, we'd weave the outer cocoon and the center part of the cocoons into thread. . . .

"Yes, well, for Tashiro here and Numabukuro, Fudai was more

convenient [to get to] than Tanohata-oaza (the central part of the village). Various merchants from Fudai came through with dry goods, clothing, and notions, also fishmongers. They came from Fudai, Miyako, even from as far away as Kesennuma down south. They'd come once a month, or every two months. People from the Toyama area who sold medicine would come once a year. The same people always came. There were five or six of them. They'd leave medicine. They still come, though now it's only one or two.

"We didn't call a doctor all that much. Usually we just used the medicine from the Toyama apothecaries. If you talked about a doctor coming, well, people assumed that the sick person was about to die. My recollection is that there was a doctor in Tanohata-oaza. If he came all the way from there on horseback or walking, how much would it have cost, do you suppose? I have no idea. As for childbirth, everyone gave birth at home. They'd ask the wife of a nearby neighbor who'd had a baby to come and help. The mother in labor would squat and give birth that way. Rather than lying down in bed, women giving birth by themselves thought it was easier to do it squatting. If birthing was too painful, someone would press on the woman from behind. I had all five of mine at home. People would see the midwife once a month [during pregnancy], and if there was nothing unusual they'd have the baby at home. Not everyone went to see the midwife, though, that's for sure. Nowadays when people get pregnant, they tell others. In the old days, that was shameful and women would hide it. Women would work up to the day before giving birth, everyone did it that way. To think that that was the way we all did it in those days! There were lots of stillbirths then, and besides the stillbirths there were also many babies who died right after a difficult birth. There were babies who didn't develop at all and died soon, and mothers who had to go out the day after childbirth and cut feed for animals. Most families had cows and horses to feed. In the summer they fed them mountain grass, in the winter hay. When you have animals to feed, there's no rest.

"We just worked the whole year through. For the men, it was making charcoal in the mountains. From my grandfather's time to my husband's youth, they would take a horse-drawn cart to the coast and haul salt up, carrying wood and bark on the way down. Then in the winter they would hitch up a pack-train of horses and haul the salt to Morioka. They'd buy rice and bring it back. But when it came to hauling wood and charcoal out of the mountains, the women would all go along to help.

"Around here, as for religious or seasonal festivals or days off from farm work, there was nothing special like that. The thing that was most enjoyable? It was Obon or New Year's. In the old days, things went by the old lunar calendar. At times like New Year's, we'd have thirty to forty guests. The special food was pretty much the same each time.

". . . You want to know about meat? We never thought of it as something to eat. Right after the war, I heard that some people were eating cows that had died. Only lately do households eat pork. I believe there were no butchers in Fudai or Iwaizumi.

"We started buying food for side dishes in about Shōwa 30 (1955). Now we have a fish truck that comes by every day. Garden vegetables we mostly grow ourselves. But we've started eating ham and sausage in the mornings.

". . . These days there are lots of gatherings of just women, but in the past, all the farmers met together. Nowadays it's just women. Anyway there is the *fujinkai* (the women's association). When the weather is bad they gather in the community hall, and about ten people come. They chat, they bring pickles too, and ask how other people make or do things. We didn't have time for that in the old days, I think. Whatever came up, you had to do it your own self. Increasingly we depend on machines. Everyone pounded their own rice at home [for rice cakes]. Now women's housework can be done with machines, but for that reason people have come to need cash. No wonder they run out of money."[11]

In the mid-nineteenth century, the central government in Edo eagerly sought new sources of iron ore and established foundries in various parts of the country. (Both the Tokugawa regime and after 1868 the new Meiji government pursued this policy.) Iron was discovered in the Tashiro area, and from the 1840s until the late 1880s the Kumagais were able to lease land for a foundry and for placer mining of iron ore in the streams of their valley. One document dated 1874 stipulating the boundaries of the lease-land and the amount and price of the ore that could be mined is signed and sealed by Itō Hirobumi, the Minister of Construction of the new Meiji government. There were similar mining operations in other parts of Tanohata and in neighboring villages in the middle decades of the nineteenth century.

Thus, forces from the nation at large sporadically impinged on life in Tanohata. The Nambu fief, in economic straits in the 1840s, tried to squeeze more taxes from the people, in the end eliciting a violent protest. And the Meiji government, in search of wealth and military power, promoted the development of the resources of the region.

Nineteenth-Century Tanohata

Isolated though it was, Tanohata was clearly not completely divorced from the larger trends of late Edo and early Meiji history. People in the three villages of Numabukuro, Tanohata, and Hamaiwaizumi struggled to keep body and soul together, often in vain. Those in the major coastal hamlets of Raga, Hiraiga, and Shimanokoshi engaged in fishing, salt-making, and subsistence farming; those on the plateau eked out an existence at farming, and sold wood and charcoal when they could. In the 1840s

Japan was in the throes of a political and economic crisis. The Edo government had entered a period of serious decline and was beset by enemies within and without. Attempts at reform all too often only placed further burdens on the peasants, and the Tōhoku District was no exception. In fact the fortunes of the Nambu Han, with its castle stronghold in Morioka, were on the wane, aided by a succession of young and weak daimyō in Morioka. Everywhere in the country, pressure mounted to squeeze more tax revenue from the commoners, but on the Rikuchū coast the pressure apparently became unbearable, for people had no paddy land and little else from which to generate the resources to pay taxes. In 1847, led by a commoner named Yagohei from Ōashi (now part of Tanohata), a protest group of two to three hundred farmers took their grievances to the authorities, gathering supporters as they went. In the end there was a force 2,000 strong. They confronted clan officials and demanded a reduction in the special tax *(go-yōkin)* that had recently been levied by clan authorities in Morioka. Receiving no satisfaction, they went through Miyako and on down the coast, hoping to petition the Date clan officials in Sendai for support and redress. When that effort failed, they turned back to deal with Nambu officials. By that time, the protest group numbered 12,000. Maneuvering and negotiations went on for weeks, with Nambu clan officials attempting to break up the movement. In early January 1848, they arrested Yagohei. He was imprisoned for two months and died in prison in March 1848. The movement faltered and was dormant for several years, but was revived in 1853 under the leadership of Tanohata Taisuke (whose family name was Hatakeyama). Taisuke was able to raise a large force of supporters, and with the support of the Date clan in Sendai petitioned successfully for relief from Nambu taxes. Following this, he returned to his farmwork and remained in Tanohata until his death in the first decade of the Meiji period.

The memory of these peasant farmer uprisings *(hyakushō ikki)* is burned indelibly into the collective consciousness of this region, and Yagohei and Taisuke are still household names on the Rikuchū coast. People celebrate those proud and fiercely independent spirits who demanded justice for their people, using them as examples for school children even today.

In the years following the Meiji Restoration, the fortunes of rural people in the area fell rather than rose.[12] The new economic system, which exacted taxes impersonally and allowed those with power and status to gain title to land, removing it from public use, exacerbated the economic woes of people who were already at the subsistence level.

In 1889, when the Meiji government enacted the national law that consolidated towns and villages into larger and more efficient and manageable administrative units, the effect of this consolidation locally was to unite a large geographic area and bring together three distinct and separate traditional villages. Numabukuro on the north, the best established and most prosperous community, was separated from the others by the Itabashi Pass, a high ridge running east from the mountains to the ocean. Numabukuro had fairly easy access to Fudai to the north along the Fudai River, and most of its inhabitants were oriented in that direction (e.g., the central shrine, Unatori-*jinja,* and the Buddhist temple as well, to which most of them still relate, are in Fudai). Old Tanohata on the central uplift plateau included two small fishing hamlets on the coast, Raga and Hiraiga, but it was the poorest and most sparsely populated. Hamaiwaizumi to the south included the coastal fishing hamlet of Shimanokoshi. It was separated from Tanohata on the north by Matsumaesawa, one of the deep, precipitous ravines that serrates the plateau, and from Omoto, the village to the south, by Makisawa, another ravine so deep that the bridge which now spans it had, until the completion of Shii Bridge, the deepest drop to the stream below of any bridge in Japan. These three villages made an unlikely match, with little in common except their poverty. But to administrators and policy-makers in Tokyo and Morioka, the paper plan made sense. Little if anything changed in people's lives for the next twenty years. A few young men went off to fight in the Sino-Japanese War of 1894–95 and the Russo-Japanese War of 1904–05. Certainly Tanohata as a village had no identity. People continued to consider their identity to be with the local hamlet or at most with the old village. In fact there was no Tanohata in the sense that it was defined by the 1889 law except on paper until after 1960. Mayors came and went in rapid succession (appointed by higher government authority until 1945). Beginning in 1947 under the postwar constitution they were elected, and no one served more than two four-year terms, with most having only one term. How could one mayor represent the whole village when there were really three quite separate entities and a host of smaller hamlets?

TANOHATA IN THE EARLY TWENTIETH CENTURY

Natural disaster visited Tanohata early and repeatedly. In 1896 (Meiji 29), a great tidal wave wiped out large numbers of houses and people in the coastal hamlets of Shimanokoshi, Hiraiga, and Raga. (Shimanokoshi, with a population of 297, lost 140—nearly half of its people.) The mouths of the ravines where the fishing hamlets are located are roughly V-shaped; thus, when a tidal wave hits, it rises geometrically and there is no escape. (The 1896 wave hit as high as 17 meters up the valley cliffs.) The main line of the present mayor's family was wiped out by the 1896 tsunami; it had to be reestablished by a son from one of the branch families living up on the plateau. In 1933 another ferocious tsunami struck, with successive lesser waves in its wake. It reached a height of 22 meters in Raga. (It was in the aftermath of this disaster that the Buddhist temple was established in Tanohata.) In between these dramatic disasters, less spectacular troubles plagued the village. Poor harvests, cold summers, severe winters all added to its burdens. Health services were nonexistent, schools few and poor in quality, cash income difficult if not impossible to come by. People were mired in the all-too-common rural cycle of poverty, sickness, and hopelessness.

Suzuki Naono, a great-grandmother who eloquently testifies to that reality, was interviewed by Professor Hashimoto. Here, he introduces her:

> Accompanied by an infant girl, Suzuki Naono appears as the light spreads across the beach. Seagulls rest on the high breakwaters. While keeping an eye on the play of her great-grandchild, she squats down to begin setting the salmon nets, weighing them down with bags of stones. As she waits an hour for her oldest son's boat to return from gathering *konbu* (an edible seaweed), she chats about the life of the beach women.[13]

She then relates her story:

> I was born in Meiji 41 in Shimanokoshi, and I became a bride in Shimanokoshi. For those of us born in Meiji, education, required education, was through the sixth grade. Even when we were busy, children were pushed off to school. If you cried, you had to stand in the corner, and then you couldn't study anything at all. Though six years were required, children who went for three or so were no better than illiterates.
>
> "I was the oldest of four children. So of course my parents put me to work. When I was this little, I was taken along with them.
>
> "The work was just the work of the sea and the beach. There weren't any rice fields here, so we went to other hamlets and got sacks of wheat or barley, *hie* (millet), and rice. In those days there were three grains, people would say. Whatever nice stories they tell, in Meiji, Taishō, and early Shōwa, all we did was survive.
>
> "I was nineteen when I came as a bride. In this area sixteen or seventeen was the usual, so I was a bit older. My mother came from a place where fourteen or fifteen was okay, but she was so young when she came she couldn't yet carry the loads or do the work. So she told me that as her daughter, it was fine to wait awhile.
>
> "I married into that *minshuku* (family inn) household, the one next to the Banya Inn. I'd known my husband from way back. He is five years older. There were younger children, so his other siblings worked at home and then went off to form branch households.
>
> "In Shōwa 8 (1933), when the great tsunami came, how old was I? I already had two children. After the big earthquake, we all got up, and waited without going back to sleep until after 3:00 A.M., when it got light [*sic*]. My grandfather-in-law shouted, 'It's a tsunami!' and we fled barefoot.
>
> "There were even more households then than now, you know. Even so, we had no deaths in this hamlet. My house was cleanly

washed away, without a trace. Some relatives who lived over near Iwaizumi cut trees from their own mountains and brought them to us. The tsunami washed away everything on March 3rd; by June 10th they helped us build a new house. It has been fifty years, and it has gotten old. My son talks about building a replacement, but the chestnut pillars are eight *sun* (9 to 10 inches; there are 10 *sun* in 1 *shaku,* which is roughly an English foot) square and run to the second floor. Pine, cedar, chestnut—we didn't use any other lumber anywhere. Other houses have been rebuilt, but this house—any carpenter who sees it will tell you it hasn't warped anywhere. It just won't come apart. This is the 53rd year.

"That's the way it is. The boats were all swept away in the tsunami. Boats, everything. We had to make or fix everything. The whole world blessed us with their help—that's why we've come so far today.

"In the old days, a bride and her mother-in-law always had problems of one kind or another. But now, in places like our house, the people we ask (to marry in) as well as daughters, and even grandchildren, live together considerately.

"My father got drunk and fell off the cliffs; he died from a broken neck and back. I was about fourteen or fifteen. After that, my mother talked with us, and me, my two sisters, and my younger brother lived together doing field, forest, and mountain work and making *surume ika* (dried squid) on the beach.

"At nineteen, after I became a bride, I worked in the fields, up in the mountains—little jobs. I worked at almost anything. When the children were born, we wove bamboo baskets, put them [the children] on our backs, and went to the fields on the mountainside. I nursed them, put them to sleep in the basket, and kept working.

"Then during the war, troop ships would come by, far out in the ocean. Sometimes while we fished, enemy planes would bomb and sink them.

"When I was young, you had to raise your children, to take care of your grandchildren, but no one ever left Shimanokoshi. These days, though, they've gone to Matsushima in Sendai, Tazawa-ko, Osoresan in Aomori. Even the old people travel. They go and visit strange outside places.

"We used to do our shopping in Miyako, going down by boat. Now, thanks to the railroad coming through. . . . When the train was put through, I wished that grandfather was alive to see it. . . . He worked so hard on the local fishermen's co-op, and with the firefighters. He was a representative to the village council: he really gave of himself to Tanohata, and he received an imperial citation, merit of the sixth rank. Really. While grandfather was out doing village work, my oldest son's wife would do all the housework for me, and I would work the fields by myself. Somehow or other we managed to live and get by.

"Today, what would you say, the village offers jobs and salaries. In the old days, whatever you did was for no remuneration. Whether it was work reclaiming the land or when people went off to Tokyo to petition, we all used our own money.

"When they built that jetty of land out from the harbor that you can see over there, a lot of Koreans came. That was during the war and there wasn't any food. I made potato flour, and dried rice. . . . Hmmm. I wonder how many Koreans came—it was really something.

"Lately Koreans have done a lot of this heavy construction work on the harbor breakwaters. They are gradually piling up the concrete tetrahedrons, and they've fixed it over here. . . . It looks terrific today. . . .

"Do you understand what I am talking about?

"Tanohata is divided into mountain and coastal regions, and further divided into *buraku*,[14] but during the war life at the beach was easier. There wasn't enough food to go around in the hills, so they would come down to the beach, and we would pick them *konbu* or *wakame* (another type of edible seaweed).

"The mountain people took their cows and ate them—we heard stories. Here we had rice with *konbu* or *wakame* on top. The fields gave us potatoes and wheat. Since we grew *hie* (a kind of coarse millet) we had enough to eat. There were people who went hungry. The old women fed these people miso. . . .The miso you're eating now was made ten years ago, and I still have two barrels of it that haven't been touched, you know.

"When I was young, what did I enjoy? Nothing special. . . . I couldn't say what was enjoyable, but during the time I was raising my children, whether something was happy or sad, when dawn came, I'd go down to the beach, and if it weren't the beach, to the field or garden, taking along the children, but I didn't find them bothersome, nor did they make me unhappy. I like the local shrine holidays and Obon and New Year's. Today they have one-day senior citizen trips, but then I still have responsibilities. I should say I enjoy them, but I guess I don't really. Ha. Everybody has to work in life, I think. . . . The laundry—I could only do it at night, but my son's wife, it's not like it used to be, she and the kids are always telling me to stop talking about how things were. . . .

"Aha! It's about time. See—a bunch of boats are coming in."[15]

Sasaki Masa, born in 1912, is known affectionately as "the Granny of Ōshita" because she likes to take care of people. She has many visitors, including students from Waseda who come to work in Shii no Mori. She speaks with feeling about shrine festivals and life on the plateau in Suge-nokubo, the geographic center of present-day Tanohata.

"Ha! This is the fifth Sasaki house on this spot. I don't know the stories about the first grandfather, but I do know about his wife. They say she came from Tashiro (one of the northern hamlets in the village). I remember the second grandmother (the first couple's daughter-in-law). Here is her gravestone. She came from a long-lived family they called Ōshita. Because the Ōshita family were long-lived, no one wanted to come to be a bride there. Look at me. Ha. You can joke, but I have lived a long time. Ha. I was born the first year of Taishō (1912).

"My father loved to drink sake, and died of a bad liver. My siblings were all girls—there are four of us. When I first knew Sugenokubo, there were twenty-two or twenty-three houses here. When my father was district head, Shimanokoshi and Matsumae were part of the Suge-nokubo district. This household is where the original Sugenokubo was; the branch houses cultivated new land and spread out. My father was illiterate, but for thirty years, people honored him by putting their confidence in him as district head. Today you'd call it the head of the *buraku* council.

"My father was brought up a spoiled youngest child. Things weren't so troublesome then; they had enough property, they went to prostitutes. It may have been a problem within households, but they tried for the sake of the *buraku* to be cultured people—to maintain some public stance. The Sasaki family used to have lots of mountain land and fields. Anyway, from Shimanokoshi up between the road and the creek, all of that land was ours. That's what they say. Nowadays we live poor.

"There were no hired hands in my household. We just cultivated the fields together. Ha. The ones who did it weren't tenants; the crop was divided sixty-forty or seventy-thirty, and the beach folks, the people from Shimanokoshi, came and cultivated. That way, at harvest time, they just piled all the harvest together and divided it. People from Fukushima consumed it—yes, Fukushima Prefecture, Fuku-shima city—they came to make charcoal. *Fukushima hoido* (a term of derision) they were called; they were like beggars, those people who came to make charcoal, and they lived in our houses. So then, those people's sons and daughters, those kids were left to be raised in the village. That's the way it was, yes. Those children didn't go to school. When I was in elementary school, there was a bunch of them.

"In the old days, my father went to the Tarō area and bought a mountain and hired people to make charcoal.

"The elementary school was in Hiranamisawa. There were six in my class, two other girls and three boys, then four when one failed. In those days there was one teacher for first through sixth grades. It was an era when you could take supplemental subjects or not as you pleased. Those classes were held in a rented room in a nearby *min-shuku,* taught by the same elementary school teacher who came and went.

"It was at the beginning of Shōwa. The mayor of Tanohata was an imported mayor from Iwaizumi, named Sasaki Seiichi. He and his wife would come riding in by horse, with the others walking behind. They left late at night and arrived the next morning. The mayor's wife came from Nagoya, and she tired easily, so they rested lots on the way, and all the crowds of guests had to wait around for them. They came up across from what is now called Takisawa Caves, passing over the Tetzusan (Iron Mountain) area.

"In general, we did our shopping at the beach hamlet of Hiraiga, where there was a store. Kusei-san ran the store for its owner, Kudō Seisaku-san, the mayor. It was called Shimotsuba; it had dry goods and was like a five-and-ten. I think there were two or three other little stores. There was also a brothel in Hiraiga. I know people who say that the people who worked there came from the city of Hachinohe. I never heard talk of local people selling themselves there.

"At the beach, the boys and girls did *kosage* and *koage* work. *Kosage* meant unloading the boats when they came into the harbor; the loading was called *koage*. In the past there was no national highway, so charcoal and everything was sent by boat. The mountain regions sent things down by horse to the Hiraiga or Shimanokoshi beaches, so in my day every kid worked at *kosage* and *koage*. That's the reason they had the brothel there, you see.

"Ha. What did I enjoy? I'd have to say *kagura*—the shrine festivals. . . . In the old times, *kagura* meant traveling around and staying overnight. Any house was expected to take the people from the troupe in. We had a much bigger house then, not this present one. The *kagura* troupe always stayed in Sugenokubo. They'd come in December or around New Year's, too. We had about twelve people for the local shrine *kagura,* but sometimes *kagura* from Miyako would come with thirteen or fifteen people. That was a once-a-year all-out fun event. Ha. We'd gather all the *gongen* (statues of Bodhisattvas), not at the temple but at home.

"The *kagura*'s *kasumi* (mist place) had a sphere of influence or affect. So, when the *kagura* from other places would come to this village, there were local *kami* (Shinto spirits) and *gongen-sama* (Buddhist spirits) who would fight with the other *kami* that didn't suit them. They said that when you put the *gongen-sama* up in the *tokonoma,* if there was a *kami-sama* that didn't get along with it, it would fall from there with a crash. It was for that reason that Tanohata people didn't go to some *kagura*. In this village when the *kagura* folks were coming, they'd blow shells to give the local *kami-sama* warning.

"When the *kagura* came in, everyone from the *buraku* came, adults and children. And from other *buraku,* too, they came to see. In those days, the young people weren't like what you see and hear today, so we all enjoyed ourselves. That's the way it was, going to see the *kagura* come dancing through the village and stay over.

"To exorcize bad spirits, you always had to make *manju* (dumplings) and bring them to offer to the *kagura*. Then you said, 'These *manju* came from my mother.' Yes, it was the custom to have *manju* from the mother of the household. They offered them to people who came from other places, and we'd get them when we went somewhere else. Then the whole *buraku* together would offer up sake and flowers. Ha. I don't remember how many flowers you were supposed to bring. And then we'd all have a big reception.

"Once they'd gotten cheery from drinking sake, they'd go on, not just for one night but often for another one of *kagura*. So we'd feed the *kagura* visitors a feast."[16]

There were people in Tanohata with ambition, initiative, and vision for themselves and their children. As we have seen, Kumagai Kumajirō was one of these people. Born in 1893, the third son in the *Wayama-ke,* at an early age he set off to make his fortune in Fudai, the village to the north of Tanohata. He established himself in business and was well-launched in a successful career as an entrepreneur when his elder brother Gisuke, who had succeeded to the family headship, died. It was then assumed that Kumajirō's other elder brother, the second son, would carry on the line. However, he turned out to be a ne'er-do-well, a gambler who squandered the family's resources. After family members had rescued him twice from bad debts to no avail, the call went out for Kumajirō to return to the farm to head the family. Over the next sixty years, he put his business experience and his entrepreneurial skills to good use. The Kumagais prospered, individually and collectively, and when he died in 1982 at the age of eighty-nine the *Wayama-ke* was strong and respected as the continuing leader of the Tashiro Valley.

In the 1920s, as Professor Hashimoto noted, Kumajirō had pioneered in cutting and selling timber for railroad ties that were used both at home and abroad. The receipt for a Ford truck (the first in the valley) that he bought in 1928 to haul out the logs is carefully preserved, and the family proudly showed it to me. (The price was ¥500, which at the time represented about $200.) In a variety of ways over the next twenty years Kumajirō was a community leader. He was always ready to experiment with new ideas. His experiment in generating electricity using manure to produce methane gas worked, but the tank leaked so badly he had to abandon the project. In 1940 he set up a water-powered generator on a stream on the farm and generated electricity all through the war and after, until public power came to the valley in 1947.

As we have seen, Kumajirō had six children, of whom all but the youngest were girls. He had solved the problem of succession to the headship of the *ie* in good Japanese style by having his eldest daughter, Tsuya, take a husband, Shōzō, from a collateral Kumagai line. Shōzō's branch of the family lived in Fudai. The fact that it had earlier taken a son of the Kumagai main family as a *mukō yōshi* (a groom who marries into the bride's family) made this solution to the problem all the more natural. Shōzō and Tsuya have five children, two boys and three girls. Although Kumajirō had had little formal education (he completed elementary school in 1906), he was determined that his grandchildren, at least, would be well educated. All five, including the women, have had some form of higher education. The eldest grandson, Ryūkō, who is the present head of the family, graduated from Tokyo University of Agriculture, the most prestigious university in the field of agricultural education.

The Kumagais prospered by seizing economic opportunities as they appeared, and moving with the times or a little ahead of them. After his marriage in 1940, Shōzō spent several years in the army during the Pacific War, serving in Manchuria in 1941–42. Kumajirō kept the farm going with his experimentation and entrepreneurship, cutting trees for railroad ties and supplying Mizuno with lumber for baseball bats. He became a member of the Tanohata village council and participated actively in hamlet and village affairs. The openness and response to the new that Kumajirō displayed had become a hallmark of the family. It continued to be expressed in a variety of ways. Ryūkō's work in agriculture college, exposed him to new methods, which he brought back and implemented successfully. They accepted his decision to marry Sachiko, an outsider from near Tōkyō, and accepted her in the family. Further evidence of this openness, and of the Kumagais' interest in the world beyond Tashiro, came in the summer of 1973. At that time they took in a family of five Americans (two adults and three children) for a period of more than two weeks, providing housing and sharing kitchen space, having some meals together and giving the Americans an unforgettable introduction to Japanese family life. Whenever I visited the family after that one of Kumajiro's first questions would always be "How is Smith-sensei (Professor Smith)?" Truly, he was a remarkable man. The whole family exhibits this same openness; we shall return to them later since in many ways they represent best in private life what the present mayor represents in public life.

Postwar Tanohata

August 1945 brought an end to the long trauma of war and a chance to put life back together, but for Tanohata, the first postwar decade was one of further decline in its economy and in the quality of life. With few resources and little that could be turned into cash income, people survived on subsistence farming and fishing. Since the population of the village was small and there was open space available, Iwate Prefecture and the national government arranged to acquire land in the village where they resettled groups of repatriate Japanese from Karafuto (southern Sakhalin). These families also began to do subsistence farming. It was a grimly difficult life, much more demanding physically and emotionally, they said, than their life in Karafuto had been.[17]

Joining these families in pioneer farm work were families from other parts of Tanohata. In Professor Hashimoto's interview, Kuwagata Nobuko remembers those difficult times:

"I was born in Shōwa 7 (1932) in Sugenokubo, so I'm now fifty-four (1986). When I was in third grade, the war began and we began to open up the Nishiwano area. At first all we had was a small hut. I'd stop there on my way back from school, put down my book bag, and work with my parents in the field. At nightfall we'd go back home together. I think we were able to buy a little more than two *cho* (about 5 acres; 1 *cho* is 2.45 acres) of land for about ¥1,200 from an organization called the Development Enterprise *(Kaitaku jigyō-dan)*. My hardheaded father planned to save money and pay for it. He placed the money with good interest, and when it came time to pay he went off in a flurry and paid something like ¥1,200. From the beginning it was tough—hill after hill—terrible. We had to cut the trees down, and then we planted between the stumps.

"At that time *hie* was the staple food, so we planted *hie*. After *hie* came wheat. Even today, tree roots are a problem, so they use bull-dozers. In those days you had to use a hoe. Even when you cleared a garden, you could chop and chop but the root sprouts still came up. You would work most vegetable fields three times as hard and get one-third as much out of them. Plus, listen, we didn't have fertilizer at that time, so we used rotting tree leaves and we hauled human excrement up from the harbor hamlets, carrying it in cake-shaped pieces on our backs. It is a dirty thing to talk about, but we had agree-ments with fishing households that had no gardens. At spring plant-ing and again when the wheat was sown, we hauled the cakes up. And the slope up from the beaches is really steep. We children who had finished upper elementary school [were big enough] to carry them on our backs from the beaches all the way up here. We didn't even have any sweat left by the time we got here. Really.

"I was the oldest of four sisters, so I also had to babysit. . . .

"Before we built this house here, my father and mother had to dig a well and put up pillars for the house, and then we had to go to the river to carry back stones for the foundation. We used small pine roots for lights. There were no boys in the family, so they relied on us [girls] for all the work.

"When we settled here, there were about twenty houses. After that, new people came in, some branch houses formed, and today there are about sixty, I think. It has taken about twenty years for the roots to be all pulled out of the fields, so they actually bring in income. But there are still some big roots left. The tree seeds came from all kinds of trees, so we had every kind of tree, good and bad. The land wasn't good enough for raising pines or cedars. The total land area we opened up was about 120 hectares (about 470 acres). Everybody worked painfully hard. From what today is the junior high school to the mouth of the Hiranamizawa River, we planted *hie, awa* (millet), wheat, soybeans, adzuki beans, vegetables—the house-holds ate whatever they had. I don't know how many years ago, tobacco flourished around here. The farmers' co-op took the lead. People needed cash income, so there was a time when they planted tobacco and peanuts. But making charcoal was the most important.

"My mother came from Sugenokubo, but my father was from Tanohata. My husband married into our family as an adopted son, in Shōwa 30. He was twenty-four. I'm not his equal any more, but for many years we went to the same school, were in the same classroom, and we're going to be together till we die." (She laughs.)

"My class had fifteen boys and girls, I think. Once they graduated from school, most stayed behind at home to help; some went on, became nurses, went into munitions factories, and some have died. Today about ten are left in the village. My father was hardheaded, so he wouldn't let me leave. Always a real farmer.

"Before the end of the war, at times like when we dug potatoes, the enemy planes would come up the coastal area. It was frightening. I'd pull along my younger sisters, and we'd flee into the mountains. For two or three days we lived in bomb shelters, but now I think it must have been truly frightening to have been in the Tokyo area.

"I married in Shōwa 30, and bore two boys and one girl. Among the same group of settlers there was a midwife named Kumagai, whose services I used for my first child. The other two were delivered by Iwami Hisako from the Women's Society of pioneer farmers."[18]

Port facilities in the fishing hamlets were still primitive, so fishing was not yet a lucrative trade. Charcoal production was the only major source of cash income for the village. Transportation and roads were worse than primitive. Even in the early 1950s, to go the three or four kilometers from the village office up on the plateau to the fishing hamlet of Shimanokoshi would take about 40 minutes on foot, but an hour and a half by truck. This was typical of the situation throughout the village. As late as 1965, roads were still in desperately poor condition, and to go from one place to another took inordinate amounts of time.

Tanohata's situation was so bad in the early 1950s that few people inside or outside the village held out much hope for it. It seemed to be a village with little past and even less future. In 1953 the Iwate Prefectural Board of Education, in collaboration with village school authorities, published a study entitled "Tanohata: Educational Plans for the Entire Village."[19] This study documents the educational situation in the village and the nature of life in this remote spot. It pointed out that the only way to enter the village by scheduled public transportation was via Numabukuro on the northern edge of Tanohata. All other entry was either on foot or by boat. Communication between the hamlets of the village took two hours on the average and had to be on foot.

When one looks at another measure of the plight of the village, employment patterns, the picture was equally dismal. Over three-quarters of the population was involved in primary economic activities (i.e. agriculture or fishing), almost all of it at the subsistence level. Productivity was so low that there was seldom a surplus, but even when there was one, there was no way to get it to market. Interviews with old-timers in the village confirm, with anecdote after anecdote, the sense of hopeless futility with which most people in Tanohata viewed life. Schools were hard to reach, even on foot, and the quality of education was low. Families with any means and ambition sent their children out of the village for middle school education, and the ambitious among these usually did not return, creating a "brain drain" that the village could ill afford.

By 1955, when Iwate Prefecture came out with a study entitled *Shichōson no kanrensei chōsa hōkoku-sho* (A report of a study of relationships among cities, towns, and villages), people saw little prospect that Tanohata could continue to exist as an independent village. It had no tax base; nor did it have the transportation system to support even a modest village development. The study was designed to provide data and analysis, rather than to formulate specific recommendations, but its implications were clear. The government policy that emerged from the study was to promote mergers of the towns in Shimohei-*gun* in order to create viable administrative entities, each with a sufficient tax base to provide reasonable local government administration and services.

Surprisingly, it is from this point on that one can identify and trace the beginnings of a Tanohata with substance, identity, and an emerging sense of hope for the future. The evidence suggests that Tanohata emerged as a viable entity as a result of a situation created by desperate internal weakness, on the one hand, and external pressure to merge with the neighboring village, on the other. This situation is described by Kudō Fusako, a village woman, who relates:

"I was born here in Shimanokoshi in 1941. I was the last of seven kids. Ours was a half-farming, half-fishing family. When I was in elementary school, I had a free rein. I played when I wanted to play and did what I wanted to do. In those days we had no clubs like the kids have now. We'd go back up into the mountains or down to the coast, play around the school, go to other kids' houses, play hide and seek, scale rocks on the water. When we went up to the hills, we'd take rope and make a swing and play Tarzan. When I was little, there was a threshing floor when they would thresh rice or millet. I'd help with that—half-playing, half-helping. I remember going into a little seaside house and pretending we were flying planes and bombing ships. A long time after that, when I became bigger, I remember saying, 'I know about war.' My older siblings said, 'You don't know what you're talking about. You were too small. Don't be saying things like that.' I remember lots of things. Another time we went up to the hills. There was nothing to eat, and we heard the planes overhead. My mother said, 'I'm going to dig potatoes. You wait here in the shade of this tree,' and she went and did it. We stayed there while the bombs were falling. I remember that. Now it seems almost like a dream.

"At that time, what we had to eat was millet, wheat, soba, and potatoes, as I remember it. My father caught fish, and we had a little crop land. By boat we'd get fish, *kombu, wakame, uni,* and *awabi.*

"When I finished middle school, my father said I could go to sewing or cooking school to study women's things, not to regular school. I said as a young person I wanted to go to regular high school, not a sewing school, but he said, 'Not on your life.' At that I said that I wouldn't just stay at home, that I'd go to work by myself. But he wouldn't even agree to that. Finally, a teacher I knew whose family was in Miyako told me that if I really wanted to study that badly, he would take responsibility and talk to my parents. In the end they still would not say yes—wouldn't help if I got sick and wouldn't give me any allowance. But no matter, I said 'all right—I'll do it myself,' and I got a fishing family to let me work for them, and for four years I went to Miyako high school. I rented a three-mat tatami room, did my own cooking. The rent was ¥1,000. I made ¥4,700 a month and had to pay school fees and buy books, and there wasn't enough for my other expenses. I didn't say anything, but my teacher was worried and asked me about it. He then arranged for me to have a scholarship of ¥1,000 a month. By the time I graduated my salary was up to ¥5,700, and then it went to ¥6,000 and I was able to make it through. I returned to the village and for three years worked as an assistant in the nursery school. During that time I turned twenty-three and was married.

"My husband had gone to Kesennuma after finishing middle school, and had worked for a bread and sweet shop and bakery for seven years. He had returned to Tanohata and had started a small shop of his own. He was from Shimanokoshi and was two years older than I. His aunt had arranged for us to meet. Now our shop is the chief supplier of lunches to the school. . . .

"I keep thinking about raising children—the expenses, the food— it's a real problem. You can't deal with it all by yourself. Two or three people are better than one; ten are better yet. They can get together, compare ideas and problems. The Women's Club is really good for that, you know. Without it each person has to fend for herself. No matter how good your idea is, if there's nowhere to take it and share it—well, nothing will come of it. In this area we have to have that kind of interaction to get anything done. It's the same with festivals. Whenever an accident happens and we need emergency feeding, then we need everyone to work and cooperate. I really think that everyone—all of us—has to remember how important this is.

"The Shimanokoshi Women's Club has about seventy members. People in their thirties and forties are the largest groups. There are only a few in their twenties. Those who are in their fifties and sixties move to the Old Folk's Club. In Shimanokoshi the number of farming families is dwindling, and the fishing co-op women's group is really combining with the local Women's Club. We have made an effort to eliminate synthetic cleansers and to work on good health practices. Beginning last year (1985), when we discovered that people were not eating much fish, the fishing co-op study group and the youth group people all mounted a vigorous campaign to get people to change their ideas and improve these things. We began to advocate the use of healthy foods, to keep out those with additives, and we started an instructional program called the 'seminar on food processing and use.'

"For a long time in Tanohata, if you were from Shimanokoshi you thought only of Shimanokoshi. There was an isolated hamlet mentality. People were aware of only their own place. Even when there were connections with other hamlets, nobody thought about them. It was a fact that ways of thinking and ways of living in the coastal hamlets were different from those in the hills. There were differences in the way people did and returned favors, and I think we had to do something to change that situation for the better. The question of what would be the best way to do that was difficult. There was no common way of approaching daily life throughout the village. Sporadic contact took place, but no one paid much attention to it. When people addressed the issue of village affairs as a whole, that's what they discovered. Wouldn't it be better if people had a certain sense of shared feelings. When it came to education and health, there would be one part of the village working hard on them and another paying no attention, and the village as a whole suffered.

"So I think we might put it this way. Men don't have any real concern for the way they live, but women don't want to live their whole lives this way. They have to take care of the children. They want the men to help out in some way. The burdens women carry are really heavy. It seems as if, from beginning to end, they have to pick up everything that men have 'forgotten' to do.

"The men in the coastal hamlets won't give an inch. They're stubborn! Working in the sea, they learn that every minute, every decision, is a risk, and they put their lives on the line all the time. So when there's a gathering the women don't speak out. It's only the men's voices we hear, and the women just have to sit there and take it. Let's face it, women are just tools to be used, that's all. In a household where the wife is treated well and respected—in those places you find good kids. In that kind of a household, the whole family is well cared for."[20]

The visitor to Tanohata in the 1990s finds a village that, although still remote and struggling to create viable economic and social patterns for development, bears little resemblance to the village of the 1950s. Cars and trucks abound; 80 percent of the village's roads are paved. Two budding supermarkets, a coffee shop, a comfortable tourist hotel, numerous *minshuku* (family-run inns) and other tourist facilities have sprung up. A thriving reforestation program, a furniture factory, numerous dairy and vegetable farms, new fishing port facilities, and a sea products experiment station (for both fish and vegetable products) all testify to the vigorous thrust of economic development and social change that engulfs the village. While there are still remote backwater areas in the village, the unifying effects of economic development and educational progress are in evidence everywhere, even to the casual visitor. Observers who stay in the village for a time are astounded by the seeming disjuncture between the Tanohata of the 1950s and the Tanohata of the 1980s. How could this be?

Having observed a decade and a half of change in Tanohata personally, I became increasingly intrigued by this question. When we relate the process to the larger trends of the four postwar decades in Japanese national life, a number of other issues arise. Were the changes the result of dynamic leadership or of fortuitous circumstance, or both? What were the ingredients that triggered these changes, and what does the evidence suggest were the causes? What follows is an attempt to spell out this process and explain not only why Tanohata is different from what it was thirty years ago, but why it is different from its neighbors today.

ピンクありオレンヂありて刺網の
色とりどりに時代を映す

拓洋

Pink! Orange!
The colors of the fishing nets
How the times are changing!

Kuri Takuyō

Pinku ari orenji arite sashiami no
Iro toridori ni jidai o utsusu

Takuyō

Chapter Two

THE PROCESS
OF DEVELOPMENT,
1955–82

The perspective of hindsight helps the social scientist as well as the historian. In the 1950s, life in Tanohata was so difficult that it is hard to imagine how it could have gotten worse, but it did. Nowhere is this fact more evident than in an analysis of the circumstances prevailing in Tanohata in 1955. Two facts, seemingly unrelated, underscore the truth of such an assertion. First, an Iwate Prefecture study of 1955, carried out in preparation for the implementation of the national program to consolidate local government units, implied that there was no future for the village. Second, that same year the Shimanokoshi fishing co-op collapsed in a chaotic state of bankruptcy. Who would have predicted anything except further economic decline and social disruption for Tanohata and its constituent hamlets? However, two new elements entered the picture. First of all, from 1955 on, political pressure for consolidation was put on Tanohata from above. This pressure came as a result of the prefecture-sponsored study (see Chapter 1). In addition, in 1955 the young Hayano Senpei was selected as the new head of the Hamaiwaizumi fishing co-op in Tanohata. These two developments can be seen as fundamental to the establishment of Tanohata as a viable local entity—a village with a future, even if it lacked a real past.

When the prefectural authorities pressured the village to unite with its neighbor to the north, its leaders were forced to consider their identity. Over the next five years, in response to this outside pressure, there emerged for the first time a real Tanohata. At the same time, a young man of twenty-five was persuaded to become head of the nearly defunct fishing cooperative, largely because no one else wanted the job. (It normally would not have been given to anyone so young.) This man was Hayano Senpei, later to become mayor of Tanohata. In the next ten years, he put the co-op on its feet and began to work actively in village affairs. He was elected to the Village Assembly, chaired the Shimanokoshi PTA, and immersed himself in learning how to run a complex social and economic institution. It is clear that Hayano's decade of training in what was essentially a private corporation, but one with an important social and political role and responsibility, gave him the skills and experience that he needed when he was elected mayor of Tanohata in August 1965. Hayano was not the only new leader to emerge, but he represented a new wave of leadership, people with new skills and a new perspective on Tanohata.

These two factors, pressure from Iwate Prefecture authorities to merge with Fudai and the emergence of new leadership within the village, go far to explain why Tanohata began to change. In addition, three other ingredients contributed substantially to the changes. First of all, nationally Japan was embarking on a decade of explosive economic growth in 1960, and from the middle of the 1960s Tanohata began to benefit from and relate directly to the mainstream of that development. Second, in 1963 a new governor, Chida Tadashi, was elected in Iwate, and he launched a full-scale campaign to raise living standards and lead Iwate up from its position as one of the two poorest of Japan's prefectures (the other was Kagoshima). Leaders in Tanohata had developed close ties to Chida, and the village benefited substantially from this relationship over the next fifteen years. Third, once Chida was elected, he appointed a new Prefectural Superintendent of Education, Kudō Iwao. Kudō launched a campaign to raise the level of education all over Iwate, but especially in some of the remote areas. Tanohata benefited in a host of ways from this movement (the "Movement to Promote Education," *Kyōiku shinkō undō*).

Bearing these five elements in mind, we can now trace the development of Tanohata over the years from 1955 to 1982, noting the ways in which such forces influenced and in turn came to be reflected in the attitudes of local people and in local conditions.

The seven-year period between 1955 and 1962 can be seen in a kind of macabre irony as setting the stage for what was to come. The bad luck that plagued Tanohata continued with several natural disasters, including a serious forest fire in 1956. This was compounded by deteriorating economic conditions and mounting pressure from the prefecture for consolidation, which culminated in a bizarre breakdown of that process. With no hard-surface roads and no fishing port facilities, opportunities to earn cash income continued to decline. As Tanohata entered the 1960s, a further blow hit the village. This was the so-called kerosene revolution, in which, all over Japan, people switched from coal and charcoal to kerosene for heating and cooking. It destroyed a major source of cash income in Tanohata.

As one analyzes developments in Tanohata over the two decades from 1961 to 1982, four phases of change emerge, each initiated or dominated by a major event or issue in village life marking a turning point in the development process. Phase I (1961–64) was initiated by the breakdown of negotiations for merger with Fudai. Phase II (1965–72) was triggered by the election of Hayano as mayor. Phase III (1973–76) was dominated by the controversy over the establishment of a consolidated middle school. Phase IV (1977–82) was highlighted by the emergence of a new phase of economic development and the establishment of the village as a pioneer in international education. Actual events do not always lend themselves to neat time capsules, and, of course, certain issues carry over from one phase to the next. However, looking at the history of Tanohata in those two decades, one can clearly identify dramatic shifts in the way of life in Tanohata and in the focus of people's attention as the village moved from one phase to the next.[1]

Phase I (1961–64): Prelude

Tanohata in the early 1960s appeared to its few visitors to be a dismal place. In the spring of 1960, the negotiations sponsored by Iwate Prefecture for the merger of Tanohata and Fudai reached a climax. These negotiations, begun in January 1957 at the behest of the prefecture, had proceeded sporadically for three years. In March 1960, there was an exchange of documents, with each village submitting to the other a detailed proposal as the basis for consummating the merger. The Tanohata proposal, undated but apparently written in January 1960 and approved by the Village Assembly, contained the following conditions:

1. The central office of the new village would be located in Tanohata-*mura*.
2. A new branch office would be constructed in Fudai-*mura*.
3. For a period of time, a branch office *(shisho)* would be maintained at the present location of the Fudai village office.
4. The functions that would be carried on at the *shisho* office would include twelve matters related to everyday activities, for instance, registration of births and funerals, welfare payments, distribution of information, etc.

This set of conditions became the key sticking point in the negotiations, since Fudai people naturally assumed that the main village office would be in Fudai. The Tanohata people also included in their proposal a long shopping list of requests for school buildings, roads, and telephone communications. The prefectural authorities interpreted these proposals as indicative of substantial progress and assumed that the merger was assured, with only a few details yet to be ironed out.

By the end of March, the negotiations had proceeded to the point where prefectural authorities in Morioka believed that the merger would go through, and they sent the congratulatory telegram to Tanohata and Fudai that is quoted in Chapter One. They clearly either misjudged the situation and their ability to control it, or else misunderstood what the Tanohata people had said in the Tanohata draft, which proposed that the central village office be in Tanohata with a branch office in Fudai.

Negotiations continued in a desultory way through July 1961, and then all trace of them disappears. There is nothing in the records to indicate that any formal decision to drop the plan had been made. The merger did not take place, obviously, but what happened? The telegram from Morioka indicated that everything was in order. (Such formal action as a congratulatory telegram would not have been sent if the prefectural officials had not been sure that this was the case.) When a number of the people who served on the negotiating team were interviewed, the dramatic climax to the story unfolded.

Apparently the pressure from the Iwate authorities was so severe that the Tanohata people felt they could not oppose the merger formally or reject it outright. A final meeting of the negotiators to settle the last details was planned for mid-May 1960; it was to be followed by a party to celebrate the successful completion of four years of arduous negotiations. Representatives from the prefecture and the two villages were present. Instead of a celebration, however, the meeting turned into a disaster. Mayor Makuuchi of Tanohata, who was also head of its negotiating team, having exhausted all other ways of blocking the merger, stood up at the meeting to say that since it was obvious that Tanohata was the larger and more populous place, the village office should, of course, be in Tanohata. To say this directly and openly was to insult the Fudai people and, by implication, the Iwate officials who supported them. At the party following the formal meeting, Tanohata's mayor proceeded to get drunk and directly insult people from Morioka and Fudai. This, of course, broke up the party, but it also brought an end to serious talk of merger between the two villages. Between the end of May 1960 and July 1961, the documents contain references to phone calls and proposed meetings, but only one substantive session seems to have been held (on February 24, 1961) and the last document with any reference to the merger, dated March 23, 1961, proposed that the governor be asked to participate in deciding the location of the office for the consolidated village. From then on, Fudai and Tanohata each went its own way. The incumbent mayor in Tanohata, a man named Makuuchi, was replaced at the end of his term in August 1961 by Hironai Kotarō; in the election, Makuuchi ran a distant fourth among the four candidates.

Nationally, 1961 saw the emergence of Prime Minister Ikeda's "Income Doubling Policy" and a scramble throughout Japan for economic growth. For Tanohata, however, life continued its course, with little to give cause for hope in people's lives. On May 24, 1961, soon after

overemphasize, for Tanohata still had little private motor-driven transportation. As of April 1, 1964, the population of Tanohata was 6,656, but there were only 103 power-driven four-wheeled vehicles in the whole village.[4] There were still 80 horses in Tanohata. Relatively little change had occurred since 1953, when the village had had 15 four-wheeled power-driven vehicles, 110 bicycles, 141 horses, and 21 horse-drawn vehicles.

To highlight the importance of the opening of regular bus service, one need only look at the public health care situation. In the 1950s, Tanohata had no hospital and almost no health care facilities. In 1956 one person, Iwami Hisako, was hired with prefectural government funds to work in the village as a public health nurse. She had to make the rounds of the various hamlets on foot, since there were neither roads nor vehicles to run on them. In 1962 an outpatient and prenatal clinic was established in old Tanohata in the center of the village, and in 1963 another clinic was set up in Numabukuro (making one each in two of the three old constituent villages). These developments had a clear impact on infant mortality, lowering it from 75 per 1000 in 1959, to 55.6 per 1000 in 1962, to 17 per 1000 in 1964. (The national average in 1959 was just over 30 per 1000.) Another fundamental indicator of health conditions was the source of drinking water. In October 1964 a town-run system for drinking water was completed, the first in the village; it was built in Hiranamisawa, the central hamlet of the old Tanohata, where the village administrative offices are located. In September 1963, a new village office was completed, providing space for expanded services and testifying to a change in the outlook of the village from the days of the merger negotiations with Fudai.

Also in 1963 a young councilman from the coastal fishing hamlet of Shimanokoshi named Kudō Takeo was elected chairman of the Village Assembly. His family were fishermen and ran a coastal inn. His election brought to the fore a new generation of village leaders. Kudō retained the chairmanship of the assembly for twenty-five years and continues to play a vital role in the political and economic life of Tanohata.

Few of these developments in themselves—with the exception, perhaps, of the Makisawa Bridge—signaled dramatic change for Tanohata. Together, however, they laid the foundation for the rapid changes of Phase II. It is especially important to note this because otherwise these changes would seem to be the result of the work of one man, Hayano Senpei, who was elected mayor of Tanohata on August 20, 1965. In fact, although Hayano was the catalyst and the architect of much that happened, he was not the sole cause.

By the summer of 1965, one can see, even if only in outline, the thrust of the changes that were to come in the next five years. Clearly transportation and health had first priority. Undergirding them was the beginning of a change in educational patterns, and a growing sense of the urgent need for economic development projects to generate cash income in the village. In the next phase of development, these elements of policy would be conceptualized, articulated, and implemented.

Phase II (1965–72):
Building the Base: Infrastructure and Identity

On March 16, 1966, Mayor Hayano gave his first administrative policy speech to the Village Assembly. It contained an interesting mixture of philosophical exhortation and practical policy proposals. The following excerpts show the flavor of the mayor's approach and the thrust of his leadership.

> Last August the Makisawa Bridge was opened to traffic, construction of National Route 45 is under way . . . and the construction of improved port facilities for fishing at Hiraiga and Akedo is being implemented, so it may not be an exaggeration to say that our formal designation as an *hekichi* (remote area) no longer holds. However, what are we to say about the conditions of our daily lives? In Shōwa 38 (1963) the average income per person in Tanohata-*mura* was ¥75,000 per month [just over $200 at the current exchange rate]. Compared to Iwate Prefecture as a whole, where the average was ¥134,000 per month, and to the national average of ¥162,000, we would have to say this is low and we must admit to ourselves that we are very poor people. . . . Isn't it clear that all 6,000 of us in this village must throw ourselves with great dedication into the task of building a new village? Isn't this the chance to do it? . . . We have ample land, sea, and forest resources, and I believe deeply that . . . we have the possibility of significant development before us.
>
> This means that each one of us must completely divest ourselves of this sense of being "people from an *hekichi*" and, adopting and promoting a spirit that desires vigorous development, we must face the future. . . . From here on, the promotion of effective and speedy development for this village is our task. . . .
>
> The three pillars of policy, that is, promotion of education, promotion of economic development, and progress in social welfare, are where emphasis will be placed. I shall exert every effort to realize these goals concretely. I pledge these as my policy goals for the fiscal year Shōwa 41 (1966).[5]

In the body of his speech, the mayor outlined specific goals for the year in each of these three areas. He announced that he had already arranged for Tanohata to participate in a prefectural program for pre-school and primary school children, citing the need to raise the low performance level of village children on national tests. He also announced plans to build a physical education addition to the central elementary school. In economic development, he reported the establishment of a forestry products cooperative, indicated that work on soil improvement and paddy development to provide self-sufficiency in food production was being rapidly carried forward, and reported on the road-building activities planned for the coming year. His social welfare plans focused on building a clinic to help reduce the infant mortality rate and continuing the construction of facilities to provide safe drinking water.

This speech and the succeeding ones are, of course, partly political rhetoric, put forth for the record. However, read in sequence, they yield threads of continuity and a record of the specific accomplishments of his administration. Hayano's second speech, given on March 22, 1967, after a year and a half in office, was even more specific in cataloguing work in progress and listing new projects for the coming year. Work on roads and fishing port facilities was in full swing, and a midwife center, a day-care center, and a school lunch program center had all been completed in the fiscal year ending March 31, 1967. (The Japanese fiscal year runs from April 1 to March 31.) Seven projects were continued from the previous year (almost all of them dealing with the village's infrastructure), and seven new ones were to be started. The new projects were also largely infrastructure-related, but they included providing high school education within the village and, in cooperation with Waseda University, establishing a permanent facility for the reforestation project. The prefecture had designated the village as a site for developing a model dairy farm operation, and a five-year plan for this to be completed by the end of Shōwa 46 (1971) had been launched. The mayor noted that for the first time ever, village children applying to high schools (there were seventy applicants) had a 100 percent acceptance rate.[6]

By the spring of 1967, the village was buzzing with activity and the pace of change was quickening. The mayor's basic decision as he took office had been to focus on projects that would build the infrastructure and provide stimulus for further growth. These were largely in the fields of health, education, and communication (e.g., provision of clinics, drinking water, school buildings, roads, telephones, fishing port facilities). His yearly speeches demonstrate a solid grasp of what was needed to generate and sustain momentum. They have a philosophical, rhetorical thrust to them, yet he always points to specific problems and weaknesses.

> . . . It is my belief that we must again redouble our efforts so that at an early date we can realize this goal . . . of developing people with the skills to care for dairy cattle and other domestic animals. We have put funds in the budget to do this, and we must begin this work under the supervision of the Agricultural Co-op. Otherwise, even if we have the cooperation of the prefectural authorities and financial backers, we will not be able to ensure the success of the project.[7]

The twin themes of Phase II were infrastructure and identity. Before real economic development could take place, there had to be roads and a communication network. Installation of public telephones in every hamlet was given priority, and road building had the highest priority of all. The issue was simple: without roads and telephones there could be no real Tanohata. For more than seventy years (since 1889) Tanohata had existed only on paper. The people in each hamlet had done their best to survive, but without everyday communication links between them, the larger sense of village identity that was needed could not develop. No wonder Mayor Hayano came to be known to critics and supporters alike as the "road building" mayor *(Dōrō sonchō)*. From education to dairy farming to fishing port facilities, the issue of communication dominated the scene in Tanohata.

The great symbol of Phase II was the national highway, Route 45. Construction crews worked ceaselessly to forge this link to the outside world. Critically important fringe benefits of this and other construction work in the village were the jobs—and cash income—for local people that were provided. The ribbon-cutting ceremony marking the opening of the full length of Route 45 took place in the fall of 1972. For the first time Tanohata was fully linked from north to south by a first-class, all-weather road, and people could travel easily from one end of the village to the other. No longer would people in the north have to turn their backs to the center of the village; now, literally and figuratively, it was accessible to them. The Kumagais of Tashiro exemplified this growing sense of belonging. Young Ryūkō participated in the ribbon-cutting ceremony as a representative of the Numabukuro Young People's Association *(seinen kai);* finally his home and Numabukuro were linked to the rest of the village.

Interesting as the story of Tanohata's emergence is, the question of how the process was initiated and sustained is equally fascinating. An analysis of the mayor's approach reveals three elements to the strategy that he evolved in Phase II of Tanohata's development. First and fundamental to all else was Hayano's ability to tap sources of revenue outside the village. The village had no real tax base on which to build. As the 1955 prefectural study had revealed, 94 percent of its budget came from outside sources. Very early in his tenure, Hayano developed effective channels of communication with prefectural and national authorities. Through these channels he was able to obtain large sums of investment assistance, first to build the infrastructure and then to stimulate economic development. (See Figure 1 of the Appendix for statistics on these funds.) Second, as a shrewd judge of people he was able to mobilize leadership from within the village as well as bring in outsiders to help in the process. Third, he had a keen sense of the value of symbolic gestures and publicity to focus attention within the village and lift people's sights beyond the immediate issue. By the end of Phase II, his judicious use of these three methods had generated significant momentum, and fortunately this momentum was sustained over the succeeding decade. There are many examples of how his approach was applied.

Judicious and effective use of outside channels for capital investment and subsidy produced funds for projects all over the village, from the seacoast to the mountains. Nowhere was Hayano's skill and judgment in these matters better used than in education. The earliest evidence appears in the development of preschool facilities and programs. Japan's unitary system of government provides national subsidies for preschool programs through two ministries, Education and Welfare. The Ministry of Education provides help for kindergartens; the Ministry of Welfare provides funds for child-care centers. Tanohata has seven child-care centers spread all over the village, but no kindergartens. Why not? Ministry of Welfare funds are more generous and require less onerous application and reporting procedures. Almost all preschool children in Tanohata today attend the centers, which are well-run institutions with cooperative work days for mothers and excellent educational facilities. (By 1982, 100 percent of the five year olds were attending preschool, and between 80 and 90 percent of four year olds were in the first year classes.)

In the field of economic development, the first subsidies were sought to improve fishing port facilities, since they would have an immediate payoff in increases in personal income. The mayor is a member of the support group *(kōen-kai)* of Suzuki Zenkō, prime minister of Japan from 1980 to 1982, though he is not a member of the Liberal Democratic Party (LDP). Pork barrel politics are as much a part of the Japanese scene as of the American and, in his years in the Diet, Suzuki served his constituency well. Shimanokoshi, Hayano's home hamlet, was designated a "fourth class fishing port" in the mid-1960s, the only one on the Iwate coast. (Miyako and Kuji to the south and to the north respectively are bigger, all-purpose harbors.)

Of equal importance in the long run was the subsidy the village received as a result of its designation in 1967 as the location of a model dairy stock experiment station.[8] Fishing was already a stable occupation in Tanohata, bringing in some cash income, but farming was not. In order for it to become so it needed not only saleable products but access to markets. Road-building provided the latter, but it took village investment and modeling to accomplish the former. Dairying had potential, but only if a surplus could be generated. This required adequate supplies of local feed and pasture and care for young stock. The prefectural subsidies mentioned in the mayor's speech in March 1967 provided the capital to establish the Nagamine Stock Farm *(Nagamine bokujo)* on village land, which would demonstrate ways to raise hay and silage and provide pasture and care services for dairy farmers' young stock. By the time of my first visit to Tanohata in 1972, the demonstration farm was operating and small silos were being built all over the village to ensure year-round availability of good, local fodder for dairy cows.

Such subsidies as these for economic development began to flow into Tanohata in large amounts in the late 1960s, and by the time Mayor Hayano was elected to his second term in 1969 the results were dramatic and quantifiable. The direct impact was most obvious in the new facilities —roads, fishing ports, and school and social service buildings. The presence of these new facilities demonstrably improved people's everyday lives. For individual families, probably the most important change was the amount of cash available. Project subsidies created jobs and payrolls, and now people in many families were working at regular jobs for cash wages. One startling statistic underscores what was happening: when the figures for village tax income in 1968 and 1969 are compared, one sees a 100 percent jump in local money raised through taxes (see Appendix, Figure 2). This happened not as the result of higher taxes; rather, it resulted from a combination of a dramatic increase in taxable cash income in the village, brought about by payroll wages, and a rise in property values, the result of new construction of all kinds. Here was concrete evidence of village-wide change in people's lives.

The second element in Hayano's three-pronged approach to change was personnel policy and management. From the beginning he hammered at his theme: *mura-zukuri* (village-building) would require first of all *ningen-zukuri* (people-building).[9] His approach was to do the two things simultaneously. He identified able local people who were open to change and made them part of his team, and he also brought in a few able people from outside and transplanted them in Tanohata. This second part of his personnel policy was particularly shrewd. Outsiders brought in new ideas and methods to serve as models to stimulate growth in the village. If they were able and sensitive people, they could challenge old ways and help to introduce new ways without threatening old-timers so much that their presence was counterproductive. While there were failures in this policy and there was plenty of deadwood among the old-timers to create inertia and resistance, on the whole the mayor's tactics worked well. He established this approach early in his first term and has continued it ever since. An examination of the roles of three people who represent this approach to people and to leadership will illustrate concretely how it worked. First, consider the role of an old-timer in the village, Hatakeyama Shōichi.[10]

Shōichi was born in 1929 and grew up in Tanohata in an old, though not particularly prosperous, family. He has been to Tokyo once or twice, but his world of experience is really Tanohata, though two of his children now live in Tokyo. He and his wife live in the central hamlet of Tanohata, Sugenokubo, where they have a small plot of land and a large garden, and raise pigs and chickens for their own food. In the early 1980s they were able to rebuild their house. Shōichi attended primary and middle school in the village but had no further schooling. He went to work in the village office in 1965 and gradually rose in the bureaucracy until, in 1980, he became *Sōmu-ka-chō* (chief of the General Affairs Section). This is the most important career administrative post in the village.[11] It makes him the number four person in the official village hierarchy, responsible for general oversight of administrative affairs related to budget and personnel. He is the internal channel of access to the mayor for all important matters including new budget proposals, and so can be either a bottleneck or a facilitator of change and development in the village.

Shōichi is a remarkable human being, wise, humane, steeped in the lore of Tanohata, and devoted to its welfare and development. A consistent thread runs through his career: he is constantly alert to and ready to consider new things and willing to accept and work with new people. In July 1966, it was he whom the mayor chose to join him to meet with Professor Oda and others from Waseda University to brainstorm about the plans for the reforestation project that later became Shii no Mori. He and his wife welcomed the Waseda students in their home regularly all through those early years. Thus he became a channel both officially and personally for new ideas and new ways to come into the village. The significance of his role as a vigorous young "old-timer" in the village can hardly be overemphasized. He and others like him provide the explanation why the mayor's plans for Tanohata have been implemented successfully. This is not to suggest that there has been no resistance to change and no problems. There is great inertia and resistance and the problems are legion. However, my research colleague, Professor Hashimoto Ryōji, an experienced Japanese sociologist who has done field work in rural areas in various parts of Japan, confirms my assessment that the presence of people like Shōichi has made change easier in Tanohata than in most places.

However, local leadership was not enough. New skills and new ideas were needed. Illustrative of the adroit way in which Mayor Hayano met this need is the career of Takahashi Yukio, an engineer who has served as chief of the Construction Section *(Kensetsu-ka-chō)* throughout Hayano's tenure as mayor.

Takahashi brought to Tanohata needed skills and understanding of a wider world. By 1982 he was supervising and promoting construction projects with a total yearly budget of ¥928 million (roughly $240,000, and 40.8 percent of the village budget in 1982). He is neither a philosopher nor someone with wide interests. He is a technician, a practical "doer" who seems to have both a knack for getting the job done and a sensitivity in human relations that enabled him to gain acceptance in the village. He and his family are now part of Tanohata. In January 1983, his teenage daughter, Kazuko, spent three weeks in the United States in a village-sponsored and financed program for middle school students. When they moved to the village in 1966 before Kazuko was born, who could have foreseen that such opportunities would ever be available to Tanohata youngsters. Takahashi illustrates how the "new" citizens of Tanohata have become a part of the ongoing processes of village life.

Closely related to the problem of village development is the phenomenon *dekasegi*, going out of the village to take good paying jobs in urban construction projects on a seasonal basis. These workers retain their basic residence and ongoing ties at home and return for extended periods. Able young people are both drawn out of the village by the magnetic pull of urban life and propelled out by the lack of decent jobs at home. (See Chapter 5 for a detailed treatment of *dekasegi*.) These socioeconomic problems (not unique to Japan, of course) plague Tanohata along with scores of other villages all over Japan. In the 1980s people began talking about a countervailing phenomenon, the "U-turn" phenomenon, in which young people go to the cities for education and jobs and then return to their home villages to find careers and settle down.

Date Katsumi represented the U-turn phenomenon long before the term was current. When I first met him in December 1972 I had little concrete knowledge of how issues like *dekasegi* and brain drain affected life in rural Japan. Date's role in Tanohata contrasts to both Hatakeyama Shōichi's and Takahashi Yukio's. But he too has been a key player in Hayano's plan.

Date grew up in a remote hamlet of the neighboring town of Iwaizumi. He got a high school education and passed the entrance exams for Waseda University. While at Waseda in the late 1960s he took a course from Professor Oda, went to Tanohata to work in the reforestation project and joined the Shii no Mori Kai. After graduation in 1970 he married a Waseda classmate and then spent a year in the Waseda Graduate School of Commerce. On completion of that year, he applied and was selected to enter one of the top national companies, a road-building corporation (the *Kokudō Keikaku K.K.*). Then fate—and Mayor Hayano's personnel plans—intervened. Date was offered a job in the Tanohata Village Office and became a village employee in April 1971. For more than seven years he worked in a variety of posts in the village office, the Board of Education *(Kyōiku iin-kai)*, the General Affairs Section *(Sōmu-ka)*, and the Economic Development Section *(Keizai kaihatsu-ka)*. In 1979 he moved out of the village office to become managing director of the Tanohata branch office of the semi-public development corporation in which the village owns substantial stock.[12] By the time I met him, Date was already on his way to becoming the mayor's right-hand man and troubleshooter for education and economic affairs, providing, especially, close liaison with Waseda and other agencies in Tokyo and abroad. Dynamic, able, wise in the ways of the world, well-connected inside and outside the village, he is remarkably effective in promoting village policies. He has no patience with small minded people and bureaucratic inefficiency or inertia, but he knows how to deal with them, bypassing them and avoiding unnecessary friction when that suffices or confronting them and overriding their objections when necessary.

The nature of the challenge that Date and his wife, Toshiko, faced as young outsiders moving into Tanohata is reflected in Toshiko's comments about their life in those early years. Raised in a well-to-do family in Toyama Prefecture on the Japan Sea side of Honshū, she had met Katsumi while studying at Waseda.

> We came to Tanohata in 1971, at the end of March. At first we lived in Shimanokoshi. We were supposed to have one of the village office houses, but when we arrived people were already living in it. That really put us in a bad situation. There were no apartments, but a kind person in Shimanokoshi rented us room(s). We were there three months. It was a fishing village, so mornings were early and everything was pitch black by 7 P.M. I was very lonely. They got up at 3 or 4 A.M. so they were in bed by 7 P.M. It was a different pattern of living.
>
> My husband was eager to bring the living standard up to the level of other towns, and put all his energy into it. So he was gone even Saturdays and Sundays. There were times when I wondered what I had come for. At that time—and this is still true—those who had higher education usually went to live in the cities. We were twenty-three and twenty-seven, coming to this village with the energy of young college graduates. People here didn't see it that way, apparently. They thought something was wrong with us. Somebody told me about this two years later. Their explanation was that we had been part of the student agitation movement, had been driven away by policemen brandishing billy clubs, and had fled hand in hand to this village. We had a big laugh when we heard this.
>
> Because I had gone to college, I saw nothing wrong with observing critically the mothers I saw around me. I think I was still rebellious. Also I thought it was strange to act overly modestly, and I hadn't learned the "proper attitude" yet. Now that I've reached middle age, I'm more relaxed about these things, but also I take more care. In this village, people who clearly spoke their opinions were thought to be not very smart. Because of that, a personality like mine didn't fit well. There were times when people said lightly, do you know that, or are you just putting on airs? There are (organized groups of) people who are against the work my husband does. That is why they opposed me. We even got anonymous hate letters.
>
> We were told to get out of the village, and not just once or twice. Today, well, everyone understands now. As a matter of fact, it was about ten years before I felt myself, before my own body had become acclimated and I was part of the village. After how many years here? Until then I was an outsider. They made me aware of it, and I kept my distance—for whatever reasons, there was a time when

I was not allowed to be a real part of things. I think I started doing village work five or six years after I came here. At first I was part of the
community education division, then of the school district. Those
were the most difficult child-raising years. Yes. I taught the tea ceremony, I spent two years teaching home economics in the high
school, I joined the mothers' chorus, I did what I could because I
thought it might be a good idea to plan enjoyable things for the village. But those village women were hard to budge. . . . "That woman
from outside is doing something or other, so we can ignore it," they
seemed to think. There were times when I was discontented without
reason, but my personality helped me somehow enjoy myself
anyway.[13]

Date and his wife had to struggle along as outsiders in Tanohata for
some years, but gradually they came to be accepted. Long before
"U-turn" became a catch phrase in Japan, Date Katsumi had done it,
returning from the city to his home area and making a place for himself
and his family. The mayor's ability to attract and hold such people,
who are a bridge between the "old-timers" and the "newcomers,"
is a tremendous asset to Tanohata. Date has been invaluable in this
role.

As we shall see in Chapter Five, one of the big tests of the decade of
the 1980s was whether Hayano and Tanohata could create job opportunities for enough able young people to staunch the brain drain and make
the U-turn phenomenon a truly viable alternative for large numbers of
young people. It is still an unusual move. When Date did it, he was the
exception that proved the rule.

Date represents the success of one element of the mayor's approach
to personnel matters. He also has been an important force in the development of the third element in the mayor's strategy for change, to wit, the
design and use of publicity and symbolic gestures to gain attention and
recognition for Tanohata in the outside world and to raise the sights and
deepen the sense of identity of the village people themselves. Date has
developed a keen sense of timing and effectively uses the media to
enhance these village-building processes. His work for the mayor in this
area is nothing short of brilliant. He has long demonstrated a flair for unit-
ing symbols and substantive programs for the benefit of Tanohata. He
demonstrated it early on, when he was still a Waseda student in 1968 and
participated in the planning for the visit to Tanohata of the Canadian
ambassador to plant maple trees. It is further shown in his work in the
spring of 1983 on a proposal to bring a consultant in international education to work in Shimohei-*gun*.

Some people in Tanohata dismiss these publicity efforts and criticize the mayor as a pompous publicity seeker. My own assessment is that
although he understands the value and the uses of publicity, he does not

seek the limelight himself. His concern for people is genuine and is often expressed quietly behind the scenes, as when he personally stood as financial guarantor for a pioneer dairy farmer who moved to Tanohata in 1977.[14] His personal and professional involvement in the day-to-day problems of education in the village also belies that charge. He certainly uses the media to further his policies, but the focus of his attention is on the substance and implementation of policy. During his first term as mayor, he discovered and began to use effectively the news potential in dramatic new initiatives of policy and program. The visit of the Canadian ambassador, for instance, highlighted the forest resource development program in Tanohata, bringing to Tanohata the governor and other high officials from Morioka and Tokyo and putting Tanohata on the regional map. Events such as this had an important fringe benefit. People in the village, hearing of the visit and seeing the attendant publicity in press and TV coverage, said to themselves, "We are doing some interesting and important things, aren't we?" A sense of pride in being from Tanohata was beginning to replace the old diffidence that reflected the down-and-out, back-country self-image of the 1950s and early 1960s. Thus publicity from the outside raised people's sights and gave further support for the changes that were needed inside the village.

This three-pronged strategy—first, seeking and using effective channels to get investment subsidies; second, creating a personnel team that was a judicious mix of able people, some original Tanohatans, some new from outside, and some who had done a U-turn; and third, using public relations to highlight dramatic new program initiatives which enhance the village's image outside and establish its identity within—has proven successful and enduring. By the fall of 1972, when National Highway 45 formally opened, it was clear that the basic infrastructure for further economic growth in Tanohata was in place. On the other hand, many more roads remained to be built, incomes were still low, education remained poor and uneven, and there was not yet a full sense of Tanohata as a village with its own identity. Even the dramas of the Canadian ambassador's visit and of the 1972 Iwate-ken Forestry Festival, which took place in Tanohata, were, in some sense, isolated happenings not at all typical of the realities of life there. The roads were still so bad in 1969 that the Canadian ambassador left the village angry and vowing never to make such a trip again. He had had to breathe the dust of the governor's lead car all the way from Morioka, and on the way back the road north to Hachinohe was as bad or worse, a rough washboard full of potholes. Yet for all this, things had changed, and the pace of change was quickening. There was much to build on. A look at the town records for the next four years reveals a very different agenda and confirms that Tanohata was moving into the next phase of development.

Phase III (1973–76): Jobs and Social Engineering

The significance of the shift from Phase II to Phase III is highlighted by two kinds of developments, economic and social. In economic terms, personal income in Tanohata more than tripled between 1965 and 1970, and by 1975 it was nearly eight times that of 1965. Figure 1 shows this dramatic rise. In education and social welfare, equally dramatic changes had occurred. In 1972, for the first time, no Tanohata infants died. New health care programs and facilities had moved Tanohata from a rate of 55 infant deaths per thousand in 1962 to zero. Such changes set the stage for a shift in the overall agenda for village affairs. This change is reflected in the village records, both in specific provisions of the budget and in the rhetoric of the mayor. No longer was the focus of attention on relief from desperate poverty and isolation, as it had been in 1965. Now education and new projects in economic development moved to the center of the stage. And, for the first time since Hayano had become mayor, a major controversy engulfed the village. Previously there had been conflict and friction between people and sections of the village, but seldom, if ever, did these surface in public reports and they usually did not constitute part of the public record.

The stage was set for the controversy by the village's progress over the preceding seven years in providing better education and new facilities in the village. By 1972, elementary school facilities had been upgraded and preschool child-care centers (*jidō-kan*) were available to all families. (By 1972 all eligible five year olds were attending *jidō-kan*.) In 1972 the mayor confirmed plans that had been announced earlier to build

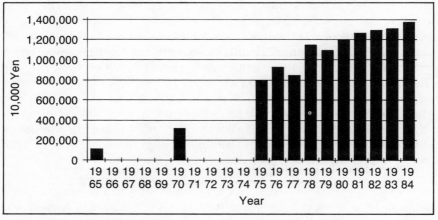

FIGURE 1. Personal income growth in Tanohata, 1965–84.
Source: Tanohata-mura, *Tanohata sonsei yōran,* 1982, p. 18.

a consolidated middle school *(tōgōchūgakkō)* that all Tanohata children would attend. This announcement gave rise to a serious controversy that would affect public life in Tanohata for the next five years; it even brought to the village an investigative reporter from one of the national dailies in Tokyo. The mayor indicated in his State of the Village address in March that land had been secured, and he announced that the Board of Education would proceed to implement the project. The idea was not a new one. He spoke of it as having been on the agenda for twenty years, and others in the village confirmed this. However, in the context of Japanese national life in the 1970s and of the particular situation in Tanohata at this time, the plan was implemented with a sense of urgency, even though it drew strong opposition from within and scathing criticism from outside the village.

The decade of the 1960s, with its phenomenal economic growth, had left Japan with environmental degradation of monumental proportions. In the early 1970s, citizens' action groups and thoughtful Japanese everywhere were challenging the concept of growth at any price and raising the issue of quality of life as the top agenda item for the decade. In this context Premier Tanaka's ill-fated "Plan to Remodel the Japanese Archipelago" *(Nihon rettō kaizō-ron)* became a symbol of all that was bad about economic growth and of the heavy hand of big government, undergirded by private greed, forcing unwanted policies and projects down the throats of helpless citizens. The press was on the lookout for any evidence of this kind of government activity and was ready to denounce it.

By the time that Tanohata's school consolidation plan began to be implemented in 1973–74 the opposition to it in the village had become public and vocal. Honda Katsuichi, a well-known investigative reporter for the Asahi Press, was at the same time touring the country visiting remote areas and writing about their problems.[15] He came to Tanohata with the assumption that what was happening was essentially the result of policies set in Tokyo by a rigid, ultra-conservative bureaucracy in the Ministry of Education, and his interviews with local people seemed to confirm this interpretation.

> The more conservative the areas and their leaders are, the more prone they are to implement central plans. They even go further, committing themselves to them politically and personally. Take the example of one village that is promoting the idea of a consolidated middle school, an idea that has come out of the Ministry of Education and is being implemented nationally with no regard for local differences. Let us see how the wishes of the village people are being trampled on.
>
> Tanohata-*mura* in Shimohei-*gun* is surrounded by mountains and its people are scattered in isolated hamlets. As a result it has six mid-

dle schools (one central one and five branch schools). At the stage
when plans for a consolidated middle school were being implemented, a strong opposition movement arose in the branch school
districts. In the spring of last year (1974) when the consolidated
school opened, the branch schools in Tsukue and Numabukuro did
not join. The mayor, who had pushed the project but failed to consummate it, had labeled the opposition a movement produced by the
propaganda of people who represented a political party or other [out-
side] organization. He said "the passage of time will solve this," but
he has been unable to get rid of the opposition of the villagers.[16]

Honda talked to people in Numabukuro and checked the questionnaires from a 1970 survey that was made as a preliminary step to drawing
up a concrete plan for the school. He strongly criticized the method and
content of the questionnaire, claiming that the sample was skewed and
the questions were a setup for those who were promoting the idea of the
school. However, his most vehement criticism was of the idea in principle and its alleged effects on the village. The *dekasegi* phenomenon had
already drawn many men out of the village into high-paying seasonal construction jobs in the cities. (Eldest sons or heads of households com-
prised the largest single group of these people.) Thus, farm families
depended heavily on teenagers to help with farm work. The consolidated
middle school with its dormitory would remove this group from the farm
work force, too. People in Numabukuro complained to Honda about this,
and he picked up on it and linked their plight to wider national trends
and to earlier historical experience.[17] Honda saw the consolidated middle
school with the dormitory as just another example in a long line of abuses
by big government. When he found out that the expenses for the dorm
and for school buses were being paid out of the village education budget,
he called this a kind of bribe.[18]

The school opened in April 1974, and the dormitory in August, in
time for the second term of the academic year. The two school districts
that had refused to participate, Tsukue and Numabukuro, held out for
some time, but today they, too, participate, most people willingly.[19] In
1982–83 my wife and I came to know a number of people in these two
areas well and we discussed this issue with them at length. By that time,
there clearly was general acceptance of the school and most people all
over Tanohata were proud of it.

Honda Katsuichi's report pinpointed serious issues. *Dekasegi* and
the heavy hand of central government ministries are continuing problems
for people in Tanohata as well as elsewhere in Japan. It is important to
examine the matter further because it turns out to be a key to understanding much of what was happening in Tanohata in Phase III.

The mayor's position on the school was clear from the beginning
and consistent throughout. He had not run roughshod over people and

ideas, but he had pushed hard and effectively, seeing the consolidated school as the linchpin in a policy of social integration that in the end would create a real Tanohata where none existed before. His analysis was as follows: he claimed (and others corroborated this) that before the consolidated school was established, ambitious families sent their children out of the village for middle school education because the Tanohata middle schools were so poor. Children leaving the village that young seldom came back—and those lost were the best ones, contributing to the endemic problem of brain drain. Ironically, it turns out that some of the leaders of the opposition to the new school were actually sending their own children out of Tanohata for middle school education, thus supporting the mayor's contention that it was politics, not principle, that motivated them. A large percentage of the middle school teachers came from outside the village, assigned by the Prefectural Board of Education. With six middle schools, all with miserable facilities and some with very few children, the quality of education was poor and teachers dreaded coming to Tanohata. (The smallest, with only thirty-eight students, was in the hamlet of Tsukue.) Something had to be done to improve that situation. Hayano's plan was to establish a consolidated middle school and build a dormitory to house most if not all of the students from Monday to Saturday. The dormitory and its program are designed to promote social integration of the various hamlets of the village. Children always have roommates from different hamlets. Teachers and former students all testify to the impact the dormitory has had in breaking down separatism and creating a sense of being a citizen of Tanohata, not just of a hamlet.

The comments of Kudō Fusako are revealing, confirming the need and the support for the consolidated middle school.

> Yes, all three of my children went to the consolidated middle school and lived in the dormitory. When they came home they'd look at TV and go to bed. In the dorm they could watch TV for only two hours, so TV was a treat for them. When they came home they'd want to sleep, and when we'd talk they'd say, "When we're at home we want to rest." They'd bring home their book bags, put them down, and not pick them up till they went back. From the first I supported the idea of the dorm and the consolidated school. I thought that it would be good for them to interact with others around them and be stimulated by this contact. There was a tendency to emphasize only discipline as a tool to growth, and I thought it would be good for them to be in the dorm.
>
> With something like the consolidated middle school, you have to wait a few years to see what's good and what's bad. It seems to me that unless the young people themselves are involved in formulating the regulations, they will not develop very far. When kids are small, if people put them down in front of the TV just to keep them quiet and

that kind of life continues for years, then the young people are not likely to take the initiative to do things on their own.[20]

Many of Tanohata's problems seemed to be economic, yet Hayano was convinced, and preached from the beginning, that the solutions lay in education. Subsistence farming or fishing did not generate cash income, and this situation had to be changed. As he saw it, the key to breaking out of a vicious circle was education. He believed that the only hope for success in Tanohata's bootstrap operation was to create local jobs and at the same time raise the general level of education so that local youngsters could take these jobs.

The controversy over the middle school was traumatic. It also highlighted both how far Tanohata had come and how far it had yet to go. This latter problem comes into focus when one examines the village agenda in the early 1970s.

The old issues—roads, telephones, drinking water—had largely disappeared. They had been replaced by two new items, dairy farming and tourism. During Phase III, a full-fledged dairy industry was established. When I first visited Tanohata in 1972, one of the things that distinguished it from other parts of Japan that I had visited were the silos for cattle feed. What made dairying possible and profitable were roads, hay, and silage. Phase II had produced the roads, and there had been experiments to identify strains of grass and corn that could be grown and harvested for feed. This work had been sufficiently successful that by the early seventies, not all feed for cows had to come in from outside the village. In Phase III, the village-sponsored work with the Nagamine Stock Farm and Extension Service paid off. Milk output was expanding. The Tanohata Industrial Development Corp. built a modern collecting station and bought small tank trucks that could navigate the local roads for daily milk collection. By the mid-1970s, the dairy business was thriving.

More than any other single activity, the burgeoning dairy business produced the explosion in personal cash income that highlighted Phase III. Income nearly tripled again between 1970 and 1975 (see Figure 1 above); this was true in part because dairying had brought new jobs as well as cash income to Tanohata. However, the work on fishing port facilities was paying off, too. Fishing and sea product income rose substantially in this period with the increases ranging from 20 percent in the case of sea urchins to 300 percent for seaweed *(wakame)*. Fishing and seafood production expanded as a result both of investment in infrastructure and direct investment in the production and sale of fish and other seafood products. New hay land, new silos, new roads, and new port facilities gave Tanohata a new look. Evidence of the results of the reforestation program began to appear also, as lines of seedlings struggled to take hold on the mountainsides and in the ravines all over the village.

Beyond the immediate signs of change, plans were being made for new projects, one in tourism and two in agriculture. The first major project in tourism was to build a toll road to one of Tanohata's two scenic spots, Kitayama-saki. Work on the road, the result of joint investment by local, prefectural, and national governments, began in the late 1960s, and the road finally opened to traffic April 1, 1974. Running parallel to it along the coast was a sightseeing boat that took people up the shore to see Kitayama-saki from that angle. These two developments had an effect on income similar to that of the dairy business, providing local jobs and bringing cash into the village. A third element was added in 1972, when a small but comfortable tourist hotel on the beach in the fishing hamlet of Raga opened.

In agriculture, plans were being made to establish vegetable farming as a source of cash income. As newly built roads gave better access to Miyako, Kuji, and Morioka, the nearest cities, it began to pay to grow vegetables as crops for direct sale to stores in these cities. This plan, implemented in Phase IV (1977–82), resulted in another infusion of cash income into the village. Another project, begun in the early seventies, was to grow specialty trees for furniture-making. Paulownia *(kiri no ki)*, considered a weed tree in the United States, makes superb lightweight furniture. Farm families have traditionally planted two paulownia trees when a daughter was born, and by the time she married these would be harvested and would make enough fine boards for chests for her new home. Paulownia already grew in Tanohata, and the plan was to plant and raise these trees in quantity. A lumber processing factory was set up by a private firm, the Maruishi Furniture Co., which came in from outside. Several hundred acres of paulownia were planted. All went well for the first five or six years, and the project seemed very promising. Then disaster struck—a viral infection carried through the root systems attacked the trees and acres of half-mature trees began to shrivel up and die. The project had to be abandoned.

The poignancy of that particular failure is reflected in the comments of Kuwagata Nobuko, whose husband still worked for Maruishi in 1986.

> Until a while ago, it was said that Tanohata was good for raising paulownia trees, but now—ha—not a thing. They got diseased and were no good. When they became diseased, we had to decide whether or not to cut them even though they were still small trees. If we left them, they'd probably wither within a year. The flowers were pretty, we treated them with medicine of course, but. . . .
>
> Maruishi now uses mostly materials brought from outside. My husband's job is all administrative work indoors. When he started, he was a salesperson and he didn't have a driver's license yet. He'd deliver by bike as far away as Kuji. At the beginning, Maruishi planned ahead

many years, borrowed the use of our farm land for paulownia, but the results turned out bad, like I said, and now they've given it back. Those farms that planted paulownia all lost out. Ha.[21]

As Phase III came to an end in 1976, there were substantial gains to be catalogued. However, it would be a mistake to suggest that development in Tanohata had "taken off" and achieved a momentum of its own. Nor would it be accurate to say that the old image of Tanohata as a poor, backward area had been replaced. There were too many reminders everywhere of problems only partially solved. In purely budgetary terms, the village was still poverty-stricken. Even as late as fiscal 1973, 94 percent of the village budget came from the *ken* or national budget as grants-in-aid or loans. In 1974, that figure was reduced to 90.2 percent, but the mayor was quick to point out to the Council that that was a bare beginning on the road to establishing a viable economy. In fiscal 1975 they actually lost ground, with outside funds providing 91.3 percent of the budget. There remained much to be done, even though the list of accomplishments during the first eleven years of the mayor's administration was impressive. As Phase III ended, however, one could see a significant shift in the village's agenda, and beginning in 1977 with Phase IV, the people of Tanohata had other things on their minds than the controversy over the consolidated middle school and roads or infrastructure.

Phase IV (1977–82): Tourists and Foreign Teachers

In 1976, Tanohata officially designated a village bird, a village flower, and a village tree[22] and adopted a village charter. The charter, containing a preamble and five vows of commitment to the village,[23] is recited in schools and on public occasions such as Adulthood Day.[24]

This kind of activity suggests that life had indeed changed in Tanohata. When people have time to think about cultural matters, then they must be feeling less economic pressure. In a conversation with the mayor in November 1982, I discussed Phase IV with him and asked him to identify the turning points that had occurred earlier during his tenure as mayor. He identified the end of Phase II and the end of Phase III immediately, saying that he knew that they were entering a new period in 1973 and 1977 because the agenda of the Village Assembly had changed. Whereas in 1973 the middle school controversy was on everyone's mind, by 1977 the issue of the middle school was no longer the emotional topic it had been. Instead, people's attention was focused on a whole new set of issues or new formulations of old ones.

With the basic infrastructure—roads, schools, port facilities, health care facilities and services—either in place or under construction, Tanohata's concerns began to converge with the concerns of towns and villages anywhere in Japan. In a sense, Tanohata had been playing catch-up with the rest of Japan, in the same way that Japan in the 1950s and 1960s had done so with the rest of the world. Tanohata's success was more limited, but the agenda of Phase IV provides evidence of this new outlook. Two issues in particular reflect these new realities: international education and tourism.

In the spring of 1976, when I visited Tanohata to confer with the mayor about plans for the Earlham students to go to Tanohata each summer, he and Date turned to me at the end of our conference and said they wanted to talk about a new project. They explained that having the students come to the village in the summer was a good thing and very important to them, but they had concluded it was not enough. They wanted a foreigner to live in the village year-round as a teacher. Their reasoning was simple and at the same time radical. When Tanohata students went on school trips to Tokyo and elsewhere they would see foreigners. Far from trying out their English on them, they were afraid of them. The mayor said, "We want to change that. Can you send us an Earlham graduate as a teacher? We want to hire one."25

The first American teacher arrived in Tanohata in April 1977 to begin a two-year term of service. The plan was so successful that in March 1979, at the request of the village, a young married couple was sent; two people should be more than twice as good as one, the reasoning went! In 1981 a third couple was sent. In July 1983, another couple (the fourth generation of foreign teachers) took over, and in 1985 the fifth generation was installed. Evidence of the effectiveness of this approach was dramatic and personal. When I visited Tanohata in 1979, people told me the following story: One day, after Jenny, the first teacher, had been there for nearly two years, several preschool children were walking along the road and saw Jenny coming toward them. One child pointed and said, "Look, a foreigner!" Another in the group turned to him and said, "That's not a foreigner, stupid! That's Jenny-san!"

In his State of the Village speech in March 1981, the mayor said:

Now I should like to speak about the creation of an educational environment in which human nature can flower.

Our aim is to nurture people who are reflective and imaginative. To that end we have worked to establish a village based on education *(kyōiku risson)*, a village that is thoughtfully conceived. The policy to do this begins with the development of facilities for the consolidated middle school and then the development of educational facilities in each section of the village. We have worked hard for the past ten years to create both the material facilities and quality education, and our efforts have been supported by the Iwate Prefecture Movement to Promote Education. . . . From now on, we must think about how we can bring into being and sustain plans for an educational administrative policy that might be termed a "soft" or sensitive policy, one that aims at nurturing quality and fulfilling [people's] inner needs.[26]

Of course, some of this is rhetoric, put forth for the record, but an examination of what was actually happening indicates that the mayor's rhetoric reflected substance. In a conversation in the fall of 1982 with a young teacher from northern Iwate who was posted to Tanohata in 1980, I was told that she was amazed when she arrived there to find that not only were foreigners teaching in the village, but they were accepted as an integral part of the educational process. This was true, she said, not only in the middle school where she taught but elsewhere, too. In December 1982, she was part of a group of five Tanohata teachers who went for four days to Guam on vacation. Afterwards she told us that no one would have thought of doing that in the last school where she had taught. An inner quality, an atmosphere, had been generated in Tanohata that set it apart in her mind.

In tourism, too, Tanohata began to make plans at a level that belied the state of the village ten years before. The tourist hotel, Ragasō, was catering to tour groups from all over Japan (thanks to the new roads and facilities completed in the mid-seventies). Facilities were also being developed for a family vacation park near the ocean with bungalows, a playground, a swimming pool, and a hiking trail. In his most expansive mood, the mayor began to talk of building an international conference center that would produce revenue without drawing so many visitors as to threaten the environment.

It is this environmental issue that in the 1980s represented one of the fundamental challenges to economic development in Tanohata. The fragility of the natural environment meant that attracting industry was out of the question. New ways would have to be designed to create jobs. The mayor recognized it as an issue, though most people in the village probably did not.

Concretely, Phase IV brought continued efforts to upgrade the infrastructure. All the usual projects appear in the budget and planning reports: port facilities, roads, social services, health care. However, in addition two new kinds of economic activity were becoming important. A booming mushroom-growing business was bringing new cash income, and experimentation in growing food in the sea (edible seaweed and sea urchins, among other things) was being designed to generate new and larger sources of income for the future.

Vegetable crops became a major source of income during Phase IV. The biggest single source of new money in family budgets was from contract vegetable growing. The most impressive evidence of what this meant in people's lives was the rapid increase in the number of new houses. By 1982, even the casual visitor to Tanohata was struck by the fine new houses in most parts of the village. Another important source of income was part-time work outside the home for wives, mostly in the grocery stores and restaurants along Route 45.

Growing mushrooms brought prosperity to a number of Tanohata families. I interviewed one of the newly prosperous farmers, and the story he and his wife told was very interesting. The Fujishiros had come to Tanohata as refugees from Karafuto in southern Sakhalin in 1948 along with many other families. They were married in Tanohata, and for twenty-five years they struggled to make a living at subsistence farming. It was a hard life, and there was mostly failure and discouragement for the refugees, individually and collectively. In the mid-1970s, with village help, a group tried building *minshuku* (family-run inns) for the tourist trade that was beginning to come to Kitayama-saki, Tanohata's major scenic spot. Due to poor management and unimaginative buildings as well as slow growth in the tourist industry, however, the project failed to prosper. The hard working Fujishiros, however, were determined to make it. They joined an experiment in growing black mushrooms *(shiitake)* and finally found the right formula for success. They built a small one-room factory for processing the logs and inserting the spores. The work was seasonal and fit in well with innkeeping, which provided them with good housing but only about 10 percent of their income (90 percent came from *shiitake*). The Fujishiros' experience is illustrative of what happened in Tanohata in Phase IV as people worked on the problems of economic development. Their experience illustrates what opportunities were, by then, being generated in the village.

When we assess the results of Phase IV, we find a village whose new-found identity and unity were recognized by people from the outside and, even more important, by the villagers themselves. By 1982 there were already three generations of Tanohata youngsters who had gone to the same middle school and rubbed elbows with each other. The acceptance of that pattern of education was essentially complete. Two events perhaps best sum up the situation in Tanohata at the end of Phase IV.

In 1981 the village was cited by the National Council of Villages and Towns as a model village (one of five in the country) and awarded a "Prize of Excellence" *(Yūryō-shō)*. In his yearly report to the council in March 1982, the mayor proudly said:

> This village and its people, with its small population, which have been cited nationally for their excellence, have demonstrated the value of working hard together, combining their strength and wis-

dom. It is because we have done this, linking people and the village administration and raising the level of local government, that we have received this nationwide recognition.[27]

Here was evidence of the bright side of Tanohata, and the village could rightly be proud.

There was, however, a dark side, too. Tanohata still had serious economic problems that defied easy solutions. There were still not enough jobs to attract and hold young people. The upland areas of the village lagged behind the coastal hamlets. Further, Tanohata's geography and the times were against it. Resources and infrastructure were still inadequate; many people in the village lacked vision for themselves or for the community; Tanohata was also being bombarded by stimuli from the outside world. With new roads and mass communication bringing in new people and new ideas every day, Tanohata was not immune from the malaise of Japanese society as a whole, which in 1982 boiled over in middle schools all around the country. *Hikō mondai* (the problem of bad behavior) was on the nightly news week after week. Outbreaks of petty thievery, destruction of property, and violence by teenagers, striking out blindly, engulfed the country. In Tanohata the outbreaks were mild, but they profoundly disturbed the village. In the fall of 1982 a small group of ninth graders committed a series of pranks and mildly anti-social behavior in the middle school that elicited shock and disbelief. How could they do this?—our children!

Would Tanohata's newfound prosperity and equality with the rest of Japan, successful in so many ways, turn to ashes in the mouths of the villagers? The pride that village people felt as they basked in the publicity accompanying Prime Minister Suzuki's visit to the Rikuchū coast in September 1982, as well as the national citation and the favorable press and TV coverage of village activities, was tempered by the social and economic difficulties that still faced them.

The concerns felt by people in Tanohata are revealed clearly in the comments of Kudō Fusako.

Nowadays, when TV is over, kids don't know what to do with themselves, and they just hang around. There they are—so young, with nothing to do!

So unless we take our way of life seriously—if we don't feed them when they should be fed, get them up when they should in the morning to wash, brush their teeth, do chores, etc.—things will go from bad to worse. In a word, if we don't do that, when they get to the point of really wanting to do something themselves, we won't be able to talk with them. We'll find them impossible, and they'll do what they please. This is a shameful situation. We have to say among ourselves, "A job is a lifelong thing; raising children is a one-time thing," and that's the truth of it.

My household may be the only one, and really I've wracked my brains about this kind of thing. People give all their attention to their work and pay no attention to the rest of their lives. People all just do their work, giving no thought to the reality of human existence. It ought to be different. When they go to bed, they say to themselves, "Today was terrible again. Today was terrible again," and off they go to sleep. People are just too busy. There's no give anywhere. As a result they get all churned up emotionally, and children, seeing that, become the same. Even young wives are like that, I think. Just working to earn money—that's all they do. That's not good. They don't have time even to think about anything else. To read a book, talk to the kids—there are all kinds of things they could do, but they just work, feel the pain of it, watch TV, and go to bed. If that's all there is to life, what a waste! No matter how hard you work, your money will always be used up. Here in Shimanokoshi women have their babies, and when they're old enough they go to work outside the home, leaving the children with someone. Really, that's a foolish thing to do.

When both husband and wife have jobs they think only of their own needs, but when they have children that way of thinking isn't enough. They can't just say, "if the kids are fed then they're OK." These are the kinds of problems that are cropping up these days.[28]

In the nearly thirty years from 1955 to 1982, Tanohata became a reality as a unit of local government on the northeast coast of Honshu. No longer was it a paper entity, made up of constituent elements with no sense of identity or shared ideals and goals. It changed from a backward and remote spot on the map, a true *hekichi* buried in the so-called Tibet of Japan, into a struggling, bustling coastal mountain village that was an acknowledged leader in international education in the region. It was now a place with a future if not a past, even though the future still had clouds on the horizon. Perhaps the darkest cloud was produced by the lack of middle- and upper-level leadership, but for the moment there was more sunshine than clouds.

How did all this come about? Five causal agents explain the "why" behind what had occurred. The first two reflect the importance of timing, in both negative and positive terms. First, in negative terms: there was no Tanohata in the 1950s, but the pressure applied by the Iwate prefectural authorities as they pushed Tanohata to merge with Fudai as part of the implementation of the 1953 Town and Village Consolidation Law forced people in the village to discover their identity. Out of that crucible, new leaders emerged, who were determined to create a real village. The negative factor of timing was that Tanohata had to choose to become a village or else disappear as a separate entity. Second, in positive terms Tanohata discovered itself while Japan was in the boom decade of the 1960s. Thus, by the time it was ready (1965), national and regional financial resources were available to it in large quantities for a sustained period of growth. Had the village emerged either earlier or later, it is doubtful that it could have gone as far or as fast as it has.

Given the pressure from higher authority and the supportive external environment, the way was open for dynamic leadership to produce results in a short time. I would identify three specific individuals as the third, fourth, and fifth agents in this process. To these two external factors, then, was added the role of leadership. At the prefectural level, the election in 1963 of Chida Tadashi as governor and his appointment of Kudō Iwao as superintendent of education that same year set the stage for Hayano, who became mayor of Tanohata in 1965. Chida gave Iwate dynamic leadership on a broad front, and Kudō took the lead in education and provided Tanohata with a structure to which it could tie its own efforts. Kudō selected Tanohata as a testing ground for what became the prefecture-wide Movement to Promote Education *(Kyōiku shinkō undō);* the sustained support that he and his successors gave to the movement and to Tanohata should not be underestimated. This support became an important channel for ideas and relationships with the outside world. A prime example of it is Chida's relationship with Shii no Mori. As a Waseda graduate, Chida saw support for Professor Oda's work in Tanohata as a significant way to express his support for his alma mater. Chida and Kudō, then, were the third and fourth agents.

Each of these outside agents of timing and leadership contributed substantially to what happened. Without them, it is unlikely that change in Tanohata would have come as fast or gone as far. It is important to recognize them because, once one begins to examine what happened inside the village, the role of Hayano as the fifth agent bulks large and these other agents seem to pale in significance. Much of the Tanohata story revolves around the mayor—his ideas, his vision, his connections, and his ability to get things done. His abilities are impressive testimony to the continuing potential of the role of the self-made man in Japanese society. The dynamic of his leadership is all the more impressive in light of the usual analyses of Japanese leaders as faceless and passive. Hayano has his weaknesses. He is not a warm person, and village people see him as distant and unapproachable. He is ambitious for Tanohata (though, curiously, he does not seem to covet higher political office for himself), and some of his development schemes have been overly ambitious. He does not seem to be grooming anyone as a successor, and his single-handed dominance of Tanohata politics for so long has undoubtedly inhibited the growth of new leadership in the village. Yet the fact remains that he is a gifted and generous human being who has brought Tanohata a long way. He welded together a team of people that included those with roots in Tanohata, skilled technicians from outside the village, and a new generation of young people who exemplify the U-turn phenomenon. And he developed the knack of using public relations and attention from the outside world not just as window-dressing but as a means to focus village attention, to challenge people to a larger vision for themselves, and to help them define who they are and where they are going.

吾は未だ 模索のまゝに十年経ちぬ
この地にしっかと 根を張るはいつ

年子

Here I am still wallowing
　　　around after ten years!
Will I ever be able to put my roots
　　　down in this place?

Date Toshiko

Ware wa mada mosaku no mama ni
jūnen tachinu
Kono chi ni shikka to ne o haru wa itsu

Toshiko

Chapter Three

THE POLITICS OF DEVELOPMENT: HAYANO IN THE LEAD

For many years the conventional wisdom about Japanese local politics has spoken of top-down decision-making and policy initiatives. The term "vertical insularity" has been used to describe the structure through which politics operated, reflecting the assessment of American scholars of the Japanese national political structure. They note that it is a unitary system of government very different from that of the United States but similar in some ways to the French.[1] Observing the structural controls of local government and the clear lines of authority and initiative that the national government holds in Japan, one may easily assume that there is little room for distinctive political leadership at the local level. The expression of leadership in Japanese political life, too, is different from that in the United States. The silver-tongued orator is looked on with suspicion, and charisma is not highly valued. The Japanese saying "The nail that sticks out is pounded down" reveals a different mind-set. Further, the influence of the early work of Ruth Benedict in *The Chrysanthemum and the Sword* and the work of Nakane Chie in her book *Tate no shakai,* which was published in English as *Japanese Society,* has been so pervasive that most people with interest in Japan have accepted the assumption that the "action" in Japanese politics is at the national level and is led by an elite hierarchy of politicians and bureaucrats.

Without disputing the truth of some of this analysis, the work of political scientists in the late 1970s and early 1980s brought new insight to our understanding of the role of local politics and of local politicians. The picture that has emerged is quite different from our earlier one. We find that local initiative and charismatic leadership do play important roles. One demonstration of the effectiveness of this approach can be seen in a recent study of Suzuki Heizaburō, the mayor of one of the sub-

97

urban cities in the Tokyo area. A change in central-local relations occurred in the 1980s, and with it came a new style and substance in local politics.[2]

In addition to seizing the initiative vis-à-vis the central government, local leaders are reaching out horizontally to establish ties with their counterparts regionally and nationally. There have long been regional and national organizations of mayors and educators, but these are now becoming vehicles for policy initiatives at the grass roots level. These initiatives have gone far to break down the old vertical insularity. According to Richard Samuels, in his book *The Politics of Regional Policy in Japan,*

> This converging evidence, when taken together, suggests three things. First, it suggests what several American scholars have also forcefully argued, namely, that local initiative is of fundamental importance in the local policy process in Japan.
>
> Secondly, it suggests that localities also rely upon each other in a variety of nontrivial ways throughout that process in the initiation and evaluation of new ideas. Finally it also suggests that *both* of these elements—localism and translocalism—are integral to local policy-making.

He concludes: "the notion of a lack of autonomy in a nominally centralized state has been vastly overstated."[3]

Tanohata's experience since 1960 gives further support to the idea of the importance of local leadership and local initiative in Japanese politics. Tanohata's emergence on the regional scene and the attention it has received in the national media are the result, above all, of the leadership of an able, dynamic, even charismatic mayor, Hayano Senpei. His work illustrates what can be done, even though it may not yet be the norm in local politics.

In the ten years preceding Hayano's election as mayor in August 1965, Tanohata had been visited by one disaster after another, some natural, some man-made. After the passage of the 1953 national law for the consolidation of towns and villages, Iwate Prefecture undertook studies to generate data on which to base the decisions required by the law. The 1955 study of the Rikuchū coast clearly implied that there was no future for Tanohata as an independent village. The prefecture subsequently proposed the merger of Tanohata with Fudai, its neighbor to the north. From 1955 to 1960, as continued and increasing pressure was applied to the village by the prefecture, backed by the authority of the national government, people in Tanohata felt beleaguered. The mayor of Fudai was a young bureaucrat turned politician who had served in the prefectural government in Morioka. This gave Fudai, which was smaller than Tanohata in area and population, potential leverage and access to prefectural and national sources of power and money, which seemed sure to tip the scales in its favor in the merger process. In large part because of this and in spite of the heavy pressure brought to bear on the two villages by the prefectural authorities, Tanohata refused to consummate the merger. As we saw in Chapter Two, negotiations broke down disastrously in the meeting in which formal arrangements for consolidation were to be confirmed. This episode vividly illustrates certain aspects of the political process in Japan.

The prefectural authorities from Morioka were determined to see the merger consummated. They were under pressure from Tokyo to complete the consolidation process mandated by the 1953 national law. They favored Fudai and were supporting Fudai's desire that the office for the new village be located there. This was unacceptable, especially to the people in Hamaiwaizumi (the southern region of Tanohata, farthest from Fudai). There seemed to be no legitimate way to block the merger.

In his formal speech, at the May 1960 meeting Mayor Makuuchi made carefully chosen comments about the location of the new village office that would preclude a settlement of the issue. Then there was the party, presumably to celebrate the successful completion of the negotiations. Makuuchi used the party as a forum for a speech which constituted a studied insult to the Fudai representatives and, by extension, the prefectural team that supported them. This speech broke up the party. As far as the records show, there were no more substantive negotiations, though fitful exchanges of memoranda among the three groups continued until July 1961. (See Chapter Two for further discussion of this episode.) Here we see local government representatives defying higher government authority.

Structurally, initiative and the balance of power in Japan tend to lie with higher authority, to which local government is beholden both economically and politically. Thus, when the chips are down, local leaders find it very difficult to resist pressure from above. If the pressure is severe enough and the local leaders desperate enough, they will take steps that might be termed quintessentially Japanese. The role of alcohol as a lubricant in Japanese social relations is legendary. It can also be used as a way to express an ultimate form of resistance to pressure from higher authority. Makuuchi's message was clear and unmistakable. He conveyed it in a context that provided a socially effective outlet for complaint and resistance when more formal structures had proven inadequate. The situation must be desperate for a man in Makuuchi's position to act as he did, but less dramatic examples of this kind of behavior abound.[4]

The short-term result of the merger debacle was the resounding defeat of Makuuchi in the mayoral election of August 1961. Some people say that it occurred as much because he was ill and was perceived as being too narrowly supportive of the interests of the coastal hamlets as because of backlash from the merger incident, but the fallout from the breakdown of the merger negotiations must have been severe.

The long-term result of the debacle was the emergence of a group of young village leaders committed to the creation of a real Tanohata. Between 1961 and 1965, new leadership took over at the prefectural level as well, providing a new political context for Tanohata. It is clear that the next mayoral election, in August 1965, marked a dramatic turning point for Tanohata. Symbolic of this new context was the opening of Makisawa Bridge in Hamaiwaizumi in the fall of 1964. This bridge, spanning a deep ravine that had for centuries cut Tanohata off from the city of Miyako to the south, opened up new avenues of contact with the rest of the prefecture and was the first physical evidence of a new context for life in Tanohata.

The merger episode had left a legacy of bad relations with the neighbors and higher authority. The village had already been physically devastated by a forest fire in the spring of 1961 and then had been economically hard hit in the first half of the 1960s by the national shift from the use of charcoal to kerosene as the major fuel for cooking and heating, the so-called kerosene revolution. In bad odor politically, besieged by the forces of natural disaster and drastic economic change, the villagers seemed to have little hope for a better life. Many left to seek employment elsewhere. Throughout the 1960s the population of the village declined steadily (from 6,590 in 1960, to 6,160 in 1965, to 5,320 in 1970), eroding the tax and manpower base. This brain drain was something the village could ill afford. Combined with the economic crisis and the merger debacle, it created a situation so desperate that a small group of village leaders were drawn together to mobilize resources and to attempt to create a real village where none had previously existed.

These were Tanohata's political and economic realities in 1965, when Hayano Senpei was elected to his first term of office. To understand how he dealt with them, we need to examine the structure of the political equation in Tanohata within which he has functioned. What are the forces and realities that move people politically? How are the political institutions structured, and how do they work, particularly the office of the mayor, the village assembly, and the civil service?

Rural Politics, Tanohata-Style

When one looks at the dynamics of local politics in Tanohata, several factors emerge as the determinants of political interaction in the village. The most obvious factor at work is geography: coastal hamlets versus upland or mountain hamlets. People who live in the coastal hamlets have traditionally been a bit more prosperous then uplanders, since they could carry on both fishing and farming activity, and more venturesome, too, since they were constantly risking their lives doing battle with the sea. Coastal people were relatively isolated and life was hard, but the upland-mountain people were even more isolated, and more resistant to change.

The two groups had little contact with each other historically, so it is not surprising to see that when political conflict erupted in the 1960s and 1970s, the battle lines were drawn as mountain versus coastal hamlet.

While conflict between the two regions has been muted in recent years, the disparity between them remains a serious issue in economic development. Kuwagata Nobuko reflected this in a comment made in an interview in 1986.

> This time when the railroad was put through, honestly speaking, it didn't do much for us. It's useful for the fishing village people, though. When they built the bridges and put through the national road, it really benefited us, so now I guess it is their turn.[5]

Cutting across these geographic tensions are tensions of "haves" versus "have-nots." Mountain land was not redistributed in the Occupation land reform, and there remain a number of large land-holders in the upland part of Tanohata.[6] These land-holders constitute a political force in the village, though few of them are active publicly in local politics. A second and more important group of "haves" are fishing families in the coastal hamlets who also have upland holdings of land. Their resources and connections link them with the mountain people and provide, at times, a positive, integrative force in village politics. The "have-nots" are not too different from those in other villages. They lack land and family connections, and the males are prime candidates for emigration or seasonal work in urban centers far from the village.

As in local communities everywhere, but especially in rural Japan, the role of blood relationship and personal connection looms large. Those clearly are still the most important forces in Tanohata politics. Depending on how one counts, there are as many as twenty-five hamlets in the village, and each hamlet has a good many people with the same family name. In the larger centrally located hamlets there would be several such families. Blood relationships and the web of mutual obligations are strong (though not the exclusive) motivating forces in Tanohata politics.[7]

Although until recently it had been largely cut off from the direct impact of the outside forces of national politics, Tanohata was not immune to their effects. In prewar Japan the central government reached in with military conscription to recruit young men for the armed forces. In the postwar period, the "kerosene revolution" affected Tanohata disastrously.

The emergence of Suzuki Zenkō as an elected member of the Lower House of the National Diet served, through his personal relationships with village leaders, to link Tanohata politically with other towns and villages on the northeast coast of Iwate. He and Chida Tadashi, who became governor of Iwate in 1963, formed an alliance when Chida served in the

House of Councillors (the Upper House of the Diet). They were members of the respective Fisheries Subcommittees of the two houses of the Diet. Hayano established contact with them when he became head of the Tanohata Fishing Cooperative in the mid-1950s. Suzuki provided a channel through which to tap national funds for roads and fishing port facilities, which, in the late 1960s, changed the face of Tanohata.[8]

Though it is certainly true that personal relationships play a part in Tanohata politics, the forces of broader social and economic change have tended to blur the tensions between mountain and coast and between "haves" and "have-nots" and to inject national and even international issues into the political scene. With these forces in mind, let us turn to the institutional structure of politics in Tanohata.

The Structure of Tanohata Politics

THE MAYOR

In pre–World War II Japan, mayors were selected at the local level and their appointments vetoed or confirmed at the prefectural level. Thus they served as an extension of central government authority, though in fact, of course, local power relationships were carefully taken into account by the higher authorities. Under Japan's postwar constitution, they are elected to four-year terms and have built and come to depend on a local power base as their source of authority and support. In Tanohata, until the last two decades mayoral politics reflected the rivalry within the village between the various hamlets. The mountain hamlets resented the dominance of the coastal people but usually did not have enough strength or unity to do anything about it. This situation was a particularly bitter one for people in Numabukuro, the old constituent village that dominated the northern third of Tanohata. Numabukuro had been the most populous and prosperous of the three villages that were merged in 1889 under the Meiji consolidation law. The village office was originally placed there, and the central post office for Tanohata (the *yūbinhonkyo-ku*) was there until 1984. Between 1900 and 1950 the lack of adequate fishing port facilities on the coast and the presence of a simple but thriving forest products industry (charcoal and railroad ties) which flourished in the 1920s allowed Numabukuro to cling to its illusions of grandeur. However, in the early 1960s the construction of fishing port facilities and new roads that began to open up other parts of the village destroyed any semblance of that old dominance.

The climax of this rivalry came in the mayoral election of 1961. Makuuchi Shigeya, the incumbent two-term mayor, was from a coastal hamlet. He ran against three others, two from the coast and one from a combined coastal-upland hamlet. In the spring of 1960, as we saw earlier, Makuuchi had given the coup de grace to talk of merger with Fudai, a merger that Numabukuro people would have accepted if not welcomed since they were neighbors with Fudai. In what was, in part, a protest vote, Numabukuro residents and other upland people combined to elect the candidate from the upland-coastal hamlet, a quiet, inexperienced person named Hironai. Makuuchi finished a very poor last in the voting. (He had less than half as many votes as the number three candidate.) Politically Tanohata was deeply divided, and the splits reflected the vigorously held particularism of the hamlets.

The village's internal political problems were compounded by bad relations with the prefectural government in Morioka, where officials still looked on Tanohata as a pariah for having rejected the merger deal with Fudai. It took four years and elections at the prefectural and village levels to repair those relations. The new governor, Chida Tadashi, elected in 1963, was an energetic, able politician with a vision for Iwate, someone willing to let bygones be bygones. Because Chida was a Waseda University graduate, he knew of Tanohata's reforestation project and he knew Mayor Hayano from the fifties, when he was on the Diet Fisheries Committee and Hayano was head of the fishing co-op. Hayano had also established ties with Suzuki Zenkō, and when he ran for mayor in 1965 and won (he had been an unsuccessful candidate in 1961), the stage was set for renewed close ties between Tanohata and both the prefectural and the national government.

The role of the mayor is important in any Japanese town or village; in Tanohata under Hayano's leadership it became the vehicle for change. Unless a Tanohata mayor demonstrated he would serve *all* the people (mountain and coast), his tenure was bound to be short. No elected mayor had served more than two terms, and most only one. Each mayor seemed to represent his own hamlet but not the whole village. Tanohata's economic plight was desperate and getting worse. The village needed a mayor with vision, outside connections, and a sense of political reality to design long-term programs and effective strategy if it was to have a future. The last person of stature and strength, Makuuchi, had been badly defeated, in part, because of the fallout from the consolidation debacle, but also because people saw him as too narrowly representing the interests of the coastal hamlets. As the election of 1965 approached, it looked as if it would be a replay of mountain versus coast: one candidate was from Numabukuro, back in the hills, the others from Shimanokoshi, on the coast. Hayano, one of the coastal candidates, won. Since he was from the same hamlet as Makuuchi the odds were against him, and, almost as important, at thirty-six he was very young. How would he be able to deal with the inertia in the village office and the suspicions of the village assembly about so young and inexperienced a politician? How would he deal with officials in Morioka and Tokyo, where resentment of Tanohata stemming from the merger fiasco might still be smoldering? A village that depended on negotiations with higher authorities for 94 percent of its budget needed good relations with those authorities. Thus the challenges to Hayano in his first term were formidable. What kind of a person was he? What was his background? How did he approach these challenges?

Hayano Senpei was born in 1929. His family lived in Shimanokoshi, the largest fishing hamlet in Tanohata, where they combined fishing on the coast with farming and forestry on land they owned on the plateau above Shimanokoshi. This combination goes far to explain the family's prosperity and standing in the village as well as the way Hayano was able to serve the interests of a wider constituency.[9]

Hayano had minimal formal schooling. He finished the six years of elementary school and started middle school in Ichinoseki, a city in the Kitakami River Valley in southern Iwate, but after a year he had to leave school and return home to work in the family business, and never went back. His education has been essentially practical and experiential. His professional career outside the family business started in 1955 at age twenty-five, when he became head of the fishing cooperative in Shimanokoshi. Because the co-op had gone bankrupt, no one else wanted the job, which explains why someone so young would be thrust into such a post. He put the co-op back on its feet and remained its head for ten years. This work became the training ground for his later work as mayor.

During this time he served on the Village Assembly (from 1955 to 1961) and on various prefectural committees related to fishing. He also was active in educational affairs, chairing the local PTA and helping raise money privately for a new elementary school. Running for mayor in the election of 1961, he came in a fairly close second (883 votes to 919); he was becoming known in the village. In 1965 he won an impressive victory, getting 66 percent of the votes and defeating the upland candidate from Numabukuro.

His first two terms as mayor were devoted to building the infrastructure of roads, schools, and health services that could sustain continued growth. He himself described it this way:

> The first task was to bring people together and eliminate some of the basic sources of conflict so that we could have positive interaction with each other. . . . Then came roads and health facilities. . . . In my second term we had to create the organs for economic development in fishing, forestry, and agriculture *(jiba sangyō ikusei)*. . . . The third, fourth, and fifth terms have really been devoted to developing the kind of education which would sustain development. We could do that only after the basic infrastructure was in place.[10]

Hayano's success as mayor was nothing short of spectacular. The fact that he ran unopposed for his fifth and sixth terms is one measure. Another, quite different one, is the percentage of roads improved and paved in the village over the sixteen years from 1965 to 1981. In 1965 none were paved. By early 1982, 90.8 percent of the prefectural-managed roads and 34.3 percent of the village-managed roads had been paved. (In 1975, 25 percent of the prefectural roads and 10.8 percent of the village-managed roads in Iwate were paved. By 1979 these figures were 53.7 percent and 27 percent.) A third rough measure is the acceptance of the consolidated middle school by a majority of the people of Tanohata. In 1973 it was the key political issue; in 1983 it was not a political issue at all.

By 1973 as Hayano completed his second term in office, basic health services, telephones, and road building had been provided or were in process and the infrastructure for generating jobs in fishing and agriculture had been put in place. (Projects included construction of port facilities and the establishment of the Nagamine Experimental Farm.) As he began his third term, the focus of the agenda shifted to jobs and education. From then on, Hayano's vision and political skills were focused on these two challenges. The local agricultural cooperative (Nōkyō) had been asked to take over the operation of the milk-processing facility of the village-run dairy. Within a short time it became apparent that the co-op had neither the technical knowhow nor the management skills to do this work. This posed a delicate political problem. Roads built or improved under the mayor's leadership had made milk production a viable way for farmers to generate cash income, and many new dairy operations were being established. (From 1965 to 1975 the number of dairy cows in the village went up nearly 6 ½ times—from 49 to 321.) These new milk producers depended on efficient operation of the village dairy. Hayano, having arranged for the co-op to take over that operation in the early seventies, now had to backtrack and finesse the resumption of village management of the dairy. His success in doing this is reflected in the fact that in the following years (1975–80) the number of dairy animals again nearly doubled (to 611) and dairy farm income almost doubled as well.

Along the way, other challenges had been faced. In his second and third terms, the greatest challenge had been in education. This came to a climax in 1974. Opposition to the plans for the consolidated middle school and dormitory was strong and deep-seated in several hamlets, notably Numabukuro, the old center of gravity of Tanohata, and Tsukue, a poor upland area near the coast. At least one assemblyman (from Numabukuro) lost his seat in the 1975 elections because he had supported Hayano and the consolidation plan. The national notoriety Tanohata and Hayano received in 1974 because of the book written by Honda Katsuichi, the Asahi Press reporter, reveals how strong the opposition was. (See Chapter Four for a full discussion of this episode.) The dormitory opened in 1974, and it was five years before the last separate middle school closed and all Tanohata children of middle school age attended the new consolidated school.

Hayano did not force the dissidents to accept the school, but he made it increasingly attractive for them to do so. In the end his patience was rewarded. To make clear to the people of Tsukue that the fact that they had held out the longest would not be held against them, plans were drawn up by the village to build a new community hall *(kōminkan)* in Tsukue. (One of these halls has now been built in each of the major population centers of the village.) The Tsukue hall is one of the nicest and best-equipped in Tanohata. Hayano's wisdom in seeing to it that this visible symbol of Tsukue's important place in the larger community was built has paid handsome dividends in good will and, probably, in votes. Here was evidence that he was mayor of all the people and did not represent just the relatively prosperous fishermen of his own hamlet.

Hayano was carefully tuned to the nuances of local politics, and nowhere more than in the fundamental issue of road-building. Investment in roads was a vital prerequisite to most other economic activity. It was also the visible, everyday evidence of mayoral policy and leadership. In an interview in the fall of 1982, the "Road-Building Mayor" talked about the politics of road-building in the village, pointing out how important the decisions about where and when to build or improve roads were. Only after sixteen years in office did he feel he could initiate a much-needed road improvement project in Shimanokoshi, his home hamlet. In the first three terms especially he concentrated investment in the inland, mountain sections of the village where not only was the need great but political sensitivities were the highest. Major projects were completed in Numabukuro and elsewhere before he felt he could give attention to Shimanokoshi. The main road link between the upland and the coast was built to Hiraiga (another coastal hamlet) rather than to Shimanokoshi in part to demonstrate that he would not favor his home hamlet.

In the early 1980s Hayano confronted a challenge very different from the early ones. The national government was searching for a site in the Tōhoku region for an atomic generating station. The study commission report, issued in the spring of 1982, proposed several possible sites. In one newspaper report Tanohata headed the list.[11] Formal designation and acceptance of the project would give the village an unprecedented financial bonanza. There would be a lump sum payment to the village from the national government of about 4 billion yen as "earnest money." In addition, all the money for construction and operation of the project would be pumped into Tanohata. Tanohata's annual budget for 1981–82 was 2.2 billion yen. Clearly the village would benefit enormously in financial terms. In an interview in the spring of 1983 Hayano discussed this matter at length. He said,

> After the commission's findings were announced, I had a call from a reporter who asked how it felt to be the top choice for the generating station. I said to him, "I am not knowledgeable in the technical

matters related to atomic energy. I know there are some issues of safety, but, leaving those aside, I must tell you that Tanohata will reject the offer of the project. It would be the ruin of us." That one-time initial payment of a sum nearly double our annual budget would be very bad. It would destroy us. We would lose what we are working for here.[12]

Here came a political challenge of the first order. The immediate appeal of the project was great. However, Hayano saw it as a threat to his attempt to create a "do-it-yourself" spirit and an environment that could withstand even the buffetings and strains of the material prosperity generated by development. Publicly and privately, he had preached the primacy of *seishin* (spirit) over material growth. His slogan for the village, "Creating the village through education," was predicated on this stance. He often talked of "creating human beings" as the central challenge for Tanohata. This project tested his commitment to that philosophy.

Some people in the village were critical of the way he handled the issue, claiming that he waited until he saw how the winds of public opinion blew before committing himself. Iwami Hisako, for instance, the wife of the Buddhist priest in Tanohata and a leader in women's affairs, criticized him for this at the time. This charge does not seem valid. He had held an open community meeting to solicit ideas and opinions before the release of the formal commission report. At that meeting a variety of opinions were voiced, pro and con. Clearly there was strong and articulate opposition to the project. Undoubtedly Hayano was encouraged by the expression of such views, but he had been a consistent champion of careful and judicious use of the fragile Tanohata environment lest permanent damage to it vitiate development efforts. His decision to oppose the atomic plant appears to have been principled and strongly motivated by his fundamental policies for Tanohata.

It is apparent that Hayano knew how to meet the immediate needs of the village as a whole. The range of projects he conceived and designed, from roads and port facilities to a milk-processing station and the promotion of contract vegetable growing, testifies to his skills and ability. One could call them pork barrel projects, but they created jobs, provided desperately needed services, and served to generate an impressive rise in the standard of living in Tanohata. By 1983 the village ranked third among the seven towns and villages in Shimohei-*gun*.

For all his ability and success, however, Hayano was not a free agent. He had to deal with the other two elements in the political structure—the village assembly and the bureaucracy. Even though the initiative lay with him, he was constrained by these two institutions, and his work might have come to naught if he had neglected them and their role in the political process.

THE VILLAGE ASSEMBLY

As in most villages in Japan, the role of the assembly in Tanohata is probably the least important among the three constituent elements. This is true for two reasons. First of all, in Japan local government plays a relatively less important role than in the United States because of the national, unitary structure of politics (in contrast to the federal system in the United States). Local government is controlled and its role defined by a national ministry called the *Jichi-shō* (Ministry of Home Affairs). Local assemblies are hemmed in by a myriad of legal regulations, some innocently aimed at preventing corruption, others aimed at reducing local autonomy and initiative and preserving the prerogatives of the central political authority (whether in the prefectural capital or in Tokyo). While these same strictures apply to the bureaucracy and the mayor, there are other forces at work that enhance their roles, particularly vis-à-vis the local assembly.

The second force limiting the role of the assembly is the fact that aside from emergency sessions, it meets only four to five times per year and then only for one to three days at a time. Further, although it has a secretariat, which is housed in the village office, its staff is small and, at least in the case of Tanohata, not expected or willing to play a vigorous leadership role. The assembly can and does act as a check on the mayor and the bureaucracy. Ultimately it controls the budgetary process, but—as in the national government—initiative, information, and policy formation are almost all in the hands of others.

Beyond these institutional and structural factors, the realities and the dynamics of everyday political activity in Tanohata mean that the assembly plays a reactive and monitoring role. If the mayor gets too far ahead of (or behind) his constituents, the assembly reins him in, but, in the nature of things, it cannot usually be the initiator.

These facts become evident when one examines the many activities and projects that are under way or projected in the village. Priorities for roads, port facilities, schools, and economic development projects all originate with the mayor and his staff. If he and they are wise, they consult and keep assembly members informed so that the assembly is not caught by surprise with plans for a new project. However, 85 to 90 percent of the village budget each year comes from outside sources. The mayor must seek sources of funds and the bureaucracy must do the paperwork to get the funds. The assembly acts on the budget and can question plans, but members lack the time, the staff, and the access to information to be more than reactive monitors of a process that over the past twenty years has moved at a whirlwind pace.

The Tanohata Assembly has eighteen members, all elected at large on a one-person, one-vote basis. Eligible voters cast a ballot for one person among the slate of candidates, and the top eighteen vote-getters win seats. In the local elections held in April 1983, there were twenty-four candidates for eighteen seats. Competition for votes is keen, since each voter can vote for only one candidate. In the Tōhoku District (northeast Honshū) in general, there is widespread talk of vote-buying and corruption, even to the point of saying that "a vote costs ¥10,000." In Tanohata, however, although there have been a few indictments for corrupt electioneering in the past ten years, the consensus of those to whom I talked is that money and vote-buying are not widely used as a means to political power. There are gray areas of gift-giving and favors with economic implications, but all of my informants in the village said that money was not a prime mover. The key to winning an assembly seat lies in having enough "connections." This means a base constituency of blood and in-law relatives augmented by a web of personal relationships that will produce enough votes. In an electorate of approximately 3,800 voters, it took 123 votes to win a seat in April 1983. The highest vote-getter received 228.

The Tanohata Assembly's eighteen members break down as follows. There is one Japan Communist Party (JCP) member, and the rest are technically *mushozoku* (non-party) representatives. Until April 1983, there was one Socialist, but he dropped his party affiliation in that election. The membership is basically conservative and supportive of LDP policies on national and international issues, reflecting the concern about international trade typical of the Tōhoku region. For example, a resolution introduced by the Socialist member of the assembly at the December 1982 meeting advocated rejection of any further opening up of the domestic market for U.S. beef and oranges. The resolution was referred to a committee, reworked, and it passed unanimously when brought to the January 1983 special session of the assembly.

Tanohata is part of Suzuki Zenkō's base area, and Tanohata people have long supported him in national elections. At the same time there is a sense of independent accomplishment in Tanohata that reflects a growing feeling of local identity. When Suzuki visited Tanohata in September 1982, the village welcomed him warmly but with expressions of pride in local accomplishments. In a discussion I had with the mayor following Suzuki's visit, he spoke of having lunch with assembly members and made a point of the fact that their discussion centered on what Tanohata had accomplished in the past twenty years, not primarily on Suzuki and his role in regional or national politics.

The assembly is not a rubber stamp for the mayor and his policies and projects, but it is basically supportive. Even the Communist Party member, though critical of some policies, does not criticize Hayano personally. The fact that Hayano takes the role of the assembly seriously is attested by the contents of his annual State of the Village speeches, which, beyond their political rhetoric, spell out past accomplishments and specify the details of plans for future projects. At the same time, the critical link between the mayor and the assembly is the bureaucracy, which the mayor depends on to give substance to his ideas and his policies.

THE BUREAUCRACY

The heart of village politics is in the village office, where planning, data gathering, and policy implementation are done. In this sense Tanohata is typical of villages all over Japan. Here are a total of 111 employees, of whom 34 work for the Board of Education. These are almost all career civil service posts, which carry job security and fringe benefits that give stability and continuity to local government. (The same is true at the prefectural and national level.) Until 1978 the Tanohata office had five sections *(ka),* General Affairs, Financial Affairs, Economic Development, People's Service (Health and Welfare), and Construction; this is the standard organizational pattern throughout Japan.[13] Figure 2 shows the structure and personnel distribution by section.

Japanese local government offices are notorious for their red tape, bureaucratic arrogance, and lack of administrative efficiency. The classic film statement of this is found in Kurosawa Akira's 1954 masterpiece, *Ikiru* (To live). In the movie, the cynical watchwords of the local bureaucrat are *san-nai-shugi* (the philosophy of the three "don'ts"): "don't be late, don't take time off, and don't work."[14] Tanohata is not immune to that philosophy, but on the whole, after a year's observation and almost daily interaction with people in the village office, I would give them high marks. My presence created work beyond the ordinary and required, at times, a flexibility in response that people imbued with *san-nai-shugi* would have resisted.[15] I visited most of the other offices in the county during my year there, and the contrast in atmosphere was often striking. In many of the others, one often sensed the presence of disputes over turf and a *san-nai-shugi* attitude.

At the same time Tanohata seems to lack able, vigorous, middle and upper echelon civil servants. From the beginning of his first term in office in 1965, the mayor has met this need in part by bringing in from outside the village a few able top-level administrators. He has used this device in education, in construction, and in economic development. In the case of education the results are mixed. The outsiders have not become integrated into the village, and they have not displayed the mayor's flare for innovation, though they have been loyal to him and his policies. In the other two sections the plan has worked well. The present head of construction is able and efficient, and he and his family have become fully accepted members of the village. In economic development, the mayor's choice in 1971 of a young staff member from outside, Date Katsumi, has paid handsome dividends. Date became his right-hand man and chief trouble-shooter, and Date and his family occupy a role of leadership and prestige in Tanohata.[16]

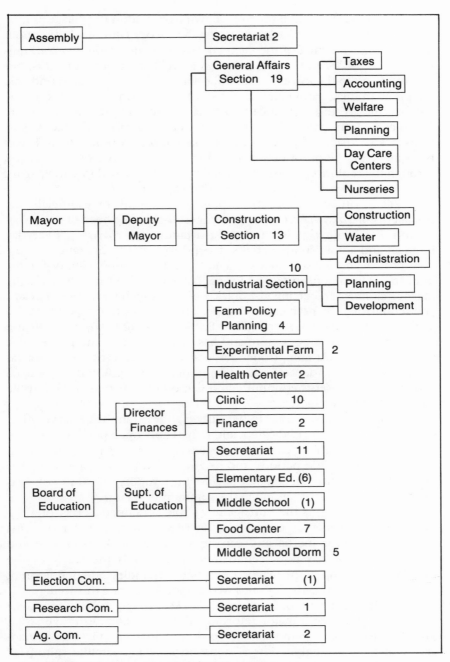

FIGURE 2. Village government administrative structure.
Source: Tanohata-mura, *Tanohata-mura nōson sōgō seibi keikaku-sho,* p. 64.

The upper-level civil servants drawn from within the village are, by and large, plodding and ordinary, doing their work faithfully but without imagination. The chief of the General Affairs Section *(Sōmuka-chō)* during the late 1970s and early 1980s was a brilliant exception to this, but one has to go to the lower levels of the staff of most sections to find able people with imagination and drive. All of my informants testified to the fact that the greatest resistance to the mayor's reform program in the late 1960s came from within the bureaucracy. People resisted change, in part from lack of vision, in part because it made more work for them. It will be some years before a new generation of able people rise to the top through the seniority system. The danger is that they will lose their spark and succumb to *san-nai-shugi* before that happens.

Village offices are organized politically around three officials, the so-called *San-yaku*. These are the mayor *(Son-chō)*, the head of finance or comptroller *(Shūnyū-yaku)* and the assistant mayor *(Joyaku)*. Everyday political and administrative affairs depend for smooth operation on the comptroller and assistant mayor. The former has responsibility for the budget, for fiscal reporting, and for tax collection; the latter serves as the mayor's alter ego, receiving visitors, keeping in touch with section heads, and monitoring the political landscape. The number four man in the village is the chief of the General Affairs Section *(Sōmuka-chō)*. He is the top civil servant with career tenure and has great influence and power. The assistant mayor and comptroller serve at the pleasure of the mayor (as does the superintendent of education in many villages), but the general affairs chief represents continuity and is the buffer between direct politics and the bureaucracy.

From the mid-seventies to the early eighties, Tanohata was very fortunate to have an able, dedicated, and remarkably open person as general affairs chief. His family ties in the village went back many generations (to the middle of the Edo period), and he and his wife personally served as village liaisons with the outside world in a variety of ways. He was respected within the office and in the community at large.

In political terms the bureaucracy's role is defined as that of a follower and implementer of political decisions. In reality it represents momentum and/or inertia and can be a severe block to change and progress. That it has not been that in Tanohata is the result of the dynamic leadership of the mayor and his understanding and definition of the proper role of the institution. Two examples illustrate this well.

In his speech to the Assembly on March 10, 1978, the mayor announced plans for a major reform of the office administrative structure. He proposed to eliminate two sections, Citizen Services and Financial Affairs, by a combination of consolidation and satellite spinoff of health and welfare services to quasi-independent status. His rationale for this was as follows:

Last of all I want to mention the plans for reorganizing the administrative structure [of the village office].

This problem as outlined in my memorandum is, of course, something that must be addressed because of the need for more efficient [structure]. . . . Cities, towns and villages are all self-governing organizations. The local people are the ultimate authority. This means that administrative structure must focus on [the needs of] those people.

Also, the purpose or object of an institution is not the structure itself but its role as a means to an end. That being the case, we must keep in mind that as the purpose and object change we must always respond flexibly.

Especially in the conditions of a small village such as ours I think we will be better off with a more flexible structure.

Furthermore, village office employees must always work as one with the mayor. It is essential that we be able to respond appropriately to questions as they arise from citizens' everyday concerns. We must do this beyond any political judgment per se.[17]

As a result of this reform plan, which was enacted by the Assembly in 1978, the number of sections in the village office was reduced from five to three. This reorganization was a bold move on the mayor's part. Officials in the prefectural capital opposed it because it made the Tanohata bureaucratic structure an anomaly and hard to deal with. He did it, however, in response to two needs. First, in the late seventies he recognized the threat that inflation and recession (often referred to as "stagflation") posed to subsidies for local government. He decided to get ahead of the game by streamlining the administrative structure and making it more efficient. Second, by spinning off village health and welfare services to a separate building with semi-autonomous status, he could provide better and more efficient health care for the village. His move paid off in April 1982, with the appointment of an able young doctor to head the health and welfare facility. Tanohata now is ahead of similar villages in the quality and breadth of its health care. Ironically, in 1983, he was criticized again by higher authority in Iwate in the wake of national proposals for administrative reorganization because, having already accomplished this in 1978, Tanohata did not need to do what other local government units were being asked to do.

In Tanohata as elsewhere in Japan the bureaucracy remains at the center of political life. Tanohata's functions well, though not spectacularly. It follows the mayor's lead and, on the whole responds humanely to the needs of citizens, despite some inertia and dead wood. The dearth of sufficient able top- and middle-level administrators is likely to create problems in the future, especially if Hayano were to leave the scene soon or suddenly.

Mayoral Leadership

In the early 1960s, torn by internal strife and beleaguered by political pressure from higher authorities, the hardships of everyday life in Tanohata gave people little cause for hope. People's desperate need created a climate of acceptance for new leadership and new ideas that prepared the ground for change if someone could define and implement a plan for concrete action. Hayano's success in rescuing the local fishing co-op from bankruptcy in the 1950s gave him credibility in spite of his relative youth. Ordinary people were ready to accept his call and follow his lead, and he had allies and supporters in the assembly. Kudō Takeo, chairman of the Village Assembly and long-time ally of Hayano, had this to say about him: "Hayano has given attention to a broad range of needs in the village. He secured money for roads and health services. Above all he had a capacity for growth. He was tough, strong, aware of Tanohata's history and deeply committed to bring development to the village."[18]

There were three basic ingredients in Hayano's success. First, he articulated very early a vision and a future for Tanohata. He did this through a shrewd combination of rhetoric and specific projects, which generated local support, and through the use of outside media and political connections, which drew attention to the village. His yearly State of the Village speeches are significant documents in their own right. His presentations are couched in idealistic rhetoric, but they outline practical policies and are larded with statistics and detailed information as well. In March 1966, six months after he took office, he said,

> For a long time this village has been referred to as a backward, remote area. Our first task, one we must address vigorously, is to remove this barrier, which, as we look back, has in the past interfered with the development of our region. The barrier is nothing but our own sense of being a backward and remote area. . . .
>
> With regard to the plans for development of fishing port facilities and road work for various economic development projects, in this fiscal year we will begin construction of tsunami protection facilities in Hiraiga and Akedo, projects that we have long waited for.[19]

In this way he regularly linked exhortations with concrete proposals for action and information about work already accomplished or projects to be accomplished. In 1969 through the good offices of Professor Oda and Waseda University he hosted a visit of the Canadian ambassador and his wife for a tree-planting ceremony, gaining nationwide publicity for Tanohata and generating a sense of pride among village people. In 1971 Tanohata hosted a prefecture-wide Arbor Day celebration, again focusing attention inside the village and out on Tanohata's accomplishments and its potential.

Second, Hayano proved exceedingly adept at tapping outside resources for investment and subsidy.[20] He began in the mid-sixties with health care, roads, and fishing port facilities. Massive amounts of capital were generated from the prefectural and national governments. In the early years, up to 94 percent of the village budget came from outside. By the early 1980s this was down to around 87 percent—still high and far above the national average for villages. (The national average is 65–70 percent.) In addition to getting investment capital for infrastructure Hayano was successful in getting funds for experimental projects in both fishing and agriculture, and he succeeded in attracting private capital investment to develop tourist facilities. The most interesting experiments have been in what have come to be known in Japan as "Third Sector" projects (projects combining government and private investment). The most spectacular of these projects is the attempt to provide rail transportation for Tanohata, which came to fruition in 1984. Others in agriculture (fodder for cattle) and fishing (raising salmon and abalone) show promise as well.

The third and most fundamental ingredient in Hayano's success has been his ability to deliver practical benefits that better people's everyday lives. Roads, telephones, drinking water, and health facilities are the most obvious of these benefits, but the building of multi-purpose *kōminkan* (community centers) in each hamlet and seeing to it that a wide variety of recreational, business, political, and social activities take place in them has made visible the growing role of Tanohata as a community. Regular trash pickup is provided for each hamlet at least once a week. Regular bus service to and from the health center and clinic is available to all twice a week, and the village doctor goes to the more remote hamlets once a week to provide health care there.

Discussions with the mayor reveal his impressive grasp of what is required to serve people's everyday needs, to make them aware that action is being taken to meet their needs, and to lift their sights to the future as the village-building process continues.

Many people in Tanohata remain unconcerned about politics. Others feel they have no time to give to it. These people wish only to be provided with basic services and left alone. But even such people, and his critics as well, give at least grudging if not enthusiastic praise to Hayano's work as mayor. They recognize what he has done for Tanohata, and many participate in the cultural and economic programs he has generated.

Kumagai Ryūkō is a good example of this kind of person. He participates actively in village affairs when necessary (for instance, in the ceremony opening National Highway 45 in 1972 and the Numabukuro Volunteer Fire Department), but essentially he wants to be left alone to do his farming. He said to me in an interview in late 1982 that he feels the Village Assembly is remote and its work unrelated to his life. He respects Hayano in an abstract way but considers what Hayano is doing to be largely irrelevant to him.[21]

Local Initiative and Horizontal Communication

Hayano's ability both to tap outside resources for investment and subsidy and to deliver practical readily perceived benefits for ordinary people raises fundamental questions of analysis and interpretation vis-à-vis Japanese politics. To what extent are local government units dependent on higher echelons of government politically and economically? Are local leaders primarily the handmaidens of national political leadership, willing implementers (some would say stooges) of Tokyo- or Morioka-generated policy initiatives? What Hayano has done in Tanohata provides evidence that local leadership can act with some independence and can generate initiatives on its own, without waiting for higher authority to suggest or act.

The evidence from the Tanohata experience from 1965 to 1985 supports the recent work of Richard Samuels and others, which emphasizes the importance of local initiative and horizontal communication among governmental units and civil servants. These trans-local initiatives often modify significantly the implementation of central government policies.

Two related examples of such initiatives show Hayano at his best. These examples provide clear evidence that local leaders and government units do not always wait for higher authorities to move, nor do they wait for money from outside to launch projects. The first example of local initiative comes from Tanohata. The second is a prefecture-wide initiative that has brought together political leaders and educators from more than twenty towns and villages. Neither of these efforts is dependent on higher authority. In fact both are designed and implemented directly by local leaders, who are explicit in saying that they do not want higher authority involved.

In 1976 Mayor Hayano and Date Katsumi came to me with an unusual request. For four years we had sent a small group of Earlham College students each summer to work in the Shii no Mori reforestation project. The mayor said, "We are very glad to have the student group here in the summer, but could you send us a graduate to live here year-round and teach?" I was surprised, I equivocated and asked why. He said, "Our children will live as adults in the twenty-first century. By then national barriers will be fewer and less important, and ordinary Japanese will need to deal frequently with foreigners. We must educate and prepare them for that." In 1977 we sent the first graduate to teach in Tanohata; this experiment was successful and the village asked for two people. Since 1979 there have been two teachers serving on two-year assignments paid by the village and conducting English and international education programs for children and adults all over the village, not just in regular English classes in school.[22]

This project has been conceived, funded, and administered exclusively by a local government entity without reference to higher authority. Since it began, representatives from other local government units, not only in Iwate Prefecture but from other parts of the country as well, have visited Tanohata to learn about it and to get information about what the village is doing and how. Beginning in 1981 two other villages requested teachers, and since then nineteen more towns and villages have committed themselves to similar programs as a result of consultation with officials in Tanohata. In most cases I have visited the town or village, met with the mayor, superintendent of education, school principals, and teachers and developed a plan with them. In each case, involvement in the program has resulted from horizontal interaction between local officials, exchanging information and learning from each other. Clearly, vertical insularity is not the only pattern either in Iwate or in other parts of Japan.[23]

Two horizontal structures appear to be the vehicles for the process described above. One is the Iwate Prefecture Council of Mayors; the other is the Prefectural Council of Superintendents of Education. These two organizations bring local politicians and educators together regularly to exchange information and ideas. Requests for teachers have come to me from officials belonging to each of these groups.

From Local Initiative to Prefecture-Wide Activity

The second example of horizontal interaction provides even more striking evidence of local initiative. In early 1983 representatives of the seven towns and villages of Shimohei-*gun* in Iwate Prefecture met to form a council to coordinate the English Teacher Program that had started in Tanohata (five of the seven units had teachers in residence or promised). Plans for the organization originated in Tanohata, but it was at the county level that the next move was made.

Before the county council was formally launched, a number of towns outside the county had already received teachers (specifically Iwate-*machi* and Isawa-*chō. Machi* and *chō* are two readings for the Chinese character meaning "town"), and two more (Noda-*mura* and Ishido-riya-*chō*) had made formal requests. Informal inquiries from several more towns led Mayor Hayano to expand the scope of the county organization to encompass a prefecture-wide plan. A year later he called an organizational meeting, which took place May 23, 1984. It was attended by mayors and superintendents from seventeen towns and villages in Iwate, and the formal prefecture-wide structure known as the Iwate Council for the Promotion of Activities in International Understanding *(Iwate-ken koku-sai rikai suishin jigyō shinkō kyōgikai)* was launched. Hayano was elected chairman of the council.[24]

All of the elements recounted in the Tanohata case are present in the prefecture-wide project. That is, the project's initiative, funding, and administration all come from local government units. In fact, the project has attracted the attention of public officials and the media in Morioka, the prefectural capital, and in Tokyo, and they are investigating what is happening. Mayor Hayano has stated, categorically, not just that initiative and funding are to be local, but that the new organization does not want any higher-echelon involvement. He and his colleagues want the organization to continue to be run by and for local towns and villages. He has even said that the local units did not want any involvement on the part of the prefectural government, because they do not want the interference or control that it might entail. One expects to hear such opinions expressed on the American scene, but they are rarely expressed in Japan.

These two examples are by no means isolated. Others, quite different in nature, in the economic sphere are appearing in various parts of Japan. An important one that vitally affects life in Tanohata has been implemented by local government units on the Rikuchū coast with the encouragement and support of the prefectural government. On April 1, 1984, the Sanriku Railroad *(Sanriku Tetsudō Kabushiki Kaisha)* began daily operations on a line linking Miyako, the port city east of Morioka, with the village of Fudai north along the coast. For the first time Tanohata had regular train service. This line had been laid out and the right of way and tunnels built by the Japan National Railways *(Kokutetsu)* in the 1970s; it was abandoned when the national railways became submerged in a flood of red ink. In 1980 a joint venture company was established. It has generated local government investment and private capital to complete the line and operate it. This is a prime example of "Third Sector" economic development. The Sanriku Railroad has attracted national attention. It is another example of regional initiative and cooperation, generated locally.[25]

Hayano's work in Tanohata is only one very dramatic example of some of the new forces at work in regional politics in Japan today. Local leaders are seizing the initiative and reaching out to other government units and creating both informal and formal organs of cooperation. Sometimes existing structures are used (for example the education office [*kyōiku jimusho*] at the county level); sometimes new structures are being created, as in the case of the Sanriku Railroad and the Iwate Council for the Promotion of Activities in International Understanding. The evidence of this trend provides an important supplement and corrective to the conventional wisdom of Nakane's "vertical society" analysis and the idea of "vertical insularity" as an explanation of the way government policy is made and implemented in Japanese society.

Politics is not, however, the only realm in which the Tanohata experience illustrates new trends and forces at work in Japanese society. In education the Tanohata program is distinctive, even path-finding, and it is Mayor Hayano who has conceived and implemented significant changes in the structure and role of education in Tanohata.

雪が降る　生徒の頃の思い出は
父の手づくり履いたぬくもり

フミ

Falling snow!
　　Memories of student days
Wearing the sandals my father made
　　Such warmth!

Onodera Fumi

Yuki ga furu seito no koro no omoide wa
Chichi no tezukuri haita nukumori

Fumi

Chapter Four

EDUCATION AS SOCIAL ENGINEERING: THE FULCRUM AND THE LEVER

Hayano conceived of his work as mayor, from the beginning, as a comprehensive educational endeavor. He coined the slogan "A Village Built on Education" *(Kyōiku Risson)* and continually referred to education as the fundamental source of long-term change and development. The challenges he faced when he took office in the mid-sixties were daunting. Essential social and economic infrastructure was lacking. Wherever he turned—communication, health care, jobs—there were desperate needs. He addressed the problems on two levels. At one level he launched a series of projects to meet the basic needs for roads, telephones, health care, and cash income. Simultaneously he began to define a long-term approach to Tanohata's problems that would use education as the fulcrum or pivot. Through this means he proposed to move the people of the whole village to acquire a sense of identity, to create a real Tanohata. On that base then could be built an educational program that would generate the ideas and the support for the broad effort that sound economic development would require.

Specific projects in road-building, the development of fishing and harbor facilities, health care, and the production of dairy feed that were carried out in his first term (1965–69) made it clear to everyone that change was on the way. This gave Hayano time to articulate a long-term development policy based on education.

Even in the 1950s Hayano was already actively involved in education in Tanohata. He had become chairman of the local PTA in Shimanokoshi, his home hamlet, while he was still head of the fishing cooperative. In that capacity he successfully campaigned to raise supplemental funds to rebuild the Shimanokoshi elementary school. As a result he knew how to define educational policy. When he became mayor it was not difficult to apply that thinking more broadly to needs at the village level.

In his first State of the Village speech to the Assembly in March 1966 after an exhortation to put aside its backward-area mentality, he presented data showing just how far Tanohata had to go (e.g., the average income was ¥75,000 per month; in Iwate as a whole it was ¥130,000; nationally it was ¥160,000). He then outlined three basic policies. First, he promised to push public service and welfare programs (e.g., day care centers) in the village. Second, he would promote economic development in primary industry (both agriculture and fishing). Third, he would nurture the "development of people" *(ningen zukuri)* through participation in the prefecture-wide Movement to Promote Education. It is noteworthy that two of these three policies focused on education.

Any examination of the actual state of people's morale and of education in Tanohata in the 1950s provides compelling evidence of why attention to education lay behind his policy priorities. A 1964 Senshu University study had pinpointed the problem exactly, saying at one point:

> . . . in a place like Akedo [the poorest coastal hamlet] it's an hour's walk to school, the number of families is small, and they are so spread out that there is little cultural contact with people from other hamlets or even with families in the area. In fact people are all isolated. One's first impression is summed up in the word "dark".[1]

As early as his first speech in 1966, Mayor Hayano proposed to establish a committee to promote a consolidated middle school. By 1967 the idea had begun to take shape and its purpose was being defined. He spoke of it as the biggest project the village had ever undertaken and urged Assembly members to help persuade people in the village of its "fateful" importance to them.

> The reason for this is that whereas economic development is what appears on the surface, by contrast "spiritual" development occurs underneath as something within people. Accordingly, I believe deeply that development always begins with people and ends with people. . . . The problem of promotion of education in the village and the problem of the consolidated middle school are one and the same. . . . I think we must strive hard to bring forth the wisdom and support of all the people in the village to find a good way to solve this problem.[2]

By 1968, thinking about the consolidated school had developed to the point that plans were being made for a dormitory to be built near it to serve students from distant parts of the village. The rationale for this project is interesting. When the mayor gave his State of the Village report in

March 1968, he had the chairman of the village's Education Committee, an advisory citizens' group, make the presentation. The chairman said:

> The third fundamental policy approach is to promote the estab-
> lishment of a consolidated middle school. This year as a way to deal
> with the problem of the long commute to school we plan to make
> provision for a dormitory. . . . Our plans are geared to those of the
> prefecture in its "Second Comprehensive Plan". . . .
>
> We are making plans for the dormitory in this fiscal year in order
> to include in the school those students who have a long commute.
> There are about sixty who cannot commute from their homes. These
> we will put in the dormitory. Through living in the dormitory, they
> will increase their social skills. We believe that we can help them to
> build good human relations and increase their understanding of their
> group *(nakama)*. They will absorb the patterns of group living
> through experience in self-government and will improve their aca-
> demic work. Without this dormitory experience, we cannot expect
> them to be able to study and absorb the real education that they
> need. This is the purpose, first and foremost, of the consolidated
> middle school and dormitory.[3]

Here we see the emergence of a strategy that makes education the fulcrum for change and the consolidated middle school and dormitory the lever to move the whole village. Hayano saw that the great obstacle to creating a Tanohata was the lack of *mura-ishiki*—a sense of belonging to a village, rather than just to one's local hamlet. He realized that this long-term problem could be attacked with a strategy that would "convert" the young people of Tanohata to this new way of thinking. By establishing the consolidated middle school, he would not only improve the quality of education but define a context in which the students would attend as residents of Tanohata, not just members of their own hamlet. The dormitory would provide the leverage to clinch that new perspective. A policy of bringing young people from all over the village to live together from Monday to Saturday, he reasoned, would break down the particularism naturally.

It took five years, from 1968 to 1973, to put the strategy in place; even then, strong opposition remained. The school building was completed in time for the school year that began in April 1973, but the dormitory was delayed another six months and could not be occupied until the fall of 1973.

The eight years between Hayano's election as mayor and the open-ing of the dormitory required strenuous efforts on a number of fronts. There was other, more basic work required in those years before con-certed attention could be given to the consolidated middle school.

Fortunately, as we have seen, Hayano was not operating in a vacuum. Governor Chida and the Iwate Superintendent of Education, Kudō Iwao, had launched the ambitious prefecture-wide Movement to Promote Education *(Kyōiku shinkō undō)*, and efforts in Tanohata could be linked to this larger program. As a graduate of both Waseda University and Heidelberg College in Ohio, Governor Chida had a deep commitment to education. Tanohata benefited greatly from his vision and the projects· he sponsored in transportation, economic development, and education. The ambitious development program that he conceptualized and launched would, over the next fifteen years, put Iwate on the national map. One of his early and most important moves had been the appointment of Kudō Iwao as Superintendent of Education. A native of Morioka, Kudō was a Tokyo University graduate (class of 1948) and had already demonstrated a commitment and a pioneering flair as an educator.[4] Kudō had a broad vision for education, and he was dedicated to serving Iwate Prefecture. With Chida's support he initiated the program, which was a broadly conceived effort to use basic education as a force for fundamental change in the prefecture that responded, on one hand, to the gathering momentum of the national effort in economic development and, on the other, to Iwate's position at or near the bottom of the heap of prefectures by almost any measure. It had two objectives: "to eliminate rapidly the differences in educational level in comparison with the rest of the country and to establish equality of educational opportunity."[5] In late 1963 and 1964, representatives from a broad range of constituent groups, both political and educational, were brought together to create special committees and draw up long-term plans. Once the movement was under way, every town and village in Iwate was required to develop its own formal long-range educational plan.

The timing of this effort was fortuitous for Tanohata. In August 1965 Hayano was elected mayor. Hayano's knowledge of education and his commitment to it was clear. His work on the Shimanokoshi PTA was well-known. In August 1982, prior to the Tanohata Adult Day ceremonies, which were held in the Shimanokoshi Elementary School, he spoke with pride of having built this school twice, once as PTA chairman, once as mayor. As mayor he launched a vigorous bootstrap operation to establish education as the cornerstone for all other development activities in the village. In his first formal policy speech to the Village Assembly, Hayano announced plans to establish a village-wide school lunch program. Referring to the fact that Tanohata's educational level was low even for the prefecture, to say nothing of the national level, he said,

> Weak bodies have a deep relationship to human resources, and the full education of our young people who will shoulder our burdens in the future is linked to the problems of the future of this village. Therefore, it is my intention to investigate fully and to push with all

my strength to solve this problem [of health as the prerequisite of education].[6]

The importance of his commitment to health and education is underscored when one remembers how high the infant mortality rate in Tanohata was in the 1960s.

It is clear from what has been said earlier that conditions of life in Tanohata in the mid-1960s were not just bad; they were desperate. For Mayor Hayano, who was in his mid-thirties when he assumed office, the issues were clear and urgent, and he launched a broad-gauged development program to deal with them. He refined and developed his analysis over the next five to six years.[7] He identified four fundamental issues:

1. We must address the twin problems of health and basic education for our children. Unless we do, there will be no future for them or for us.
2. We are committed to building a sense of identity for Tanohata-*mura*. To do this we must transcend, and eventually eliminate, the separation that results from *buraku-ishiki* (a sense of identity as a member of a hamlet rather than of the whole village).[8]
3. We must create and develop economic opportunity within the village if we are to solve the problems of *dekasegi* (leaving the village for seasonal salaried construction work in urban centers) and "brain drain" (leaving the village for good to settle elsewhere).[9]
4. To accomplish these tasks, there must be many new economic and educational opportunities for individuals.

These issues defined the challenge facing the village and indicate why education was so central to the implementation of the mayor's plans.

Education in Tanohata

From 1965 to 1972, Tanohata's educational needs were to change attitudes and to design and create basic educational facilities and services.[10] In 1965 the total of 1,100 elementary-age children in Tanohata were divided among six full-fledged primary schools and three branch schools. There was one full-fledged middle school and five branch schools for the over 500 students in that age group. Each of the geographic regions of the village had a middle school, and each of the large hamlets had an elementary school.

Two fundamental problems were not revealed by these facts. One was health, the other the quality of education. As noted earlier, the infant mortality rate was appalling, but even those who survived were undernourished and weak. The other problem was quality of education. Teachers were poor, facilities were poorer, and parents had little vision or desire for their children to have better education or to continue their education beyond middle school. In 1964 only twenty Tanohata middle school graduates (11.3 percent) went directly on to high school (as early as 1956, nationally the figure was already up to 51.3 percent).[11] In the early 1960s the village had been legally designated a *hekichi* (remote area) under a law passed by the Diet in May 1949. The law made schools in Tanohata eligible to receive special subsidies and other aid from both the national and prefectural governments.[12]

There were two outside sources of subsidy already available, and Hayano was able to plug the village into these mechanisms quickly and effectively. Tanohata was already receiving modest outside aid under the *hekichi* law. In addition, the Iwate Prefecture Movement to Promote Education almost immediately proved to be an important source of ideas as well as money.

Kudō Iwao, the superintendent of education, and Governor Chida had laid out a comprehensive program. In developing prefectural plans for education, they sought several sites for pilot projects. Conditions in Tanohata were so bad that it was an ideal spot in which to experiment. It was designated a pilot site, and thus close links were established between educational officials in Morioka and those in Tanohata. Hayano was aggressive in his search for aid on all fronts but especially in education. His commitment to his proposition that education was fundamental to economic development and his use of it as a way to draw attention to his efforts both inside and outside the village are highlighted in two ways. His early slogan for the village, "A village based on education," was used repeatedly to draw outside people's attention to Tanohata and also to focus village people's attention on program development. The strategy was effective. People in the village were so immersed in their everyday lives and problems that they had little time or energy to think about larger issues. Slogans such as this and outside publicity served to highlight what was actually happening in the village. In the long run the result was a new level of self-conscious pride in Tanohata.

Tanohata began to be known in the region for its distinctive approach to development. For instance, in 1983, when my wife and I became stranded in a snowstorm just south of Tanohata, the couple who rescued us and took us in from the storm told us later, when we were seated cozily around the *kotatsu,* "We thought you must be from Tanohata. That place is really something with the mayor's emphasis on culture and education. We admire it!"

Once in office Mayor Hayano attacked the two problems of health and educational vision vigorously. In the short run he was very successful, initiating a school-lunch program and upgrading health care and health facilities. Improvement in these basic services came quickly. The problem of vision, however, required careful, long-term planning and consistent support before fundamental change could take place. Analysis of what happened in Tanohata reveals three stages of development in educational opportunity in the village. Stage One (1966–72) saw the establishment of pre-school educational opportunities for all children, the upgrading of elementary school facilities throughout the village, and the beginning of planning for special new facilities and opportunities in middle school education.

Stage Two (1972–77) was dominated by the controversy over plans to establish the consolidated middle school. As economic opportunities began to open up for people in Tanohata their vision for education also broadened and by 1977 Tanohata had a window on the world, not just beyond the village and Iwate Prefecture itself but beyond Japan to the United States.

Stage Three (1977–85) saw a continuation of the struggle to improve educational facilities, the search for stable, long-term leadership in education, and the implementation of ambitious plans to make international education an integral part of the life of every child in Tanohata. Those plans are by no means complete or completely implemented, but there is impressive evidence of success in each stage of the process as well as evidence of ongoing problems in education that Tanohata shares as part of the larger educational scene in Japan.

Educational Change in Tanohata: Stage One (1966–72)

In the first period of development, the village authorities and people of Tanohata were primarily concerned with creating the infrastructure of the village in fundamental economic, social, and educational terms. Until the critical needs for health care and physical well-being could be met, there was no time for anything else. Village records for the period 1966–68 reflect this basic need. Upgrading health facilities and building child care centers (*jidō kan*) occupied people's time and energy and are reflected in aid requests to central authorities and in budget allocations. (Over 30 percent of the total village investment in those three years went for such things. Just under 30 percent went for roads and communications.)[13]

The plans for the child care centers are interesting to examine. A village can obtain Education Ministry funds to help build and staff kindergartens; from the Welfare Ministry come subsidies to build and run child care centers. Tanohata built child care centers because the subsidies available from the Ministry of Welfare are more generous and the red tape for application and reporting is less onerous. The mayor and his associates proved adept at establishing connections with appropriate prefectural and national offices and their strategies for tapping these sources of funds were shrewd and effective, bringing very substantial sums of money into the village as educational subsidies each year.[14] By 1972 the child care center program had progressed to the point where most eligible children (four and five year olds) were enrolled in one of the center programs.[15] An indirect benefit of the child care center system for mothers in the village was that it enabled some of them to take part-time jobs.[16]

New health care facilities, child care centers, and a school lunch program were in place by 1968, and they created a new social and educational environment. Much work was needed to improve primary school education, however; this problem was of a different order. It included issues in curriculum and the role and quality of teachers. Here Tanohata was clearly a part of a regional and national problem. These issues and what happened can best be understood when we examine what was meant by the term *hekichi,* remote area. National legislation dealing with this educational problem went back to the Meiji Period (1867–1912), and in 1949 new legislation was passed updating the old provisions.[17]

A 1982 study of education in Iwate Prefecture notes that after Hokkaidō, Iwate had the most severe *hekichi* problem; 31.2 percent of the towns and villages of the prefecture qualified as *hekichi* in 1949 when the new national law was passed. Within the prefecture, Shimohei-*gun,* which includes Tanohata and most of the northern Rikuchū coast, was the worst off, with 40 percent of its elementary schools defined as *hekichi* schools (some 58 schools).[18] During the 1950s Iwate Prefecture implemented various provisions of the national *hekichi* legislation (for example, providing special extra pay for teachers sent to *hekichi* schools).[19] By the mid-1960s the prefectural Movement to Promote Education was available to assist local educators, and Tanohata effectively availed itself of this help. All of Tanohata's eight primary schools were designated as *hekichi* schools. This meant that special funds were available for facilities and program and special pay for teachers could be secured. In this way Tanohata was able to begin the process of upgrading its primary education, and during this first stage a great deal was accomplished.

One of the most interesting and important collateral developments in education in the first stage was the establishment by Waseda University faculty and students of the reforestation project called Shii no Mori (Concerned and Reflective Forestry). The ramifications of the connection with Waseda spread in many directions (leading, for instance, to Governor Chida's interest in Tanohata, as noted earlier). Waseda was one of the two most prestigious private universities in Japan, and thus association with it gave luster to any project. (See Chapter Two for further details on the establishment of the Shii no Mori program.) When the young Waseda student from Hamaiwaizumi brought Professor Oda to Tanohata he unwittingly established a relationship between the village and the outside world which would have tremendous impact on the course of Tanohata's development—and on those who came to the village from the outside as well.

While the Shii no Mori project had no direct effect on the basic educational program in the village, its broader influence was pervasive. It led, as we have seen, to the coming of Date Katsumi to Tanohata. And Hatakeyama Shōichi, the able chief of the General Affairs Section and number four man in the village, speaks with great appreciation for what the Shii no Mori Kai has done for him and for Tanohata. Its influence on him has been deep (see Chapter Two).[20]

The fundamental problem for Tanohata was deeper than facilities, special programs, or even teachers: it was, in a nutshell, that even as late as 1970, there was still no real Tanohata, only the administrative unit and its constituent elements, the three original *mura* and a dozen major hamlets.[21] The mayor began in his first four-year term to establish a centripetal force that would overcome separatism or *buraku isshiki*. He reasoned that a consolidated middle school with a dormitory would bring together children from all over the village to study and live there. This was the device that could be used to overcome the separatism that prevented the creation of a real Tanohata.

Some people say that plans for a consolidated middle school go back more than twenty years to the early 1950s.[22] However, according to the 1964 Senshu University study: "At this time, Tanohata is not at the stage of dealing with the problem of [the need for] a consolidated middle school. People are [only] vaguely thinking about it."[23] The mayor brought it to the fore publicly in his State of the Village Speech in 1967, linking the project to his larger objectives in economic development. From then on it was part of the policy agenda for education.

By the late 1960s, as Hayano started his second term as mayor, however, enough progress had been made in meeting basic infrastructure and health needs that village leaders could turn their attention to the long-range tasks of village-building. Plans had been laid for a number of projects in economic development, and this work came to a climax in 1972 in a new planning document that was called simply an "Interim Report."

The document itself waxes rhetorical and philosophical. The following quotations give the flavor of its approach: "Human life is a reflection of the individual person and village political life is an administrative reflection of Tanohata-*mura*'s personality. . . . We must become a village that is founded on the education of people [this is a reference to the slogan *Kyōiku Risson*], a village that thinks about human beings and their relationship to the natural environment. . . . We must be made newly conscious of the value of human existence and of the tremendous natural resources we have in Tanohata-*mura*. We must express this fully in imaginative ways that will reflect the individuality and the new value of the village of Tanohata."[24]

Along with the rhetoric there were concrete plans as well. In his annual State of the Village speech of March 17, 1972, the mayor referred to earlier planning for the consolidated middle school, apologetically indicating there had been delays. Then he added:

> However, we clearly committed ourselves to do this last year and in this fiscal year we will proceed to make the necessary studies and buy the land . . . and over the next five fiscal years (1972–76) we will push forward and complete the construction of the consolidated middle school.[25]

This public commitment to a concrete plan ushered in a new stage in the development of education in Tanohata.

Stage Two (1972–77)

In a conversation with Mayor Hayano in the fall of 1982 I queried him on the key turning points in his administration. He immediately pointed to 1972 and said, "That was one of the moments. Opposition to the consolidated middle school came out into the open in the spring of 1972."[26] I discussed this matter with him at some length because I had already read about the controversy in the book by Honda (see Chapter Two). In it Honda severely criticizes Hayano for being highhanded in his policies and a mere mouthpiece for policies emanating from Tokyo. The reporter spent some time in Tanohata and talked with many people, so his report is not to be dismissed lightly. His most vehement criticism of the consolidated school was of the idea in principle and the effects he saw it having on the village.

> The people most active in opposition were the farm women. The background reason for that was the problem of *dekasegi*. In the case of Tsukue and Numabukuro, where the opposition was the strongest, 64% of the families are without male hands to help because they are away. The women and old folks left behind depend on middle school youngsters to help with the farm work. The household head who is away on a construction job can't agree [to the village plan] either. If the children are in the dorm [as they would be from Monday to Saturday] the economic burdens on the family are even greater. It is especially hard on the mothers in families where the men are away working to have children who have just finished elementary school taken away from them. The people in the mountain villages of the Tōhoku have been put upon continuously. Before World War II their husbands and children were taken to be soldiers; after the war there has been *dekasegi*.[27]

Honda saw the school as part of a national pattern of policy planning in education and in economic development in which central government would run rough-shod over local needs and force communities to march in lock-step with its policy. The Ministry of Education was notoriously conservative educationally, and had continually pressed for recentralized educational policy-making. In addition the Minister of Education was often one of the most politically conservative members of the Cabinet.[28] In the 1970s to this long-standing trend was added the Tanaka plan for regional development. Honda and other critics saw the plan as posing a further threat to local communities and their needs. Hayano's plans for the consolidated middle school seemed to fit into this interpretation. Hayano could be seen as just another local official dutifully carrying out policies laid down in Tokyo in order to pad his budget and enhance his prestige regardless of what local people wanted or needed.[29] However, this interpretation does not hold up when one examines closely both what Hayano was saying and doing and how a wider spectrum of people in Tanohata were reacting.

The school was in fact the central element in the mayor's policy of social integration, and within that plan a key role was to be played by the dormitory. The plan was that, in the dorm, children from all over the village would live together as children of Tanohata, not of a hamlet. If education was to be the fulcrum for long-term economic development, the dormitory was the lever that would move and change the self-perception of the people of Tanohata. Hayano's position on this had been clear from the beginning and he was consistent throughout. He saw the consolidated school as the linchpin in a policy of the social integration of Tanohata as an organic whole.

In his 1967 State of the Village speech, he laid out the rationale:

> For the people of this village, the fateful issue is before us. Why do I say that? On the surface it seems to be the issue of economic development, but I tell you that the real underlying issue in contrast to that superficial analysis is spiritual development *(seishin kaihatsu)*. It is just what the Chinese characters say, nothing other than the development of an inner quality of the spirit.
>
> This is why I have always stressed the idea that "development begins with people and ends with people," and I believe that deeply. Therefore, we must seek approval and support from all citizens for this development policy. At this critical moment for this village, which demands earnest application of our principles, I tell you that the problems of the promotion of education *(kyōiku shinkō)* and the plan for a consolidated middle school are one and the same. Since this is the case, rather than spend a long, agonizing period in debating the issue of whether or not it can be done, we must enlist the wisdom of all the people of the village. I believe that we must then bend every

effort to produce the very best plan that we can to fulfill this mission.[30]

Hayano claims (and others corroborate) that before the consolidated school was established ambitious families sent their children out of the village for middle school because the middle schools in Tanohata were so poor. Children leaving the village that young seldom came back —and these were the best students. Since a large percentage of the middle school teachers came from outside the village and were assigned to duty there by the Prefectural Board of Education, they resented going to these poor, small schools. The need to create a sense of belonging to Tanohata as a whole was reinforced by the realities of the existing educational pattern, in which teachers from outside reinforced local attitudes. A consolidated middle school would be a much more attractive place to teach, and in it the quality of education as well as the sense of village identity would be enhanced. The logic was compelling.

The dormitory program was planned to promote social integration, with children always having roommates from different hamlets. Teachers testify to the impact it has had in breaking down separatism and creating a sense of being a citizen of Tanohata.[31]

Hayano said that he welcomed the opposition that surfaced in the period 1972–74 because once it was in the open, it could be dealt with directly by committees and in the Village Assembly. He said, "Once the opposition came into the open I knew we would be able to deal with it successfully. People kept it hidden earlier because they saw no hope of a solution, so actually I was encouraged by this."[32]

The issue of the middle school dominated village life all through Stage Two. It was the key issue in the mayoral election of 1973. Hayano's opponent, a man named Kikuchi, was from Numabukuro, one of the original constituent villages and the center of the most vocal opposition to the school. Hayano won the election handily, assuring continuity in educational policy.

The dormitory was a radical departure in middle school education, and the complaints and opposition were understandable. Perhaps only because Tanohata's situation was so desperate could the dormitory be justified in terms of social and educational policy. The village was already losing some of its best young people before they entered middle school. There was no way to hold the good students in the village for high school because Tanohata had neither the resources nor the student population to support one. (Tanohata has a small branch high school operated under the aegis of a prefectural high school in the neighboring town of Iwaizumi,[33] but its quality is questionable and its numbers are declining. People expect it to be closed in the near future.) This situation and the testimony of the teachers and families in Tanohata confirm the wisdom of the decision. During my year in Tanohata I interviewed several dozen people on this matter, including people from Numabukuro and Tsukue where the opposition was strongest and lasted the longest. Even critics of the mayor who opposed the consolidation now grudgingly admit that it was the best thing to do. People who have observed education in Tanohata carefully over two or more decades speak enthusiastically about the positive effects of both the school and the dormitory. They point to individuals and to groups and say, "People have a sense of belonging to Tanohata, not just to Shimanokoshi or Katchi [hamlets within Tanohata]. Children have opportunities now they never had before, and the quality of teachers is much better, to say nothing of the facilities."[34]

The plan was a bold gamble, but in the long run it paid off handsomely. One element of it that reflects the mayor's overall strategy is the architecture of the school and dormitory. Through Tanohata's connection with Waseda University he was able to get a distinguished young professor of architecture to design both buildings. These striking buildings were selected in 1977 in a national competition as the best educational architecture of the year, bringing publicity to Tanohata from outside and stimulating a sense of pride and identity at home. They were further publicized in a national architecture journal, which printed a major story and picture essay about them and featured a photograph of the school on the front cover.

The school and dormitory served as symbols of a new kind of education in Tanohata. Evidence of the change is provided by the statistics on Tanohata teenagers going on to high school. In 1964 only 11.3 percent went directly to high school. By 1974 the figure had reached 63.4 percent and by 1983 it was 83 percent.

Tanohata's relationship with Waseda University through the Shii no Mori-kai continued to prosper and develop in Stage Two. The Waseda dormitory and the program in reforestation brought adults and young people from the village in contact with college students and opened a window on the larger world of Japan that had many ramifications. Governor Chida with his Waseda connections had brought the Canadian ambassador to Tanohata in 1969 for a ceremonial tree planting. Village-sponsored reforestation was promoted and stimulated by the presence of the Waseda project. Beginning in the summer of 1973 as an outgrowth of the Waseda relationship a group of American college students joined the Shii no Mori work crews in Tanohata. This project, a study abroad program in comparative education sponsored by Earlham College in Indiana, provided an opportunity for international contact for people in Tanohata. The details of this relationship will be discussed in the analysis of developments in Stage Three.

In my conversations with Hayano about the pivotal moments in his experience as mayor, he said, "I knew by 1977 that we had been successful in dealing with the problem of the school and dormitory." When I asked him why, he replied: "Because the whole agenda and the discussions in the Assembly changed. The consolidated school issue was no longer on the agenda. We were talking about and working on other matters."[35]

The agenda for education changed, too. Two matters assumed increasing importance. One was international education, in which Tanohata was and remains a pioneer. The other was the national issue referred to as *hikō mondai* (problems of bad behavior), an issue in which, fortunately, Tanohata is not yet engulfed but which is of increasing concern to parents and educators in the village.[36]

Stage Three (1977–85)

The completion of the school and dormitory project in 1974 symbolized the fundamental changes that had occurred in education in Tanohata in the first decade of the mayor's tenure. By 1977 the effects of this innovation and the substantial educational investment which had been made were evident. While many problems remained and the educational level of many Tanohata children was still low by national or even prefectural standards, Tanohata was in the educational mainstream and further development would take place in that context rather than in the old context of a remote, backward area. Most Tanohata schools were still designated as *hekichi* schools since this gave the village access to extra funds but the thrust of educational planning and thinking went far beyond that kind of educational effort.

The nature and direction of the change that occurred as Tanohata moved from Stage Two to Stage Three are illustrated by remarks the mayor made to me in the spring of 1976 when I visited the village. We talked about the plans for the students from Earlham College who go to Tanohata to work and study each summer. Toward the end of our conference he and his assistant, Mr. Date, launched into a discussion of their plan and hope to have an American teacher come to live in the village and work full-time. Ten years before the Japanese government launched a massive program to bring hundreds of foreign teachers to smalltown Japan, this was a daring step. For Tanohata, with its financial resources already stretched to the limit, it was also an act of courage. Hayano's vision again put him in the lead, this time in international education. The success of his plan was underscored not only by the reactions of the children of Tanohata to their new teacher, Jenny[37] but by the response of the young couple down the coast in the neighboring town who befriended my wife and me in the snowstorm in the winter of 1983.

Tanohata had caught up with the rest of Japan in one respect and was now a pioneer, ahead of most other locales. Others have talked about international education and "internationalizing the Japanese," but too often this is PR, and the foreigner teaching in Japan is a *kazari-mono* (a mere decoration). By 1980 one of these teaching positions had been folded into the regular village budget (Usually the foreign teacher is a temporary, contract employee.) which passes the scrutiny of the Village Assembly. The post was then included in the permanent table of organization of village employees. Beginning in 1983 the second post became a regular position under the Board of Education (before it had been a temporary contract post split between two agencies). This development, however, is only the most dramatic evidence of the shift in emphasis from education for basic literacy and job training to education aimed at the whole person and at people in all age groups, from infants to the aged.

Though the hiring of foreign teachers was, in a sense, a quantum leap for Tanohata, it was not done in a vacuum, nor was it an isolated development. Other changes were taking place, moving Tanohata into mainstream Japanese society. For instance, the rate of Tanohata students going on to high school had risen steadily from 1965 on. The most dramatic jump came between 1970 and 1975. By 1980 it had nearly reached the national average, and from then on it has been high and relatively stable. Table 1 quantifies these changes.

There were demonstrable changes in the educational patterns of individuals and families. Buildings, equipment, and program facilities had been steadily upgraded by capital investment and operating subsidies received from Morioka and Tokyo. In addition, adult education began to receive increasing attention in Stage Three.

Most local education programs in Japan include some form of adult education. It usually goes under the rubric *shakai kyōiku* (social education), and in Tanohata, as is common elsewhere there is a section in the

TABLE 1. Students going on to high school

Year	Total students graduating from middle school	Students entering high school		Percentage
		Regular	Night	
1965	186	19	37	
1970	184	43	29	
1975	160	106	15	
1977	112	84	11	
1980	89	61	9	
1982	119	103	16	86.55
1983	93	87	6	93.55
1984	100	93	7	93.00
1985	91	89	2	97.80
1986	92	86	6	93.48
1987	88	80	8	90.91
1988	117	105	12	89.74
1989	91	87	4	95.60

Source: Statistics supplied by letter from the Tanohata Board of Education, July 1989.

Board of Education office with that title. During the four years from 1977 to 1981 more and more attention was given to this part of the educational program. The annual report for 1978 entitled *Education in Tanohata* devoted two pages to outlining activities and plans for various forms of social education. It placed emphasis on recreational activities and promoted village-wide participation in a program called "The Villagers' Olympia." Ten years earlier, the emphasis was, of necessity, on preschool child care, buildings, and basic elementary education. By 1978 people in Tanohata had begun to have time and energy for recreation and adult education. Village leadership was, in one sense, responding to a need; even more, however, it was anticipating the need and attempting to generate wider social and educational interests in the village.

During the next three years, a series of small texts for adult education was written and published,[38] and a wide range of activities was planned reaching out to all the hamlets of the village.[39]

Another indication of the change in the educational environment was the increasing number of reports and statistics having to do with education. In 1979 a sophisticated comprehensive report on education in Tanohata was drawn up, containing a thorough narrative and statistical review of educational programs and educational finances. Superintendent of Education Hashimoto Tetsuo said in his preface:

> In recent years, in response to changes in societal structure and the needs of an internationalized era, there is debate over the fundamental ways in which education is organized as well as its content. At the national level there are revisions in the educational process. With a future-oriented perspective, better approaches are being added to what is being done.
>
> In our village, as we implement the last year of the "Second Phase Plan for Promoting [Education] in a Sparsely Populated Area," we find, to our great satisfaction, that we are making rapid progress in developing the needed educational facilities and in achieving our goals.[40]

Hashimoto cited the completion of the middle school facilities, a new elementary school building at Shimanokoshi, and various physical education and recreation facilities as well as the construction of public halls throughout the village as evidence of the progress. He went on to say:

> To raise the level of education in Tanohata we must combine formal schooling and social education [i.e. adult education]. When we do this with the participation of all the people, we can be sure that we can fulfill the great expectation [the people have] of education.

From 1978 on, yearly reports trace the village's educational program in detail, discussing everything from planning to implementation.

The Board of Education began to use fairly sophisticated questionnaires with parents, teachers, and others to measure program effectiveness and to gather data on which to base program decisions. In all of these documents, both international education and social education were given significant attention. The summary charts provide a view of people's perception of life in Tanohata in 1981.

In a study carried out under Board of Education sponsorship by an outside researcher from the Matsushita Research Institute, a random sample of young people were asked, "How do you feel about living in Tanohata?"[41] They were given three choices of answers under "a good place to live" (extremely good, good, all right) and two under "a difficult place to live" (difficult, very difficult). The survey sampled 71 young people between the ages of 18 and 29 (46 men and 25 women). Of the 71 people surveyed, 70 percent said it was a good place to live (though of those only 1.9 percent said it was extremely good), 22.5 percent said it was not a good place (of those 3 percent said it was very difficult), and 7.5 percent had no opinion or did not answer. Of those who responded positively the largest number (44 percent) said it was because they had been born there while more than one-third (35.6 percent) cited the good environment. Others spoke of human relations (6 percent), "easy living" *(seikatsu ga shiyasui)* (10.2 percent) and good transportation (1.7 percent). Those who said Tanohata was a difficult place to live gave reasons ranging from poor medical facilities to transportation problems, lack of culture, inconvenient shopping, and poor recreation facilities.

The individuals were also asked whether they wanted to continue to live in Tanohata in the future. Slightly more than 59 percent said "Yes," (65.9 percent of the men and 45.5 percent of the women), 40.9 percent said "No" (34.1 percent of the men and 54.5 percent of the women). The single most important reason given for staying was "the living environment is good" (27.5 percent for men and 30.8 percent for women). Next came family and friends (7.5 percent and 23.1 percent respectively) and ancestral home and traditions (15 percent and 7.7 percent). Job satisfaction was a reason for 40.4 percent of the men and 30.4 percent of the women. Only 10.6 percent and 17.4 percent said they disliked their work. Tanohata had come a long way in twenty years!

In a continuing effort to nurture a sense of community and to raise people's sense of self-worth, the village developed ambitious plans for adult education. These efforts were given formal structure through the launching of a project called *Sonmin Daigaku* (College for ordinary citizens). This organization became the vehicle for a series of programs serving the needs and interests of many people, young and old. The evidence from its first year of operation suggested that there would be a great deal of trial and error as the people in the Board of Education attempted to identify and meet diverse interests and needs. There were 125 different programs and meetings held during the fiscal year (April 1, 1982–March

31, 1983) with a total of 2,005 participants. Some programs were very sparsely attended (2 to 3 people) but many had 15 to 20. The largest had 127. Topics ranged from education and child-raising to health care, diet, sports, politics, and the meaning of life.

In a number of ways, Tanohata's program efforts in international education represent radical pioneering. The Board of Education uses English teaching as part of the formal curriculum, but adds a number of things to it. One of the foreign teachers serves as a regular staff member at the middle school dormitory, having contact with the 200 students—about two-thirds of the school body of just under 300 live there—regularly in an informal setting. The teacher shares meals, monitors study time, leads group activities, tutors (not just English but also Math), and gets to know the students personally. Beginning in 1980 this position was incorporated into the regular table of personnel as a village staff employee. This meant that the position and funding for it were formally approved by the Village Assembly in the budget review, a truly radical step.

The foreign teachers go to Tanohata on two-year contracts. From 1979 there have been two, often a married couple who are recent A.B. college graduates. For the first two two-year cycles the husband worked half-time for the Board of Education and half-time running tutoring sessions *(juku)* for village children and young adults in the region. Beginning in April 1983 this position was brought under the Board of Education full-time. This teacher generates international education and cultural activities for grade school children and adults as well as leading activities in sports and recreation for boys in the middle school dormitory.

This latter is part of a broader effort to deal with middle school student behavior problems, which are not yet serious in Tanohata but are approaching crisis proportions nationally. Though there is not yet a crisis, problems do exist with truancy, petty vandalism, and a variety of recalcitrant behavior. In the fall of 1982 seven middle school boys were severely disciplined for anti-social behavior (not violence) in the middle school. A major cause of this behavior is the plight of ninth grade students in their last term at the school. Poor students (both those from economically poor families and those who do not do well in school) or students whose parents will not allow or cannot afford further education often give up and cease to try and are bitter and angry. Since they are not preparing for high school entrance exams, they have time on their hands —time for mischief-making and anti-social activity. The system offers them nothing except boredom and discouragement. With time and teenage energy on their hands, the results are not surprising.

The superintendent of education in Tanohata for most of the 1980s was Takeda Seiichi, a man from outside the village, an engineer who had spent most of his professional life in Morioka. Mayor Hayano brought him to Tanohata as part of the effort to raise the sights of local people and to ensure that leadership in this key position was carried by someone of unquestioned loyalty to Hayano and his principles. Takeda was a quiet but effective spokesman for these values inside and outside the village. He was well-connected in Iwate and used his contacts to good effect. Since he was not an educator he was very diffident when it came to educational policy and administration but as someone who could speak for Tanohata and articulate the mayor's goals he served the village well, especially in the work in international education. (See Chapter Seven for further discussion of Takeda's role.)

The unusual characteristic of the Tanohata efforts in international education is that while English teaching is part of the formal educational plan, its use is conceived in broader terms than just acquiring language skill. Tanohata is attempting to create an environment in which contact with foreigners and learning about another culture become a part of the total educational program of the village. The English language instruction per se is solid but not inspired; it is not yet imaginative or effective beyond the norm, but the success of the program is judged by different standards. The foreign teachers have become an integral part of village life, and their roles are seen and judged in this wider context. Much can be done to improve what happens in the classroom, but when improvements are made they will be in a larger context that is very different from the educational environment of most Japanese towns and villages.

The effects of Tanohata's experiment are now being felt in the whole of Iwate Prefecture, since twenty other school systems now have foreign teachers in a prefecture-wide program. Officials in these other towns have come to Tanohata for help and advice and are beginning to use variations on the Tanohata model. A Council for the Promotion of International Understanding has been established to coordinate these efforts in international education. (For details, see Chapter Three.)

Two other developments indicate how pervasive the commitment to international education had become. Beginning in 1979 the village has sent one Tanohata teacher each year to participate in the Institute on American Culture and Education at Earlham College. Since 1981, two middle school students have been sent for a two-week home-stay experience in the United States. The village institutionalized the financing of these program efforts in March 1982 by establishing the Village People's Study Fund *(Sonmin kenshū kikin)*. Substantial village capital funds have been committed, and a regular fund drive is conducted each year to raise private contributions to increase the capital.[42]

The story of education in Tanohata is a record of achievement, but, impressive as that achievement is, severe problems remain. Some of these are peculiar to Tanohata; most of them Tanohata shares with the rest of Japan.

Among the achievements the most impressive are the advance in the level of facilities and programs for schooling within the village, the increase in the number of Tanohata children going on to high school and college, and the success of the effort at social integration through the consolidated middle school. Tanohata's efforts in international education are unique, and have been acclaimed by the national media and in educational circles. Other towns and villages in the region now look to Tanohata for leadership, a remarkable achievement when one thinks of what Tanohata was like in the early 1970s.

All of this success should not hide the serious problems that remain. Financially, the village remains overdependent on outside funding, and educational funding is no exception. The slowdown in economic growth and soaring national budget deficits of the 1980s have made subsidy cuts inevitable. These threaten educational gains, though how much is not yet clear.

The national issue of behavior problems among young people has also come to Tanohata, as we have seen. It rides the crest of the affluent society, and Tanohata families are by no means immune to it. Its sources are subtle and pervasive. Roads, bridges, and economic development projects brought cash income, leisure, new ideas, and new people to the village. Parents no longer insisted that children help with household chores or even with the care of farm animals. Children responded with sophisticated arrogance and demand more "things."[43] The tendency of teachers and administrators in the schools has been to clamp down severely with repressive measures to control behavior. (This is not unique to Tanohata, of course.) Such a response is bound to lead to more severe outbreaks of trouble.

The most basic problem Tanohata faces is leadership. This is reflected in the response to the behavior problems. It has been the mayor and a few people around him who have had the vision for a new kind of education, not primarily the educators or officials in the Board of Education. Critics would say that he has had to fight the educators all the way to implement his plans. What will happen when he goes? (He began his seventh term in 1989 and might well not seek another term, according to confidants.) Tanohata needs vigorous educational leadership at all levels, but especially at the top. However, there is little evidence of it emerging. Its innovative work has been done by swimming against the mainstream of the bureaucratic norms in Japanese public education. My own involvement and work in the village have been vigorously promoted and sponsored by the mayor, but the top educational leadership at times has resisted it or only acquiesced in it. The able young people in career positions in the Board of Education are too junior to play significant roles in leadership or policy formation for some years to come.

Prediction is really speculation. The optimist can see tremendous progress and real hope for education in Tanohata. Many of the gains have been institutionalized and have become part of the life of the village. (The work in international education is a dramatic example.) The pessimist sees the basically closed, bureaucratic nature of Japanese education, the lack of imagination, and the self-serving rather than humane quality of much that is done. Putting those general realities beside the severe specific problems Tanohata faces in financing and leadership one hopes for the best but is sobered by the difficulties that lie ahead. If Tanohata can sustain the economic growth curve that has been established, then there will be resources and the will to sustain continuing educational change. If it cannot sustain that growth, then education may well sink back to a prosaic humdrum of rote-learning and bureaucratized control of the process. This leads us back to a consideration of the fundamental questions of jobs, income, and economic planning.

出稼ぎに行かずは食えぬ　と言う友の
持ち来たる酒　沁みて酔えぬ夜　哲夫

Dekasegi or starve!
　　Tomorrow he leaves
We drink the night out and worry.
　　What can a friend do?

Sasaki Tetsuo

Dekasegi ni ikazu wa kuenu to iū tomo no
Mochi kitaru sake shimite yoenu yo

Tetsuo

Chapter Five

THE DESPERATE SEARCH
FOR JOBS

Poverty, discouragement, and isolation summed up life in Tanohata in the fifties and early sixties. Times were bad and seemed to be getting worse for those who stayed. Those who could, left, in increasing numbers. The population declined by nearly 18 percent from 1960 to 1970, thereby qualifying Tanohata to continue to be designated a *hekichi* under the national guidelines, which provide subsidies for a wide range of local investment and services for local government units so designated.[1]

To measure concretely the depth of the despair, one need only consider a few statistics on health, employment, income level, and education. In health the high rate of infant mortality (75 per 1,000 in 1959, compared to the national average of just over 30 per 1,000) was only the tip of the iceberg. The first clinic was not built until 1963. There were only two by 1965, so most people still had to walk or even be carried a minimum of two hours to get to medical help in Fudai or Iwaizumi. Most people's drinking water was untested and much of it unsafe. In employment the number of full-time farmers declined dramatically in the sixties (from 93 families in 1960 to 55 in 1970; from 10.5 percent of the total number of families in agriculture to 6.9 percent). This drop was occurring nationally as well, of course, but in Tanohata it reflected an exodus of able-bodied males from the village as well as a decline in the farming population. Income figures also highlight Tanohata's plight. In the years from 1955 to 1965, while the national average income went from ¥76,464 to ¥266,323, in Tanohata as late as 1962 per capita income was only ¥59,041. By 1965 it was up to ¥102,969, still only 38.6 percent of the national average and only 58.4 percent of the Iwate average. Table 2 shows how Tanohata people's income related to income levels in the prefecture and nationally.

TABLE 2. Average income per person

Year	Tanohata average	Iwate prefecture average	Tanohata % of Iwate average	National average	Tanohata % of national average
1955		¥53,772		¥76,464	
1960		¥83,351		¥129,962	
1965	¥102,969	¥176,226	58.4%	¥266,323	38.6%
1970	¥313,702	¥376,158	83.4%	¥571,625	54.8%
1975	¥790,609	¥887,665	89.0%	¥1,177,618	67.1%

Source: Tōyō Keizai Shinpōsha, *Shōwa kokusei sōran*, vol. 1, p. 110.

The same dismal story could be found in education. Families saw no future for themselves and had little or no ambition for their children. Here we see how inextricably education and jobs are intertwined. The 1964 Senshū University study of education in Tanohata had spoken of this poignantly, pointing out how isolated from each other the hamlets were. Focusing on Akedo, the most isolated hamlet, which includes some remote upland farm land on the plateau and at that time had no real port facilities for fishing, even though it was on the coast, the report said:

This hamlet depends on agriculture, and in economic terms they are not favored. The burdens of heavy work are so excessively demanding that there is no time for parents and children to talk with each other. In a sense, even when children are "in the sun," you have the feeling that they are "hiding in the shadows."

Parents point emotionally to the problem of the distance to school for the children, which is a real burden for younger children. Parents want their children to have education, but in a place like this, which has such an unstable economic situation, parents have to work from early morning to late at night and are trapped in a miserable existence.

In such a situation they say, "Leave school to the teachers." It may be impossible to expect them to give more time and thought to children's education in the family. However, beyond giving responsibility to the schools and teachers, isn't there some way to create a desire for more education? We have to establish the relationship between raising school standards, raising children's ability, and improving the schools themselves.

When we asked them, "What do you want from the teachers and the schools?" more than 40 percent said, "Nothing in particular." From that one could say that they are satisfied with things as they are. Their energies are so taken up in just existing that we can see that behind their answer lies the real reason that they can't do more for their children. Since economic problems are closely tied to education, there is a need to think directly of the influence on children of the process of compulsory education.

One child said, "My father and mother are busy working the whole day, and there's no one to talk to me or help with homework or play with me, so won't you play with me?" Most children yearn for more direct love from and contact with their parents.[2]

The few families who were concerned with providing better education sent their middle-school age children out of the village to live with relatives or friends in one of the cities of Iwate.

Statistics are cold and abstract. Though they give an objective and comparative view of reality, they provide little of the vital, personal sense of what life was like in those years. Mayor Hayano pointed to this side of the equation in his early State of the Village reports. In March 1966, he exhorted the Village Assembly, saying:

> For a long time this village has been known as a remote and backward place. . . . Our income level in 1963 was only a little more than half that of Iwate Prefecture, and we must recognize this poverty. . . . Now, even more, all 6,000 of us, each one, must commit ourselves anew to a desire to build a new life—this is our chance. . . . Accordingly, each one of us must put off that *hekichi* mentality and, looking to the future, strive with all our might to build a spirit that is committed to development. I believe this and I strongly urge you to join me in a cooperative effort to promote rapid development in Tanohata.[3]

Hayano's sense of urgency reflected the grave situation in Tanohata. The chairman of the assembly, Kudō Takeo, in an interview in 1983, responded emotionally when I asked him about the early sixties. "You can't imagine how desperate we were in the days before the Makisawa Bridge was built," he said. "We were cut off from the outside, especially in winter. There were no jobs. People didn't know what to do."[4] Tanohata adults born before 1950 share bitter memories from the old days. Growing up in the fifties and sixties, they heard about better times in the outer world of mainstream Japan; many were drawn to it and left the village forever. The exodus gained momentum all through the sixties, reaching a peak in 1970, when there was a net loss of 168 people.

The flight from the village was caused by two forces interacting and feeding on each other. Neither jobs nor cash income was available in Tanohata, and people looked elsewhere in desperation for some way to survive. At the same time, in the urban centers of the great industrial belt that now stretches from Tokyo to Kitakyūshū, the building boom and the seemingly insatiable demand for factory workers were sucking in the young and able-bodied from rural areas in a never-ending flood of one-way population movement. These two trends reinforced each other. People in Tanohata, desperate for jobs, heard the call of urban Japan's rush to modernize, industrialize, and overtake the advanced economies of the West, and off they went to join the action.

In broadest terms this process was no different in Japan than it has been in the United States, except for its pace and intensity, and the fact that Japan's land area is so small. Twentieth-century life has brought these stresses to all of us. Small town and village life has disintegrated and virtually disappeared as a viable alternative. In the United States, however, the process has been spread over a century. Japan's prewar changes were a mere prelude to what was packed into the forty years from 1945 to 1985. In 1945, 45 percent of all Japanese still were farmers. By 1984 only 5.4 percent were.[5] Tanohata did not join the mainstream in this trend until after 1960. By 1985 it had nearly caught up with the rest of Japan, in less than two decades rather than four. What has happened there is intensely interesting in its own right; in addition, by tracing it we can highlight perhaps more clearly some of the special characteristics of the Japanese experience. The story revolves around the phenomenon called *dekasegi* (going out of one's home place to an urban area for seasonal work, usually in major construction projects such as bridges, roads, buildings).

Dekasegi

The impact of *dekasegi* gives distinctive coloration to the process of urbanization that engulfed postwar Japan. No analysis of social change and economic development since 1945 is complete without consideration of this issue. This type of employment appealed to many young men in rural Japan because it provided better wages than they could get at home, where jobs were hard to come by anyway. The availability of this pool of able-bodied workers is an important part of the explanation of Japan's postwar economic growth. The men of Tanohata participated in *dekasegi* just as those in other villages of the Tōhoku did, and it brought the same stresses to their families that it did to thousands of others in the region.

One important effect of *dekasegi* was to exacerbate another problem, the issue of succession to the family headship. Among those working away from home in *dekasegi* the largest single group of people are heads of households; those in the second largest group are successors to the headship. By the late 1960s the problem was serious in Iwate. In 1968, 34,559 men from the prefecture were doing *dekasegi*. This constituted 9.1 percent of the male farming population, and a large percentage of these men fell into one or the other of these categories.[6] In 1979, nationally, of the 122,000 temporary workers away from home, 79,200 (64.9 percent) were heads of households and 34,000 (27.8 percent) were in line to succeed; 75.5 percent of the total were from Iwate.[7] Their younger siblings could leave home, cut their ties if necessary, and participate fully in

Japan's rush to affluence. Eldest sons *(chōnan)* must remain at home or leave only temporarily, ready to answer the call of the family council as the next head of the *ie*. Other sons and many of the daughters tended to leave home permanently. This situation results in severe distortion of the population profile of most villages. The total number of people in the 20–40 year age range declines. Proportionally the number of eldest sons in the local male population rises. This isolates the eldest sons as a kind of "orphan" group sandwiched between children and old folks, and, as a result, the *chōnan* form the largest single group doing *dekasegi* work. Even worse, though their nominal base and place of residence is the village, they are away a great deal. One study found that in 1971, of the people from the Tōhoku doing *dekasegi,* 63.7 percent were away 4–6 months and 26.3 percent were away 7–12 months of the year.[8]

Since the population in the 20–40 age range declines rapidly, that of the younger and older cohorts rises proportionally. In Tanohata there were 1,720 people in the 20–35 age range in 1965. By 1980 the number had declined by 28.5 percent, to 1,230. The statistics and charts do not reveal, however, what was happening within the 20–40 age group that remained. The number of women 20–35 declined even a little faster than the number of men, as all of the daughters and the rest of the sons in the family were, in a sense, free to leave home and go to the big city to work and to marry and settle there whereas the eldest sons must retain their ties to the family and the village. This phenomenon exacerbated what was already a serious shortage of eligible women. In this situation the eldest sons are left without a sufficient pool of potential wives. This situation creates a sense of quiet desperation in the family councils. In a study of Tanohata done in 1981, Ōno Masaya, a researcher from the Matsushita Research Institute in Osaka *(Matsushita Seiji Keizai Kenkyūjo),* examined the situation in detail.[9]

Ōno's study documents the vicious circle created by the *dekasegi* phenomenon. The need for jobs sends people out. They and their families become dependent upon those wages. Those who are married and have children become one-parent families or the children are raised by grandparents. Men who are not married cannot find women to marry. Further complicating life in village society is the plight of those who wish to continue to farm, normally the eldest sons. It becomes even more difficult to find wives for them. What young woman wants the long hours and drudgery of a farm wife? In addition to the hard work she may have to put up with a nagging, domineering mother-in-law.

The problem of finding brides *(hanayome)* highlights the social effects of *dekasegi* because it is essentially the problem of finding wives for eldest sons. We have seen that as the pull of urbanization and economic development grew stronger in the 1960s, those who could, moved to the cities, more or less permanently, finding jobs, marrying, and settling down. They became part of the statistical picture of Japanese economic growth and urbanization. One category of people among the men, the *chōnan,* could not easily do this. Most could not or would not divest themselves of their responsibility to succeed to the headship of the family upon the death of their father. Each feels keenly the responsibility to carry on the family name. The power of this demand on these people's lives has led to some of the most poignant stresses and heartache of Japan's postwar experience. Tanohata has shared in this trauma.

In a section entitled "There are no brides," Ōno's study quotes from a conversation Ōno overheard: "In A-san's household, even though their son has come back to succeed to the farm, there doesn't seem to be any way to find him a wife. They are really beside themselves."[10] He notes that farm families are desperately looking for wives for their sons; however, these same families do not want their daughters marrying into another farm family. They say the work is too hard and there's no money in farming. Even if these attitudes were not present, one stark fact would remain. The number of women of marriageable age in the village is less than the number of men. This was true, in Tanohata and elsewhere, except for a year or two around 1970, for the two decades 1960–80. In 1965 there were 910 men and 810 women in the 20–35 age range. In 1975 there were 765 men and 638 women and in 1980, 650 men and 580 women. These data indicate how difficult this problem is.[11] Ōno quotes another person in the village: "A young man, if he can't find a wife in the village, must go outside to find one and work somewhere. However, if he finds a wife where he's working, then he has to settle down there and not return to Tanohata." The *hanayome* problem weighs heavily on people's personal lives. Ōno concludes that if something is not done to address the shortage of eligible young women, it will become an ever bigger problem in the future.[12]

The toll that *dekasegi* takes on families and individuals is severe. In the winter of 1984 the *Iwate Nippō,* a major regional newspaper in the Tōhoku, ran a lengthy series of articles about the Rikuchū coast entitled "The Sanriku Road." Early in the series is a lengthy discussion of *dekasegi.* The article quotes from interviews with local people, some of them from Kuji, one of the two major port cities on the Iwate coast. The analysis puts the problem in personal terms.

> However, here [in Kuji] *dekasegi* is not seasonal and short term and supplemental–it's 99 percent permanent. More than a half work in construction in the big cities of the Tōhoku and Hokkaidō. But this year the employment offices are busy a month early with requests for help from *dekasegi* people returned for the winter. It's been bad since last year. . . . One wife says, "Our little boy has almost forgotten his father's face. If only there was work for him here, then we could be together. That's what would be best but. . . ." On the other hand, there are the young people who just want a car, and go out to work at *dekasegi* to get it. When they're laid off they come back and

draw unemployment, tooling around in their cars and playing pachinko. It's a vicious circle. We have to change the way of thinking of everyone.[13]

Dekasegi is on everyone's mind in these villages. Ōno in his 1981 study compiled a sampling of responses from people of all ages to the question, "What would you do for Tanohata if you were mayor?" Many pointed to *dekasegi* as the number one problem.

> "Lots of people from Ikena and Akedo [two of the smaller, poorer hamlets in Tanohata] have gone off to Tokyo for *dekasegi*. I'd do everything I could to make good-paying jobs nearby." (12-year-old girl, 1976)
> "I'd think about what I could do to make this a village without *dekasegi*. I'd reconsider what to do about primary sector employment." (24-year-old male store clerk, 1977)
> "I'd work to make it so people didn't have to do *dekasegi*. Planning for dairying, raising wages for laborers." (48-year-old man in agriculture, 1978)
> "I'd want to make a situation where villagers had jobs here as a policy to deal with *dekasegi*." (36-year-old salaryman)[14]

The fundamental problem with *dekasegi* is that people feel they cannot escape from the vicious economic circle it creates. It is like drug addition. Withdrawal is too painful and the urge to continue too great, as families come to depend on *dekasegi* wages for their livelihood.

A study of conditions in Iwate in 1972 showed that of the 24,780 people doing *dekasegi,* 22.6 percent depended on those wages for 60 percent of their income; another 22.2 percent were dependent on them for 30 percent of their income, and 21.5 percent were dependent on them for 20 percent of their income.[15]

Dekasegi, local jobs, and *atosugi* are inextricably linked to the whole development process. Given the present social attitudes in rural Japan, eldest sons are not free to leave and take permanent jobs elsewhere. This fact explains, in part, the strength and persistence of the *dekasegi* phenomenon. Eldest sons and their families represent, potentially, the backbone and stability of communities such as Tanohata. Instead, at present, these people are a cause of instability. The seriousness of the problem was reflected in the desperate activity generated in local village offices all over the prefecture in the late seventies and early eighties to try to address this problem and the related issue of finding wives for these eldest sons. In 1982 one village decided to establish a formal office to help these people. This decision generated a flurry of stories and discussion in the regional press.

Interestingly Mayor Hayano explicitly rejected that approach, saying that local government should not assume such a role but should provide an infrastructure and an economic climate that would produce jobs. These would then create alternatives to *dekasegi* and provide a solution to the twin problems of finding wives and of succession to the family headship.

Until the local economy develops sufficiently, the pull of big city jobs and money will be too strong for people to resist. Creating stable local employment thus becomes the most fundamental task of local government if it is to serve people's needs. The ultimate objective must be to stem the flow of young people. In the long run it requires social infrastructure and improved education. This explains the priority that Mayor Hayano gave to education from his second term on. (See Chapter 4.)

U-Turn: A Short-Term Strategy

Until these long-term efforts can take effect, however, towns and villages must develop interim policies to deal with the need to attract and hold their young people. The short-term strategy used all over the Tōhoku is to nurture a phenomenon called "U-turn," that is, getting young people who have already left to work to return to their home villages. The short-term objective of each town or village is to create jobs to attract these young people.

Villages proudly feature stories of returning young people in their local papers. One such article in the *Tanohata kōhō* in 1983 quoted a young woman, Hatakeyama Rimiko, as follows:

> The two years I worked in Gumma Prefecture were really an education for me. Being so far away from home—that was when I realized for the first time how good my own village was. I began to long to return and now I have come back here to work in adult education.[16]

The U-turn issue raises problems that are cut from the same cloth as *dekasegi* and *atosugi*. Unless there are jobs available, young people who have gone away to work cannot and will not come back. There is gathering evidence of a rising interest, even a desire, on the part of young people to return.

In the summer of 1985 there appeared a number of articles in both regional and national papers pointing to this trend. The *Iwate Nippō* carried a story on August 6, 1984, headlined "I want to return! . . . I want to be able to return!" It reported on a poll done in several towns in Iwate. Nearly 70 percent of the respondents in each case said they wanted to return and would if there were work. (About half of those said they doubted it would be possible.)[17]

An article in the national *Nihon Keizai Shinbun* in August 1985 carried the headline "Desire for U-turn Grows Stronger." It quotes an Iwate Prefecture study of 1985 college graduates on the subject.

> 88.5 percent of the graduating college seniors in Iwate who replied said they wanted to work in Iwate and live in their home town. The questionnaire was sent to 529 people, and 260 (40.8 percent) replied. Of those 192 (88.5 percent) expressed this desire.
> 74.5 percent gave as their reason that they wanted to live in their home town. 27.1 percent said their parents wanted them to do so.[18]

Later the same newspaper reported in a similar vein on a study done on the same question in Fukushima Prefecture. The headline read "Strong Desire for U-turn" and "University Students from Fukushima Studying outside the Prefecture."[19] In this case 2 out of 3 graduating seniors indicated a strong desire to return to their home prefecture to work.

The pervasive and fundamental nature of this problem is clear. One response to it at the prefectural level has been to attempt to link the recruitment efforts of prefectural businesses to those wishing to find work at home through computer lists, seminars for company recruiters and for recruits, and publicity campaigns generated by government offices and through the media.

The Struggle for Economic Stability and Growth

How does Tanohata deal with these issues? What kinds of jobs are possible in Tanohata? What shifts have there been since 1960? What have Hayano and his colleagues done to deal with this congeries of problems created by *dekasegi* and the twin issues of headship succession and the shortage of women? To answer these questions we must analyze in some detail the evolution and development of primary sector economic activity in the village.

In 1960, 83.8 percent of the gainfully employed population of Tanohata were engaged in primary production (agriculture, forestry, fishing), 4.5 percent in secondary production (mining, construction, manufacturing), and 11.5 percent in tertiary jobs (commerce, transportation, services). By 1975 a dramatic shift had taken place: the percentages were 47.4 percent, 30.2 percent, and 22.2 percent respectively.[20] By 1980 these trends were even more in evidence. The percentages were as follows: primary, 43.9 percent, secondary, 27.1 percent; and tertiary, 29 percent.[21]

Within agriculture, further shifts were taking place. The number and percentage of people in full-time farming did not change significantly between 1965 and 1980, but those in part-time farming shifted their other employment from the primary sector to the secondary sector. In

1965, 47.5 percent combined farming with another primary sector activity. By 1980 only 20.2 percent were in the primary sector and 70.8 percent were in the secondary sector. The same pattern can be found in fishing as well.[22]

One of the puzzles of economic life in Tanohata is the fishing and ocean products business. Important as it would appear to be, given the location of the village and the seeming potential of that gorgeous coastline, a variety of factors, human and environmental, have intervened to prevent or inhibit the full exploitation of this potential. In 1978 it represented only 8.8 percent of the economic production of the village. (Agriculture represented about 10 percent.)

In the hard times before Hayano's programs began to take effect, fishing was one alternative for subsistence. The families who were best off were those who lived in the coastal hamlets but had land-holdings in the upland above the coast. Hayano's family was one of these. The land-holdings were a "cushion," a reserve, a supplement—and a place of refuge and source of renewal for the family when disaster in the form of tsunami or typhoon struck, as they did every 40 to 50 years. In the terrible tsunami of 1897, the Hayano main family on the coast was devastated (half the population of Shimanokoshi was wiped out), and a younger son from one of the branch families in the upland had to be adopted and brought down to head the main family.

People fished for subsistence, but there was no way to market fish commercially. Even as late as the early 1970s families could not buy fish to eat in any of the stores of the village. As we have seen, Hayano got his chance to head the Shimanokoshi Fishing Cooperative in 1955 as a young man just turned twenty-six because it had gone bankrupt and no one wanted the job. There was another small, struggling fishing co-op in Hiraiga, next door to Shimanokoshi on the coast. However, people there were rivals of Shimanokoshi, not partners, and one could not travel between the two hamlets easily except by boat (in good weather). If you had to go in bad weather you went on foot, scaling the cliffs of the headland that separates them.

Hayano was successful in putting the fishing co-op back on its feet in the decade preceding his election as mayor. His friendship and support of Suzuki Zenkō in the Lower House of the Diet, and of Chida Tadashi in the Upper House, helped bring investment for basic fishing port facilities and safe-haven harbor construction. In his first term as mayor, these plans were expanded and harbor construction projects provided new jobs and cash income for local people. But the fishing business continued in the doldrums until the late seventies, when, finally, the long-term investments began to pay off. The 1964 village publication *Tanohata* says there were 248 family entities whose income came from fishing, of which five were full-time. The rest combined fishing with farming or forestry (71) or with construction work (172). In 1968 there were 317 family units engaged in fishing, but still only 6 worked at fishing full-time. By 1969 there were 23 full-time units out of a total of 303, the substantial jump reflecting the opening up of new opportunities. (See Appendix 1, Figure 7 for a chart of changes in the fishing population over time.)

The lack of unified structure and the existence of two rival fishing co-ops pointed to the lack of *mura isshiki* or a sense of belonging to Tanohata. The rivalry between the hamlets was given continuity by local religious institutions. The Raga hamlet shrine, Ōmiya Jinja, was the largest and had the oldest tradition in the village, its festival overshadowing all the other shrine festivals. Shimanokoshi, the larger and more prosperous hamlet, had nothing to rival the Ōmiya shrine. No doubt people in Raga and Hiraiga feared that Shimanokoshi would dominate any union of the two fishing co-ops. It was not just coincidence that the two fishing co-ops were finally unified in 1979 at about the same time that the last separate middle school was closed in Numabukuro. Only when sufficient social and economic momentum could be generated could people perceive their own interests as being served by a village-wide rather than a local hamlet organization. The consolidation of the two fishing cooperatives was further evidence of progress in building *mura isshiki*.

By the time this union was consummated Date Katsumi was working as manager of the growing village tourist industry, operating a small resort hotel. He tells of his struggle to get local fish to serve guests at the hotel. He had to reorganize the whole operation and fire the cook before he could get people to change. Every step was painful, just as it had been in the contract vegetable business (as we shall see later in this chapter).

As port facilities were developed and expanded, two new kinds of activity became possible—the cultivation of ocean products such as *wakame* (a delicious edible seaweed for which Tanohata is now becoming well-known) and tourism.

The 1968 publication *Tanohata* contains a picture of three fishermen in a boat holding up some *wakame*. The caption reads: "Creating a Fishing Industry! Second-Year Crop of Cultivated *Wakame*." In the late seventies Hayano brought in a consultant to advise Tanohata on how to process, package, and sell *wakame* under its own brand name. As the tourist traffic grew in volume, year by year, the linking of fishing with tourism in the development process began to pay off in jobs, income, and reputation for Tanohata.

It would appear, however, that much remained to be done. The 1982 planning document assessed the situation this way, pointing to the persistence of a variety of problems:

> We must press forward first of all with the development of port facilities. With the improvement of the structure of the fishing industry we will be able to promote actively the modernization of its management and can press vigorously for a variety of stable policies. In

the future we must complete the port and production infrastructure, using the facilities already completed more effectively, and with this construction and the natural resources we are blessed with we must plan to nurture those resources to achieve long-term stability. In addition, because most of what we produce is shipped out without processing, our productivity is very low. To counter this it is very important that we work to raise the "value added" dimension of our products quickly.[23]

It took thirteen years to do it, but in 1979, when the two rival fishing co-ops were finally merged, one of Mayor Hayano's major tasks in village building was accomplished. Momentum could now be generated for economic development on the coast. Today, in conjunction with tourism, aquaculture now constitutes the fastest-growing segment of economic life in the village.

Long-Term Strategies for Development

Hayano's program had three dimensions: building infrastructure, creating private sector jobs, and structuring long-term education to promote and undergird social and economic change.

The first task was to build an infrastructure capable of sustaining long-term economic growth. Nothing else was possible without that. It consisted of a variety of planning and construction projects: roads, schools, telephones, health care facilities—the institutional and communications network that would make life not just bearable but sustainable. An important by-product of this activity was that it generated local jobs and cash income for the people of Tanohata. In the first years of his tenure, 1965–70, this was of critical importance both politically and economically since it gave people a visible, material stake in the program he had initiated. An indication of the effects of these new jobs is contained in the figures for local taxes. The gross total more than doubled from 1965 to 1970, and by 1975 it had gone up more than six times.[24] Personal income in the village increased by more than 50 percent between 1964 and 1968.[25] In addition, average personal income tripled in Tanohata between 1965 and 1970, and then more than doubled again between 1970 and 1975.[26]

The most obviously needed construction projects were roads and fishing port facilities. Year after year investment money was secured from the prefectural and national budgets. From 1965 to 1975 it averaged more than 50 percent of the town's yearly budget. In gross amounts this figure is even more impressive, as Table 3 shows. Between 1965 and 1970 it went up by about 140 percent. From 1970 to 1975 it rose by nearly 300 percent.[27]

Impressive as the process and results of building infrastructure are,

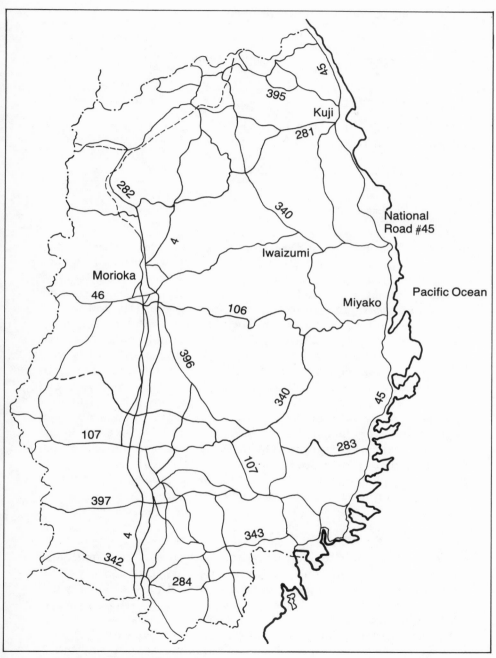

Iwate Prefecture road system.
Source: Iwate-ken, *Iwate no dōrō,* 1981.

TABLE 3. Equalization taxes and investment expenses

Year	Equalization tax as % of budget income	Investment as % of budget expenses
1965	¥75,421/170,655 = 44.2%	¥86,799/167,484 = 50.7%
1970	¥183,440/392,105 = 46.8%	¥202,237/387,312 = 52.2%
1975	¥540,680/1,195,480 = 45.2%	¥584,403/1,185,259 = 49.3%
1976	¥587,633/1,613,147 = 36.4%	¥881,078/1,595,285 = 55.6%
1977	¥650,262/1,881,078 = 34.6%	¥1,026,883/1,860,436 = 55.2%
1978	¥762,786/2,393,468 = 31.9%	¥1,413,195/2,373,552 = 59.5%
1979	¥847,354/2,108,753 = 40.2%	¥1,085,308/2,071,110 = 52.4%
1980	¥928,302/2,388,934 = 38.9%	¥1,237,977/2,346,256 = 52.8%

Source: Tanohata-mura, *Nōson sōgō seibi keikaku kōzō-zu,* p. 66–67.

Note: Unit = Thousands of Yen

the story in Tanohata in this regard is not so different from what could be found in many other towns and villages in Japan, although it happened later and at a more intense pace in Tanohata. However, creating an infrastructure was only a preliminary step, a necessary prerequisite to launching the distinctive program to generate private sector jobs and income that Hayano and his associates designed and implemented. That story revolves around three kinds of projects—dairy farming, contract vegetable growing, and tourism. Dairy farming and contract vegetables were introduced and developed through a kind of cooperative extension service run out of the village office. By the mid-1980s these projects had largely though not completely been devolved into private hands or hybrid ("third sector") companies. Tourism has gone through a number of phases with very mixed results. Efforts in the early 1970s were premature, and devolution to private individuals led to failure. In the short run, the work did not produce the hoped-for results. Only in the mid-1980s, after the completion and opening of a rail line through Tanohata, did it begin to give promise of sustained, long-term growth.

DAIRY FARMING

In terms of basic, long-term development, dairy farming came first. Some farm families in Tanohata had begun to raise dairy cattle as early as the 1940s. However, lacking good fodder to produce milk in quantity and roads to transport it to market, there still was no dairy industry even in 1965. During Hayano's first term as mayor, major resources were committed to develop a dairy industry. Beyond the need for roads, the key problems were raising the quality of animals and finding a local feed source. An experimental farm, the Nagamine Dairy Station, was established under the wing of the Economic Planning Section of the village office. Here work was done to develop strains of local grass for hay that would be hardy, productive, and nutritious. A breeding and calf care program was set up to raise milk cows to maturity and provide breeding services and advice for dairy farmers. By the end of Hayano's second term in late 1972, the dairy industry had made impressive strides. A local milk processing station was in operation, road-building had progressed to the point where there could be daily pickup of milk, and hay production was sufficient to provide the margin of profit for local farmers. (Until they could produce most of their own roughage and silage, the cost of producing milk was too high to make a milking operation profitable.) From 1965 to 1969 the number of milk cows increased by 50 percent. In the same period the amount of hay land in the village increased by one-third. As a first-time visitor to Tanohata in 1972, I was immediately struck with the number of silos and barns in place or under construction.

The success of the dairy program gave a renewed sense of hope to people all over the village. The work was hard and success did not come overnight, but what happened was soundly conceived, visible, *and* it made a difference in people's lives. It was quantifiable, too, and something Tanohata could point to with pride.

The Kumagai family, who began dairying right after World War II, had 4 or 5 cows in 1972. Ryūkō, the eldest son, after finishing his work at the university, had come home to take the lead in the work on the farm. He had convinced Sachiko to marry him. (Sachiko, a college graduate whom he had met at a university retreat seminar, had grown up in the Kantō Plain and knew nothing about farming, but she came to live in Tashiro, the hamlet dominated by the Kumagais.) Ryūkō had new-fangled ideas about pasturing cows on the hillside—unheard of in most of Japan—learned from his mentor at the university. He persuaded his father to work with him to try this method, and over the next decade they were successful. They expanded their pasture and their herd so that by the early eighties they were milking fifteen cows. Ryūkō had, by then, become a highly respected young leader in Tanohata. He is a doer, not a talker. He also is apolitical. Although he appreciates what Hayano has done for Tanohata, even grudgingly admitting that the consolidated middle school is a good thing, he worries about the fact that his children have had to go off to live in the dormitory there. More than anything, he wants to be left alone to do his work and build up the farm. He is clearly following in the footsteps of his grandfather, Kumajirō, who died in 1982, and his father, Shōzō, who still works with him actively on certain projects. While vigorously maintaining the family and its traditional structure, they seem always ready to try new things.

The Kumagais, with their traditional family structure and elite status in their region of Tanohata, have not only used the economic development that has come to the village to improve their own situation but also contributed to these developments in significant ways. For example, in the mid-seventies, Ryūkō sponsored a graduate of his university, Yoshizuka Kimio, to come to Tanohata as an apprentice to learn dairy farming. Kimio lived and worked with the Kumagais for a year and then with Ryūkō's help found land to buy in a neighboring hamlet. When he had his own dairy farm set up, he went back home to Chiba Prefecture (next door to Tokyo) and found a wife, whom he convinced to join in his pioneering venture. In the Yoshizukas, Tanohata has gained some sturdy and vigorous new citizens. Mayor Hayano personally stood as guarantor for Kimio when he purchased his land, further evidence of the personal commitment that Hayano has made to village economic development.

However, dairying is just one aspect of the effort to create jobs and develop agriculture in Tanohata. The nucleus of a tradition for dairy development was already there before Hayano took office. Another program that was started from scratch has emerged as an important segment of the Tanohata farm economy. This is contract vegetable growing. Of course people in Tanohata, as they eked out an existence at subsistence farming, grew vegetables for their own use, but the remoteness of the village, the lack of roads and transportation, and the absence of any structured channels for distribution and sales meant that no one had even thought about vegetables as a source of cash income.

CONTRACT VEGETABLE GROWING

Once there were roads and the dairy industry had been started, the potential for other activity was there, and in the early 1970s, as Hayano and his associates cast about for new ways to generate income and jobs, they devised a plan. The idea apparently was the brainchild of Hayano and his young associate from Waseda, Date Katsumi, who had joined the village office staff in April 1971. In my first trip to the village Date took me along as he made the rounds visiting farmers. It appeared that he was serving as a kind of extension agent, carrying messages, information, and even seeds and tools to people. I was fascinated by the glimpse I got of this activity, though at the time I could not grasp its significance. It was clear that Date was respected and had rapport with farmers everywhere he went. Later I found out why. In his book *Experiment in Tanohata,* he details the hard work, the frustration, and the accomplishments of his first years in the village office when he worked as messenger boy, teacher, gadfly, mediator, and entrepreneur for his venture.

> The Planning Section was responsible for research, of course, and for experimentation and implementation of plans. We felt the need to establish a new development company. For example, we couldn't continue to market products through the Planning Section Office [in the village office]. . . . Two years later I was in the Economic Section. I had direct responsibility for vegetables and special products. . . . I was still working with the Production Cooperative, too, and there

were lots of sticky problems. I saw the seamy side of the operation.
. . . As I noted before, the Public Development Corporation [*Kaihatsu
Kōsha*] had very broad functions. My work, however, while I was in
the Planning Section was with research and surveys. When I moved to
the Economic Section my work was with actual experimental projects.
We were then able to get those contract vegetable projects fully under
way. In each hamlet there was an agricultural co-op group and an agricultural improvement office. The co-op supplied materials, the
improvement office supplied advice and technical help.[28]

The whole project had to be generated by the village office as the
agent of change and development. It was the classic problem of the
chicken and the egg. Which comes first; which is the source of movement and change? The farmers were the chicken, and the outlets in cities
like Miyako and Morioka were the egg. Which do you generate first, markets or vegetables to supply them? Of course it was not an either/or question; you had to do both at once. Since Date's relationships with the farm
community were already in place, he lined up potential producers and
then made the rounds of wholesalers and green grocers in the cities,
finally landing a contract with a wholesaler in Morioka to supply *daikon*
(white radishes). He found farmers willing to raise them to sell and ener-
getically promoted the project. His report of the events surrounding the
production of the first batch of radishes reveals the nature of the problems he faced.

We had planned carefully, considering soil conditions, weather
and all that. We had consulted widely in Morioka and elsewhere. I
had talked with the farmers and gotten everything ready. They
planted the *daikon* and in a month they were three centimeters high.
Then suddenly they all blossomed.[29] It was terrible! The whole crop
was useless. This was caused by the *yamase* (the damp wind and fog).
We hadn't calculated on the cool dampness that it brings, and the
summer of 1976 was especially bad. We tried every way of disposing
of the *daikon* and sold some, but it was a bad situation. We couldn't
say to the farmers "Throw them out." (There were some the bugs had
attacked.) So we kept trying. We finally sold them for use as pickles
but we had to peel them first. The Shii no Mori students helped with
that.[30]

Date had to teach and lead and coax and cajole the farmers every
step of the way. After *daikon* came potatoes, with the same kinds of problems.

Now we tried potatoes, but it turned out that it was not just Tanohata. All over the Tōhoku they were growing them, and so the price
dropped drastically from what it had been the previous year. We had
hoped to get more than ¥80 per kilo for them, but we got less than

¥50. We had to run around begging the supermarket people to buy them.[31]

In the end this persistence, energy, and drive paid off. The contracts were renewed and expanded. Other vegetables were added—asparagus, peas, sweet corn, and lettuce. One of the early experiments that succeeded was growing chrysanthemum blossoms for restaurants. The flowers, used as a garnish, are also a potent source of vitamin C, and growing them has become a major source of cash income for some families in Tanohata.

The establishment of a commercial contract vegetable business had become possible with the completion of National Route 45, the north-south coastal highway link between Miyako and Kuji. It was formally opened in the fall of 1972. The effect of completion of this important link is revealed in the development figures for the rest of the decade. In 1970 there had been 64 hectares of vegetable land in Tanohata; by 1979 this had increased 57.8 percent to 101 hectares and the value of production had gone up 2.7 times.[32]

Success with the vegetables was not automatic or universal. Beyond the human factors related to production and distribution which Date describes there were the hard realities of Tanohata's physical environment. The village has no true rivers, only water courses and drainage down the ravines, some of them seasonal. It receives less snow and rain than most of the Tōhoku, so supplying water in large quantities for irrigation and animal husbandry is problematic. Supplies must be carefully apportioned. Further, in the summer, at the height of the growing season, comes the local weather phenomenon known as *yamase*. Offshore seasonal breezes pick up moisture from the ocean. When they hit the precipitous 200–300 foot headlands of Tanohata, they produce the fog. In July and August Tanohata is plagued morning and evening by *yamase,* reducing drastically the amount of sunshine for vegetable growing. Iwami Hisako refers poignantly of this threat to people's livelihood in a poem:

> Thick fog spawned by the oceans currents
>   envelops our village
> The cold of the summer
>   keeps on and on.[33]

As the vegetable business grew in the 1970s, people learned which crops could be produced under local conditions and which would sell. By the end of the decade, the prefecture was providing help with an experiment station to identify the crops and strains best-suited to Tanohata's severe climatic conditions.

A highlight of the contract vegetable business has been the spectacular development of mushroom growing. Started in the late 1970s, in the

1980s it became the fastest-growing segment of the whole agricultural program. Several families are on their way to making small fortunes. For one family, the Fujishiros, the opportunity came none too soon. I spent an afternoon with them one day in the winter of 1983 viewing their operation and listening to the story of their life in Tanohata.

The Fujishiros, husband and wife, were born and raised in southern Sakhalin or Karafuto, as it was known to the Japanese, who took it from Russia as one of the spoils of the Russo-Japanese War of 1904 and controlled it until 1945. They, along with about 60 other refugees, were sent to relocate in Tanohata after the war. They were married in the village and received a small homestead of land in the northern part of the village not far from Kitayamasaki, a spectacular headland that juts out into the Pacific. They eked out an existence in subsistence farming through the fifties and sixties and then participated in a not very successful attempt to develop a "*minshuku* village" to serve the fledgling tourist trade at Kitayamasaki. Poor architectural design, lack of capital and management skills, and poor timing prevented the "village" from prospering. Then came the opportunity to try raising mushrooms. This time the timing was right, and hard work and the marketing network that had been developed have made them one of a growing number of prosperous mushroom farmers in Tanohata. Success stories like theirs give substance and personality to the statistics on economic development in the village.

The Fujishiros' biggest problem now is with the local agricultural cooperative. They complain about its bureaucratic structure and the self-serving attitudes of its staff. They sell half of what they produce directly to a wholesaler in Shizuoka, south of Tokyo, and would sell more but for the restrictive policies of the co-op. They depend on it for supplies and dare not give up that connection, but they resent the fact that it takes a disproportionate profit as a middleman. Yet in spite of their problems with the agricultural co-op, the Fujishiros are prospering as never before.

The contract vegetable business turned Date into a skilled and able entrepreneur, and he became increasingly impatient with bureaucracy, chafing under its procedures and red tape. He had become the mayor's trusted troubleshooter, always ready to dive into a problem and work with tremendous energy toward a solution, bringing people together in problem-solving contexts to achieve the goals of Hayano's administration. It was he who promoted, designed, and sold the mayor on international education. His connections with Waseda made him the natural person for this. His relationship to the Shii no Mori Kai led to another development project, this one in forestry.

FOREST PRODUCTS

Date was adviser, sponsor, and local mediator for the Shii no Mori Kai. He used it not only as a means to economic development through reforestation, but also for mutual education, for the villagers and for the students from Waseda and from Earlham. Tree planting and silviculture would generate jobs and local products for sale, but they also brought outsiders and local people into meaningful contact with each other. He was demanding and impatient with the students and local residents but kind and wise as well, ready to help day or night when need arose. He saw the value of this window on the world but realized that it was a two-way glass —the outsiders would learn as much as the villagers and they must listen and learn from the wisdom and spirit of the local people. He articulated this philosophy as follows:

> We were working with the village to realize the dream together. Shii no Mori was the place for village and college students to learn together. When you are in the urgent pursuit of the ideal—then the opportunity, the place, the human heart—one must not leave out any of these. Eating corn together, working on the red pines, talking with young people about their dreams by the light of kerosene lamps—we were taught much just by being there, by being close—these are jewels, precious moments for human beings and for the future of society.
>
> When we enter the village we sense that here we have kinship with others [literally, we smell the scent of our mothers]. At one point we realized that we should invite the village people to Waseda in Tokyo.
>
> The *Shishiodori* (deer dance) has been handed down in the village since Heian times. From the rugged cliffs reflected in the sea, to the green pines which hide Japanese antelope from view, the mysterious beauty of it lives in this natural setting. The people of the village call it *Aoshishi* (The Green Deer).
>
> People associate the deer dance with both joyous and sorrowful times. It is a symbol of the culture and history of the village. It was to give a performance of this deer dance, which is so expressive of the deep feelings of people, that we thought of inviting Tanohata people to Waseda. . . .
>
> When we go to the village now we say *kaete kimashita*.[34] We stay at the Shii no Mori dormitory, but for us the whole village is a classroom. We are part of it, and morning and evening greetings to people in the village symbolize that Waseda and Shii no Mori will continue and develop their relationship further.[35]

The Shii no Mori afforestation work was conceived in this spirit of two-way education. The college students would learn forestry skills, the value of hard work, and would participate in a way of life rich in tradition and folk lore. The villagers would receive inspiration and help from the youthful enthusiasm of the students and from the spirit of service in which they came. The project itself would be a model for the development of public and private forestry land in the village.

Fundamental change was halting and slow to come, but the Shii no

Mori model has had an impact. By 1982 the majority of the public forest land (18 percent of the total of forest land) as well as nearly 25 percent of the privately held land was under a forest management program. There have been failures along the way and one of the saddest is the story of the *kiri no ki* (paulownia) plantings (see Chapter 2). This forest products project of the early 1970s seemed a natural way to capitalize on local potential.

In 1982–83 when we lived in the village people were still trying to salvage what they could of the crop, cutting immature trees before they began to rot. What had looked like a promising project, employing 40–50 local people in the factory and providing income for a group of farm families, was collapsing around them. The factory continued to operate successfully (with 55 employees in 1983), but the paulownia for it had to be imported from China. It comes by ship to the port of Miyako and is trucked to Tanohata. People don't like to talk about this disaster, but it is one of the realities of the trial-and-error development process that Tanohata has undertaken.

TOURISM

At the same time the fishing co-ops merged, the local development corporation was reinvigorated with new leadership (see Chapter Six for a full discussion of this development) and the coastal hamlets embarked on vigorous self-help development efforts sparked by the new head of the development company, Date Katsumi. He initiated a seafood product development and marketing effort that was closely coordinated with the push for tourism. This whole effort was given a significant boost in 1984 with the opening of the Sanriku Railroad. The resulting economic growth, fed especially by tourism, is creating some regional stresses in the village. As the coastal hamlets forge ahead, they leave behind people in the western inland region of the village.

The inland hamlets of Tanohata have always been the most isolated and most needy economically. (The Kumagai family in Tashiro, who are discussed in Chapter One, are an exception in this regard.) The development of the dairy and contract vegetable industries in the 1970s gave an economic boost to the inland hamlets and allowed them to keep pace with coastal development. In the 1980s, with tourism triggering fast growth in the coastal hamlets, differential economic levels began to emerge again. This constitutes a serious political as well as an economic challenge to Hayano and we shall return to it. However, first we need to examine tourism as a source of jobs and of economic development.

Many general maps of northern Honshū show Kitayamasaki, the spectacular headland that juts out into the Pacific—the point where the Japanese coast is nearest to America, as villagers like to remind us. Until recently none showed Tanohata, and there was a blank coast between

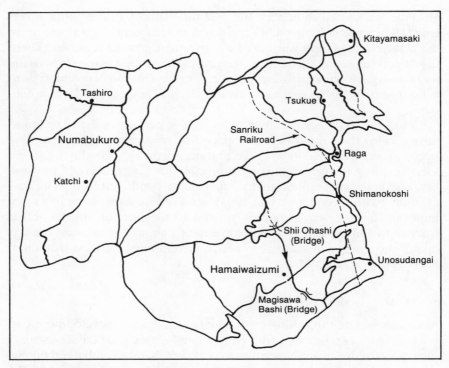

Selected hamlets and points of interest in Tanohata.
Source: Adapted from Tanohata-mura, *Tanohata-mura sonsei yōran,* 1982.

Miyako and Kuji, the two major port cities. That is changing, however, for the map-makers have "discovered" Tanohata. On April 1, 1984, the first trains began operation through Tanohata on the Sanriku Railroad, the rail line linking the Rikuchū coast through an area that was officially designated a national park in 1961. Ever since that time, the struggle has been to establish Tanohata as a tourist site. At the same time, there has been some ambiguity in the village's stance. Many people have wanted to promote tourism as a way to create jobs, but the thoughtful ones, led by Hayano, have been concerned about the fragile environment and have struggled to balance the desire for tourist traffic with the need to control environmental degradation which that could bring.

   This ambivalence was in evidence when I traveled with Franklin Wallin, the president of Earlham College, to Tanohata in the spring of 1980. Mayor Hayano took us first to Unosudangai, a promontory that juts out into the Pacific at the southern end of Tanohata, as Kitayamasaki does at the northern end. He proudly showed us the simple walking paths, the picnic area, and the unspoiled beauty of the spot. Then we went to Kitayamasaki with its souvenir shop, rest house, and the inevitable litter from tourist buses. He pointed out that the Kitayamasaki site had begun to develop before he became mayor. He said, "Now, we wouldn't allow this kind of unseemly clutter so close to the headland. That's why we designed Unosudangai as we did." Tanohata desperately needs the jobs and wants the tourists and their money but the debate continues on how to design the facilities and the context for further development. To whom should they appeal? What kind of clientele do they want? Those issues are still unresolved. A variety of approaches have been tried, with mixed results, and experimentation continues. Over time, environmental concerns have come to bulk larger as the dangers of environmental degradation have been revealed, both in Tanohata and in the country at large.

Throughout the 1960s, even after Hayano took office, little could be done directly. The real task was infrastructure and the need to change people's attitudes. There was no time to recognize the potential of Tanohata's natural beauty until people had jobs, food, and the time to develop a broader worldview. Completion of National Route 45 meant that tourist buses could come through Tanohata. Construction of safe harbor facilities at Shimanokoshi provided a site for a coastal sightseeing boat. The prefecture agreed to sponsor and underwrite the construction of a short toll road giving good access and a scenic drive along the coast from Kitayamasaki to Shimanokoshi. The one major communication link that was lacking was a railroad line. In the 1960s talk of a link through Tanohata came up sporadically. In 1967 Hayano listed the rail line as one of the projects he felt had a good chance to be started. The work was finally begun by the Japanese National Railways (JNR), and in 1972 the first section north from Miyako to Tarō opened. A section coming south from Kuji to Fudai was completed and opened in 1975. Work laying out the road-bed and building tunnels through Tanohata continued sporadically until 1981. Then, bathed in red ink, the JNR announced it was stopping work. Not only would it not complete the line, it planned to stop running trains on that portion of the coastal railroad that was already in operation, as part of the plan to restructure its national operations, a severe blow to people on the coast. But that gets us ahead of our story.

While Tanohata's basic work on infrastructure was in process, Hayano was attempting to awaken people to the natural beauty of the village and its potential. In his first State of the Village speech in March 1966, he said,

> We must admit that our productivity is low, but on the one hand we have a wide expanse (11,000 hectares) of land. Three quarters of that is forest resource land, and in addition we are blessed with the coastal land and the Pacific Ocean. I believe deeply that with these two resources we have in our grasp the potential for very great future development.[36]

By 1969 the general process of development was far enough along that Hayano could turn his attention directly to tourism as a potential source of jobs. In his State of the Village speech on March 20, 1969, he stated:

> Since 1967 various groups have wanted to do this, but in this fiscal year it appears we can realize our plan to build a hiking trail along the coast from Kitayamasaki to Unosudangai. Linked to that plan, the Kenpoku Bus Co. is now planning definitely to open a sightseeing boat service. These plans will add substantially to Tanohata's resources for tourism and will increase our visibility in this region. As a result economic development here will, I believe, enter a whole new stage.[37]

A year later he had this to say:

> The start of the work on the prefecture-sponsored toll road, I think, holds great significance for the development of the tourist industry here in our village. . . . With regard to tourism, the Northern Rikuchū Coast Tourist Development Corp. has established and is operating a "*Minshuku* Center" and a sightseeing boat here. This has truly been the year when we launched a real tourist industry. Using these facilities that have been created, tourism in Tanohata now has a solid foundation in both name and substance. I feel this strongly. At the same time, for the future we have to plan how, through our own efforts, we can produce the desired and appropriate facilities for tourism. As you all know this will be very difficult considering the economic base that we have here.[38]

By the mid-seventies, with the sightseeing boat operating, the toll road open, and a growing number of *minshuku* providing simple overnight accommodations, Tanohata was beginning to develop sufficient base of experience to sustain further growth. However, it would be the end of the decade before a full-fledged tourist industry could emerge. Several plans and experiments were tried, some more and some less successful.

Access to Tanohata was still difficult. There was no convenient public transportation. JNR buses came to the village, but there were only two or three per day and the schedules were inconvenient. Tour buses went through Tanohata, but few stopped except at Kitayamasaki, and almost none stayed overnight. Some hardy tourists drove to the village in their own cars and stayed overnight in *minshuku*. However, there was not much volume of business.

In 1972 a general development plan for the village was published. It was an interim and incomplete plan, especially when compared with the 1982 document, but it is useful in seeing where Tanohata had come from and where the leadership thought it should go at that time. Hayano had certainly made progress in getting people to focus on the natural environment, Tanohata's greatest resource. The introduction to that document states:

> We must rethink the value of people as they exist within these impressive natural surroundings that constitute Tanohata. Then we must create a new view of Tanohata's value and its individual richness. With this we must then express ourselves with true courage. . . . We must find ways to talk about the clean air and blue sky that are our legacy, the energy that flows from this traditional highland village, and focus anew the attention of each individual in the village on this.[39]

There follows more rhetoric in the same vein exhorting people to appreciate their values and traditions. Some of this rhetoric reflects the national agenda. In 1972 Japan was attempting to come to terms with massive environmental degradation in its cities, and a national debate was raging on what to do and how to do it.

At this time Tanohata was using the slogan "Your Hometown in the Highlands." There were charts and graphs presenting a structure and a rationale for development, but few hard data or concrete projects. The fact is that Tanohata was not yet ready or able to produce a full-fledged development plan. These documents, however, give us some sense of direction and show how slim the resources were for development of a tourist industry. There were then only two real inns *(ryokan)* and a total of twenty-five family-run *minshuku*. These were scattered all over the village. Many had no real tourist facilities and needed repair and renovation. It is no wonder it took another decade for tourism to take hold.

However, the direction was being hammered out. Tanohata was searching for a way to draw tourists by playing up its potential strengths: environment and scenic beauty. It had primary economic activity in agriculture and fishing, which, people hoped, could be used to draw tourists. For instance, the 1972 planning documents suggested raising edible wild plants for food and establishing a farming program for city children.

The experiments of the 1970s with tourism took a variety of forms. The most useful was something called "Cabin Heights," a group of simple overnight cabins. It had a store for supplies and a buffet-barbeque ("all you can eat") on weekends and catered to families and small groups. As family travel by car became more common, the facility was crowded on weekends. The overnight accommodations were less in demand and barely paid for themselves. Date Katsumi took hold of the operation in the late 1970s and used it to experiment with programs for summer camp groups from the big cities. Students from Nihon University of Physical Education were recruited to work with Earlham College students to run an English and outdoor activities experience for youngsters from Iwate. While these experiments did not generate permanent jobs or much income, they were useful in spreading the word about Tanohata and its potential.

In the upland area near Kitayamasaki, another kind of tourist experiment was tried. A group of families were recruited who would run *minshuku,* and a *minshuku* village was built, with a dozen modest establishments erected. Tennis courts, volleyball, softball, and other sports facilities were planned nearby. The hope was to attract large numbers of people who would enjoy the scenic beauty and outdoor recreation. A coastal hiking course was also completed, but the project never generated a sufficient volume of activity and people were not able to make a living running *minshuku.* Our friends the Fujishiros, the mushroom growers, said their *minshuku* operation produced about 10 percent of their income. It appears that in the 1970s the time had not yet really come for much of this activity.

Another experiment that has not yet proven itself is a facility for seaside family recreation called Hamanasu Park. Built in the late seventies, it provided family housing units, a swimming pool, and other recreational facilities. The hope was to attract family groups for several days of camping, generating cash income for the service people and nearby store keepers and increasing the flow of traffic through the village. The emphasis on family groups and outdoor activity reflects Tanohata's attempt to define the clientele it would attract, in order to avoid environmental degradation and the social evils of drunk driving and carousing associated with young singles groups. The use of Hamanasu Park grew slowly, and even in 1985 the park was still not a viable economic entity.

Still in progress in the mid-1980s was an experiment involving a tie-in with the management of the Imperial Hotel in Tokyo whereby the hotel took young people from Tanohata as trainees in food service and hotel management. At one time in the early 1980's there was a rumor that the hotel would build a resort center in Tanohata, and apparently the hotel corporation has an option on some land in the village. However, so far no specific project has emerged.

The most important activity in the village related to tourism revolved around the development of the resort hotel Ragasō. It was built in 1977–78 under the auspices of the Northern Rikuchū Coast Tourist Development Corporation *(Hokubu Rikuchū Kaigan Kankō Kaihatsu K.K.).*[40] The corporation had been established in 1969 with Hayano as president. Half the capital came from the Northern Iwate Motor Lines *(Iwate Kenpoku Jidōsha K.K.),* a commercial firm, and half from Tanohata. Its job was to develop the tourist trade in Tanohata. As a hybrid public/private company, it was a forerunner of what in the 1980s came to be known as third sector economic activity. (This phenomenon will be examined closely in Chapter Six.) However, this corporation played an with village kids. When they went back they told their parents about their experience. While they were here we made *tezukuri no tabi* [handmade straw sandals]. People stayed in *minshuku*. We provided program. In some ways it was like a *shūgaku ryokō* [school excursion]. Now I borrowed this experiment to use with the tourist company. There remained problems such as staff, publicity, etc. I drew on contacts with Nihon University of Physical Education, Professor Hirano, the *Iwate Nippō,* etc. Now with better facilities, the sightseeing boat and all, it was different from before. Also, with Shii no Mori and the Waseda and Earlham students, we had people to draw on. We tried things like a "Summer Vacation Children's Village," "Family Camp," "English Camp." A pattern emerged: three nights, four days— using the environment (farming, fishing), crafts, making butter, milking, fishing. We had young people as counselors, but we got farmers, fishermen, old people involved.

The problem was, we designed and ran the program but not many local children got involved. As an enterprise it went well, but in evaluating it the fourth year we decided to focus it exclusively on the local scene. With the preparation and all, we've been able to do it only once so far, but in content and in the effect on local kids it paid off.

From the perspective of contact between town and country, and in terms of regional development, these experiments seem to hold great promise.

SEEKING A PLACE FOR NEW KINDS OF HUMAN CONTACT

In the course of these developments Professor Hirano from the University of Physical Education became the center of a plan for building a *shizen daigakkō* [university of the natural environment] at Kitayamasaki. He also had a connection with the Matsushita Research Institute as a Lecturer in Physical Education. I had known him since 1974. Shii no Mori had been influenced by him, and we were inspired to try to build the *shizen daigakkō*. Leaving aside the question of whether we should view these things as tourism or as education, this could be seen as a new form of industry for Tanohata.

Creation of a new form for human interaction must be at the core of Tanohata tourism, I believe. That kind of industry cannot be simply divided up as "primary," "secondary," "tertiary." It may be more appropriate to call it *fukugō sangyō* [composite industry], which includes all three categories. For example, take the case of agriculture. It is not just a product of activity; you can consider it from the point of view of school education, or you can also consider it fully from the point of view of tourism.

FROM INNKEEPER TO FISHMONGER
The Birth of Marukita Ocean Products

From the problem of providing good hotel food service to the way to get fresh fish I found myself involved in the whole question of supply. I explained all this to the Board of Directors, and we changed the articles of incorporation so that we could get into this work. . . . In February 1981, when I got the okay for this, we established two new posts, assigning people to buy from local fish markets. To do this we needed an official brand name so we chose *Marukita*. Then the *Bussan jigyō-bu* [the Production Section] came to be known everywhere as Marukita *Kaisan* [Marukita Development Production].

BEGINNING BARTER TRADE

The purpose of this section was to provide fresh fish. Therefore we needed to have permission to trade outside the village. However, to get formal status in places like Miyako or Hachinohe was very difficult. So we began to barter—fish from our catch for fish from theirs. Gradually we expanded to other areas as well. From this time on, local fish became a staple in our food service and we had accomplished our purpose.

BEGINNING TO WORK AS A JOBBER FOR LOCAL PRODUCTS

Now we found ourselves working as jobbers for local products. It was a tough business to break into. If you have a factory and can provide "value added," it is possible to sell, but we had neither the facilities nor the equipment. We could only provide a path for disposal of fish locally caught. Thus we would have to ship out in the hope that the fish would sell in other markets. And there were packing and shipping expenses. We had no idea how to package, where to ship, what fish to send. As newcomers, we'd have to sell for less than established brands.

However, we did have the information and experience from the contract vegetable business. We sent our people out on that circuit to visit markets and learn. We talked to other market people.

EXPERIMENTS IN PRODUCING SEA PRODUCTS
THE ROAD TO INDEPENDENCE FOR THE BUSSAN JIGYŌ-BU
Raising the Value of Our Brand

We were selling tourist souvenirs in the restaurants and hotels, but there were virtually none with the Tanohata name. Of course, for the tourists who had come to the Rikuchū coast there was no particular difference in the towns and villages from Aomori to Sendai. The same sea products—*wakame, kombu, awabi, uni*—came from all of them. And the fish were about the same. However, when Tanohata people saw *"Miyako Meibutsu"* or "Hachinohe Special Product" printed on things, they said, "It's not a Tanohata product." The same product with a different label would be received differently. Even when I was in the village office, I had been aware of the problem. Then when we established the *Bussan Jigyō-bu,* when I saw products in their final market form, I realized what was needed. We tried packaging sea products ourselves and selling them in the shops. People coming from inland who bought seafood products especially liked these and bought them to take home. By 1983 about 20 percent of our sales were of our brand. We plan to do even more of this. This will increase the value of them. We have to strive for good quality and low price. If we can do this we can improve the image of Sanriku tourism.

The need to establish an identity for Tanohata is a thread reaching all the way back to the fight over consolidation in the late 1950s. Date rightly grasped the potential of putting the Tanohata logo and brand on local products. By the early 1980s, as the fishing industry and the contract vegetable business began to generate new sources of income, Tanohata had products it could call its own. *Wakame* and *konbu* joined milk and mushrooms as Tanohata *meibutsu* (famous products). As tourism became a viable source of jobs and income for people, it supported the primary production from ocean and farm and Tanohata began to have what Date calls *fukugō sangyō* (composite industry). Date makes an interesting point in explaining what he means by *fukugō sangyō*. In another context he calls it "fourth sector" economic activity, meaning a mixture of primary production (vegetables, fish and sea products, etc.) and tertiary activity (commercial or service work), which, when combined creatively, produce a viable local economic base for jobs and income locally generated. He and Hayano recognized that Tanohata could not attract (and did not want) the usual kind of industry. They had been struggling to design an alternative mix of economic activity to capitalize on local resources and characteristics and yet succeed in providing stable long-term employment. They have not succeeded—yet—but they have established a base and a direction. They have been willing to gamble and experiment and to abandon projects that fail, to chalk the failures up to experience, and to forge ahead with something else.

Liberation

Hayano, Date, and the other leaders in Tanohata are always looking for ways to tap into regional and national efforts to promote such things as U-turn. At the same time, they try to generate momentum within the village for long-term economic development. This is what has made the building of the infrastructure of roads and communication so essential. As long as Tanohata was physically isolated, the process could not even start. One word on everyone's lips was *kaihō* (liberation). It was a long time in coming, but in this sense the culmination of their work for development in Tanohata came in the six months between April and October of 1984. In the *Tanohata kōhō* for January 1984, Hayano put it dramatically in a New Year's message entitled "The Year of Liberation."

In the new year the century-long efforts of so many of our people, who have worked so hard to liberate us from isolation, will come to fruition with the completion of two major projects. It has seemed like a never-ending task to accomplish this and make this coming year truly the "Year of Liberation." One of these projects is the opening of the Northern Riasu Line of the Sanriku Railroad. The second project is "Tanohata Ōhashi," which spans that inaccessible ravine, Matsu-maesawa.

The completion of these two projects will, of course, serve to unlock the unlimited resources of the Rikuchū coast that have awaited development. Even beyond just guaranteeing activity and economic development for the region, it holds great promise. I believe that it signals the dawn of the twenty-first century, which we on the Sanriku coast are now facing.[42]

The opening of the Sanriku Railroad and the dedication and opening of Shii Ōhashi, as the great bridge on Route 45 was named, symbolized not just Tanohata's release from isolation but its new position on the leading edge of economic development in Iwate Prefecture.

By the end of October a record-breaking total of over one million tourists had visited Tanohata. People on the coast were kept busy just providing the goods and services demanded by such numbers. The excitement generated by the opening of the railroad made all other activity pale into insignificance, but in reality the railroad was only the tip of the iceberg of two decades of development, without which it would never have been completed.

Even so, the benefits flowing from the presence of the railroad reach in many directions. The two most obvious in their social and economic effects are, first, that young people can commute everyday to high school (north to Kuji or south to Miyako). They don't have to live away from home any more. Second, adults can commute to jobs in either direction, unhindered by weather or driving conditions even in the winter. These two things highlight the sense of liberation that Tanohata feels. A third important benefit is to tourism and jobs inside the village. The dramatic increase in the flow of tourists underscores this. The two stops on the railroad in Tanohata have themselves spawned new business of various kinds, from coffee shops to the sale of souvenirs and packaged seafood products.

By early 1985 plans were announced to establish a second "*min-shuku* village" at Akedo on the coast. Overnight stays in the hamlets on the coast by tourists had nearly doubled, from 29,000 in 1983 to 50,000 in 1984. There was a need to expand facilities. Learning from the earlier experience at Kitayamasaki, this project, a spinoff from the third sector initiatives of Date's company, is an interesting blend of a family-run business and commercial catering service. The company puts up the capital for a family to renovate its home and provide simple overnight accommodations for guests. The company runs a catering service, providing food and other support services. Initial response to the project was enthusiastic. Families in Akedo, one of the hamlets hardest hit by *dekasegi,* were eager to join the project. Said one resident: "If we have a *minshuku* then our young people can make a U-turn, and there's a chance we can get rid of *dekasegi.* We have to make this project succeed."[43]

This activity on the coast was good news for Tanohata overall, but it created problems, too. Back away from the coast, pockets of economic depression remained, and the long-term tasks of building a viable economic base in agriculture and forest products continued to occupy the time and energy of a majority of the people of Tanohata. These are continuing issues and we shall return to them.

However, the opening of the railroad focused nationwide attention on Tanohata. The Sanriku Railroad was the first third sector company to be used to launch such an ambitious project. The fact that this was an attempt to salvage a local rail line, one which was actually stillborn under JNR auspices, has given it even greater significance. Literally the whole country was watching the opening on April 1, 1984. There were special program segments on the national news, reporters flocked to Tanohata to witness and report the event, and Tanohata became the object of country-wide attention—and envy. The third sector phenomenon is so important in contemporary Japan that it is worthy of special attention. The Sanriku Railroad as well as the Northern Rikuchū Coast Tourist Development Corporation provide interesting case studies of what is being done to create jobs and bring economic development to the region.

A Tanohata road, 1955.
Photo from *Tanohata 101*.

Hotel Ragasō as seen from the tourist highway, 1990.
Photo from *Tanohata 101*.

Seaside road in Shimanokoshi hamlet, 1960.
Photo from *Tanohata 101*.

Seaside road in Shimanokoshi hamlet, 1990.
Photo from *Tanohata 101*.

Kumagai Yasuke in Tashiro hamlet with one of Tanohata's first milk cows, 1913.
Photo from *Tanohata 101*.

Tanohata milk and ice cream festival, 1988.
Photo from *Tanohata 101*.

Charcoal bearers headed for market, 1963.
Photo from *Tanohata 101*.

Sanriku railroad, one-car train, 1990.
Photo by the author.

Pulling in a fishing boat in Raga hamlet harbor, c. 1964.
Photo from *Tanohata 101*.

A fishing boat in for repairs in Raga hamlet harbor, 1990.
Photo by the author.

Railroad ties being carried to the shore for shipment, 1952.
Photo from *Tanohata 101*.

Hotel Ragasō in Raga hamlet, 1990.
Photo by the author.

若者の顔も水面も赤く照らし

精霊舟は流れに傾く

敬子

Young faces reflected
    Water flashing red
The candle-lit boats of Obon
    Drift out into the current
        Nakamura Keiko

Wakamono no kao mo minamo mo
Akaku terashi Shōrōbune wa nagare
ni katamuku

        Keiko

Chapter Six

THE HYBRID ENTERPRISE AND REGIONAL DEVELOPMENT

Tsugi no teisha eki wa Tanohata . . . (Next stop, Tanohata). This announcement in a one-car diesel train travelling up the Rikuchū coast on April 1, 1984, signaled the success of nearly a century of effort by the people of the coast to acquire rail transport. Critics said "It's a boondoggle. It will never pay for itself." For the residents of Tanohata and other coastal towns it brought jobs, easy access to the outside world, and hope. Mayor Hayano proclaimed 1984 "the Year of Liberation," and called on the villagers to bend every effort to make *Mai Reeru* (My Rail) a viable enterprise. Indeed plans had been carefully laid in an attempt to prevent the new line, the Sanriku Railroad, from being engulfed by the same wave of red ink that was overwhelming long-established local JNR lines all over the country.

The opening of the new line drew national media attention as the first attempt to deal with local mass transit needs through the device of the hybrid enterprise, the so-called third sector *(daisan sekutaa)* company. This was not a new device structurally. Such hybrid enterprises had been used all over the country for years. Tanohata had created one as early as 1969, and it reflected a trend that had appeared in the 1960s during Japan's high-growth boom years.

In his book *Japan's Public Policy Companies,* Chalmers Johnson takes brief note of hybrid public-private enterprise corporations but dismisses them as relatively unimportant.

185

The mixed enterprise form the *tokushu kaisha* exemplify became quite popular in Japan during the 1960s. It was called the "third sector" *(daisan sekutoru)* because it was alleged to be more efficient than either the purely public or the private sector. However, many authorities feel the potentialities of the form have been retarded by excessive government interference.[1]

In the years since Johnson did his research, this pattern has been resurrected and given a new "reading" or pronunciation. (Johnson calls them *daisan sekutoru;* the loan word "sector" is now pronounced *sekutā* and written differently in katakana.) By the mid-eighties *daisan sekutā* companies were again being talked about as a potential "wave of the future" for regional development. Johnson rightly points out the danger that government bureaucratic inertia will strangle such companies before they can accomplish their missions. Date Katsumi in his book on Tano-hata spells out these dangers further in his discussion of the approach that Mayor Hayano took to development.

> "Mother Japan" [*Oyakata Hi no Maru*]—That's the way people talk about inefficiency all the way from the nation to small towns, saying, "There's no bankruptcy." Leave aside the question of inefficiency, is it not possible for bankruptcy to occur? Without even looking at the case of the developing countries, there will be bankruptcy. In Japan, if not at the national level, at lower levels, reorganized groups, the "company reorganization law" will certainly produce cases of this. There is a difference between private companies and public companies in accounting practices with regard to deficits such that public companies which actually have deficits can adjust accounts to show themselves in the black. To simplify the problem, one can just say "embellished accounts are possible."

THE DIFFERENCE BETWEEN CONTROL OF FIXED EXPENSES AND FIXING EXPENSES

With projects, one way to manage loss and profit was to think of costs as fixed, and income as the variable. In private companies you have to work to control costs. In public enterprises it is common to promote the idea of fixed costs. To take one example: at the end of a fiscal year you have unused funds for what is called *shutchō* [travel on official business] and the tendency is to use them somehow (since they're already budgeted). Having budget left over suggests poor planning and will hurt next year's budget. As a result purposeless activity and spending for unneeded things occur. From this comes the problem of fixed expenses no matter whether conditions and needs change or not.

THE POTENTIAL FOR BANKRUPTCY TO SPREAD FROM
MISTAKES IN LINKED PROJECTS

Another thing that brings bankruptcy is "linked companies." For the towns in the Rikuchū Coast National Park there are many projects linked to tourism.

So what happened with linked enterprises when there were deficits? Most local government offices took funds out of ordinary tax budgets to cover them. It became a matter of balancing the books by taking in funds from outside the enterprise. This is really just another form of consumption. One can't expect growth or expansion from that. If it goes only a year or two and ends, then the burden is not too heavy, but if the management situation does not improve, then such requests become almost perpetual.

Today, almost all mayors have these collateral enterprises, and if you look at the service aspects of them and their management, you find that they are *oyakusho-teki* [full of bureaucratic red tape].[2]

Both Johnson and Date make it clear that the hybrid enterprise structure is no panacea for regional and local development. At the same time it is a potentially useful device if it is well conceived and well managed. One example of this on the Rikuchū coast provides a useful case study.

Third Sector Enterprise:
The Sanriku Railroad

The story of the century-long effort to link the coast by rail culminated in 1981 in the formation of the Sanriku Railroad *(Sanriku Tetsudō Kabushiki Kaisha),* but this was only the formal evidence of dramatic behind-the-scene maneuvering that had gone on for twenty years. The story revolved around the work of Suzuki Zenkō, the Dietman who represented the Rikuchū coast for nearly 40 years, first as a member of the Socialist Party, and since the early 1950s as a member of the ruling LDP. The process is worth examining, since it reveals much about the interaction of local and national political forces.

In the early 1960s Suzuki had become a highly regarded member of the Ikeda Hayato faction in the LDP. In July 1960, when Ikeda became prime minister in the aftermath of demonstrations that engulfed Japan and swept Kishi Nobusuke out of office, Suzuki became minister of post and communications. He later served as cabinet secretary. As a member of the inner councils of the LDP and confidant of Ōhira Masayoshi, who became head of Ikeda's faction after the latter's death in 1965, Suzuki played an increasingly important role in national politics. He became premier in 1980 following the sudden death of Ōhira. Suzuki was also the key negotiator and policy-maker in domestic and foreign affairs related to fishing, and he represented the Rikuchū coast well in these matters.

Inevitably he was caught up in the politics of the National Railway's troubles as JNR went from riches to rags in the two decades between 1960 and 1980. As the success and glory of the Shinkansen of the sixties gave way before the waves of red ink of the 1970s, it became increasingly unlikely that the final sections of the coastal rail line would be completed by the JNR. Actively promoted as far back as the Taishō period by Hara Kei (who was also from Iwate) before he became premier, the project was taken up in the 1960s and supported by Suzuki when he was head of the General Affairs Bureau of the LDP. When the National Railway Building Commission *(Tetsudō Kensetsu Shingikai)* recommended completion of the line, Suzuki had sent a telegram with that welcome news to his supporters on the Rikuchū coast.[3] By the early seventies, plans were off the drawing boards and construction was moving forward, with short sections linking Miyako to Tarō and Kuji to Fudai opening by 1975. In the late seventies construction ground to a halt, though not until the entire road-bed had been laid out and all the tunnels built.

In late 1980 the JNR announced plans to close a whole group of money-losing local lines, including those to the Rikuchū coast. The response in Iwate was immediate. On November 25, 1980, a prefecture-wide meeting attended by 500 people was held with representatives from all 62 towns and villages present. At this meeting people expressed their anger at what they considered the cavalier way in which the JNR and the national government were washing their hands of local and regional transport needs. The chairman of the meeting, the mayor of Kuji City, put it this way: "The law to restructure the National Railways destroys before our very eyes the dream of three generations, going back a hundred years to Meiji times."[4] As if this were not enough, the meeting was rocked by the presentation of a draft resolution which proposed that the coastal railroad be operated by "an entity other than the JNR." The mayor of Kamaishi, sitting next to him, is said to have leaned over to him and said: "Mr. Kuji, what do you think of this resolution? What in the world will you say to your people back home to explain this?!"[5] It turned out that Suzuki Zenkō, by then party president and prime minister, had adopted this strategy and had played his cards this way (by having the draft resolution submitted) because in his judgment, "there was nothing for it but to use the third sector structure."[6] So here these mayors were, faced with a draft resolution into which the phrase "an entity other than the JNR" had been slipped. They were beside themselves and heavy-hearted. This sudden turn of events had put them in the position of having to consider how the Sanriku Railroad could be built and operated, not by the JNR, but by a new entity that they would have to create.

The shock and anger of the coastal people were fierce. By all measurements they were the latecomers to development on the national scene and it seemed they were being made the victims—again. From their perspective the national government, while preaching an even-handed national development policy for all, was turning its back on one region in an arbitrary way. One person put it this way: "You people in the cities! You hire our young people, the middle school graduates, calling them the 'golden eggs.' You've built your cities with them, right? Now you come to us saying you have to close down the local lines, which are losing money. This surely is an arbitrary, citified way of thinking."[7]

These people put the issue as urban versus rural, but the writer of an article about the situation, Ueno Toshiakira, saw it as even more a conflict within Iwate between the developed central and southern areas and the undeveloped northern coast. His analysis pointed to the sorry state of public finance in the late seventies as the source of the problem, and his opinion was that there was no choice but for the JNR to divest itself of those lines and leave their development and operation to some other group.

Faced with this reality, the towns and villages on the coast rallied to the task. In the next few months they created a new entity, the *Sanriku Tetsudō K.K.,* a hybrid corporation with capital from local and regional, public and private sources.

The behind-the-scenes story of this process is outlined in Ueno's article. It revolved around Suzuki and a close associate of his, Tsutsumi Yoshiaki, president of the Seibu Group of transportation companies.[8]

Suzuki had become premier in late 1980 as a result of severe political in-fighting in the LDP. The three front-runners had each been unsuccessful in capturing majority support, and the party elders turned to Suzuki as a compromise, dark-horse candidate. He staked his cabinet's life on the slogan "Administrative Reform" and appointed a blue-ribbon commission to investigate and recommend policy and action. The commission was headed by Dōkō Toshio, a highly respected older business leader. When the commission made its report, it recommended, among other things, breaking up and privatizing the JNR. This recommendation at the national level by his hand-picked commission tied Suzuki's hands as far as any further support by him for completion by the JNR of the Iwate coast rail links was concerned. This explains his assessment that "There's nothing for it but to use the third sector structure." He did not just say this and walk away from the problem, however. He had a plan, and, once the regional leaders in Iwate accepted the inevitability of the third sector approach as the only way they would ever have a railroad, Suzuki went into action behind the scenes.

In the world of Japanese politics, connections mean even more than in other democratic societies. Suzuki had had a lengthy relationship with Tsutsumi Yoshiaki and with Tsutsumi's father before him through Suzuki's mentors Ikeda and Ōhira. As the plans for the Sanriku Railroad evolved in the spring of 1981, Suzuki turned to Tsutsumi for advice and help, feeling that private business had much to contribute to this pioneering venture and hoping that Tsutsumi might even take the fledgling line under the wing of the Seibu Group. Tsutsumi responded by sending a team to Iwate to assess the project. The team reported negatively, saying that no outside group should even think of taking on the line. Tsutsumi is reported to have told Suzuki categorically, "After all, it will be best for local people to be central in the development of the project."[9] Tsutsumi saw no way for a purely tourist-based operation to be successful given the distance from population centers and the difficulty of developing facilities in that remote area. Further, he didn't see how outsiders could go in and run the line given the long history of the project and the way local people felt about it. However, although he refused to involve the Seibu Group directly, Tsutsumi did promise Suzuki personal help and access to know-how. He is quoted as saying, "If it would be helpful I would be glad to cooperate with people and with know-how."[10]

When the time came and Suzuki asked for help, Tsutsumi sent one of his trusted lieutenants, Shimizu Takeshi, who was running the Itami-Hakone Railroad, to Iwate on loan to assist in the project. Shimizu became chief adviser and de facto director of operations for the final phase of construction and the launching of the line. He plunged into the task with vigor and organized the whole thing from scratch, operating from a one-room office attached to the General Transportation Policy Section of the prefectural offices in Morioka.

Shimizu apparently initiated a number of radical policy decisions. The most important was to run "one-man cars" in which the motorman would take the tickets, just as drivers do on buses. Other innovations were planned as well, all with the objective of cutting personnel and other operating expenses. Shimizu and his associates eliminated separate ticket-takers at all but two or three of the largest stations and arranged to franchise that function to local businesses. New diesel-powered cars, with the latest most fuel-efficient engines and maintenance-free design, were ordered. This apparently was accomplished in spite of pressure from the JNR to take over some of its old rolling stock. The wisdom of this decision was confirmed by rider reaction. People from outside the region who rode the line marveled: "This doesn't seem like a car on a remote local line. It seems like a *densha* [electric car]. The cars are so up-to-date."[11] Riders were so used to the run-down inefficiency of local line JNR operations that they could hardly believe what they were seeing.

Experts and observers had projected a minimum of five years before the Sanriku Line could expect to turn a profit; some estimates were as high as seven years. To everyone's astonishment it ran in the black the first year and the second year, too. This seems too good to be true, and believers in the project were cautious in their assessments even after the line had operated in the black for two years.[12] While it is still much too early to know whether this success can be sustained it is a significant accomplishment, one that has changed people's lives and expectations even more than anyone anticipated. We need to examine both the structure of the project and the new dynamic that this third sector company has created for economic life on the coast.

The first year of operations was a time of great hope and expectation, but it was fraught with worry and insecurity as well. The Sanriku Railroad was an improbable undertaking. Fully 55 percent of the entire line of 271 kilometers was actually tunnels so even though much of the time the line ran along a gorgeous coastal escarpment, it could not be seen. (The solution was to equip the cars with VCRs and TV monitors that play video cassettes showing the coast line on TV as the train passes through the tunnels.) The region also had no year-round attraction such as ski resorts or mountain climbing. And the JNR had thrown up its hands and walked away from the project, convinced that it would be a money loser. It seemed to have little going for it.

Because of its success despite these realities, the basic structure and the dynamics of the enterprise have attracted much attention and it is viewed as a potential model for other places. What is this "hybrid" company, how was it created, and how is it operated? What are its effects on life in this region? These are some of the questions that were being asked in Tokyo and other parts of Japan.

In structure the Sanriku Railroad is a *kabushiki kaisha,* that is, a joint stock company that operates as a private commercial enterprise. It is thus very different from the *kōsha* or public companies that have been created both at the national level (e.g., the monopoly corporations such as that for tobacco) and the regional level. There are *kaihatsu kōsha* (public development companies) in many parts of Japan. (Tanohata has one of these, which runs the local dairy collection and marketing operation.)

The *Sanriku Tetsudō Kabushiki Kaisha* was established November 10, 1981. There are 58 stockholders. It has a capitalization of ¥300 million (about $200,000 at ¥150 = $1).[13] Of this 48 percent was provided by Iwate Prefecture, 27 percent by the towns and villages on the line, and 18.7 percent by private business in the region. The remainder (6.3 percent) came from private regional entities such as the fishing and farming cooperatives. This means that about one-fourth of the capital is private with nearly half from the prefecture and the other one-fourth from local government. The governor of Iwate Prefecture serves as the president of the company, with the mayors of the towns and villages and presidents of private companies making up the board of directors. National Railways representatives serve as advisers to the company, and the mayors of the three cities on the coast served by the line (Miyako, Kuji, and Kamaishi) serve as vice presidents. This structure is not remarkable in itself. It is weighted heavily in favor of local government representation. That would suggest the danger that the line would become just another arm of inefficient local government with a tendency to indulge in bureaucratic foot-dragging.

However, so far this has not been the case. Operationally the Sanriku Railroad is not only not featherbedded, it has a very lean table of organization. The central office has only 17 employees and there are only 80 more full-time employees for the whole line, a total of 97 people. For a company with a capitalization of ¥300 million, this is a very small roster —perhaps one-third the number of employees a comparable segment of the JNR would have. With those numbers, however, the line ran 2.5 times the number of trains the JNR would have run. There are 23 stations on the line, but only the ones in the three cities are staffed by people on the company payroll. Each of the others is served by a local business with a kind of franchise to sell tickets and run the station. Each station has a parking lot and small shops including a coffee shop and a kiosk. Every effort has been made to give each station a local flavor. From architecture to color scheme to distinctive tickets and station names, they reflect the history and culture of the region. Some places held contests to select a motif and a name, attempting both to capitalize on and to strengthen pride in the local area.

Estimates for the first year of operation (April 1, 1984–March 31,1985) projected a deficit of approximately ¥98 million. Instead, at the end of the fiscal year accounts showed a profit of ¥26 million. This startling figure included nonrecurring start-up costs totaling ¥58 million, so the company had come out ¥182 million ahead of the estimates.

The line had attracted national attention at its opening in April of 1984, but in its second year of operation, after the stunning financial success of the first year, the Santetsu, as it became known (the term is a contraction for *Sanriku Tetsudō*), was the object of unprecedented attention. Its success was attracting more than just idle curiosity. The JNR had plans to use the third sector device as a means of shedding other lines, and this gave a sense of urgency to the interest of visitors from other regions. There emerged what one report called the "rush to study the Santetsu" *("Santetsu kengaku rasshu").*[14] It was not surprising, perhaps, to have groups from the JNR, from local government, from private rail lines, and from unions come to investigate what was happening. What was more remarkable was the number of people from the research departments of banks and universities who came. They were particularly interested in the tax and budget implications of the Santetsu's success. In the first half of the second year of operation about 800 different groups visited the line and the Santetsu ran out of pamphlets describing its operations. Some Santetsu officials joked that they should begin charging a consultant's fee to these groups. "Santetsu style" became a buzz-word. In some places people imitated the things that the Santetsu was doing, like printing different colored tickets and selecting special names for stations. However, these were superficial evidences of a much deeper interest.

Ueno summed up his analysis of what happened as follows:

> The thing we must not forget is the role of the Seibu Group "know-how." That, combined with the local environment where the people of the region cooperated in a spirit that reflected a sense of identity with "My Railroad, the Santetsu," brought unprecedented success to this first effort to run a portion of the JNR under private auspices. If we call the executive and administrative strength of the prefectural and local government units the trunk of the tree, and if the cooperative efforts of local people are the flowers, we can say then that the cooperation of Seibu constitutes the roots, which we can't see.[15]

In Ueno's view, Tsutsumi Yoshiaki's reading of the situation was exactly right. Tsutsumi saw that outsiders would only be meddlers if they took the lead in the project, so he refused to involve the Seibu Group directly. A writer for the national economic daily, the *Nihon keizai shinbun,* giving a speech in Kyūshū spoke of the Santetsu as an entity in which "people invested their own money in the company and felt that this was their railroad."[16] The computer projections that talked of five to seven years of deficits had no way to factor in the role of the local people's commitment and involvement in the project. Apparently, that plus factor was what accounted for the stunning financial success of the first year of operation.

The intense interest of the media and of outsiders from all over Japan was evidence of the potential significance of the Santetsu experiment. However, much more fundamental was what was happening in the region as a result of the line's opening. If the success of the first two years is sustained, then fundamental changes will take place in life on the Rikuchū coast. Tanohata is the place where this is most evident because it was the one place where there had never been rail service, nor good public transportation of any significance. (JNR buses had come into Tanohata, but they served only a few people and resulted in little socioeconomic change.)

Three major new forces are at work now in Tanohata as a result of the opening of the Santetsu. The first is the force generated by the availability of regular, convenient commuting service to the cities of Kuji to the north and Miyako to the south. For the first time, Tanohata young people can live at home and commute to regular high schools. (The branch high school in Tanohata has not served as a viable alternative. Only less able students go there, because able students are counseled to go elsewhere.) Also, for the first time people can commute regularly to jobs outside Tanohata without driving long distances. The availability of this service will change perceptions and expectations about life in Tanohata for both families and individuals.

Second, the tourist industry and the creation of jobs in Tanohata are now directly linked, and the potential for further development is substantial. The Santetsu itself generates some new jobs directly in the service sector. More than 1,000,000 tourists visited in 1984; this was an increase of more than 50 percent from 1983. As the volume of tourist traffic increases, demand for ancillary support services also increases, and this will generate more jobs. The impact of the Santetsu on tourism is shown graphically in Figure 3.

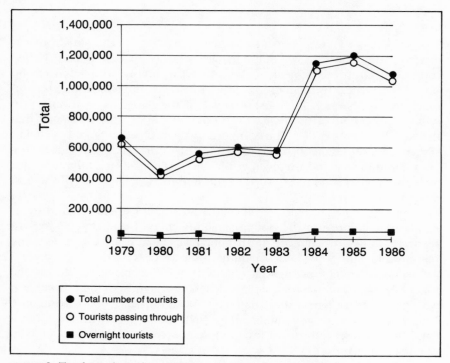

FIGURE 3. Total number of tourists.
Source: Tanohata-mura, *Shisatsu setsumei shiryō* (Documents for a graphic presentation of Tanohata), p. 10.

The third force for development and change results from the second: It is the opportunity that the tourist trade provides for the farmers and fishermen of Tanohata. These people are faced with a new challenge. They have the opportunity to sell their products directly to the visitors—if they can develop a steady supply of attractively packaged, distinctively identified, and appropriately marketed goods.

The first and second factors were predictable and, to some extent, are already measurable. The third is so new and open-ended that it is hard to deal with analytically. There are, however, some indicators of the significance of this force. As noted in Chapter 5, contract vegetable and seafood product development had received attention for some years in Tanohata. In the five years from 1979 to 1984, as that effort gained momentum, a structure for further growth was created by another third sector company, this one based in Tanohata. The fanfare associated with the Santetsu obscured the important behind-the-scenes work being done by another hybrid enterprise. This one was older. Since 1979 it had been run by Date Katsumi, in his capacity as managing director of the Northern Rikuchū Coast Tourist Development Corporation.

The company was established in 1969 in the boom years of the 1960s, as the effects of national economic development penetrated ever deeper into the hinterland. The hope was that the company would provide the capital, know-how, and structure to create jobs in Tanohata and link it with general economic growth in the Tōhoku. However, the company languished for ten years, never fulfilling its promise, struggling to stay alive, and producing a steady stream of red ink. It lacked two essential ingredients and was short on a third. First of all, in the early years Tanohata was not ready to take advantage of the presence of the company. The infrastructure of roads and facilities was not yet sufficient to draw and sustain the volume of tourist traffic necessary to make its operations viable economically. Hayano had hailed the opening of the toll road to Kitayamasaki and the building of the Banya Inn in the early 1970s as the dawn of an era of tourism for the village, but he was premature in his assessment.

Second, the company lacked imaginative and effective leadership, and suffered from the bureaucratic attitude. In Date's words: "For public corporations if there is no income then you can't work; for private companies if income goes down you have to work. In the worst case with public companies, if after you pay salaries there's nothing left, then it's all right not to work."[17] For ten years the company was in that position. It appears that the company also lacked sufficient capital to initiate and develop the kind of projects that would generate jobs and economic momentum in Tanohata.

Finally in 1979 Mayor Hayano and President Yaegashi of the parent commercial company asked Date to take over as managing director and give the company the managerial leadership it needed to achieve the kind of growth and to play the role that they had originally envisioned for it. Evidence that he did so is provided by his success with the resort hotel Ragasō in Hiraiga hamlet, next door to the main Tanohata fishing port of Shimanokoshi. Between 1979, when Date took over, and 1986, there were three major additions to the hotel and its facilities. Sleeping rooms, meeting rooms, and shops were added in rapid succession, and the quality of facilities and services upgraded. The five year plan that Date presented to the board of directors in the fall of 1985 called for further expansion of both program and physical plant. Dynamic local leadership in the person of Date along with the success of the Santetsu Railroad, began to create the potential for real economic growth. Momentum was being generated. The income data for the village provide evidence of this. In 1978 Tanohata was 33rd among the 62 towns and villages in Iwate in per capita income. By 1984 it had risen to 20th.[18] Another measure of the momentum that was being generated was the volume of tourist traffic through the village. In 1985 it rose 5.8 percent over 1984, with a total of 1,208,000 people coming through Tanohata.[19] Date's leadership in economic development was being felt. The specific impact of the opening of the Santetsu Railroad and the Shii Ōhashi are graphically revealed in the statistics on tourism.[20]

Date is a restless, driving person to whom incompetence, procrastination and lack of drive are utterly unacceptable. He leads by example. For years, as I got to know him, I admired this energy and ability and appreciated his understanding and commitment not only to Tanohata but to the cause of international understanding. It was not until he published his book on the Tanohata experiment, however, that I could grasp the vision and the larger picture of what Hayano and he were trying to do and the methods they were using. That statement which combines a philosophical definition of objectives and means as well as data and descriptions of the various projects they had undertaken gives invaluable insight into what has been done in Tanohata. It is also very revealing of the ways in which the third sector structure can be harnessed to serve the needs of a village and a region.

The earlier discussion in chapters Three and Five examined Date's work, first in the Tanohata Village Office with dairying and contract vegetables, and then when he took over the Tourist Development Company to make use of local seafood. Often frustrated by bureaucracy, he was drawn to work for the Tourist Development Company because it offered an opportunity to use his talents in a much more free-wheeling way than the bureaucratic procedures of the village office allowed.

Date considered the management of local and regional development to be the analogue of running a *sōgō shōsha* (general trading company), and his analysis rings true. In his book he goes on to develop that idea more fully. He also examines the methods and objectives that are

He said, "In a certain sense moving Tanohata away from the idea of being an isolated inland island was accomplished by putting the actual practice of making education for people at the center. At the same time, we had to put into practice contact with people outside. We were very lucky in being able to promote contact with people from the outside to break down the isolation of the village."

By *lucky,* he meant contact and interchange between Waseda University and the village people, which began in a kind of educational experiment. That interchange with people on the outside included students from Nihon University of Physical Education, and from Earlham College in the United States, gradually expanding as it developed.

The work with Waseda was focused in the reforestation project called Shii no Mori and the Seikaryo Dormitory. The contact with Nihon University of Physical Education was with their environmental college or college of nature. For these people and for the Matsushita Research Institute, the village provided the place for actual study. Earlham College and international exchange then followed. Education to create a new kind of people and exchange with people from outside the village contributed to and provided the opportunity to press forward in this building process. "Rather than thinking about the rice cake that is in front of your eyes, you have to think about a feast that will be ready twenty years, thirty years in the future." This kind of training of the villagers, one by one, the mayor says, comes from doing what you can right now, always taking the next step and using it as a building block. So it is a step-by-step process.

THE DREAM OF THE TWENTY-FIRST CENTURY

In all of this, there were the strong feelings on the part of the village people of dissatisfaction and unhappiness because of the problem of their feeling inferior to those in the interior of the prefecture—feeling that they were an isolated island, that they were in a remote, backward place. However, nowadays, people will say, "Oh yes, there are lots of things that we have to do here in the village. There is a great deal more that can be done."

To put it in the opposite way, the dramatic change in the self-perception of the villagers is [toward] one that now says, "If we work at it, we can do it." That is what they have produced. There is no question that this is what has produced the tremendous drive of the village of Tanohata. There is none of the fragmentation one sees in the other villages and towns on the Sanriku coast. . . .

Education for people that is directed by the slogan "A village based on education" has developed now to the point where the vision of Mayor Hayano is focused on the twenty-first century, and he is attempting to design and plan with that in mind.

"Even though we are still poor, we can carry burdens on our backs and work away. True wealth and prosperity are not something based on material things or money. They are based on *kokoro* or spirit, which knows no limits in the way it can develop. We cooperate with each other. We are building a base that will establish Tanohata as a result of our joining our spirits."

The idea is to build a village that is produced by Tanohata self-help. It does not matter that we are poor. We can say that we are building successfully step-by-step, moving from one small effort to the next. "We must move ourselves without giving up over small things if we wish to do the larger things." This saying of Ninomiya Sontoku is the motto that teaches us. This is the mayor's position.[1]

It is revealing that Hayano quoted from Ninomiya Sontoku. Ninomiya was a mid-nineteenth century homespun philosopher who emphasized education and self-help. His writing was later distorted by ultranationalists in the 1920s and 1930s, and in the postwar period he has been decidedly out of vogue nationally. In the Tōhoku, however, he has continued to be revered as a patron and advocate of education.

The vision and call to action that Hayano articulated to the *Iwate Nippō* reporter continue to provide the philosophical ground on which Tanohata stands. Yet problems remain.

In his State of the Village report in March 1985, Hayano sounded a note of concern, pointing to issues in education that still bulked large. He said, "Now that we have achieved some modicum of comfortable living in this environment in terms of the necessities of clothing, food, and shelter, are we giving our children the wisdom they need to live in the new age that is dawning? Are we nurturing tough, strong human beings? I think that each of us, in the family, in the schools, and in village administration, must reevaluate our roles and must carry more fully our overall responsibilities in this regard."[2] He was undoubtedly pointing to three specific problems: behavior problems in the middle school and especially in the dormitory, the continuing insularity of the schools, and the problem of educational leadership in the village.

Tanohata's middle school was caught up in the same behavioral problems that have plagued middle schools all over the country. In the mid-1980s these issues centered in the phenomenon that had come to be known as *"ijime"* (literally "teasing" but probably better translated as "bullying"). Unfortunately most teachers and administrators in Tanohata, as elsewhere, thought that the way to deal with this phenomenon was to tighten discipline and control, thereby giving young people even less opportunity for self-expression. In Tanohata, just as elsewhere, this usually exacerbated the problem.

Even if there had not been behavioral problems Japanese education faced severe challenges. Japanese school structure tends to be rigid and inflexible even at the elementary school level. This structure produces resistance to change. Much as Tanohata changed in the twenty years from 1965 to 1985, an inward-looking, "maintain the status quo" mind-set still remained in many of the schools. It continued to be difficult for new ideas and new methods to enter. The foreign teachers in the village testified to this reality year after year. The issue is related to the transient nature of most teacher appointments in rural areas, as well as those of the administrators.

Since Tanohata, like most small towns and villages, does not produce enough people of its own interested in becoming teachers to supply its needs, it has always been dependent on outsiders. These teachers come and go, many of them just "putting in their time." Why should they be open to innovation and new ideas that might make others uncomfortable?

The most serious educational problem, however, was administrative. Tanohata schools continued to suffer from a lack of imaginative, vigorous leadership in the middle ranks. The superintendent of education in the first half of the eighties was a dedicated supporter of the mayor's leadership and vision, but he had few, if any, enthusiastic and able supporters in the Board of Education. At the lower levels of that group of officials were young, vigorous, and able people, but they received little opportunity to demonstrate their talents or to act on their ideas. The *Ji-chō* (vice superintendent) and *Shidō shuji* (the number two and number four administrators in the hierarchy) have always been relatively short-term people from outside. The number three person (the assistant to the vice superintendent), while from Tanohata, took little initiative. So the problem remained endemic.

In short, despite giant strides in improving facilities, opportunities, and educational outlook in Tanohata, in 1985 the village was still subject to the forces of inertia within and of national trends from without, and the battle for better education would continue to be a severe test of will and vision for Hayano and his associates.

Jobs

In the third of the 1984 series of *Iwate Nippō* articles on Tanohata, the reporter focused on the fundamental economic problems faced by the village. It was remote, its environment lacked resources such as harbors and flat land, and it lacked the infrastructure needed to generate and sustain momentum in economic development. In the article, Mayor Hayano articulated the philosophical basis for his work, and one of his associates describes what Tanohata had accomplished.

TREES, THE LIFE OF THE VILLAGE

"Green is the life of the village" is Mayor Hayano's idea. Green is the undergirding of the spirit of man. This is the foundation of Hayano's philosophy. He considers this to be the bedrock and tremendously important, the link between the natural environment and the life of the people. All of the planning for economic development is predicated on the idea that economic productivity must be linked to this.

For example, this thinking produces the idea that the benefits of forestry are linked to the work of the fisherman. So as they think about the addition of forest land and the planting of trees, they see that as a case of people in forestry doing something for their own benefit, but something that also [indirectly] benefits the fishing industry, and so they want to promote the development of forestry and of fishing as intimately linked. One object is to increase radically the number of salmon.

Mayor Hayano says, "The mountain which I myself am caring for also helps the person who is fishing. If we keep that in mind, then the attitudes of those who follow us will certainly be changed." This is the way he explains his thinking: "From now on, economic activities, whether on the land or having to do with fishing, are not separate things. In the larger meaning as part of the full socioeconomic picture we must consider them in that light."

Beginning in September 1973 the four groups—the village itself, the fishing co-op, the agricultural co-op, and the forestry co-op—joined together to put up the capital (¥10 million) to create the Tanohata Economic Development Public Corporation *(Tanohata Keizai Kaihatsu Kōsha)*. The purpose of this, according to the by-laws, was "to protect the resources of the village, including the land, from outside capital, to raise the level of activity of labor and capital resources, to raise the productivity of all this and to establish a socioeconomic base that would be truly productive."

We might call this an attempt to establish an independent economic base in the village, one which would preserve the environment and protect that environment from the unwanted or destructive invasion of big capital from outside.

Also, if you look at the activities that have been carried on, whether in the use of land for forestry or fishing or agriculture or the production of special products or the dairy business, you see that this all points toward activity that is aimed at development of an economic base for the people, owned by the people and done by them.

Within this, the sale of special local products is a strategy that attempts to use agricultural, forestry, and sea products so that value is added to them. If it were just a matter of preserving the environment, they would not be able to justify the work of the public corporation. However, we can see now that, even though there are only around twenty products, this is going to be a very significant venture.

"Because our village was isolated for a long time, farm families had no idea of the value of agricultural products. It all ended with just subsistence farming. They had no time even to think about ways of selling their own products by adding value to them."

The public corporation section chief, Ishihara, speaking of the situation in the village at the time of the establishment of the public corporation, said, "We started from zero." From zero, in the five years from 1975 to 1980, the public corporation, through contracts with local farmers, gave them an understanding of what they could do, and at last, beginning in 1980, they were able to plug into the prefectural distribution network.

SELLING THROUGH THE SANRIKU RAILROAD

The development of special local products began from an effort to make some of the local flavor available. There is a very difficult side to doing this, but now *wakame, kombu, awabi, uni* and such seafood products are the focus of attention, and people are moving into such value-added food products as chrysanthemum flowers and leaves, cucumbers, mushrooms, etc., and expanding the number of saleable things through which they can have value-added profit.

Up to now, the sale of these things had been largely through the grocery stores in the village, but since April 1, 1984, they have been able to sell them at the station kiosk in Tanohata, which they call Kampaneru, and in Shimanokoshi, where the kiosk is called Karubonado. There they have a tourist gift center and they are handling all these things as well as other goods.

However, there aren't enough of these goods at the moment. Therefore, they need to find ways to expand the number of local products that they can make independently with value added, and Ishihara, the section chief, says, "We still have a great many things to do. The public corporation is just beginning its work. We have launched it." And we can see from this the forward-looking, future-oriented stance of the village.

Even so, this policy in Tanohata of giving emphasis to linked economic development suggests that, leaving aside the extent of what has been done in Tanohata so far, in many ways we have to rethink the whole question. Economic activity raises the question of the fundamental ways in which one promotes the attitude of preserving the environment when one adds tourism as well. For the towns and villages on the Sanriku coast, which are emphasizing economic development, it is important to think once again about just what it is they are trying to do.[3]

The issue identified here is obviously the threat to the environment that economic development poses when tourism is a major element in it. This situation constitutes a serious dilemma for Tanohata. Hayano and his associates spent the last half of the seventies and first half of the eighties wrestling with that issue. They have by no means resolved it, even now, but by 1985 the direction had become clear. They were committed to a course of development based on melding primary agriculture and seafood production with service activity based on tourism. Date Katsumi, the head of the third sector company responsible for economic development, has called this *Daiyon sekutā* (fourth sector) development. In the planning document that he submitted to the company's board of directors in October of 1985, Date drew up a comprehensive plan for development in the region. Included in that plan was a proposal for new entities that would link producers and retailers of village products and give each a direct stake in the success of the venture.

A STRUCTURE TO PROMOTE [COMMERCIAL] ACTIVITY

> With regard to activities related to tourism and the hotel operation, the Tourist Development Co. should manage those directly. However, as for other enterprise activities, I propose that we adopt a new device for management and establish a new, separate organization. When we do that, the Tourist Development Co. and Tanohata village will provide the principal capital ownership. However, we should adopt a so-called fourth sector organizational structure that includes the producers and others who benefit from it.[4]

In the document Date went on to outline what he had in mind. He suggested that private subcontract supplier companies be established for agricultural and seafood products and that these become the structural links with the third sector Tourist Development Company. This structure would provide a channel for training the producers in the new work while giving them a direct stake in the success of the whole effort.

Here we see the evolution and linking of regional development structures in an attempt to solidify the base for job development and thereby promote long-term economic viability for the village and the region.

With the experience of the preceding fifteen years to build on and with such structural devices in place, Hayano and Date along with their associates Takahashi, the head of construction in the village office, and Ishihara, the head of the village public development corporation, apparently felt that the task ahead was to capitalize on existing opportunities. They were not without worries. Takahashi confided to me in October 1987 when I visited the village that he was concerned about how to sustain the momentum. He said that the opening of the railroad and the completion of the great bridge across Matsumaesawa in 1984 had given a real thrust to economic development. What could they use now to generate upward economic movement in the late 1980s?

The old endemic problems of flight to the cities for jobs *(dekasegi),* succession to family headship *(atotsugi),* and finding wives for local men *(hanayome)* continue to plague villages like Tanohata. Hayano, however, steadfastly refused to establish a section in the village office to address the latter two issues as other nearby towns had done, believing that it is not the proper role of government to do so. Instead, he remained committed to education and the building of economic infrastructure as the only long-term solutions to these issues. The reaction of local people to Date's work with them as suppliers of food for the embryonic tourist industry suggests that Hayano is right (See Chapter 5). Families in Akedo (one of the coastal hamlets) were quoted as saying, "If we have *minshuku* then our young people can make a U-turn and there's a chance we can get rid of *dekasegi*. We have to make this project succeed."[5]

Political Leadership

Difficult as the challenges of education and jobs are, underlying all else in the Tanohata equation is the role of Hayano and the issue of political leadership. Hayano was elected to his sixth four-year term as mayor in the summer of 1985 and to his seventh in the summer of 1989. Tanohata celebrated the centennial of its formal establishment in 1989. Hayano's election to a seventh term only delayed the day of reckoning. Even his friends and staunch supporters in the village question how long he can sustain the quality of his leadership which has, so far, been of a high order. However, these are questions beyond the scope of this study. An analysis of the twenty years 1965–85 in terms of political leadership in Tanohata leads us in two directions. The first focuses on Hayano himself and his role; the second on the wider issue of leadership in the village as a functional phenomenon. An examination of this latter question brings to the fore a kind of contradiction, or *mujun,* as Japanese analysts would term it. With such a powerful and charismatic figure at the top, how can other leaders grow and emerge?

HAYANO AS LEADER

For thirty years Hayano was the right person at the right place and time. In 1955 when he was asked to take over the fishing co-op he was unproven, but he soon demonstrated that he had ability. His ten years of experience in the co-op and in PTA work constituted the formative decade of his career. He acquired experience and was tested in both economic terms (in the co-op) and political terms as an elected member of the Village Assembly. By the time he ran for mayor in 1965 he was ready to articulate a vision for Tanohata, having acquired the connections, regionally and nationally, and the know-how to make things happen. From the time of his first State of the Village speech in March 1966 onward, he projected powerful missionary zeal and presented practical proposals that could be and were implemented in relatively short order. From the need for drinking water, telephones, roads, and schools in his first term, to international education in his third term, to tourism and the "year of liberation" in his fifth term, he identified and seized themes and harnessed them to generate practical results. In some sense his most impressive discovery was that one could harness public relations and media attention to achieve significant goals within the village as well as outside. Using this technique he prepared village people to make the psychological jump from thinking of themselves as country bumpkins to being citizens of a village that was recognized for leadership in economic development regionally and in international education nationally. On a variety of occasions, from the visit of the Canadian ambassador to Japan in 1969 to that of the president of Earlham College in 1980 to the visit of the governor of Tokyo in 1985, Hayano used the occasion to convey to Tanohata's people that their village, and what they are doing, was not just worthy and useful but was noteworthy and admired, even envied. In 1984 the *Iwate nippō* reporter testified to what had happened as follows:

> In this way they pursued the policy of liberation of people's consciousness and were able, to a certain extent, to make progress. National Road 45, which links the whole village, was followed by the development of a road network throughout the village and by building fishing port facilities and completing work on the Sanriku Railroad. But all these things followed as a material outcome of the freeing of people's minds. . . .
>
> The villages and towns of the Sanriku coast now feel strongly the discrepancy between their situation and conditions in the inner part of the prefecture, which is the beneficiary of the high-speed era (of the Shinkansen). They are demanding even more strongly the completion of work on a direct link to the center, but that in a sense is an evidence of dependence on material things, and suggests that they are not as enlightened as the people in Tanohata.
>
> However, are the plans for freeing of people's self-perception sufficient as yet? They do not have the same sense of emphasis and linkage that Tanohata has. Their situation in their everyday lives is limited to their immediate surroundings and they are rather strongly dependent on material things. In that sense, then, they have certainly not been liberated.[6]

Native ability Hayano had, experience he acquired as he went along. The articulation of the vision was a further essential ingredient, and he articulated it early in his career as mayor. The final quality necessary for successful political leadership, personal appeal, the ability to "bring people along"—charisma we call it—Hayano also possessed, as he demonstrated in a number of concrete ways. By the end of his first term he had convinced all segments and regions of the village that he would be mayor of *all* the people, not just serve the interests of the coastal hamlets. His appeals for unity were heard because each hamlet saw that its needs were taken seriously. The evidence was clear and continuing. In the elections for his fourth and fifth terms he ran unopposed. In my interviews with members of the village assembly in 1982–83, all testified to the appeal of his leadership. Even the one Communist assembly man, admitted it, however grudgingly. It was evidenced early in his career as mayor by his ability to attract and hold three people from outside Tanohata as key leaders in his administration. One was Takahashi Yoshio, who became head of the Construction Section of the village office. The second was Date Katsumi, who served as his right hand man and troubleshooter in the village office from 1971 to 1979 and thereafter as manager of the Tourist Development Corporation. Date was a Waseda University graduate with other professional options but chose Tanohata and stayed with Hayano through thick and thin. The third was Takeda Seiichi, superintendent of education from 1980 to 1988. Takeda was an engineer who had lived in Morioka most of his career. Hayano convinced him to come and join him to give educational leadership to the village. While not charismatic himself (He was actually a rather frail person, physically, and very diffident in his style of operating.) Takeda was drawn by Hayano's vision for education, absorbed it, and became a staunch advocate and even a spokesman for it in Iwate educational circles. In an interview in 1982 he said,

> The important thing is not just whether people will remain here, but what kind of people will remain here.
>
> To look only to the adults to solve our problems is a bad thing. When the twenty-first century comes, the people who must take the initiative are today's children. For this reason it is important that our children not only be talented, but also associate with lots of people and have broad minds. This is the goal of the exchange program with Earlham College. . . .
>
> Twice each week, about 75 students of grades four and above join together for the class. The primary object is simply to have these students associate with a foreigner. Making them skilled in English is a secondary goal.
>
> Passing people on the street and actually encountering them are different things. We hope to make people recognize that. We don't want our people simply to look past the people they meet; we want them to have an encounter. This kind of active approach can make a big difference. . . .
>
> The important thing is, what kind of people will remain? When we enter the twenty-first century, if our people have good judgment and determination, if they are equipped with the best knowledge and wisdom, then we can walk with our heads high.[7]

Takeda played a key role in the establishment and nurturing of the Iwate Prefectural Council for the Promotion of International Understanding and, remarkably, in spite of an almost complete lack of English language ability, was a fatherly mentor to several generations of American teachers in Tanohata.

Hayano's charismatic appeal is attested to by two other developments. In establishing the Iwate Prefectural Council, Hayano attracted the attention and participation of Seki Kōjurō, then mayor of the town of Ishidoriya, south of Morioka. Seki was a prosperous businessman turned politician, a graduate of the University of Tokyo. He was from an old-line local family of high status. His acceptance of Hayano's leadership was confirmed when he became vice-chairman of the council. At meetings of the council I have heard him hold forth in enthusiastic support of what he called the "Hayano philosophy". His public stance of deference to the formally unlettered Hayano testified to Hayano's appeal. In 1985 Hayano was elected chairman of the Iwate Mayors' Council, a prestigious post, further testimony of the respect in which he was held and the appeal of his message.

For all of these strengths and accomplishments, however, one fact continues to cloud the future for Tanohata. Hayano has not been able to discover, establish, or nurture much new local leadership. There is a gap between him at the top and the next level of leadership in the village. He has drawn associates from outside and young people in the village to work for him, but a new generation of top leaders in their late forties and early fifties is clearly lacking. Perhaps he has been too strong, too charismatic. His strength is such that in the period 1970–85 no one of substance sought to challenge his leadership, nor has a single new leader or any group of leaders emerged. Date Katsumi seems to have no taste for politics and he is the one person who would seem to possess the capacity to provide dynamic leadership. Herein may lie the contradiction inherent in strong leadership. Those who wield leadership may find it difficult if not impossible to relinquish it or to nurture it in others. As of 1985 Hayano's position and his strength were clear, and he still had wide respect and support inside and outside Tanohata. His next big test was likely to be that of leadership succession.

ASSESSING HAYANO'S LEADERSHIP

Beyond the story of Tanohata, which is certainly interesting in its own right, lies the issue of political leadership in postwar Japan. Where does the local leader fit? How should we place Hayano? What does his work tell us about the role of local political leaders in a unitary society in which so much initiative and so many resources emanate from above, and ultimately from the national government? Any analysis of these questions leads us to examine the particular case of Hayano's role in two ways. First, how does his role relate to the issue of local autonomy and initiative versus central policy and leadership? And, second, what does he represent in terms of local political leadership in its own terms? These two dimensions of the problem keep crisscrossing with each other; they seem to be almost two sides of the same coin. Yet it was only when Hayano became mayor in 1965 that it became so. His predecessors were unable to come to terms even with the idea of Tanohata as a single entity until the 1953 National Law for the Consolidation of Towns and Villages forced them to do so. They apparently took little initiative in relating to the larger, national system until it impinged on their own world in Tanohata through the implementation of that law. When that happened, they vigorously resisted being used by the system.

Two larger issues which have been examined widely by political scientists studying Japan provide a "grid" on which to measure Hayano. One is the issue of vertical insularity and hierarchy (the writing of Samuels on the one hand and Nakane on the other, to oversimplify the issue). The other is the role and relationship of local politics and political leaders to the larger system. By examining these two issues we can come to some assessment of Hayano and his work.

On the first issue, Hayano's role and his work clearly support the thesis that vertical insularity is not necessarily the normative structure and mode of operation for local political leaders. Hayano addressed Tanohata's problems with initiative and vigor, establishing horizontal ties not just regionally but nationally. He reached up the system vertically and has been part of it, but he has not waited for the system, nor has he been merely its handmaiden.

We saw, in the case of the middle school consolidation crisis, that Hayano in no sense acted just as an extension of national government policy, as appealing as that interpretation was to some people both inside the village and outside. He took the initiative in several instances to forge new policy. These policies, although they were not necessarily counter to expectation or to policy emanating from above, either anticipated policy or moved Tanohata into a role of leadership regionally and nationally. Two examples confirm this analysis.

First, in 1978 Hayano took the initiative to reorganize the Tanohata village office to establish more efficient administration. He reduced the number of sections by consolidating services, and placed health services in a semi-autonomous, separate category, thereby removing them from village office politics. (See Chapter 3.) In so doing he anticipated the whole regional and national policy initiative that emerged in the 1980s to reorganize and rationalize local government in an attempt to cope with rising government deficits and to meet local needs.

Second, in 1976 Hayano initiated a locally sponsored and funded program in international education, anticipating by nearly a decade programs at the national level. Tanohata began by hiring one American to live and teach in the consolidated middle school. By 1982 the number of teachers in the region under this program had grown to five, and by 1985 to more than twenty. Only in 1986 did the national government initiate its massive JET program to bring young foreigners to teach in Japan's schools (some 1,200 or more by 1989). The Tanohata-led Iwate Program was by then so well established that additional towns were clamoring to join it and it had spread to Tochigi and Yamagata prefectures, where local authorities asked to participate even though they had access to the JET program, sponsored by the Ministry of Education. The Tanohata program has given the village national publicity and recognition as a leader in international exchange and international education.

Hayano very early learned how to use the regional and national systems effectively. He did not fight them, but found ways to channel their benefits into the work he was doing in Tanohata, beginning with roads, port facilities, and schools and moving on to meet infrastructure needs and to create a hybrid development corporation which would in turn generate and sustain economic growth and jobs. Hayano used the system to get funds from the various prefectural and national ministries. Money came in many forms—equalization taxes, loans, grants-in-aid, and funds for special projects from a sea products experiment station to reforestation work and bridge building.

When necessary he was prepared to buck the system. He even had the political courage to turn down massive subsidies that were offered by the national government if Tanohata would accept a planned nuclear power generating station.

He was not, however, a naysayer to the prefectural or national government. He nurtured and used close ties to regional and national political and bureaucratic leadership. As noted in Chapter Three he has been a long-time member of Suzuki Zenkō's support group. He has the ability, it seems to make the critical distinction between policy decisions from above that would be good for Tanohata and those that would not be in Tanohata's best interest.

When we attempt to assess Hayano's leadership in terms of local government in general, he emerges as an effective manager. In addition, he is a charismatic person with a vision and dynamic appeal in the prefecture and the region (as evidenced by his chairmanship of the Iwate Prefectural Council for the Promotion of International Understanding and of the Iwate Mayors' Council). Finally, he is a person who knows how to design, to build, and to move institutions. It is clear that he is not typical of local government leaders, but it also seems clear that he is illustrative of a group of people emerging here and there around the country, signaling, perhaps, a different kind of normative behavior in Japanese local government that challenges regional and national government to serve local needs better.

Local and Regional Development

Another question remains. What is the meaning of the Tanohata experience when viewed in the larger perspective of regional development. Is it just a "biological sport," produced by unusual, charismatic leadership, serendipitous outside events, and lucky timing? Each of these elements clearly were present in what happened in Tanohata between 1965 and 1985. Hayano's leadership was charismatic and he was unusual, especially in 1965. The decade of the 1960s—Japan's "income doubling decade"—produced a national environment of expectations about change and growth. At the same time, nationally and regionally, budgetary resources were made available in large amounts to support infrastructure building and development activities in local communities. Thus, outside events and the timing of Hayano's emergence as leader combined to support a powerful thrust for change in Tanohata.

It would appear, however, that Tanohata was not a mere rocket shot up in the sky only to burn itself out and fall back to earth in ashes. Its problems are far from being solved and they are serious in both economic and social terms. The need for more jobs and for better education each produce a never-ending quest. Yet in the decade 1975–85 Tanohata became a kind of model, a pilot experience, an example of what could be done with grass roots initiative, energy, and leadership.

The best early evidence of the thrust toward development which Tanohata represents was the dairy business. Hard-surface roads began to provide access to markets by the early seventies, enabling Tanohata, through the mechanism of the Economic Development Section of the village office, to promote the development of private dairy herds. The next step was the creation of the Public Corporation for Development *(Kaihatsu Kōsha),* a village-run entity that developed a milk processing station and established Tanohata milk as a distinctive product for retail in the area. By the late seventies, the third sector development company established in 1969 was reorganized, and became under Date Katsumi's leadership the vehicle for economic development for agriculture and fishing. It pioneered in the development of "value added" production for retail sales under the Marukita label. Another structural development occurred when Tanohata joined with other government and private entities to form a new third sector company, the *Sanriku Tetsudō K.K.* to complete the construction and run the Sanriku Railroad. The next step in Tanohata's plans was the creation of what Date called "fourth sector" companies to provide jobs and promote the sale of agriculture and aquaculture products locally and regionally. These were spinoffs of his third sector company that were designed to provide the entrepreneurial skills and capital formation for local farmers and fishermen to produce value-added products for retail sale from the raw materials they produced on farms or took from the sea. It was too early, in 1985, to know whether these new structures would be successful, but local people viewed them optimistically.

Taken as a whole, this progression in the twenty years from 1965 to 1985 represented a significant breakthrough in economic terms for Tanohata. New jobs were created and people began to have a sense of hope that jobs could be found near home. High school students stayed in Tanohata and commuted to high school in Miyako or Kuji. New *minshuku* (family-run inns) were established in the coastal hamlets. The interplay of these elements, all created primarily by local initiative and leadership, began to generate momentum in economic development. The Sanriku Railroad ran in the black each of its first three fiscal years. Ragasō, the Tanohata resort hotel, embarked on major expansion of its facilities and completed two major additions to the hotel in the period 1984–86. (Another major expansion of the hotel was successfully completed in 1988.) Local leadership, joining horizontally in the region and using the third sector structure to mobilize and concentrate capital to build infrastructure and create jobs and marketing devices for "value added" local products, was the key to this surge of economic development.

By 1985 national attention focused on Tanohata and the coastal region as a result of the opening of the Sanriku Railroad on April 1, 1984. In its first year the railroad authority printed hundreds of brochures and other documents to explain what was happening; even so, it ran out of material to give visiting delegations from public and private entities from other parts of the country. Local people joked that the Sanriku Railroad should start charging consulting fees to those who came on inspection tours.

That these developments were part of a wider national trend is suggested by the existence today of more than twelve third sector rail line companies scattered around the country. These were established as part of the process of privatization of the national railways. In 1986 two others besides the Sanriku were already running in the black.

From what has been said, it is clear that Tanohata is not typical of villages in rural Japan. It is however, illustrative of what is being done through a combination of local leadership, local and regional infrastructures, and private and public sector capital that are mobilized to stem the flow of people and economic activity to the crowded urban areas. The U-turn phenomenon (discussed in Chapter 5), which was under way by the beginning of the 1980s, fed this movement, giving local leaders specific incentives to design new programs and, in turn, giving hope to young people who desired to return to jobs in their home areas. Where this trend will lead and how far it will go remains to be seen. As Japan enters more and more fully into the mainstream of the world economy of the late 1980s and 1990s and as the process of internationalization permeates ever deeper into everyday life in Japan, one can hope that these new trends in regional economic development will be a positive force in enhancing that process. People like Mayor Hayano seem to understand how important and necessary that process is. They are demonstrating an ability to be leaders and models for Japan, not just follow the lead of Tokyo and the national government. The analysis and the statistics that I have presented quantify and document the process of social and economic change and development that has come to Tanohata. Important as that process is, especially as it illustrates and illuminates national and international trends of which Tanohata is now an integral part, ultimately this is a record and a story of people and their lives, ordinary people but people with extraordinary spirit. Mayor Hayano is one of those people. Two others perhaps most appropriately represent the new Tanohata. They are the Yoshizukas, Kimio and Toshiko. Kimio came to Tanohata as an apprentice farmer, and Toshiko came to marry him and join him as a pioneer farmer. Toshiko's description of their life in Tanohata (with their small children) brings the whole process back to its proper focus on the individuals whose lives have been so changed over the two decades I have chronicled.

Professor Hashimoto introduces his interview with Toshiko as follows:

> Back in the farthest hills up a mountain road two kilometers from the village-maintained road between Katchi and Negishi, there is a dairy farm run by a young couple. Yoshizuka Kimio (35), the second son of a Chiba businessman got the idea of becoming a dairyman when he was trying to decide where to go to high school. He shocked his teachers and friends, but he went on to Tokyo University of Agriculture and then apprenticed himself to Kumagai Ryūkō in Tashiro to get experience in mountain dairying. Three years later he bought ten hectares of wooded upland, bought two cows, and began dairying himself. Two years after that Toshiko, a kindergarten teacher in Funabashi in Chiba, came to marry him and join his primitive life. She knew nothing about cows and dairying. Now, seven years later, this little family on that upland farm demonstrates the potential of the humanity in us all.[8]

Then Toshiko relates her story:

> "My original home was in Kumagaya in Chiba. Both my parents died when I was young and I was raised by my older brother. He knew the Yoshizuka family and introduced me to Kimio's mother and he and I had a formal *miai* [interview with a prospective spouse]. What did I think of Kimio? Well, my parents had died and I was given a good deal of freedom by my brother and his wife. They would let me marry whomever I wanted. But I knew nothing about farming in Iwate, let alone mountain dairy farming. I thought a farm was a wonderful place, spacious; it evoked a good feeling and I wanted to go there. Ha! Ha! I came up here once to visit with his mother, and that decided it. It was March and everything astonished me—no electricity! But it attracted me—the freedom and all. My family all said it was too far away and opposed my coming at first.
>
> "We were married at Unotori Shrine in Fudai. Kumagai Ryūkō was our formal go-between. We were both from Chiba and our families were there so the two of us could have just gone back there and done it. But my husband said that we were going to live up here and it would be people up here who would have to look after us so we'd

better do it here, and I had to agree with him. So both our families came up here in a chartered bus. All the people around here came, and we had the reception at the Kitayama-sō over at the promontory. It was January 4, 1979.

"Until then I knew nothing about farming. I had seen cows from a distance on a school excursion, but I'd had no contact with them. When I first began to work with them I'd do crazy things—things that Kimio knew not to do as a matter of course. I'd pull on them and get stepped on. So after we were married for several years I'd make him angry and we had a lot of conflict. We had no relatives nearby—just the two of us all the time. When things went well it was wonderful, but when there was trouble there was nowhere to go. Even if I'd made up my mind to pick up and go back to Chiba it would then have been terrible to have to come back. Anyway, we fought a lot in those early days. When we were filling the silo I was loading silage into the truck with a fork and a snake appeared. I hated snakes and there was one dangling on my fork right in front of me. I threw it and ran like everything. I wasn't going to fork any more silage out in that grass—I couldn't do it. My husband really got angry and said that when you find snakes in the grass it means that the land is fertile and productive. I ought to be really happy—what was I afraid of? I came here to work with cows. If I was going to be afraid and upset by snakes, I'd better go back to Chiba. That kind of conflict between us was frequent at first.

"In summer, things go well—we're working outdoors. When it rains lots and we can't fill the silo then our spirits go down. A lot depends on the weather.

"I was willful and said whatever came to me and he said to me, 'Don't say things which will kill your husband's dreams. Talk about wanting to work.' We were just the two of us—when things went well it was heaven, but when we fought it was hell. Really!

"Soon after we were married he was hurt and spent twenty days in the hospital. I still knew nothing (about how to run things) and when people came I couldn't even understand the local dialect. I couldn't start the generator for the milking. I didn't know how much grass to feed the cows or how to put them out [to pasture]. The mailman came to deliver the mail and said, 'You have the cows out everywhere, don't you?' I felt desperate. Kumagai Ryūkō came to help some. I thought, 'even if he gets mad he's here, thank goodness.' Looking back, that twenty days was a great experience.

"At that time we had only two milking cows, and we received a unit price of only ¥7 for milk from the co-op. No matter what came up to pay for, we were stuck with that price. I was shocked at the situation. I wracked my brains and kept coming back to that ¥7 wall. At the same time even though we didn't have money, other people helped us with vegetables and eggs, and somehow or other we were able to eat.

"Now [1986] we are milking five cows and we have five young ones. We're covered up with debt to be sure, but somehow or other each year our income has gone up, and we're getting by. Before, when we went to the co-op to borrow they would say, 'You folks— you can't expect to make enough up there to pay off a loan,' so we couldn't borrow. Even now we keep wondering if we can really afford to borrow.

"The Kumagais and other village people also helped us a lot. When heavy snow fell and our backwoods mountain road shut us in, the telephone would ring—people would ask if we had food and fuel. Yes, we had a telephone put in first thing. People would come up here helping us carry things in, and they'd say, 'When we see you up here we think of our own experience long ago doing the same thing.'

"At first when the telephone rang I couldn't understand what people were saying. They'd only give their 'house name' and I'd have no idea who it was. I'd pick up the phone when it rang and say, 'How do you do; this is the Yoshizuka residence,' just as I would have done in Chiba. My husband said, 'You'd better stop that,' and I began to say 'Yoshizukas' when I answered the phone.

"In a sense, since our relatives are not nearby the local neighbors here have become our family—or even closer. My husband's college friend and sponsor, Kumagai Ryūkō, is the leader of a group of seven mountain dairy households that have formed the Yamami Association. They meet each year, visit each other's farms, gossip, have a big meal together—husbands and wives—and share plans. Then the mothers in this group also get together separately, in what we call the '¥200 Group.' Those are joyful times. If it's once a month, that's often. There's no set day. Ryūkō's wife will call us on the phone and say 'what about such and such a day?' We all look forward to those gatherings. We go in our workaday clothes and we talk about daily life, our husbands, our children, how to make inexpensive tasty dishes. We cry, we laugh. We're all from the same place here, women doing the same work. Others have children the same age as our boy, Kōtarō, so we can communicate as mothers—and that's what we want. The talk goes on and we forget what time it is. If I were to go back to my family, I wouldn't be able to talk about these things—not wanting to worry them. Their life is so different that even if I talked they wouldn't understand. But here we can easily communicate. When I get too stressed my husband will say, 'Shouldn't you and the other wives get together pretty soon?'

"What's the hardest for me? Well, perhaps, in terms of convenience, electricity. Till I came here I always assumed that one had it as a matter of course. When it comes to food and making do, in the winter you can put things in the snow, but in the summer meat or vegetables have to be eaten or at least cooked the day they are bought. If you don't eat them by the second day—well. . . . When people give us things—vegetables, fish, etc.—we get lots—the question is how to save it and keep it from spoiling and how to prepare it in a tasty way. Some we prepare in soy sauce or garlic, others in *miso* [bean paste]. I've finally gotten used to not having a refrigerator.

"Naohara Sensei [the founder and theorist of the mountain dairy method] teaches that we shouldn't use sugar. From before we were married, my husband wouldn't eat sweets. At first I didn't take that seriously. I loved sweets, and for a while I thought I would have to have sweets even if I did it on the sly. Now I've become completely used to it. My husband was very strict about correcting my habit at the beginning. We eat them when people give them to us nowadays. We give the children no sweets up to age five. Now that our oldest daughter, Miyako, is more than five we let her have some, but Kōtarō is only four and we don't give him any. When Miyako eats something sweet he'll say, 'I'm four so I can't.' He's happy with what he has for snacks.

"My husband doesn't give in on things once they're decided. We have to do it that way. I'm kind of wishy-washy, and there have been some tough times. Anyway, it's been more than seven years and I've changed. I can eat anything and be satisfied. Vegetables, anything just as it is, not pretending, just enjoying the natural taste, even squash—just boil it, add a little salt—it's good. Here on the farm there are pear trees—volunteers, I guess. The pears are small and hard, but the kids pick them and really enjoy eating them. Mulberry fruit, chestnuts—when they ripen, these two kids—only four and five—go pick them, hit them with a hammer to open them, and eat them.

"At night I'm really busy. I start the generator, go and do the milking, put on the cooler fan, heat the bath, make supper. That's the only time the kids can watch TV. It must be the uneven voltage, because the TV has lines, but they watch anyway. At other homes kids watch during the day. Miyako, asked me, 'Why only at night at my house?'

"So our kids watch anything—education programs, news, Chinese language lessons. There's 'Little House on the Prairie' on NHK. We love it. When I'm preparing supper I watch.

"When milking's done and the rice is cooked, we turn off the generator and eat by a kerosene lamp. The generator takes a barrel of fuel a month in winter when we have to start it at 5 P.M. In the summer it'll go two months on a barrel. We use it about two hours in the evening and then use the lamps or battery lights. When we come back late from a distant field it's pitch dark, and there are the kids waiting with a battery lamp. It makes me want to cry when we start the generator. Everyone, down to the baby, everyone shouts with joy.

"Since there's no one around us, the kids take their moods from us —the light and the dark. That means that nothing is more important than our health and good relationship. When we have harsh words with each other, just from that the kids will burst out crying. When we're doing well with each other, the children are happy doing almost anything and they eat well, too. My husband's father is a salary man. When the family would go to the ocean for an outing he'd have to work the next day so he'd have to go back early. That was really hard on the children.

"Miyako began nursery school in Numabukuro this spring. She'll have friends and be in an environment where children are the focus for the adults. She's so happy. She says, 'Even if I don't feel well I'll always go!' It's four kilometers, but she'll walk it every day. My husband says, 'It'll be good for her—make her strong.' Coming home she'll play here and there along the way, and it'll be nearly nightfall by the time she gets home. 'One rice ball for lunch is good, so make that and give it to her,' he says.

"When the kids grow up if they decide they want to do mountain dairying like this—that would be great! We don't have money, but as parents if we can just pass this on. . . .

"When we look back, we have really warm feelings. If the kids can only have those kinds of memories!

"There is something written by a farmer poet from Yamagata who died some years ago. No matter how many times I read it, it still moves me deeply. He writes,

" 'We see the Tōhoku as a region. We have within us the will to reject the idea that a region is just an adjunct of the center. A region is the space that holds the essence of the lives and culture of a distinct group, but this is not a matter of being shut off in any essential way from another region. Instead we should think of this as a way of clarifying identity through interchange and the linking of one region with another. The whole world, in a sense, is fundamentally divided into a number of regions. Each region has its own individual role or value, and through that the world is enriched. The Tōhoku in this way can be a part of and participate in Japan as a whole and in the world.'[9]

"This is a constant, a universal, I think. I share the feeling that this is the right perspective. For instance, take the term *hekichi* (remote, backward area) that is used today. I think that when people in the city or in the villages use the term, it contributes to the resurgence of the spirit of isolation. Neither pride nor humility is a one-way attitude. When we adopt one or the other, what remains is either autonomy or cooperative association. To take another example, that of men and women, this idea applies also. What we need is both cities and villages, men and women. Isn't that always the problem when we take only a part of something, in this case just the region [and not the organic whole]?"

It's 7:00 A.M. and Miyako-chan is leaving the Yoshizuka home. It is four kilometers to the nursery school along a mountain road. The parents are busy with the milking and four-year-old Kōtarō, with a determined look, is giving green grass to each of the milk cows. There he is, a four year old, grass on his little hands and legs working away unspoiled. Shōji-kun, the youngest, is still asleep.

Leaving her parents and her brother, off goes Miyako-chan. She must be at nursery school between 8:30 and 9:00. As she goes along, from one side road and then another come her classmates, in yellow caps and blue smocks, running out and joining the wave. Her home is the farthest, so her return will take more than two hours, yet she has never missed a day since she entered.

Everyone—her teachers, her classmates, passersby, animals, trees, flowers—loves her.

She says, "This is Miyako's field, this is Taku-chan's house. I saw a bear, you know!" The name Miyako she got from her Chiba grandpa. No doubt he has a sense of satisfaction in his grand-daughter's living up there in that distant Tōhoku mountain country. This is not a matter of city people pitying those in the regions. The grandfather with his roots in the city, her parents with their independent life in the village—I think these are expressions of linkage and interchange between them.

There goes Miyako-chan trudging down the leaf-strewn autumn road. There is the lowing of the milk cows, and Kōtarō-chan's high-pitched voice echoes after her. On this fall morning the sky is blue, as are the mountains. Miyako-chan is just one of the 2,775 women who live in Tanohata village."[10]

Miyako and her pioneer parents bespeak the rugged individualism that for centuries has been a thread of life in Tanohata. Their way of life is tough and physically demanding, and their material comforts are minimal. Yet they also feel themselves to be part of the larger Tanohata community. As latecomers, they did not have to learn to think of Tanohata as a whole; the unified village is what they came to. Their work illumines the new Tanohata that was created in the two decades from 1965 to 1985. With other family members living in Chiba, they feel a part of Japan as a whole, too, in a way that most residents of Tanohata do not. It is in this sense that they represent Tanohata as it moves into the last decade of the twentieth century.

APPENDIX 1

TABLE 1. Public finance, budgeted expenses

Year	Total budgeted	Education	Construction	Investment
1950	¥24,853,305	¥2,952,888	¥14,205,875	¥727,402
		8.4%	5.71%	2.9%
1955	23,925,266	6,100,161	1,120,000	
		3.9%	4.6%	
1958		6,418,792	18,489,452	472,568
1964	98,839,000	19,471,000	7,314,000	31,529
		19.7%	7.4%	Ag., etc. 30.4%
				Comm. 1.5%
1968	244,500,000	79,468,000	33,257,000	57,114,000
		32.5%	13.6%	23.4%
1970	377,518,000	65,688,000	39,996,000	138,171,000
		17.4%	9.8%	36.6%
1972	551,743,000	132,760,000	134,883,000	131,094,000
		24.0%	24.4%	23.7%

Source: Tanohata-mura, *Tanohata-mura sonsei yōran,* passim. Composite chart drawn from statistics presented in various of these reports, 1950–1972.

TABLE 2. Public finance—budgeted income 1950–72

Year	Total budgeted	Equalization tax	National and prefectural support	Village tax	Loans
1950			¥23,605,086		
1955	¥23,925,266	¥8,700,000 36.3%	¥2,325,002 1,060,002 14.1%	¥3,342,057 13.9%	
1957	46,789,765	11,095,000	2,313,958 9,604,673	3,882,233	¥5,000,000
1964		48.5%	26.9%	6.6%	6.9%
1965		44.2%	27.3%	5.0%	12.3%
1968	207,708,000	95,000,000 38.9%	79,790,000 32.6%	11,433,000 4.7%	36,600,000 15.5%
1970	377,518,000	46.8%	31.0%	3.9%	8.7%
1972	551,743,000	218,240,000 39.6%	113,491,000 Ken 56,849,000 Natl 30.9%	18,450,000 3.4%	104,300,000 18.9%

Sources: Tanohata-mura, *Tanohata-mura sonsei yōran* (Tanohata yearly reports); Tanohata-mura, *Tanohata-mura sōgō seibi keikaku-sho* (General planning report for Tanohata), 1982, p. 66.

Note: In these years statistics are spotty and disorganized, so it is difficult to obtain consistent categories of data for comparison. This chart provides rough comparisons of key categories and reveals the dramatic growth of income from all sources in the late sixties and early seventies.

TABLE 3. Comparative income levels

Year	National	Iwate-ken	Tanohata	Tanohata-ken relationship
1961	¥165,600	¥102,560	¥65,235	63.6%
1962		115,354	57,950	50.2%
1965	325,800	166,609	102,969	61.8%
1970	680,400	350,144	313,702	89.6%
1975	1,141,400	894,013	679,420	76%
1980	2,166,600	1,308,985	1,186,321	90.6%
1983	2,282,790	1,569,927	1,303,301	83%

Source: Iwate-ken Tōkei Kyōkai, *A Survey of Towns and Villages,* 1983, passim.

TABLE 4. Third sector companies

Third Sector Tourist Company
Northern Rikuchū Coast Tourist Development Company
Established: Shōwa 44 (July 1979)
Stockholders: 3

	Shares	*Face Value*
Total Stock 286,000		¥143,000,000
Stockholders		
Tanohata-mura	143,000	¥1,500,000
Northern Iwate Motor Co.	140,000	¥70,000,000
Hamaiwaizumi Hamlet Committee	3,000	¥1,500,000

Personnel as of December 31, 1984

	Men	Women	Total
Central Office	1	1	2
Shimanokoshi Banya Inn	3	3	6
Hotel Ragasō	8	18	26
Cabin Heights Park	1	1	2
Sightseeing Boat	3	1	4
Special Products	3	23	26
Total	19	47	66

Total Sales

1983	¥382,000,000
1984	¥571,000,000
1985	¥540,000,000
1986	¥668,000,000

Source: Tanohata-mura, *Shisatsu setsumei shiryō,* 1986.

TABLE 5. Third sector companies

A Public Interest Legal Entity
Tanohata Production Development
Established: Shōwa 50 (August 19, 1975)

Operations
  Agriculture, forestry, fishing improvement
  Agriculture and forestry conservation
  Dairy processing and school lunch
  Special products development and sales
  Agriculture, forestry and fishing activity, and public conservation
    Nagamine Experimental Farm
    Fish and sea products
    School lunch center
    Middle school dormitory
Other

Constituent Members
  Tanohata-mura
  Tanohata Agriculture Cooperative
  Tanohata Fishing Cooperative
  Tanohata Forestry Cooperative

Capitalization: ¥10,000,000
Investment Shares: ¥10,000,000

Tanohata-mura	¥8,000,000
Tanohata Agriculture Co-op	¥500,000
Tanohata Fishing Co-op	¥1,000,000
Tanohata Forestry Co-op	¥500,000

Employees: Total of 25 (16 men, 9 women), 15 in Central Office

Source: Tanohata-mura, *Shisatsu setsumei shiryō,* 1986.

TABLE 6. Twenty years of development in Tanohata, a comparison

	1965	1985	Comparison
Roads paved	0.7%	79.6%	78.9% Numerical difference
Telephones/100 people	3.6%	29.1%	25.5% Numerical difference
Running water	23.5%	60.4%	36.9% Numerical difference
Infant Mortality/ 1,000 people	73.4	0	
Medical professionals	2	4	2 People added
Health workers	0	3	3 People added
Rank in Iwate	60 out of 63	57 out of 62	
% going to high school	38.9	93.5	54.6 % Increase
Total village taxes/¥1000	¥8,613	¥195,395	22.7 Factor of increase
Village taxes/person	¥1,398	¥37,583	26.9 Factor of increase
Total budget/¥1000	¥180,384	¥2,568,229	14.2 Factor of increase
Budgeted funds/person	¥29,288	¥493,985	16.9 Factor of increase
Income/person	¥118,987	¥1,376,434	
People doing *dekasegi*	500	286	214 Decrease
Production/¥1000	¥648,250	6,323,221	9.8 Factor of increase
Primary sector	288,067	1,467,608	5.1 Factor of increase
Agriculture	126,448	519,178	4.1 Factor of increase
Forestry	73,948	160,040	2.2 Factor of increase
Fishing	87,671	788,390	9 Factor of increase
Secondary sector	118,705	1,452,892	12.2 Factor of increase
Tertiary sector	241,478	3,643,145	15.1 Factor of increase
Population	6,159	5,199	960 Decrease
Number employed	3,018	2,569	85.1% Decrease
Primary sector	2,404	1,005	40.6% Decrease
Secondary sector	188	695	20.9% Increase
Tertiary sector	425	869	19.7% Increase

Source: Tanohata-mura, *Shisatsu setsumei shiryō,* 1986.

TABLE 7. Tanohata tax revenues, 1965–73

Date Shōwa	A.D.	Total received	% of budget	Amount of increase
40	1965	¥8,613	5.0%	
45	1970	19,008	4.8%	Up 2.2×
50	1975	51,877	4.3%	Up 2.73×
51	1976	76,363	4.7%	Up 1.47×
52	1977	90,866	4.8%	Up 1.18×
53	1978	89,636	3.7%	
54	1979	105,156	5.0%	
55	1980	116,810	4.9%	Up 2.25× from 1975
56	1981	133,206	5.2%	
57	1982	116,600	5.1%	
58	1983	164,536	6.9%	

Sources: Tanohata-mura, *Tanohata-mura sōgō seibi keikaku-sho* (General planning report for Tanohata), 1982, p. 66; Tanohata-mura, *Tanohata-mura sonsei yōran,* 1984.

TABLE 8. Tanohata farm family distribution

	Total in village	Total on farms	Full-time	Part-time Ag. is central	Ag. is sideline
1975	1322	796	72	158	566
1980	1376	732	66	148	518
1981	1352	707	79	111	517
1982	1357	685	75	125	485
1985	1377	654	74	125	455

Source: Tanohata-mura, *Tanohata sonsei yōran,* 1987, pp. 2, 4.

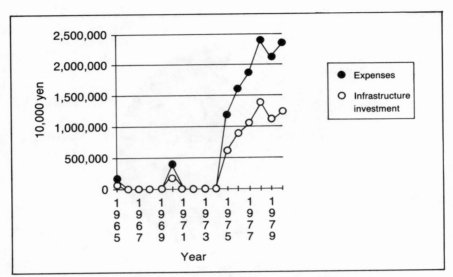

FIGURE 1. Relationship between expenses and infrastructure investment.
Source: Tanohata-mura, *Tanohata-mura nōson sōgō seibi keikaku-sho,* p. 156.

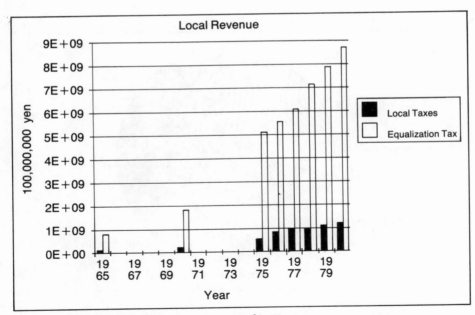

FIGURE 2. Tanohata growth in tax revenue, 1965–79.
Source: Tanohata-mura, *Tanohata-mura nōson sōgō seibi keikaku-sho,* p. 68.

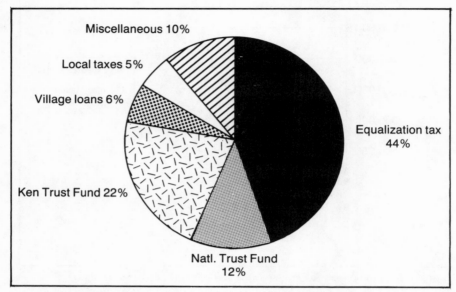

FIGURE 3. Tanohata 1982 income.
Source: Tanohata-mura, *Tanohata sonsei yōran,* 1982, p. 20.

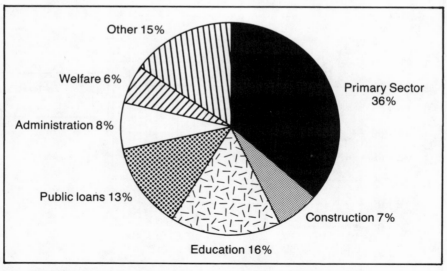

FIGURE 4. Tanohata 1982 expenses.
Source: Tanohata-mura, *Tanohata sonsei yōran,* 1982, p. 20.
Note: "Primary sector" refers here to forestry, agriculture, and fisheries.

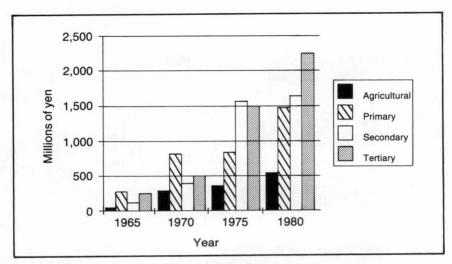

FIGURE 5. Changes in production by economic sector.
Source: Tanohata-mura, *Tanohata-mura nōson sōgō seibi keikaku-sho,* p. 27.

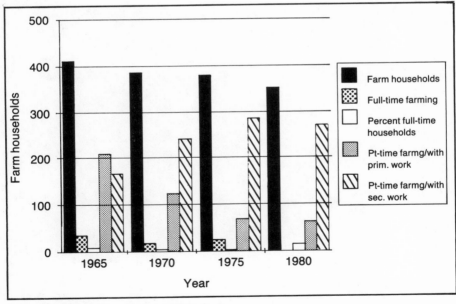

FIGURE 6. Farming population in Tanohata.
Source: Tanohata-mura, *Tanohata-mura nōson sōgō seibi keikaku-sho,* p. 128.

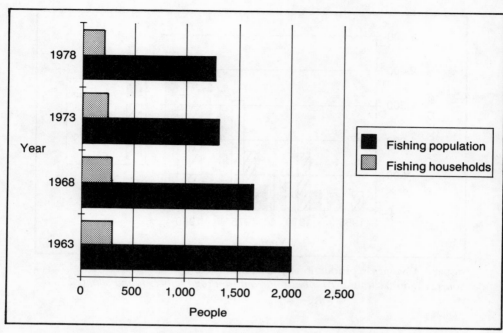

FIGURE 7. Fishing population in Tanohata.
Source: Tanohata-mura, *Tanohata-mura nōson sōgō seibi keikaku-sho,* p. 36.

APPENDIX 2

The Charter of the People of the Village

We, the people of Tanohata, do hereby establish the following Charter, promising to work day by day to build a strong and progressive village, one which will seek peace, emphasize cooperation, and think deeply in this emerging new era. Mindful that we are the inheritors of the traditions built by the efforts of those who went before, we shall strive to preserve our natural surroundings and our rich heritage and in this environment to nurture people with a simple and honest way of life.

1. We, the citizens of Tanohata, resolve to create families and a village which are productive and in which we are careful to preserve a safe and healthy environment.
2. We, the citizens of Tanohata, resolve to create families and a village in which there is joy, where hazards to life are eliminated, and where we treat our beautiful environment with respect and care.
3. We, the citizens of Tanohata, resolve to create decent and orderly families and a village where people observe the social amenities and return thanks with direct honesty to all with whom they deal.
4. We, the citizens of Tanohata, resolve to create families and a village where harmony prevails, where public morality is high, and where freedom and rights are carefully respected.
5. We, the citizens of Tanohata, resolve to create families and a village which provide happiness for our children who hold the key to our future, helping them to develop their knowledge and their creative thinking.

NOTES

PREFACE

Unless otherwise attributed, all translations from Japanese sources are my own.

1. Hashimoto Ryōji, "The Women Speak: *Rikuchū Tanohata mura*," *Aruku, miru, kiku* 238 (Dec. 1986): 5.

INTRODUCTION

1. The term *enjutsu* is a variant of the more usual term for a speech, *enzetsu*.

2. After World War II, as Japanese were brought back from overseas, many of them really as refugees, the government looked for places to resettle them. The remote, sparsely populated areas of such villages as Tanohata were identified as "pioneer settlement" areas. In Tanohata, people repatriated from Sakhalin were resettled in these areas.

3. Hashimoto, "The Women Speak," p. 39.

4. It is still quite common in Japan for the husband to "marry into" a family where there are no sons and take his wife's family name to ensure the preservation of the paternal family line.

5. Date Katsumi, *Tanohata-mura no jikken* (Experiment in Tanohata), pp. 70 ff.

6. Ibid., p. 44.

7. Hashimoto, "The Women Speak," p. 36.

CHAPTER 1

1. Translated from a copy held in Tanohata-*mura* files and dated March 24, 1960.

2. Translated from notes of a conversation with Mr. Makuuchi, November 6, 1982.

3. Mayor's speech to the Village Assembly, March 16, 1966.

4. Mayor's speech to the Village Assembly, March 23, 1967.

5. Interview with the mayor, November 1982.

6. Hara was an able politician who played a central role in Japanese political life from 1900 to his assassination in 1921. He was president of the Seiyūkai, the dominant political party, from 1913 and premier from 1918.

7. Sasaki Kyōichi, a history teacher in Iwaizumi, the town next to Tanohata, has edited some of these documents for use by junior high school students. His pamphlet "Heii-gun musen kōshiki" is a fine Japanese history primer.

8. Like Hatakeyama, Kumagai is a common family name. Apart from this family name, each *honke* or main family *ie* has an *ie* name. Thus the Hatakeyama *ie* cited above is called *Nakasaki-ya*. The Kumagai *ie* is called *Wayama-ke*. The eldest son carries special responsibility to preserve and enhance the fortunes of the *ie*.

9. See the seminal study by Iwao Ishino and John Bennett.

10. Hashimoto, "The Women Speak," p. 11.

11. Ibid., pp. 12–15.

12. This was a national phenomenon in rural Japan in the 1870s and 1880s. It resulted in large part from the change from in-kind to cash tax levies.

13. Hashimoto, "The Women Speak," p. 6.

14. In many parts of Japan it is not acceptable to use the term *buraku* (hamlet) because *burakumin* (hamlet people) is a code word for the 2–3 million people sometimes called "untouchables" who have been segregated and discriminated against. The generic term *shūraku* is now used for hamlet. People in Tanohata continue to use the term *buraku* without the perjorative connotation it has elsewhere.

15. Hashimoto, "The Women Speak," pp. 6–8.

16. Ibid., pp. 8–11.

17. Interview with one of the repatriate couples, March 1983.

18. Hashimoto, "The Women Speak," pp. 15–19 passim.

19. *Tanohata-mura: Zen-son kyōiku keikaku,* 1953, pp. 8–14.

20. Hashimoto, "The Women Speak," pp. 19–23.

CHAPTER 2

1. This analysis emerged from my reading of the village records, especially those of the Village Assembly and the transcripts of the mayor's yearly address to the assembly. It was confirmed through interviews with a number of key people, including the mayor and the chairman of the Village Council.

2. Date, *Experiment in Tanohata,* pp. 39–44.

3. In March 1983 my wife and I were unable to return to the village because of a driving snow storm and had to stay overnight some five kilometers down the coast. However, by early morning the roads were plowed and we drove across Makisawa Bridge, thankful for it as so many other residents of Tanohata have been.

4. Even this figure masks the stark reality. There was only one private car for every 100 households—most of the vehicles were public or commercially

owned, and so did not provide access to the outside world for ordinary people. These statistics are drawn from the 1964 edition of the Sonsei Yōran (A review of conditions in the village).

5. Mayor's State of the Village speech, March 16, 1966, pp. 1a–3a.

6. In the early 1960s Tanohata had had a very low percentage of children going on from middle to high school. In 1964 only 1 in 8 or 12.5 percent went on to high school. By the mid-seventies the village was at or above the national average of 92 percent.

7. State of the Village speech, March 16, 1967, p. 8a.

8. The mayor announced this in his speech to the council, March 23, 1967, p. 8.

9. This term is a buzzword all over Japan. Its thrust and nuance are difficult to convey in English. The mayor used the term frequently in speeches and in private conversation. He once said to me that it was the most important discovery of his years as head of the fishing co-op. He felt that developing the leadership capacity of people was the key to his success in that job.

10. Hatakeyama is one of three of the most common family names in Tanohata; the others are Kumagai and Sasaki. To speak of "Mr. Hatakeyama" in a group of a dozen people is not very useful, since a number in the group are likely to have that name. Accordingly I will refer to him by his given name, Shōichi, in the American way.

11. The most important post theoretically is the number three person in the village hierarchy, the village comptroller *(shūnyū-yaku)*; however, it carries with it little policy or leadership initiative and the comptroller normally serves at the pleasure of the mayor.

12. The name in Japanese is *Hokubu Rikuchū Kaigan Kankō Kaihatsu Kaisha*.

13. Hashimoto, "The Women Speak," pp. 23–25.

14. This was Yoshizuka Kimio, a protege of Kumagai Ryūkō. See Chap. 7 for more on the Yoshizukas.

15. His findings were published in 1975 in the book *Soshite, waga Sokoku Nippon* (What can we say about our fatherland, Japan), in which he denounced the Tanohata authorities and the mayor in particular for the consolidation plan and the way they were implementing it. His argument is interesting and, on the surface, persuasive.

16. Honda claims to be quoting from the mayor's speech to the Village Assembly in 1974, but these words do not appear in the text, though he does discuss the problem on p. 187.

17. Honda, *What Can We Say,* p. 190.

18. Ibid., p. 191.

19. Tsukue gave up its middle school in March 1978, and Numabukuro in 1979.

20. Hashimoto, "The Women Speak," p. 22.

21. Ibid., pp. 16–18.

22. The bird is the pheasant *(yamadori),* the flower, the white rhododendron *(shirabana shakunage),* and the tree, the paulownia *(kiri no ki).*

23. A translation of the charter appears in Appendix 2.

24. In most of Japan, Adulthood Day is January 15. In Tanohata it is August 15, so as to coincide with the Obon festival, when most villagers are at home.

Tanohata has been successful in using this ceremonial day to build a sense of village identity. In 1982, 62 of the 106 young people who had attained adulthood (that is, age twenty) during the year attended the village-sponsored ceremony.

25. I presented the story of this exchange relationship and an analysis of this program in international education in two articles in the *Japan Quarterly,* vol. 30, no. 2, April–June 1983 entitled "Bridging the Cultural Gap."

26. Mayor's State of the Village speech, March 1981, p. 13.

27. Mayor's State of the Village speech, March 1982, p. 1.

28. Hashimoto, "The Women Speak," pp. 22–23.

CHAPTER 3

1. See Mark Kesselman, *The Ambiguous Consensus.*

2. See Ronald Aqua, "Mayoral Leadership in Japan: What's in a Sewer Pipe," in MacDougall, *Political Leadership in Contemporary Japan.*

3. Samuels, *Politics of Regional Policy,* pp. 246–47.

4. For instance, stories abound of white collar workers complaining to and about their superiors in the bar at night after a few drinks.

5. Hashimoto, "The Women Speak," p. 19.

6. It is almost impossible to get statistics on this land-holding pattern since much of it is hidden. People with whom I talked estimated that only about half of such land is in the public record.

7. In the hamlet of Tsukue, for example, the common family names are Kamitsukue (Upper Tsukue), Nakatsukue (Middle Tsukue), and Shimotsukue (Lower Tsukue). This gives evidence of the way family names were acquired in the Meiji period (commoners had no family name in pre-Meiji times): many people simply took the name of their hamlet. In Tashiro the most common name is Kumagai; in Tanohata, the central hamlet in the village, it is Hatakeyama.

8. Suzuki is an interesting figure. He was forced out of office as prime minister in the fall of 1982 but he remained a powerful force in Liberal Democratic Party (LDP) politics. He inherited the mantle and the faction of Ōhira Masayoshi, who died suddenly in 1979. He has been very adept at the game of pork barrel politics, though with none of the suggestions of corruption associated with former Prime Minister Tanaka in Niigata Prefecture.

9. The material in this section is based on several lengthy interviews with the mayor held on November 22, 1982, May 16, 1983, and June 17, 1983, with a follow-up interview in April of 1986.

10. Interview with Hayano, June 17, 1983.

11. *Iwate nippō,* March 25, 1983.

12. Interview with Hayano, June 20, 1983.

13. See below for a discussion of the 1978 reform.

14. In Japanese, *Okurenai, yasumanai, hatarakanai.*

15. For example, making arrangements to see the mayor or taking care of special requests for photocopying, introductions, and contact with local people all required extra work. Workers in the village office frequently took the initiative and offered to help me.

16. Date's wife, Toshiko, also from outside, is a member of the Advisory Committee to the Board of Education and is active in the women's club. Though she once complained about being an outsider, my observation is that she and her

husband are now fully a part of the community. See Chapter Two for a fuller discussion of the Dates' status in the village and Chapter Five for an analysis of Katsumi's leadership in economic development and for Toshiko's comments on their life in Tanohata.

17. Mayor's State of the Village speech, March 10, 1978, pp. 6b–7a.

18. Interview, June 1, 1983.

19. Mayor's State of the Village speech, March 16, 1966, pp. 1, 1a.

20. See Appendix 1, Figure 1 for statistics on infrastructure investment.

21. Interview, December 23, 1982.

22. See Chapter Four for more details about this project.

23. Two of the most interesting of such efforts are in Oita Prefecture in the northern and Kagoshima in the southern part of Kyūshū. In Ōita the governor took the lead in the "each village, one product" project. In Kagoshima it was the governor who initiated what came to be called the Karaimo Exchange Program (Karaimo Kōryū) with young people from all over Japan and the world invited to spend two weeks in towns and villages in Kagoshima.

24. By 1989 the council membership included 21 towns and villages, with several others clamoring to get in.

25. See Chapter Six for a full discussion of this project.

CHAPTER 4

1. Narita, *Kyōiku* p. 15.

2. State of the Village speech, March 22, 1967, p. 11.

3. *Kōhō Tanohata* (News from Tanohata), April 1968, p. 3.

4. Kudō is a signally able and humane person, generous in spirit and open to new ideas and people. He served as superintendent of education for nearly five years (December 1962–June 1967) and then was elected mayor of Morioka where he served for eight years (1969–1977). In 1978 he was elected a member of the Lower House of the national Diet.

5. Kurosawa, *Iwate kindai kyōiku shi* (A modern history of education in Iwate), vol. 3, p. 745.

6. Mayor's speech to the Village Assembly, March 16, 1966, p. 8.

7. My basic sources for this analysis are his yearly State of the Village speeches to the Assembly, in which he reports very specifically on the accomplishments of the past year and the plans for the next year and explains his budget requests.

8. See note 14, Chapter One.

9. The crucial importance of this issue is seen when one notes the steep decline in population between 1965 and 1970. The population dropped from 6,170 to 5,320 (13.7 percent). In the period 1960–65 it had declined from 6,590 to 6,170 (6.5 percent). The accelerated decline in the second half of the 1960s reflects the momentum of forces set in motion by Tanohata's desperate economic straits in the aftermath of the merger debacle and the kerosene revolution.

10. The basic information and data for this section of Chapter Four are drawn from three sources: (1) Yamanaka, *Zenson kyōiku keikaku*, 1953; (2) Narita, *Kyōiku*, 1964; (3) Tanohata Kyōiku Iinkai, *Tanohata sonsei yōran*, 1964.

11. Mori, *Nippon: A Charted Survey of Japan*, 1984/85, p. 292.

12. Article II of this law states that certain areas of the country shall be des-

ignated as *hekichi* when they are "regions which are surrounded by mountains, are remote islands or other places which have unfavorable conditions culturally, economically or in terms of natural environment or access by [public] transportation." Narita, *Kyōiku,* p. 3. Designated areas were to receive aid by various categories under the law, and schools within such areas were classified according to criteria such as commuting distance, population density, local tax base, etc.

13. Budget figures for investment are presented in Appendix 1, Table 1. Statistics were supplied by the Construction Section of the Village Office, 1986 chart.

14. From 1971 to 1979 a total of ¥1.277 billion (roughly $423,000) was invested in educational and cultural development alone.

15. Attendance is, of course, voluntary. The centers are a service offered to citizens by the village. One hundred percent of the five year olds were attending in 1982 and a majority of the four year olds.

16. It was not until the early 1980s that this became a frequent pattern. Before that, not many part-time jobs were available, and the local social ethic frowned on such work by young mothers.

17. The original *hekichi* law was promulgated August 20, 1900, as part of the general rescript on primary school education. Kurosawa, *Iwate kindai kyōiku shi,* vol. 3, p. 256.

18. Bad as things were in Tanohata in the 1950s they had been even worse in some of the other villages in Shimohei-*gun.* Earlier Kawai-*mura,* which is landlocked, had one hamlet in which, at about the time the Meiji *hekichi* law was implemented, not even one primary school age child was in school. At that time the prefecture's rate of attendance for primary school age children was already 90 percent.

19. A discussion of this legislation and the conditions under which it was applied in Iwate is contained in vol. 2 of Kurosawa, *Iwate kindai kyōiku shi,* pp. 255–60.

20. In the fall and winter of 1982–83 Hatakeyama supported the incorporation of the post for the second foreign teacher in the village in the Board of Education's regular budget and guided that proposal through the budget procedures. It was clear that he was ahead of the people in the Board of Education on this matter.

21. In certain planning documents as many as thirty hamlets are listed, but the cluster of households which have some real social cohesion and history and could be termed real *shūraku* (hamlets) is more like seventeen or eighteen. There are seventeen *kōminkan* (community centers) in the village and their presence suggests the reality and potential of hamlet life.

22. Conversation with the postmaster of Raga hamlet, February 1983.

23. Narita, *Kyōiku,* p. 24.

24. Preface to the 1972 planning document (Tanohata-mura, *Shin sōgō kaihatsu keikaku kōsō hokoku*), p. 1.

25. State of the Village speech, March 17, 1972, pp. 3a–4.

26. Notes from an interview on November 22, 1982.

27. Honda, *What Can We Say,* p. 189.

28. In the postwar period there has been a series of episodes involving textbook revision and recentralization in which the Minister of Education has publicly taken severely revisionist positions on such things as interpretation of Japan's wartime aggression in China and on ethical education in the schools. In

1986 Premier Nakasone actually dismissed the minister of education because he refused to retract his publicly enunciated revisionist position.

29. Honda, *What Can We Say,* p. 191. He develops this thesis at some length in his book.

30. State of the Village speech, March 22, 1967, pp. 11–12.

31. In 1984, a member of the dormitory staff went to the United States to participate in the January Institute on American Culture and Education, an exchange program for public school teachers held annually at Earlham College. He had been on the staff of the dormitory from the beginning. At the institute he emphasized repeatedly, in conversations as well as in his formal report, what an integrative role the consolidated middle school and dormitory had played in the village.

32. Notes from a conversation with the mayor, November 22, 1982.

33. Most high schools in Japan, except in the biggest cities, are run by prefectural boards of education.

34. Interview with Kumagai Ryūkō in Numabukuro, November 1982. A reluctant convert, Ryūkō would have preferred to have his own children go to middle school in Numabukuro. However, by 1989, after two of them had lived in the dormitory, he came to recognize its value.

35. Notes from a conversation, November 22, 1982.

36. By 1985 the focus of this problem nationally was the phenomenon *ijime,* literally "teasing, vexing." *Ijime* is the bullying of one student by a group. It has become a widespread problem in middle schools all over Japan.

37. See Chapter Two for the details of this specific episode.

38. Typical of these was one called *Hanayome gakkyū* (A text for brides).

39. By the end of the 1970s *kōminkan* (community centers) had been constructed by village funds in the most populous hamlets. In 1982 there were seventeen such facilities. These provide space for community meetings, for recreation and for youth and adult education activities. The mayor also holds briefing and dialogue sessions at them on a regular basis to keep the formal lines of communication open between the village office and local constituents.

40. *Kyōiku shinkō kihon keikaku,* p. 1.

41. A *Report on a Survey of Young People's Perception of Their Lives,* 1983, privately printed by the Tanohata Board of Education.

42. Tanohata received national publicity in a lengthy article in the national daily *Nihon keizai shinbun* on April 27, 1982. The article, headlined "Village Education Toward the Twenty-first Century," told of the various efforts in international education and described the establishment of the Study Fund.

43. One set of parents told us their children refused to help take care of pigs and complained when the family continued to raise them. "They stink!" the children said.

CHAPTER 5

1. For the legal criteria for *hekichi* designation, see Chapter Four, n. 12.

2. Narita, *Kyōiku,* p. 15.

3. State of the Village speech, March 1966, pp. 1–1a.

4. Interview, June 1, 1983.

5. Statistics measuring the farming population are confusing. Full-time

farmers in 1988 constituted only 8.4 percent of the total population and constituted only 14.5 percent of the total farm population. Part-time farming has become a way of life for a substantial number of Japanese. Over 85 percent of those who farm do so part time and they yield nearly 80 percent of Japanese agricultural production. This phenomenon has been one of the major national economic trends of the period 1970–85. Statistics from *Deeta de miru kensei* (A statistical view of the prefectures) (Tokyo: Kokuseisha, 1987–90), p. 196.

6. Iwate-ken *Iwate-ken ni okeru dekasegi no jittai* (Actual conditions of *dekasegi* in Iwate-ken) (Morioka: Iwate-ken Shōkō Rōdō-bu Shokugyō Antei-ka 1985), p. 5.

7. These figures are from the *Norin Suisan Nenkan,* 1980–81, pp. 48–49.

8. Yamashita Yūzō, *Dekasegi no shakaigaku,* p. 113.

9. Ōno Shinya, "What Makes Tanohata a Depopulated Village?"

10. Ibid., pt. 2, sect. III-3, p. 1.

11. Ibid.

12. Ibid.

13. *Iwate nippō,* January 5, 1984.

14. Ōno, "What Makes Tanohata a Depopulated Village?," pt. III-2, pp. 1–2.

15. Ōkawa Taketsugu, *Sengo Nihon shihon shugi to nōgyō,* p. 302.

16. *Tanohata kōhō,* no. 182, January 1983, p. 11.

17. *Iwate nippō,* August 6, 1984.

18. *Nihon keizai shinbun,* August 13, 1985.

19. Ibid., September 10, 1985.

20. Tanohata-mura, *Komyunitei karejji kōsō,* p. 10; Tanohata-mura, *Tanohata-mura nōson sōgō seibi keikaku-sho* (cited hereafter as 1982 Study), p. 29.

21. Tanohata-mura, 1982 Study, p. 27. See Appendix 1, Figure 3.

22. See Appendix 1, Figures 3 and 4.

23. Tanohata-mura, 1982 Study, p. 36.

24. Ibid., p. 68. See Appendix 1, Figure 2.

25. Tanohata-mura, *Sonsei yōran,* 1964, 1968.

26. For comparison nationally, personal income doubled between 1965 and 1970 and doubled again between 1970 and 1975. Shōwa Kokusei Yōran, Vol. 1, p. 110. See Appendix 1, Tables 2 and 3.

27. Tanohata-mura, 1982 Study, pp. 66–67.

28. Date, *Experiment in Tanohata,* pp. 92–95 passim.

29. Once the root vegetable blossoms, it begins to go to seed and the tuberous root no longer grows.

30. Ibid., pp. 96 ff.

31. Ibid., p. 100.

32. Ibid.

33. In *Nenkan Kashū* (1981), p. 53.

34. The verb *kaeru (kaete kimashita)* is used to refer to return to one's own home place. Thus, the emotional tone of this phrase expresses the relationship the young people from Waseda felt with Tanohata.

35. Date, *Experiment in Tanohata,* pp. 39–44.

36. Hayano, State of the Village speech, March 1966, p. 3.

37. Hayano, State of the Village speech, March 20, 1969, p. 5.

38. Hayano, State of the Village speech, March 13, 1970, pp. 5, 8–9.

39. Tanohata-mura, *Shin sōgō kaihatsu,* p. 1.

40. See Appendix 1, Table 4 for an outline of the structure of the company.

41. The following lengthy excerpts are from Date's *Experiment in Tanohata,* pp. 108–19 passim.

42. *Tanohata kōhō,* no. 194, January 1984, pp. 4–5.

43. *Yomiuri shinbun,* January 25, 1985.

CHAPTER 6

1. Johnson, *Japan's Public Policy Companies,* p. 45.

2. Date, *Experiment in Tanohata,* pp. 99–202 passim.

3. Ueno Toshiakira, "The Quiet Campaign of Tsutsumi Yoshiaki," *Purejidento,* December 1985, p. 323. The details of the story of the establishment of the Sanriku Railroad are drawn from this article.

4. Ibid., p. 324.

5. Ibid.

6. Ibid.

7. Ibid., p. 325.

8. The Seibu Group includes department stores and private rail lines in the Kanto area as well as a department store and hotels in Hawaii. It is considered one of the most successful and enterprising of such conglomerates, which are a distinctive phenomenon in Japanese economic life.

9. Ueno, "Quiet Campaign," p. 327.

10. Ibid., p. 328.

11. Ibid., p. 322.

12. In August 1987 the National Land Agency published the results of a study it had done of 13 third sector or privatized transportation companies nationwide. The Sanriku Railroad was one of the three that were already running in the black. *Asahi shinbun,* August 31, 1987.

13. This small capitalization seems strange. However, the company is only running the line, not constructing it, since that job had essentially been done.

14. Ueno, "Quiet Campaign," p. 335.

15. Ibid., p. 336.

16. Quoted in ibid., p. 335.

17. Date, *Experiment in Tanohata,* p. 330.

18. Hokubu Rikuchū Kaigan Kankō Kaihatsu K.K., *Eigyō hōkoku sho,* 1985.

19. Hayano, State of the Village speech report, March 1986.

20. See Figure 3.

21. Date, *Experiment in Tanohata,* pp. 195–98.

22. *Tanohata kōhō,* November 1985, p. 6.

23. e.g. This meeting was one of the first times, if not the first, that Fudai and Tanohata had come together to work cooperatively on the initiative of one of them since the merger fiasco of the early sixties. Representatives of both villages meet regularly in larger prefectural groupings, of course.

24. It is interesting to note that in the end Hayano decided to celebrate the 101st anniversary of the creation of Tanohata instead. He said, "We must look to the future, not the past." So 1990 was chosen as the year of celebration rather than 1989.

CHAPTER 7

1. Excerpted and translated from "The Sanriku Road," pt. 1, *Iwate nippō*, April 25, 1984.

2. Hayano, State of the Village speech, March 1985, p. 2.

3. "The Sanriku Road," pt. 3, *Iwate nippō*, April 27, 1984.

4. Date, A Proposal submitted as a basis for adjustments, Shōwa 60 (1985), October 5.

5. *Yomiuri shinbun*, January 25, 1985.

6. "The Sanriku Road," pt. 2, *Iwate nippō*, April 26, 1984.

7. Interview with Takeda Seiichi, *Japan Economic Journal*, May 25, 1982, p. 24.

8. Hashimoto, "The Women Speak," p. 28.

9. Makabe Jin and Nozoe Kenji, eds., *Customs beyond Culture*, p. 10.

10. Hashimoto, "The Women Speak," pp. 28–33.

BIBLIOGRAPHY

BOOKS AND ARTICLES

Andō, Tarō. *The Fourth Comprehensive National Development Plan.* Tokyo: National Land Agency, 1987.

————. *Daiyonji zenkoku sōgō kaihatsu keikaku* (The fourth comprehensive national development plan). Tokyo: Kokudō-chō, 1987.

————. *Ruiji dantai betsu shichōson zaisei shisu-hyō* (An indexed and charted comparison of differences in public finances among cities, towns, and villages). Tokyo: Chihō Zaimukyōkai, 1985.

Aoki, Shotarō. *Tanohata fudōki* (A gazetteer of Tanohata). Rev. ed. Tanohata: Fudōki Kankō Kai, 1979.

Asahi Shinbunsha. *'84 Minryoku* ('84 people power). Tokyo, 1984.

Ashita no Nihon o Tsukuru-Kai. *Machi-mura, jichi-kai, chōnai-kai jōhōshi: chiiki to kokusai kōryū* (The regions and international exchange). Dec. 1986.

Beardsley, Richard. *Village Japan.* Chicago: University of Chicago Press, 1959.

Befu, Harumi. "The Group Model in Japanese Society and an Alternative." *Rice University Studies* 2, no. 1 (1980).

Bestor, Theodore. *Neighborhood Tokyo.* Stanford: Stanford University Press, 1988.

Brown, L. Keith. *Shinjō: The Chronicle of a Japanese Village.* Pittsburgh: University Center for International Studies, University of Pittsburgh, 1979.

Chihō Zaisei Chōsa Kenkyūkai (Association for research on regional finance). *Ruiji dantai-betsu shichōson zaisei shisu hyō* (An indexed and charted comparison of differences in public finance among cities, towns, and villages). Tokyo: Chihō Zaimu Kyōkai (Association for regional finance), 1985.

Chiiki Shakai Kenkyūsho (Institute for the study of regional society). *Sanson josei no seikatsu hando komyunitei* (Changes in the lives of women in a mountain village). Tokyo: Kokuseisha, 1978.

Date, Katsumi. *Tanohata-mura no jikken: Chiiki kaihatsu manejimento no ikiru* (Experiment in Tanohata: Regional development lives in management). Tokyo Sōgō Rōdō Kenkyūsho, 1984.

Dore, Ronald P. *Shinohata: A Portrait of a Japanese Village.* New York: Pantheon, 1978.

Ebihara, Hiroshi. "Shii no Mori" (The reflective forest). Tokyo: privately printed for Shii no Mori Kai by Tōkōdō, 1969.

Embree, John F. *Suye Mura: A Japanese Village.* Chicago: University of Chicago Press, 1939.

Embree, John F., and Wiswell, Ella Lury. *The Women of Suye Mura.* Chicago: University of Chicago Press, 1982.

Hokurikuchū Kaigan Kankō Kaihatsu K.K. *Eigyō hōkoku sho* (Report on operations). Tanohata: privately printed, nos. 13–18, 1981–86.

Honda, Katsuichi. *Soshite waga sokoku Nippon* (What can we say about our fatherland, Japan?). Tokyo: Suzusawa Shōten, 1975.

Ishino, Iwao, and Bennett, John W. *Japanese Social Relations.* Interim Technical Report, no. 6. Columbus: Research Foundation, Ohio State University, 1953.

Iwate-ken. *Iwate no dōrō* (Roads of Iwate). Morioka: 1981.

Iwate-ken Tōkei Kyōkai (Iwate Prefecture Statistical Association). *Iwate-ken tōkei nenkan, 1983* (Iwate-ken statistical yearbook, 1983). Morioka, 1983.

Iwate-ken Shōkō Rōdō-bu Shokugyō Antei-ka (Iwate-ken Employment Stabilization Section, Commerce and Labor Bureau). *Dekasegi rōdōsha shuro jōkyō jittai chōsa, 1984* (An investigation into the actual conditions of employment of seasonal workers in 1984). Morioka: Iwate-ken Office for Stabilizing Commercial Labor, 1985.

Jichi Daigakkō (Home Ministry Institute for Education). *Jichi yōgo jiten* (A dictionary of terminology for self-government). Tokyo: Kyosei K.K., 1978.

Jichi Kenshū Kyōkai. *Local Public Enterprise System in Japan.* Tokyo: Ministry of Home Affairs, 1984.

———. *Regional Development Policy in Japan.* Tokyo: Ministry of Home Affairs, 1980.

Johnson, Chalmers. *Japan's Public Policy Companies.* AEI-Hoover Policy Studies, no. 24. Washington, D.C.: American Enterprise Institute, 1978.

Kabayama, Koichi, et al. *Taiwa "Tōhoku" ron* (A symposium on theories of the Tōhoku). Tokyo: Fukutake Shoten, 1984.

Kaneko, Ippei. *Annual Report on the National Life for Fiscal 1984.* Tokyo: Printing Bureau, Ministry of Finance, 1985.

Kaneko, Ko. *Iwate no shichōson dō* (Roads in Iwate cities, towns, and villages). Morioka: Iwate-ken Dōboku-bu (Iwate-ken Engineering Section), 1983.

Kanno, Tahara, and Hosoya, eds. *Tōhoku nōmin no shisō to kōdō* (The behavior and thought of Tōhoku farmers: A report of research in the Shōnai district). Tokyo: Ochanomizu Shobō, 1984.

Kesselman, Mark. *The Ambiguous Consensus.* New York: Knopf, 1967.

Kodama Tanka Kai (Kodama Tanka Club). *Nenkan kashū* (An annual collection of poems). Tanohata: privately printed, nos. 3–8, 1981–88.

Kojima, Shigeki. *Rokaru aidenchitei* (Local identity). Tokyo: Daiichi Hoki Shuppan K.K., 1985.

Kokumin Seikatsu Sentā (Center for the people's livelihood). *Kurashi no tōkei '85*

(Statistics on life in Japan, 1985). Tokyo: Keizai Kikaku-chō Kokumin Seikatsu-Kyoku, 1985.

Kurosawa, Makoto, ed. *Iwate kindai kyōiku shi* (A history of education in Iwate in modern times). Vols. 2, 3. Morioka: Iwate-ken Kyōiku Iinkai, 1985.

MacDougall, Terry E., ed. *Political Leadership in Contemporary Japan.* Michigan Papers in Japanese Studies, no. 1. Ann Arbor: University of Michigan Center for Japanese Studies, 1982.

McNelly, Theodore. *Politics and Government in Japan.* 2nd ed., Boston: Houghton Mifflin, 1972.

Makabe Jin, and Nozoe Kenji, eds. *Kegai no fudō: Tōhoku* (Customs beyond culture: Tōhoku). No. 270. Tokyo: NHK Books, 1976.

Marshall, Robert C. *Collective Decision-making in Rural Japan.* Michigan Papers in Japanese Studies, no. 2. Ann Arbor: University of Michigan Center for Japanese Studies, 1984.

Mori, Kahei. *Iwate-ken no rekishi* (A history of Iwate Prefecture). Tokyo: Yamakawa Shuppansha, 2nd printing, 1982.

———. *Michinoku bunka ron* (A theory on Michinoku culture). Tokyo: Hōsei Daigaku Shuppan Kyoku, 1974.

Mori, Su. *Nippon: A Charted Survey of Japan.* Tokyo: Kokusei-sha, 1962, 1972, 1984.

Murakami, Masako. *Sōdai no yume no jitsugen* (Realizing the grand dream). Tanohata: privately printed, 1983.

Nagai, Michio. *Ie and Dōzoku: A Preliminary Study of the Japanese Extended Family Group and Society and Economic Function.* Interim Technical Report, no. 7. Columbus: Ohio State University Foundation, 1953.

Nakahara, Ryoichi. *Iwate-ken chiiki tōkei shihyō: tōkei kara miru 62 shichōson* (A graphic presentation of regional statistics in Iwate Prefecture: A statistical look at the 62 cities, towns, and villages). Morioka: Iwate-ken, 1985.

———. *Iwate-ken no kenmin shotoku, 1982* (Income of citizens of Iwate Prefecture, 1982). Morioka: Iwate-ken, 1984.

———. *Iwate-ken no shichōsonmin shotoku* (Income levels of citizens of the cities, towns, and villages of Iwate Prefecture). Morioka: Iwate-ken Kikaku Chōsa-bu, 1954.

Nakamura, Tadashi. *Shin Iwate-ken sōgō kaihatsu keikaku, Shōwa 59* (A new comprehensive plan for development in Iwate Prefecture, 1984). Morioka: Iwate-ken, 1984.

———. *Iwate-ken sōgō hatten keikaku* (Plans for overall development of Iwate Prefecture). Vol. 1, *Basic Plans;* Vol. 2, *Implementation.* Morioka: Iwate-ken, 1984.

Nakane, Chie. *Japanese Society.* Berkeley: University of California Press, 1970.

Nakatami, Shinya. Iwate-ken nōgyō dōkō nenpō (Yearbook of trends in agriculture in Iwate Prefecture). Morioka: Iwate-ken, 1984.

Narita, Hiroshi. *Kyōiku* (Education). Vol. 2, *Jittai chōsa hōkoku kenkyū rombun* (A report on actual research in Tanohata). Tokyo: Senshū Daigaku Gakujutsu Bunkakai, Kyōiku Kenkyūkai, 1964.

Nenkan kashū. See Kodama Tanka Kai.

Norbeck, Edward. *Takashima: A Japanese Fishing Village.* Salt Lake City: University of Utah Press, 1954.

Nōson Sōgō Seibi Taisaku Shitsu. *Aru Tanohata sonmin no tegami* (Letters from people in Tanohata). Tanohata: Tanohata Yakuba, 1981.

Ohta, Takashi. *Sengo Nihon kyōikushi* (A postwar history of Japanese education). Tokyo: Iwanami Shoten, 4th printing, 1981.

Oikawa, Jun, ed. *Tanohata sonshi* (A history of Tanohata). Vol. 1. Tanohata: Privately printed, 1985.

Ōkawa Taketsugu. *Sengo Nihon shihonshugi to nōgyō* (Postwar Japanese capitalism and agriculture). Tokyo: Ochanomizu Shobō, 1979.

Ōno Shinya. *Nani ga Tanohata-mura o kaso ni suru no ka?: Tanohata-mura no kakaeru kadai to tembō* (What makes Tanohata a depopulated village?: The perspective and concerns of Tanohata). Tanohata: Matsushita Institute for Politics and Economics, privately printed, 1981.

Rekishi Kyōikusha Kyōgikai Tōhoku Burokku, ed. *Tōhoku minshū no rekishi: Nihon shi o minaosu tame ni* (A history of ordinary people in the Tōhoku: An attempt to rethink Japanese history). Tokyo: Minshū Sha, 1977.

Samuels, Richard J. *The Politics of Regional Policy in Japan: Localities Unincorporated.* Princeton: Princeton University Press, 1983.

Shichinomiya, Keizō. *Iwate saishō ron* (A discussion of Iwate prime ministers). Tokyo: Shinjinbutsu Orai-sha, 1981.

Shichōson Zeimu Kenkyūkai. *Kojin shotoku shihyō, Shōwa 60* (An index to personal income, 1985). Tokyo: Nihon Maketingu Kyōiku Senta, 1985.

Shokugyō Antei-ka (Section for Stabilization of Employment). *Iwate-ken ni okeru dekasegi no jittai* (Conditions regarding *dekasegi* in Iwate). Morioka, Iwate-ken Shōkō Rōdō-bu, 1985.

Smith, Robert J. *Kurusu: The Prince of Progress in a Japanese Village.* Stanford: Stanford University Press, 1978.

Sōrifu (Prime Minister's Office). *Jumin kihon daichō jinkō idō hōkoku, Shōwa 41–50* (Report on fundamental movement of population, 1966–75), Tokyo: Sōrifu Tōkeikyoku, n.d.

———. *Annual Report on Internal Migration.* Tokyo: Office of the Prime Minister, 1969, 1973, 1976, 1981.

———. *Japan Statistical Yearbook.* Tokyo: Office of the Prime Minister, 1966, 1971, 1976, 1985.

———. *Population Census of Japan.* Tokyo: Office of the Prime Minister, 1965, 1970, 1975, 1980.

Statistics Bureau. *Nihon tōkei nenkan 1985* (Japan statistical yearbook, 1985). Tokyo: Sōmuchō Tōkeikyoku, 1985.

Steiner, Kurt. *Local Government in Japan.* Stanford: Stanford University Press, 1965.

Takeda, Seichi. *Kokusai rikai kyōiku ni tsuite* (Regarding education for international understanding). Tanohata: Tanohata-mura Kyōiku Iinkai, 1987.

———. *Tanohata shōgakkō shakai-ka fuku tokuhon* (Tanohata supplemental text for elementary school social studies). Tanohata: Tanohata Office of Education, 1987.

Tanohata Kikaku Sōmu-ka. *Tanohata 101.* Morioka, 1990.

Tanohata Kōchō Kai. *Kokusai rikai o fukameru tame no kyōiku wa dō areba yoi ka?* (What should we do to deepen education for international understanding?). Tanohata, 1985.

Tanohata Kyōiku Iinkai. *Hanayome gakkyū* (A text for brides). Tanohata, n.d.

————. *Kenkyū kiyō* (Research notes). Tanohata: Tanohata Chiku Hekichi Kyōiku Sentā, 1981.

————. *Kyōiku shinkō kihon keikaku* (Fundamental plans for the promotion of education). Tanohata Kyōiku Iinkai, 1979.

————. *Myōnichi no oya ni naru tame no gakkyū* (A text for tomorrow's parents). Tanohata, n.d.

————. *Tanohata no kyōiku* (Education in Tanohata). Tanohata: Tanohata Kyōiku Iinkai, 1984.

Tanohata-mura. *Komyunitei karejji kōsō* (The concept for a community college). Tokyo: Seikatsu Kōzō Kenkyūkai, 1979.

————. *Kihon kōsō Tanohata sōgō kaihatsu keikaku* (An outline of fundamentals for a comprehensive plan for development in Tanohata). Tanohata, 1980.

————. *Kokusaisei yutaka na jinzai o sodatete iru tame ni* (In order to foster world citizens). Tanohata, 1984.

————. *Nōson sōgō seibi keikaku kōzō-zu* (A map of the comprehensive concept and plan to provide agricultural development in Tanohata). Sendai: Sendai Chizu no Mise, 1982.

————. *Shin sōgō kaihatsu keikaku kōsō hōkoku* (An interim outline report on the new comprehensive plan for development in Tanohata). Tanohata, 1972.

————. *Shinzanson kensetsu moderu jigyō kihon kōsō* (Basic concept for building a model mountain village). Tanohata, 1975.

————. *Shisatsu setsumei shiryō 1965–1985* (Documents for a graphic presentation of Tanohata), 20 Years of Village-building in Tanohata, 1965–1985. Tanohata Village Office, 1986.

————. *Tanohata-mura nōson sōgō seibi keikaku-sho* (Comprehensive planning document for Tanohata as a farming village). Tanohata, 1982.

————. *Tanohata sōgō kaihatsu keikaku* (Comprehensive plans for development in Tanohata). Tanohata, 1981.

————. *Tanohata sonsei yōran* (A survey of Tanohata village affairs). Tanohata, 1964–.

Tanohata Sonshi Hensan Iinkai. *Tanohata sonshi gaiyō* (An outline of a memoir of Tanohata history). Tanohata, n.d.

Tōyō keizai shinpōsha (The Oriental Economist). *Shōwa kokusei sōran* (A survey of national statistics in the Shōwa period). Tokyo, n.d.

Wylie, Laurence. *Village in the Vaucluse*. 3rd ed. Cambridge: Harvard University Press, 1974.

Yamanaka, Goro. *Zenson kyōiku keikaku* (Educational plans for the whole village). Tanohata: Tanohata Kyōiku Iinkai, 1953.

Yamashita, Yūzō. *Dekasegi no shakaigaku* (The sociology of *dekasegi*). Tokyo: Kokusho Hakkō Kai, 1978.

Yano, Tsuneta Kinenkai. *Kensei '89–'90* (Conditions in the prefectures '89–'90). Tokyo: Nihon Kokuseizukai Chiiki Tōkei-han, 1988.

PERIODICAL LITERATURE

Aruku, miru, kiku (Wander, look, listen). December 1986 (238).

Asahi shinbun. August 31, 1987.

Enaji fōramu (Energy forum). December 1977 (21).

Iwate keizai kenkyū-sho (Iwate economic research institute). February 1983 (4); October 1983 (12); November 1984 (25); June 1985 (31); July 1985 (32); December 1985 (37).

Iwate nippō. January 1–May 4, 1984.

Japan Quarterly. April–June 1983. 30 (2).

Mainichi shinbun. April 30–May 13, 1984.

Nihon keizai shinbun. April 27, 1982.

Purejidento (The president). June 1985; December 1985.

Tanohata kōhō (Report from Tanohata). 1980–90.

Yomiuri shinbun. January 25, 1985.

INDEX

Sunday Missal
for Young Catholics

2016 – 2017

I want to know Jesus better.

This missal will help you take part in the Mass on Sundays and important feast days. Pages 2 to 33 contain the words and explain the gestures that are the same for every Mass. The rest of the book gives you the readings for each Sunday of the year.

Look over the readings with your family before you go to church. This is a wonderful way to prepare for Mass.

The most important thing about this little book is that it will help you to know Jesus better. Jesus came to bring God's love into the world. And his Spirit continues to fill us with love for one another.

We hope the short notes in this book will help you to participate more fully in the Mass. You will find an explanation for the bold-faced words at the end of each week's readings. May the Mass become an important part of your life as you grow up, and may the readings and prayers you find in this missal inspire you to love and serve others just as Jesus did.

What We Need to Celebrate the Mass

The **priest** makes Jesus present and acts in his name.

The **altar** is the table where the priest consecrates bread and wine.

A group of Christians. You are a Christian by your baptism.

Two **books** are used at Mass: the missal contains the prayers of the Mass, and the lectionary contains the readings.

One **cruet** contains water, while the other cruet contains wine.

Holy vessels

chalice   ciborium   paten

Bread and wine

The Mass is the commemoration of what Jesus did during the Last Supper with his disciples, before he died. The bread is shaped like a small disc and is called a "host."

The **ambo** is the place where the word of God is proclaimed.

The Four Main Parts of the Mass

On the following pages you will find the words that the priest says and the responses we say together during each part of the Mass. You will also find explanations and responses to many questions that people ask about the Mass.

Gathering Prayers

The Lord brings us together.
We ask God for forgiveness.
We give glory to God.

The Word

We listen to the word of God.
We profess our faith.
We pray for the whole world.

The Eucharist

We offer bread and wine to God.
We give thanks to God.
We say the Lord's Prayer.
We share the peace of Christ.
We receive Jesus in communion.

Sending Forth

The Lord sends us forth to live the Gospel.

The Lord Brings Us Together

We come together in church with family, friends, neighbours, and strangers. We are here because Jesus has invited us to be here.

When the priest comes in, we stand and sing. Then we make the sign of the cross along with the priest.

Priest: In the name of the Father, and of the Son, and of the Holy Spirit.

Everyone: Amen.

Sometimes, the words can change a bit, but usually the priest will say:

Priest: The grace of our Lord Jesus Christ, and the love of God, and the communion of the Holy Spirit be with you all.

Everyone: And with your spirit.

Questions

Why do we celebrate Mass on Sunday?

Jesus rose from the dead on Sunday, the day after the Sabbath. This is why Christians gather on that day. Over time, people started to call it "the Lord's day."

Why do we celebrate Mass in a church?

Churches are built specially for Christians to gather in. If needed, Mass can be celebrated in other places: a home, a school, a plaza, a jail, a hospital, a park...

Why do we need a priest to celebrate Mass?

We believe that Jesus is present in the person of the priest when Christians gather for the Mass. He presides over the celebration of the Lord's supper in the name of Jesus Christ.

Gestures

Standing

We stand to welcome Jesus, who is present among us when we gather in his name.

The sign of the cross

With our right hand we make the sign of the cross (from our forehead to our chest, from our left shoulder to our right) and say "In the name of the Father, and of the Son, and of the Holy Spirit." This is how all Catholic prayer begins.

Singing

This is a joyful way to pray together.

We Ask God for Forgiveness

We speak to God and we recognize that we have done wrong. We ask forgiveness for our misdeeds. God, who knows and loves us, forgives us.

Priest: Brothers and sisters, let us acknowledge our sins, and so prepare ourselves to celebrate the sacred mysteries.

We silently recognize our faults and allow God's loving forgiveness to touch us.

Everyone: I **confess** to almighty God, and to you, my brothers and sisters, that I have greatly sinned, in my thoughts and in my words, in what I have done and in what I have failed to do, *(tap the heart)* through my fault, through my fault, through my most grievous fault; therefore I ask blessed Mary ever-Virgin, all the Angels and Saints, and you, my brothers and sisters, to pray for me to the Lord our God.

Priest: May almighty God have **mercy** on us, forgive us our sins, and bring us to everlasting life.

Everyone: **Amen.**

Priest: **Lord,** have mercy.

Everyone: Lord, have mercy.

Priest: **Christ,** have mercy.

Everyone: Christ, have mercy.

Priest: Lord, have mercy.

Everyone: Lord, have mercy.

What does it mean?

Confess
We recognize before others that we have turned away from God, who is love.

Mercy
We know God is full of mercy — that he loves us even when we have sinned. God's mercy is always there for us.

Amen
This is a Hebrew word meaning "Yes, I agree. I commit myself."

Lord
This is a name that we give to God. Christians call Jesus "Lord" because we believe he is the Son of God.

Christ or Messiah
In the Bible, these words designate someone who has been blessed with perfumed oil. This blessing is a sign that God has given a mission to the person. Christians give this name to Jesus.

Gestures

Tapping our heart
This is a way of showing we are very sorry for our sins.

We Give Glory to God

We recognize God's greatness when we say "Glory to God."
This prayer begins with the hymn the angels sang when they
announced Jesus' birth to the shepherds.

Everyone: **Glory** to God in the highest, and on earth peace to
people of good will.

We **praise** you,
we bless you,
we adore you,
we glorify you,
we give you thanks for your great glory,
Lord God, heavenly King,
O God, **almighty** Father.

Lord Jesus Christ, Only Begotten Son,
Lord God, Lamb of God, Son of the Father,
you take away the **sins of the world**,
    have mercy on us;
you take away the sins of the world,
    receive our prayer;
you are seated at the right hand of the Father,
    have mercy on us.

For you alone are the Holy One,
you alone are the Lord,
you alone are the Most High,
Jesus Christ,
with the **Holy Spirit,**
in the glory of God the Father.
Amen.

Priest: Let us pray.

*The priest invites us to pray. He then says a prayer in the
name of all of us, and finishes like this:*

Through our Lord Jesus Christ, your Son, who lives
and reigns with you in the unity of the Holy Spirit,
one God, for ever and ever.

Everyone: Amen.

What does it mean?

Glory
With this word, we indicate the greatness of a person. It shows that a person is important. When we say "Glory to God" we are recognizing that God is important in our lives.

Praise
To praise is to speak well and enthusiastically of someone.

Almighty
When we say that God is almighty, we mean that nothing is impossible for God.

Sins of the world
This expression refers to all the evil that is done in the world.

Holy Spirit
This is the Spirit of God, our heavenly guide, who fills us with love for Jesus.

We Listen to the Word of God

This is the moment when we listen to several readings from the
Bible. We welcome God who speaks to us today.

*You can follow the readings in this book. Look for the Sunday that
corresponds to the day's date.*

The First Two Readings

*We sit down for these readings. The first reading is usually taken from
the Old Testament. The second is from a letter written by an apostle
to the first Christians. Between these two readings, we pray with the
responsorial* **Psalm,** *which we do best when it is sung.*

The Gospel

We stand and sing **Alleluia!** *as we prepare to listen carefully to a
reading from one of the Gospels.*

Priest: The Lord be with you.

Everyone: And with your spirit.

Priest: A reading from the holy **Gospel** according to N.

Everyone: Glory to you, O Lord.

*We trace three small crosses with our thumb: one on our
forehead, one on our lips, and another on our heart. When
the reading is finished, the priest kisses the book and says:*

Priest: The Gospel of the Lord.

Everyone: Praise to you, Lord Jesus Christ.

The Homily

*We sit down to listen to the comments of the priest, which help us to
understand and apply the word of God in our lives.*

What does it mean?

Bible
This is the holy book of all Christians. The Old Testament tells the story of the covenant God made with the Jewish people before Jesus' time. The New Testament tells the story of the covenant God made with all people through his son, Jesus Christ.

Psalm
The Psalms are prayers that are found in the Bible. They are meant to be sung.

Alleluia!
This Hebrew word means "May God be praised and thanked."

Gospel
The word "gospel" means "good news." Jesus himself is the Good News who lives with us. The first four books of the New Testament are called "Gospels." They transmit the Good News to us.

Gestures

The sign of the cross which we make on our forehead, lips and heart
This sign means that we want to make the Gospel so much a part of our life that we can proclaim it to all around us with all our being.

Kissing the book of the Gospels
When the priest does this, he says in a low voice: "Through the words of the Gospel may our sins be wiped away."

We Profess Our Faith

We have just listened to the word of God. To respond to it, we proclaim the "**Creed**."

We stand up and profess our faith:

The Apostles' Creed

Everyone: I believe in God,
the Father almighty,
Creator of heaven and earth,
and in Jesus Christ, his only Son, our Lord,
who was conceived by the Holy Spirit,
born of the Virgin Mary,
suffered under **Pontius Pilate**,
was **crucified**, died and was buried;
he descended into hell;
on the third day he rose again from the dead;
he ascended into heaven,
and is seated at the right hand
    of God the Father almighty;
from there he will come to judge
    the living and the dead.

I believe in the Holy Spirit,
the holy **catholic Church**,
the communion of saints,
the forgiveness of sins,
the **resurrection** of the body,
and life everlasting.
Amen.

What does it mean?

Creed
From the Latin verb *credo*, meaning "I believe." The Creed is the prayer that expresses our faith as Christians.

He suffered
This refers to the torture Jesus endured before he died on the cross.

Pontius Pilate
This is the name of the Roman governor who ordered that Jesus be crucified.

Crucified
Jesus died by crucifixion, meaning he was nailed to a cross.

Catholic
In Greek, this word means "universal." The Church is open to all people in the world.

Church
The "Church" with a big C refers to the whole Christian community throughout the world. The "church" with a little c is a building where we gather to worship God.

Resurrection
This means coming back to life after having died. God raised Jesus from the dead and gave him new life for ever. Jesus shares that life with us.

We Pray for the Whole World

This is the moment of the universal Prayer of the Faithful when we present our **petitions** to God. We pray for the Church, for all of humanity, for those who are sick or lonely, for children who are abandoned, for those who suffer through natural disasters...

After each petition we respond with a phrase, such as:

Everyone: Lord, hear our prayer.

Reader: For the needs of the Church ...

For peace in every country ...

For the hungry and the homeless ...

For ourselves and for all God's children ...

What does it mean?

Petitions
Petitions are prayers asking for something specific. Each week at Mass, the petitions change because the needs of the world and our community change. We stand for the petitions and answer "Amen" at the end. Sometimes we call these prayers intentions.

Why do we call the Prayer of the Faithful "universal"?
It is a universal prayer because it includes everyone: we pray for all the people of the world.

Why do we take up a collection?
Christians help out with the maintenance of the church building and also help people who are in need. These gifts are brought to the altar with the bread and the wine.

We Offer Bread and Wine to God

The celebration of the Lord's Supper continues at the altar. Members of the community bring the bread, the wine, and the gifts collected to relieve the needs of the Church and the poor. The priest presents the bread and wine to God and we bless God with him.

We sit down. The priest takes the bread and wine, and lifts them up, saying:

Priest: **Blessed** are you, Lord God of all creation, for through your goodness we have received the bread we offer you: fruit of the earth and work of human hands, it will become for us the bread of life.

Everyone: Blessed be God for ever.

Priest: Blessed are you, Lord God of all creation, for through your goodness we have received the wine we offer you: fruit of the vine and work of human hands, it will become our spiritual drink.

Everyone: Blessed be God for ever.

The priest washes his hands and says:

Priest: Pray, brothers and sisters, that my sacrifice and yours may be acceptable to God, the almighty Father.

Everyone: May the Lord accept the **sacrifice** at your hands for the praise and glory of his name, for our good, and the good of all his holy Church.

We stand while the priest, with hands extended, says a prayer over the bread and wine. He usually ends the prayer by saying:

Priest: Through Christ our Lord.

Everyone: Amen.

What does it mean?

Eucharist
A Greek word that means "gratefulness, thanksgiving." The Mass is also called the Eucharist.

Blessed
To bless means to speak well of someone. To bless God is to give thanks for everything God gives us.

Sacrifice
God does not ask for animal sacrifice, as in the old days written about in the Bible. Nor does God ask us to die on a cross, like Jesus did. Instead, God asks us to offer our daily life, with Jesus, as a beautiful gift.

Gestures

Procession with the bread and the wine
With this gesture we present to God the fruit of our work and we give thanks for the gift of life that comes from God.

Drops of water in the wine
With this sign, the priest prays that our life be united with God's life.

Washing of hands
Before saying the most important prayer of the Mass, the priest washes his hands and asks God to wash away his sins.

We Give Thanks to God

At this moment we give thanks to God for his Son, Jesus Christ, for life, and for all that he gives us. This is how the great Eucharistic Prayer begins.

Priest:	The Lord be with you.
Everyone:	And with your spirit.
Priest:	Lift up your hearts.
Everyone:	We lift them up to the Lord.
Priest:	Let us give thanks to the Lord our God.
Everyone:	It is right and just.

Here is one way of celebrating the Eucharist with young Catholics. On page 22, you will find Eucharistic Prayer II, which is a common way of celebrating the Eucharist with grown-ups.

Eucharistic Prayer for Masses with Children I

Priest: God our Father,
you have brought us here together
so that we can give you thanks and praise
for all the wonderful things you have done.

We thank you for all that is beautiful in the world
and for the happiness you have given us.
We praise you for daylight
and for your word which lights up our minds.
We praise you for the earth,
and all the people who live on it,
and for our life which comes from you.

We know that you are good.
You love us and do great things for us.

[So we all say (sing) together:

Everyone: Holy, Holy, Holy Lord God of hosts.
Heaven and earth are full of your glory.
Hosanna in the highest.]

Priest: Father,
you are always thinking about your people;
you never forget us.
You sent us your Son Jesus,
who gave his life for us
and who came to save us.
He cured sick people;
he cared for those who were poor
and wept with those who were sad.
He forgave sinners
and taught us to forgive each other.
He loved everyone
and showed us how to be kind.
He took children in his arms and blessed them.

[So we all say (sing) together:

Everyone: Blessed is he who comes in the name of the Lord.
Hosanna in the highest.]

Priest: God our Father,
all over the world your people praise you.
So now we pray with the whole Church:
with N., our Pope and N., our Bishop.
In heaven the Blessed Virgin Mary,
the Apostles and all the Saints
always sing your praise.
Now we join with them and with the Angels
to adore you as we say (sing):

Everyone: Holy, Holy, Holy Lord God of hosts.
Heaven and earth are full of your glory.
Hosanna in the highest.
Blessed is he who comes in the name of the Lord.
Hosanna in the highest.

Priest: God our Father,
you are most holy
and we want to show you that we are grateful.
We bring you bread and wine and ask you to
send your Holy Spirit to make these gifts
the Body and Blood of Jesus your Son.
Then we can offer to you
what you have given to us.

On the night before he died,
Jesus was having supper with his Apostles.
He took bread from the table.
He gave you thanks and praise.
Then he broke the bread,
gave it to his friends, and said:

Take this, all of you, and eat of it,
for this is my Body
which will be given up for you.

When supper was ended,
Jesus took the chalice that was filled with wine.
He thanked you, gave it to his friends, and said:

Take this, all of you, and drink from it,
for this is the chalice of my Blood,
the Blood of the new and eternal covenant,
which will be poured out for you and for many
for the forgiveness of sins.

Then he said to them:

Do this in memory of me.

We do now what Jesus told us to do.
We remember his Death
and his Resurrection
and we offer you, Father,
the bread that gives us life,
and the chalice that saves us.
Jesus brings us to you;
welcome us as you welcome him.

Let us proclaim our faith:

Everyone: We proclaim your Death, O Lord,
and profess your Resurrection
until you come again.

or

When we eat this Bread and drink this Chalice,
we proclaim your Death, O Lord,
until you come again.

or

Save us, Saviour of the world,
for by your Cross and Resurrection
you have set us free.

Priest: Father,
because you love us,
you invite us to come to your table.
Fill us with the joy of the Holy Spirit
as we receive the Body and Blood of your Son.

Lord,
you never forget any of your children.
We ask you to take care of those we love,
especially of N. and N.,
and we pray for those who have died.

Remember everyone who is suffering from
pain or sorrow.
Remember Christians everywhere
and all other people in the world.

We are filled with wonder and praise
when we see what you do for us
through Jesus your Son,
and so we give you praise.

Through him, and with him, and in him,
O God, almighty Father,
in the unity of the Holy Spirit,
all glory and honour is yours,
for ever and ever.

Everyone: Amen.

(Turn to page 26)

Eucharistic Prayer II

Priest: It is truly right and just, our duty and our salvation,
always and everywhere to give you thanks,
Father most holy,
through your beloved Son, Jesus Christ,
your Word through whom you made all things,
whom you sent as our Saviour and Redeemer,
incarnate by the Holy Spirit and born of the Virgin.

Fulfilling your will and gaining for you a holy people,
he stretched out his hands
as he endured his Passion,
so as to break the bonds of death
and manifest the resurrection.

And so, with the Angels and all the Saints
we declare your glory,
as with one voice we acclaim:

Everyone: Holy, Holy, Holy Lord God of hosts.
Heaven and earth are full of your glory.
Hosanna in the highest.
Blessed is he who comes in the name of the Lord.
Hosanna in the highest.

Priest: You are indeed Holy, O Lord,
the fount of all holiness.

Make holy, therefore, these gifts, we pray,
by sending down your Spirit upon them like the dewfall,
so that they may become for us
the Body and Blood of our Lord Jesus Christ.

At the time he was betrayed
and entered willingly into his Passion,
he took bread and, giving thanks, broke it,
and gave it to his disciples, saying:

> Take this, all of you, and eat of it,
> for this is my Body
> which will be given up for you.

In a similar way,
when supper was ended,
he took the chalice
and, once more giving thanks,
he gave it to his disciples, saying:

> Take this, all of you, and drink from it,
> for this is the chalice of my Blood,
> the Blood of the new and eternal **covenant**,
> which will be poured out for you and for many
> for the **forgiveness of sins**.
> **Do this in memory of me.**

The mystery of faith.

Everyone: We proclaim your Death, O Lord,
and profess your Resurrection
until you come again.

or

When we eat this Bread and drink this Cup,
we proclaim your Death, O Lord,
until you come again.

or

Save us, Saviour of the world,
for by your Cross and Resurrection
you have set us free.

Priest: Therefore, as we celebrate
the memorial of his Death and Resurrection,
we offer you, Lord,
the Bread of life and the Chalice of salvation,
giving thanks that you have held us worthy
to be in your presence and minister to you.

Humbly we pray
that, partaking of the Body and Blood of Christ,
we may be gathered into one by the Holy Spirit.

Remember, Lord, your Church,
spread throughout the world,
and bring her to the fullness of charity,
together with N. our Pope and N. our Bishop
and all the clergy.

Remember also our brothers and sisters
who have fallen asleep in the hope of the resurrection,
and all who have died in your mercy:
welcome them into the light of your face.
Have mercy on us all, we pray,
that with the Blessed Virgin Mary, Mother of God,
with blessed Joseph, her Spouse,
with the blessed Apostles, and all the Saints
who have pleased you throughout the ages,
we may merit to be co-heirs to **eternal life**,
and may praise and glorify you
through your Son, Jesus Christ.

Through him, and with him, and in him,
O God, almighty Father,
in the unity of the Holy Spirit,
all glory and honour is yours,
for ever and ever.

Everyone: Amen.

What does it mean?

Covenant
When two people enter into a covenant, they promise to be faithful to one another. God entered into a covenant with us. He is our God and we are his People.

Forgiveness of sins
This is the forgiveness that comes from God, whose love is greater than our sins.

Do this in memory of me
Jesus asked the disciples to remember him by reliving what he said and did during the Last Supper.

The mystery of faith
Together we proclaim our belief in Christ who was born and died for us, rose to life, and will return one day.

Eternal life
This is life with God, which will be given to us fully after death.

Gestures

Extending the hands
When the priest extends his hands, he calls upon the Holy Spirit to consecrate the bread and wine, so that they become for us the Body and Blood of Christ.

Raising the bread
The priest lifts the consecrated bread and then the chalice, so that the community may see and respectfully adore the Body and Blood of Christ.

Kneeling
This is a common way to show respect and to worship.

We Say the Lord's Prayer

Jesus has taught us that God is the Father of all human beings
and that we can call upon God at any time. Together we recite or
sing this prayer.

Priest: At the **Saviour's** command and formed by divine
teaching, we dare to say:

Everyone: Our Father,
who art in **heaven**,
hallowed be thy name;
thy kingdom come,
thy will be done
on earth as it is in heaven.
Give us this day our daily bread,
and forgive us our **trespasses**,
as we forgive those who trespass against us;
and lead us not into **temptation**,
but deliver us from evil.

Priest: Deliver us, Lord, we pray, from every evil, graciously
grant peace in our days, that, by the help of your
mercy, we may be always free from sin and safe
from all distress, as we await the blessed hope and
the coming of our Saviour, Jesus Christ.

Everyone: For the **kingdom**,
the power and the glory are yours
now and for ever.

What does it mean?

Saviour
This is one of the names we give to Jesus because he saves us from evil and death.

Heaven
Heaven is a special way of being with God after our life on earth is over.

Trespasses
These refer to our lack of love and to the sins we commit.

Temptation
This is a desire we sometimes feel to do things we know are wrong.

Kingdom
Jesus speaks of God as king when he says: "The kingdom of God is at hand." With his life, Jesus shows us that God is present in our midst as a king who loves us. When we live as Jesus did, we welcome the kingdom of God.

We Share the Peace of Christ

God is our Father and we are brothers and sisters in Christ. In order to show that we are one family, the priest invites us to offer each other a sign of peace.

Priest: Lord Jesus Christ, who said to your Apostles: Peace I leave you, my peace I give you, look not on our sins, but on the faith of your Church, and graciously grant her peace and **unity** in accordance with your will. Who live and reign for ever and ever.

Everyone: Amen.

Priest: The peace of the Lord be with you always.

Everyone: And with your spirit.

Priest: Let us offer each other the sign of peace.

At this time, by a handshake, a hug or a bow, we give to those near us a sign of Christ's peace. Immediately after, we say:

Everyone: **Lamb of God**, you take away the sins of the world, have mercy on us.

Lamb of God, you take away the sins of the world, have mercy on us.

Lamb of God, you take away the sins of the world, grant us peace.

What does it mean?

Unity
When we get together each Sunday to celebrate the Lord's Supper, we recognize our unity, or oneness, since we are all children of the same loving Father.

Lamb of God
In the Old Testament, believers offered a lamb to God. We call Jesus the Lamb of God because he offers his life to God.

Gestures

The Sign of Peace
We shake hands, hug or bow to one another to share the peace that comes from Christ. It is a sign of our commitment to live in peace with others.

We Receive Jesus in Communion

When we receive communion, the Bread of Life, we are fed with the life of Christ.

The priest breaks the host and says:

Priest: Behold the Lamb of God, behold him who takes away the sins of the world. Blessed are those called to the supper of the Lamb.

Everyone: Lord, I am not worthy that you should enter under my roof, but only say the word and my soul shall be healed.

It is time to come up to receive communion. The priest or the communion minister says:

Priest: The Body of Christ.

Everyone: Amen.

Questions

Why do we go to communion?
When we eat the bread, we receive Jesus. He gives himself to us this way so we can live for God. Sharing the Body and Blood of Christ in communion creates among us a special 'one-ness' with God and with each other.

Why is the bread we share during Mass called a "host"?
The word "host" means "victim who is offered." The consecrated host is Jesus Christ, who offers himself in order to give life to others.

Gestures

The priest breaks the bread
The priest breaks the bread in the same way that Jesus did during the Last Supper, in order to share it. The early Christians used to call the Mass "the breaking of the bread."

Receiving the host
The priest or communion minister places the host in your open left hand. You pick the host up with your right hand, put the host in your mouth, eat the bread carefully and return to your place. You take a few moments of quiet prayer to thank God for this Bread of Life.

The Lord Sends Us Forth

After announcements, the priest blesses us in the name of God. We are then sent to live out our faith among all the people we meet during the week.

Priest: The Lord be with you.

Everyone: And with your spirit.

Priest: May almighty God bless you, the Father, and the Son, and the Holy Spirit.

Everyone: Amen.

Then the priest sends us out, saying this or something similar:

Priest: Go in peace, glorifying the Lord by your life.

Everyone: Thanks be to God.

What does it mean?

The word "Mass"
The word "Mass" comes from the second word in the Latin phrase that was once used by the priest to announce the end of the Sunday celebration: *Ite missa est* — Go forth, the Mass is ended.

Communion for the sick
Sometimes people who are sick cannot be present at Sunday Mass. Certain members of the parish, known as communion ministers, can take consecrated hosts to the homes of sick people so that they can receive communion and be assured that the rest of the community is praying for them.

Gestures

Blessing
The priest makes the sign of the cross over the people in church. With this blessing we are sent out with the loving strength of God to live a life of love and service to others.

Dismissal
We cannot stay together in the church all week. When the Mass is ended, we must go our separate ways, in peace and love, to witness to the risen Jesus in the world today.

November 27

1st Sunday of Advent

A reading from the book of the Prophet Isaiah
(2.1-5)

The word that Isaiah son of Amoz saw concerning Judah and Jerusalem. In days to come **the mountain of the Lord's house** shall be established as the highest of the mountains, and shall be raised above the hills; all the nations shall stream to it.

Many peoples shall come and say, "Come, let us go up to the mountain of the Lord, to the house of the God of Jacob; that he may teach us his ways and that we may walk in his paths."

For out of Zion shall go forth instruction, and the word of the Lord from Jerusalem. He shall judge between the nations, and shall arbitrate for many peoples; they shall beat their swords into ploughshares, and their spears into pruning hooks; nation shall not lift up sword against nation, neither shall they learn war any more.

O **house of Jacob**, come, let us walk in the light of the Lord!

The word of the Lord. **Thanks be to God.**

Psalm 122

R. **Let us go rejoicing to the house of the Lord.**

I was glad when they said to me,
"Let us go to the house of the Lord!"
Our feet are standing
within your gates, O Jerusalem. R.

To it the tribes go up, the tribes of the Lord,
as was decreed for Israel, to give thanks to the name
    of the Lord.
For there the thrones for judgment were set up,
the thrones of the house of David. R.

Pray for the peace of Jerusalem:
"May they prosper who love you.
Peace be within your walls,
and security within your towers." R.

℟. **Let us go rejoicing to the house of the Lord.**

For the sake of my relatives and friends
I will say, "Peace be within you."
For the sake of the house of the Lord our God,
I will seek your good. ℟.

A reading from the Letter of Saint Paul to the Romans (13.11-14)

Brothers and sisters, you know what time it is, how it is now the moment for you to wake from sleep. For salvation is nearer to us now than when we became believers; the night is far gone, the day is near. Let us then lay aside the **works of darkness** and put on the **armour of light;** let us live honourably as in the day, not in revelling and drunkenness, not in debauchery and licentiousness, not in quarrelling and jealousy.

Instead, put on the Lord Jesus Christ, and make no provision for the flesh, to gratify its desires.

The word of the Lord. **Thanks be to God.**

A reading from the holy Gospel according to Matthew (24.37-44)

Jesus spoke to his disciples: "As the days of **Noah** were, so will be the coming of the Son of Man. For as in those days before the flood they were eating and drinking, marrying and giving in marriage, until the day Noah entered the ark, and they knew nothing until the flood came and swept them all away, so too will be the coming of the Son of Man. Then two will be in the field; one will be taken and one will be left. Two women will be grinding meal together; one will be taken and one will be left.

"**Keep awake**, therefore, for you do not know on what day your Lord is coming. But understand this: if the owner of the house had known in what part of the night the thief was coming, he would have stayed awake and would not have let his house be broken into. Therefore you also must be ready, for the Son of Man is coming at an unexpected hour."

The Gospel of the Lord. **Praise to you, Lord Jesus Christ.**

Key Words

When the prophet Isaiah speaks of **the mountain of the Lord's house**, he is referring to the temple of Jerusalem. In saying it is the highest of the mountains, Isaiah wants to communicate that there will come a time when the God of Israel will be known and revered by all the people of the world.

Jacob was a grandson of Abraham and father of twelve sons, after whom the twelve tribes of Israel were named. The **house of Jacob** was another way to refer to all the people of Israel.

The **works of darkness** are bad actions that break our friendship with God and other people. We prefer to keep them hidden or out of the light, because we're not proud of what we have done.

The **armour of light** is our willingness and desire to follow the teachings of Jesus. To be friends of Jesus we must be ready to struggle against all that might distance us from God.

Noah was the just man chosen by God to be saved from the flood, along with his family and two of every animal. God asked Noah to build a huge boat, called an ark, in which he, his family and the animals lived during the flood.

To **keep awake** is to avoid sleep throughout the night. But it also means to be alert so that nothing can surprise us. Christians must live in such a way that we're ready at any moment to meet our Lord.

December 4
2nd Sunday of Advent

A reading from the book of the Prophet Isaiah
(11.1-10)

On that day:
A **shoot** shall come out from the stump of Jesse,
and a branch shall grow out of his roots.
The spirit of the Lord shall rest on him,
the spirit of wisdom and understanding,
the spirit of counsel and might,
the spirit of knowledge and the **fear of the Lord**.
His delight shall be in the fear of the Lord.

He shall not judge by what his eyes see,
or decide by what his ears hear;
but with righteousness he shall judge the poor,
and decide with equity for the meek of the earth;
he shall strike the earth with the rod of his mouth,
and with the breath of his lips he shall kill the wicked.
Righteousness shall be the belt around his waist,
and faithfulness the belt around his loins.

The wolf shall live with the lamb,
the leopard shall lie down with the kid,
the calf and the lion and the fatling together,
and a little child shall lead them.
The cow and the bear shall graze,
their young shall lie down together;
and the lion shall eat straw like the ox.
The nursing child shall play over the hole of the asp,
and the weaned child shall put its hand on the adder's den.
They will not hurt or destroy
on all my holy mountain;
for the earth will be full of the knowledge of the Lord
as the waters cover the sea.

On that day the root of Jesse shall stand
as a signal to the peoples;
the nations shall inquire of him,
and his dwelling shall be glorious.

The word of the Lord. **Thanks be to God.**

Psalm 72

R. **In his days may righteousness flourish,
and peace abound forever.**

Give the king your justice, O God,
and your righteousness to a king's son.
May he judge your people with righteousness,
and your poor with justice. R.

In his days may righteousness flourish
and peace abound, until the moon is no more.
May he have dominion from sea to sea,
and from the River to the ends of the earth. R.

For he delivers the needy one who calls,
the poor and the one who has no helper.
He has pity on the weak and the needy,
and saves the lives of the needy. R.

May his name endure forever,
his fame continue as long as the sun.
May all nations be blessed in him;
may they pronounce him happy. R.

A reading from the Letter of Saint Paul to the Romans (15.4-9)

Brothers and sisters: Whatever was written in former days was written for our instruction, so that by steadfastness and by the encouragement of the Scriptures we might have **hope**.

May the God of steadfastness and encouragement grant you to live in harmony with one another, in accordance with Christ Jesus, so that together you may with one voice glorify the God and Father of our Lord Jesus Christ.

Welcome one another, therefore, just as Christ has welcomed you, for the glory of God. For I tell you that Christ has become a servant of the circumcised on behalf of the truth of God in order that he might confirm the promises given to **the patriarchs**, and in order that the Gentiles might glorify God for his mercy. As it is written, "Therefore I will confess you among the Gentiles, and sing praises to your name."

The word of the Lord. **Thanks be to God.**

A reading from the holy Gospel according to Matthew (3.1-12)

In those days **John the Baptist** appeared in the wilderness of Judea, proclaiming, "Repent, for the kingdom of heaven has come near." This is the one of whom the Prophet Isaiah spoke when he said, "The voice of one crying out in the wilderness: 'Prepare the way of the Lord, make his paths straight.'"

Now John wore clothing of camel's hair with a leather belt around his waist, and his food was locusts and wild honey. Then the people of Jerusalem and all Judea were going out to him, and all the region along the Jordan, and they were baptized by him in the river Jordan, confessing their sins.

But when he saw many **Pharisees** and **Sadducees** coming for baptism, John said to them, "You brood of vipers! Who warned you to flee from the wrath to come? Bear fruit worthy of repentance. Do not presume to say to yourselves, 'We have Abraham as our father'; for I tell you, God is able from these stones to raise up children to Abraham. Even now the axe is lying at the root of the trees; every tree therefore that does not bear good fruit is cut down and thrown into the fire.

"I baptize you with water for repentance, but one who is more powerful than I is coming after me; I am **not worthy to carry his sandals**. He will baptize you with the Holy Spirit and fire. His winnowing fork is in his hand, and he will clear his threshing floor and will gather his wheat into the granary; but the chaff he will burn with unquenchable fire."

The Gospel of the Lord. **Praise to you, Lord Jesus Christ.**

Key Words

When the prophet Isaiah speaks of a **shoot** coming out from the stump of Jesse, he is making a comparison between a branch that seems withered and dead, and the hope and new life of the people. When Isaiah refers to the appearance of branch growing from the roots of Jesse, he is referring to Jesus who is descended from Jesse.

To have the spirit of **fear of the Lord** does not mean to be afraid of God. Rather, it signifies having a heart that is full of respect for the greatness of the Creator.

Hope is the confidence we have as Christians that God will always support us. God made this promise in many ways, but especially when he sent us his son, Jesus Christ.

The patriarchs are the ancestors of the people of Israel. Abraham, Isaac and Jacob were all known by this name. They received God's promise that his people would become a great nation.

John the Baptist was the son of Zechariah and Elizabeth, who was a cousin of the Virgin Mary. He preached the coming of the Messiah. He was called John the Baptist because those who were converted by his preaching were baptized in order to prepare themselves for the coming of the Saviour.

The **Pharisees** and the **Sadducees** were people who belonged to two Jewish religious sects. Pharisees were very strict and believed religion consisted in obeying the rules, sometimes forgetting that love is the greatest rule. The Sadducees did not believe in the resurrection of the dead.

When one person was recognized as being much less important than another, it was said they were **not worthy to carry his sandals**. Untying and carrying the sandals of a visitor was a job for a slave; if you are not worthy even to do the work of a slave, then the important person is very great indeed.

A reading from the book of the Prophet Isaiah
(35.1-6, 10)

The wilderness and the dry land shall be glad,
the desert shall rejoice and blossom;
like the **crocus** it shall blossom abundantly,
and rejoice with joy and singing.
The glory of **Lebanon** shall be given to it,
the majesty of **Carmel** and **Sharon**.
They shall see the glory of the Lord,
the **majesty** of our God.

Strengthen the weak hands,
and make firm the feeble knees.
Say to those who are of a fearful heart,
"Be strong, do not fear!
Here is your God.
He will come with **vengeance**,
with terrible recompense.
He will come and save you."

Then the eyes of the blind shall be opened,
and the ears of the deaf unstopped;
then the lame shall leap like a deer,
and the tongue of the mute sing for joy.
And the ransomed of the Lord shall return,
and come to Zion with singing;
everlasting joy shall be upon their heads;
they shall obtain joy and gladness,
and sorrow and sighing shall flee away.

The word of the Lord. **Thanks be to God.**

Psalm 146

R. **Lord, come and save us.**

or **Alleluia!**

It is the Lord who keeps faith forever,
who executes justice for the **oppressed**;
who gives food to the hungry.
The Lord sets the prisoners free. R.

The Lord opens the eyes of the blind
and lifts up those who are bowed down;
the Lord loves the righteous
and watches over the strangers. R.

The Lord upholds the orphan and the widow,
but the way of the wicked he brings to ruin.
The Lord will reign forever,
your God, O Zion, for all generations. R.

A reading from the Letter of Saint James
(5.7-10)

Be patient, brothers and sisters, until the **coming of the Lord**. The farmer waits for the precious crop from the earth, being patient with it until it receives the early and the late rains. You also must be patient. Strengthen your hearts, for the coming of the Lord is near.

Brothers and sisters, do not grumble against one another, so that you may not be judged. See, the Judge is standing at the doors! As an example of suffering and patience, brothers and sisters, take the Prophets who spoke in the name of the Lord.

The word of the Lord. **Thanks be to God.**

A reading from the holy Gospel according to Matthew (11.2-11)

When John the Baptist heard in prison about the deeds of the Christ, he sent word by his disciples who said to Jesus, "Are you the one who is to come, or are we to wait for another?"

Jesus answered them, "Go and tell John what you hear and see: the blind receive their sight, the lame walk, the lepers are cleansed, the deaf hear, the dead are raised, and the poor have good news brought to them. And blessed is anyone who takes no offence at me."

As they went away, Jesus began to speak to the crowds about John: "What did you go out into the wilderness to look at? A **reed** shaken by the wind? What then did you go out to see? Someone dressed in soft robes? Look, those who wear soft robes are in royal palaces. What then did you go out to see? A **Prophet?** Yes, I tell you, and more than a Prophet. This is the one about whom it is written, 'See, I am sending my messenger ahead of you, who will prepare your way before you.'

"Truly I tell you, among those born of women no one has arisen greater than John the Baptist; yet the least in the kingdom of heaven is greater than he."

The Gospel of the Lord. **Praise to you, Lord Jesus Christ.**

Key Words

A **crocus** is among the first flowers that bloom in springtime.

Lebanon is a country at the eastern end of the Mediterranean Sea, bordering on modern-day Israel.

Carmel refers to a coastal mountain in Israel. Mount Carmel marks the northern reach of the plain of **Sharon**, a flat region that includes the modern city of Tel Aviv.

The **majesty** of a king or queen is their grandeur and power.

In the Old Testament there are many stories of battles and wars. **Vengeance**, which is a terrible thing, means getting back at someone after they have offended or hurt you. In today's reading, the prophet Isaiah is trying to encourage the people to believe in God, who will eventually come to their aid and save them from their enemies.

If someone is **oppressed**, then they are being treated very badly by others. Oppression deadens the soul and must be opposed by working for peace and justice.

The **coming of the Lord** is a reference to the Second Coming of Jesus, at the end of time. The first Christians thought that Jesus would be returning in their own lifetime; they expected it to happen soon.

A **reed** is a thin shoot of a plant, often found near water. It is flexible, and bends with the wind.

Prophets were holy men and women who spoke publicly against poverty and injustice, and criticized the people whenever they refused to listen to God's word. Many of the books of the Old Testament were written by prophets (Isaiah, Jeremiah, Amos, and Micah, for example).

December 18
4th Sunday of Advent

A reading from the book of the Prophet Isaiah
(7.10-14)

The Lord spoke to **Ahaz**, saying, "Ask a sign of the Lord your God; let it be deep as Sheol or high as heaven." But Ahaz said, "I will not ask, and I will not put the Lord to the test."

Then Isaiah said: "Hear then, O **house of David!** Is it too little for you to weary the people, that you weary my God also? Therefore the Lord himself will give you a sign. Look, the young woman is with child and shall bear a son, and shall name him Emmanuel."

The word of the Lord. **Thanks be to God.**

Psalm 24

R. **May the Lord come in; he is king of glory.**

> The earth is the Lord's and all that is in it,
> the world, and those who live in it;
> for he has founded it on the seas,
> and established it on the rivers. R.
>
> Who shall ascend the hill of the Lord?
> And who shall stand in his holy place?
> Someone who has clean hands and a pure heart,
> who does not lift up their soul to what is false. R.
>
> That person will receive blessing from the Lord,
> and vindication from the God of their salvation.
> Such is the company of those who seek him,
> who seek the face of the God of Jacob. R.

A reading from the Letter of Saint Paul to the Romans (1.1-7)

From Paul, a servant of Jesus Christ, called to be an Apostle, set apart for the **Gospel** of God, which God promised beforehand through his Prophets in the holy Scriptures: the Gospel concerning his Son, who was descended from David according to the flesh and was declared to be Son of God with power according to the spirit of holiness by resurrection from the dead, Jesus Christ our Lord.

Through Christ we have received grace and **apostleship** to bring about the obedience of faith among all the **Gentiles** for the sake of his name, including yourselves who are called to belong to Jesus Christ.

To all God's beloved in Rome, who are called to be saints: Grace to you and peace from God our Father and the Lord Jesus Christ.

The word of the Lord. **Thanks be to God.**

A reading from the holy Gospel according to Matthew (1.18-24)

The birth of Jesus the Christ took place in this way. When his mother Mary had been **engaged** to Joseph, but before they lived together, she was found to be with child from the Holy Spirit. Her husband Joseph, being a righteous man and unwilling to expose her to public disgrace, planned to dismiss her quietly.

But just when he had resolved to do this, an Angel of the Lord appeared to him in a dream and said, "Joseph, son of David, do not be afraid to take Mary as your wife, for the child conceived in her is from the Holy Spirit. She will bear a son, and you are to name him Jesus, for he will save his people from their sins."

All this took place to fulfill what had been spoken by the Lord through the Prophet: "Look, the virgin shall conceive and bear a son, and they shall name him Emmanuel," which means, "God is with us." When Joseph awoke from sleep, he did as the Angel of the Lord commanded him; he took her as his wife.

The Gospel of the Lord. **Praise to you, Lord Jesus Christ.**

Key Words

Ahaz was a king of Israel who was not well thought of. He was not true to the people's covenant with God, he worshipped other gods that he himself had created, and he closed the temple.

When the prophet Isaiah speaks to the **house of David**, he is speaking to all the Israelites. This is one of the names by which all the people of Israel were known.

The Letter of Saint Paul to the Romans is the longest surviving letter that Saint Paul wrote. The Christians who lived in Rome belonged to a small community. Paul wanted to travel to preach in Spain and stop on the way in Rome to visit the Christians. He sent this letter ahead in order to encourage them, and to remind them of the teachings of Jesus.

The word **Gospel** means the whole message that Jesus brought us. It is a word meaning the 'Good News.'

Apostleship is a mission that God gave to Saint Paul, to announce the Good News of the resurrection of Jesus — that Jesus conquered death. This is also the mission of all Christians: we are all apostles through our baptism.

The **Gentiles** are people who are not Jewish. When Saint Paul speaks of Gentiles, he means Greeks and Romans living within the Roman Empire.

Saint **Matthew** was the author of one of the four Gospels. Today's gospel clearly tells us about the life of Jesus and emphasizes that he is the promised Messiah, and that the Church is now the Chosen People, the new Israel.

Joseph and Mary were **engaged**, but they did not live together before marriage. For this reason, when Mary became pregnant, Joseph at first thought they shouldn't get married. But Joseph obeyed what the Lord told him in a dream, and he kept his promise to Mary and became Jesus' earthly father.

December 25

The Nativity of the Lord
Christmas

A reading from the book of the Prophet Isaiah
(9.2-4, 6-7)

The people who walked in darkness have seen a great light;
those who lived in a land of deep darkness —
on them light has shone.
You have multiplied the nation,
you have increased its joy;
they rejoice before you
as with joy at the harvest,
as people exult when dividing plunder.

For the yoke of their burden,
and the bar across their shoulders,
the rod of their oppressor,
you have broken as on the day of Midian.

For a child has been born for us,
a son given to us;
authority rests upon his shoulders;
and he is named
Wonderful Counsellor, Mighty God,
Everlasting Father, Prince of Peace.

His authority shall grow continually,
and there shall be endless peace
for the throne of David and his kingdom.
He will establish and uphold it
with justice and with righteousness
from this time onward and forevermore.
The zeal of the Lord of hosts will do this.

The word of the Lord. **Thanks be to God.**

Psalm 96

R˷ **Today is born our Saviour, Christ the Lord.**

O sing to the Lord a new song;
sing to the Lord, all the earth.
Sing to the Lord, bless his name;
tell of his salvation from day to day. R˷

R̸. **Today is born our Saviour, Christ the Lord.**

Declare his glory among the nations,
his marvellous works among all the peoples.
For great is the Lord, and greatly to be praised;
he is to be revered above all gods. R̸.

Let the heavens be glad, and let the earth rejoice;
let the sea roar, and all that fills it;
let the field exult, and everything in it.
Then shall all the trees of the forest **sing for joy**. R̸.

Rejoice before the Lord; for he is coming,
for he is coming to judge the earth.
He will judge the world with righteousness,
and the peoples with his truth. R̸.

A reading from the Letter of Saint Paul to Titus (2.11-14)

Beloved: The grace of God has appeared, bringing salvation to all, training us to renounce impiety and worldly passions, and in the present age to live lives that are self-controlled, upright, and godly, while we wait for the blessed hope and the manifestation of the glory of our great God and Saviour, Jesus Christ.

He it is who gave himself for us that he might redeem us from all iniquity and purify for himself a people of his own who are zealous for good deeds.

The word of the Lord. **Thanks be to God.**

A reading from the holy Gospel according to Luke (2.1-16)

In those days a decree went out from Caesar Augustus that all the world should be registered. This was the first registration and was taken while Quirinius was governor of Syria. All went to their own towns to be registered. Joseph also went from the town of Nazareth in Galilee to Judea, to the city of David called Bethlehem, because he was descended from the house and family of David. He went to be registered with Mary, to whom he was engaged and who was expecting a child.

While they were there, the time came for her to deliver her child. And she gave birth to her firstborn son and wrapped him in swaddling clothes, and laid him in a **manger**, because there was no place for them in the inn.

In that region there were shepherds living in the fields, keeping watch over their flock by night. Then an **Angel of the Lord** stood before them, and the glory of the Lord shone around them, and they were terrified. But the Angel said to them, "Do not be afraid; for see — I am bringing you good news of great joy for all the people: to you is born this day in the city of David a Saviour, who is the Christ, the Lord. This will be a sign for you: you will find a child wrapped in swaddling clothes and lying in a manger."

And suddenly there was with the Angel a multitude of the heavenly host, praising God and saying, "Glory to God in the highest heaven, and on earth peace among those whom he favours!"

When the Angels had left them and gone into heaven, the shepherds said to one another, "Let us go now to Bethlehem and see this thing that has taken place, which the Lord has made known to us." So they went with haste and found Mary and Joseph, and the child lying in the manger.

The Gospel of the Lord. **Praise to you, Lord Jesus Christ.**

Key Words

Christmas Day is celebrated on December 25th, but the Christmas season lasts for three weeks, ending with the Baptism of Jesus in January. The liturgical colour for this season is white, the colour of joy and celebration.

Prophets like **Isaiah** were good men and women who spoke for God. Sometimes their messages were demanding: they asked people to change their lives and attitudes to grow closer to God. At other times, they brought words of comfort.

We **sing for joy** because our hearts are full of happiness: God has come to be with his people. In today's psalm, we see that all creation — even the trees! — rejoices in the glory of the Lord.

A **manger** is a wooden crate filled with hay to feed the animals in a stable. It comes from the French word *manger*, to eat. The baby Jesus was placed in a manger soon after he was born. It is amazing that God would choose to be born in such a simple place.

An **Angel of the Lord** is a messenger of God. Angels appear many times in the Bible, as we see angels revealing God's plan in the lives of Jesus, Mary and Joseph.

Merry Christmas!
Glory to God in the highest
and on earth peace to all people!

January 1
Solemnity of Mary,
the Holy Mother of God

A reading from the book of Numbers (6.22-27)

The Lord spoke to **Moses**: Speak to **Aaron** and his sons, saying,
Thus you shall bless the children of Israel: You shall say to them,

The Lord bless you and keep you;
the Lord make his face to shine upon you, and be gracious to you;
the Lord lift up his countenance upon you, and give you peace.

So they shall put my name on the **children of Israel**, and I will
bless them.

The word of the Lord. **Thanks be to God.**

Psalm 67

Ṟ. **May God be gracious to us and bless us.**

May God be gracious to us and bless us
and make his face to shine upon us,
that your way may be known upon earth,
your saving power among all nations. Ṟ.

Let the nations be glad and sing for joy,
for you judge the peoples with **equity**
and guide the nations upon earth.
Let the peoples praise you, O God;
let all the peoples praise you. Ṟ.

The earth has yielded its increase;
God, our God, has blessed us.
May God continue to bless us;
let all the ends of the earth revere him. Ṟ.

A reading from the Letter of Saint Paul to the Galatians (4.4-7)

Brothers and sisters: When the **fullness of time** had come, God sent his Son, born of a woman, born under the law, in order to redeem those who were under the law, so that we might receive adoption to sonship.

And because you are sons and daughters, God has sent the Spirit of his Son into our hearts, crying, "**Abba!** Father!" So you are no longer slave but son, and if son then also heir, through God.

The word of the Lord. **Thanks be to God.**

A reading from the holy Gospel according to Luke (2.16-21)

The shepherds went with haste to Bethlehem and found Mary and Joseph, and the child lying in the manger. When they saw this, they made known what had been told them about this child; and all who heard it were amazed at what the shepherds told them.

But Mary treasured all these words and **pondered** them in her heart.

The shepherds returned, glorifying and praising God for all they had heard and seen, as it had been told them.

After eight days had passed, it was time to circumcise the child; and he was called Jesus, the name given by the Angel before he was conceived in the womb.

The Gospel of the Lord. **Praise to you, Lord Jesus Christ.**

Key Words

The **book of Numbers** is part of the Bible. It is called Numbers because it talks about many numbers and times when the people of Israel were counted. In Hebrew, it is called "In the Desert," because it tells of the travels of the Israelites in the desert, after they left slavery in Egypt.

Moses was a friend of God who was born in Egypt when the Israelites were slaves there. When God asked him to lead the people to freedom, Moses said yes because he loved God and didn't want the people to suffer any more. The people left Egypt on a journey called the Exodus about 1,250 years before the time of Jesus.

Aaron, Moses' older brother, helped him free the Israelites. When Moses went up Mount Sinai to receive God's law, Aaron stayed with the people.

Children of Israel is the name of the people God chose to help everyone in the world know God's love.

To judge with **equity** is to be fair to everyone. In the Psalm, the psalmist is praising God for God's fairness to all people on earth.

Fullness of time means when the time was right for God to send Jesus into the world.

In Aramaic, the language Jesus spoke, **Abba** means 'Daddy.' By calling God 'Abba,' Jesus shows that we can talk to God with the same trust and love that small children have for their father.

To **ponder** means to think about something a lot. Like all mothers, Mary remembered all the details surrounding the birth of her child, and recalled these memories over and over.

January 8

Epiphany of the Lord

A reading from the book of the Prophet Isaiah
(60.1-6)

Arise, shine, for your light has come,
and the glory of the Lord has risen upon you!
For darkness shall cover the earth,
and thick darkness the peoples;
but the Lord will arise upon you,
and his glory will appear over you.
Nations shall come to your light,
and kings to the brightness of your dawn.
Lift up your eyes and look around;
they all gather together, they come to you;
your sons shall come from far away,
and your daughters shall be carried on their nurses' arms.

Then you shall see and be radiant;
your heart shall thrill and rejoice,
because the abundance of the sea shall be brought to you,
the wealth of the nations shall come to you.
A multitude of camels shall cover you,
the young camels of **Midian** and **Ephah**;
all those from **Sheba** shall come.
They shall bring gold and frankincense,
and shall proclaim the praise of the Lord.

The word of the Lord. **Thanks be to God.**

Psalm 72

R̵. **Lord, every nation on earth will adore you.**

Give the king your justice, O God,
and your righteousness to a king's son.
May he judge your people with righteousness,
and your poor with justice. R̵.

In his days may righteousness flourish
and peace abound, until the moon is no more.
May he have dominion from sea to sea,
and from the River to the ends of the earth. R̵.

> May the kings of Tarshish and of the isles render
>   him tribute,
> may the kings of Sheba and Seba bring gifts.
> May all kings fall down before him,
> all nations give him service. R.
>
> For he delivers the needy one who calls,
> the poor and the one who has no helper.
> He has pity on the weak and the needy,
> and saves the lives of the needy. R.

A reading from the Letter of Saint Paul to the Ephesians (3.2-3, 5-6)

Brothers and sisters: Surely you have already heard of the commission of God's grace that was given me for you, and how the mystery was made known to me by **revelation**.

In former generations this **mystery** was not made known to humankind as it has now been revealed to his holy Apostles and Prophets by the Spirit: that is, the Gentiles have become fellow heirs, members of the same body, and sharers in the promise in Christ Jesus through the Gospel.

The word of the Lord. **Thanks be to God.**

A reading from the holy Gospel according to Matthew (2.1-12)

In the time of King Herod, after Jesus was born in **Bethlehem of Judea**, wise men from the East came to Jerusalem, asking, "Where is the child who has been born king of the Jews? For we observed his star at its rising, and have come to pay him **homage**."

When King Herod heard this, he was frightened, and all Jerusalem with him; and calling together all the chief priests and scribes of the people, he inquired of them where the **Messiah** was to be born. They told him, "In Bethlehem of Judea; for so it has been written by the Prophet: 'And you, Bethlehem, in the land of Judah, are by no means least among the rulers of Judah; for from you shall come a ruler who is to shepherd my people Israel.'"

Then Herod secretly called for the wise men and learned from them the exact time when the star had appeared. Then he sent them to Bethlehem, saying, "Go and search diligently for the child; and when you have found him, bring me word so that I may also go and pay him homage."

When they had heard the king, they set out; and there, ahead of them, went the star that they had seen at its rising, until it stopped over the place where the child was. When they saw that the star had stopped, they were overwhelmed with joy.

On entering the house, they saw the child with Mary his mother; and they knelt down and paid him homage. Then, opening their treasure chests, they offered him gifts of **gold, frankincense, and myrrh**.

And having been warned in a dream not to return to Herod, they left for their own country by another road.

The Gospel of the Lord. **Praise to you, Lord Jesus Christ.**

Key Words

Epiphany is a Greek word that means 'unveiling' or 'revelation.' God revealed his love for all people by sending us his Son, Jesus, as a human being — as a baby.

Midian, Ephah and Sheba were three ancient kingdoms near Israel. In the book of the prophet Isaiah in the Bible, they represent all the nations outside Israel.

The **Ephesians** were a group of Christians in the city of Ephesus. A letter Saint Paul wrote to them is now part of the Bible. Ephesus is located in modern-day Turkey.

To know something by **revelation** means that God has shown or given someone this knowledge. It is not known by human means.

A **mystery** is something that is very hard to understand. In Saint Paul's letter to the Ephesians, the mystery Paul speaks of is God's plan to create a human community in Christ.

Bethlehem of Judea is the city of King David, one of Jesus' ancestors. Joseph and Mary went to Bethlehem for a census (an official counting of all the people). Jesus was born during their stay there.

To pay someone **homage** is to show your respect or honour for them in a public way, such as by bowing or bringing gifts.

Messiah is an Aramaic word meaning 'anointed.' A chosen person was blessed with holy oil and given a special mission. The Greek word for 'anointed' is 'Christ.'

Gold, frankincense, and myrrh were three very expensive gifts: gold is a precious metal; frankincense and myrrh are rare, sweet-smelling incenses. Myrrh is the main ingredient in holy anointing oil.

January 15
2nd Sunday in Ordinary Time

A reading from the book of the Prophet Isaiah
(49.3, 5-6)

The Lord said to me,
"You are my **servant**, Israel, in whom I will be glorified."

And now the Lord says,
who formed me in the womb to be his servant,
to bring **Jacob** back to him,
and that Israel might be gathered to him,
for I am honoured in the sight of the Lord,
and my God has become my strength.

He says,
"It is too small a thing that you should be my servant
to raise up the tribes of Jacob
and to restore the survivors of Israel;
I will give you as a light to the nations,
that my salvation may reach to the end of the earth."

The word of the Lord. **Thanks be to God.**

Psalm 40

R. **Here I am, Lord; I come to do your will.**

I waited patiently for the Lord;
he inclined to me and heard my cry.
He put a new song in my mouth,
a song of praise to our God. R.

Sacrifice and offering you do not desire,
but you have given me an open ear.
Burnt offering and sin offering
you have not required. R.

Then I said, "Here I am;
in the scroll of the book it is written of me.
I delight to do your will, O my God;
your law is within my heart." R.

R. **Here I am, Lord; I come to do your will.**

I have told the glad news of deliverance
in the great congregation;
see, I have not restrained my lips,
as you know, O Lord. R.

A reading from the first Letter of Saint Paul to the Corinthians (1.1-3)

From Paul, called to be an Apostle of Christ Jesus by the will of God, and from our brother **Sosthenes**. To the Church of God that is in Corinth, to those who are sanctified in Christ Jesus, called to be saints, together with all those who in every place call on the name of our Lord Jesus Christ, both their Lord and ours:

Grace to you and peace from God our Father and the Lord Jesus Christ.

The word of the Lord. **Thanks be to God.**

A reading from the holy Gospel according to John (1.29-34)

John the Baptist saw Jesus coming toward him and declared, "Here is the **Lamb of God** who takes away the sin of the world! This is he of whom I said, 'After me comes a man who ranks ahead of me because he was before me.' I myself did not know him; but I came baptizing with water for this reason, that he might be revealed to Israel."

And John **testified**, "I saw the Spirit descending from heaven like a dove, and remain on him. I myself did not know him, but the one who sent me to baptize with water said to me, 'He on whom you see the Spirit descend and remain is the one who baptizes with the Holy Spirit.' And I myself have seen and have testified that this is the **Son of God**."

The Gospel of the Lord. **Praise to you, Lord Jesus Christ.**

Key Words

A **servant** is someone who carries out the wishes of their master. God's servant will bring together the tribes of Israel. Christians believe that Jesus, the Messiah, came to bring all people back to God.

Jacob was the grandson of Abraham and the father of many children. His children were the first people in the twelve tribes of the Jewish people. In this reading, Jacob represents all the people of Israel.

Sosthenes was a friend and companion of Saint Paul who helped him spread the Good News of Jesus Christ to the people in Corinth in Greece.

When Saint Paul says "**grace to you and peace**," he is expressing his wish that we will all live according to the gifts that Jesus' salvation brings, especially peace.

The **Lamb of God** is Jesus. Jewish people made sacrifices of animals to God. Because Jesus' sacrifice brought us back to God, John the Baptist compares Jesus to a lamb.

To **testify** is to announce a truth with words or deeds, so that others will know the truth. We testify that Jesus lives when we live as he taught us.

John the Baptist calls Jesus the **Son of God**, showing that Jesus is the Messiah, the long-awaited one sent from God to bring us salvation.

A reading from the book of the Prophet Isaiah
(9.1-4)

There will be no gloom for those who were in anguish. In the former time the Lord brought into contempt the land of **Zebulun** and the land of **Naphtali**, but in the latter time he will make glorious the way of the sea, the land beyond the Jordan, Galilee of the nations.

The people who **walked in darkness** have seen a great light; those who lived in a land of deep darkness — on them light has shone. You have multiplied the nation, you have increased its joy; they rejoice before you as with joy at the harvest, as people exult when dividing plunder.

For the yoke of their burden, and the bar across their shoulders, the rod of their oppressor, you have broken as on the day of Midian.

The word of the Lord. **Thanks be to God.**

Psalm 27

R. **The Lord is my light and my salvation.**

The Lord is my light and my salvation;
whom shall I fear?
The Lord is the stronghold of my life;
of whom shall I be afraid? R.

One thing I asked of the Lord, that will I seek after:
to live in the house of the Lord all the days of my life,
to behold the beauty of the Lord,
and to inquire in his temple. R.

I believe that I shall see the goodness of the Lord
in the land of the living.
Wait for the Lord; be strong,
and let your heart take courage; wait for the Lord! R.

A reading from the first Letter of Saint Paul to the Corinthians (1.10-13, 17-18)

I appeal to you, brothers and sisters, by the name of our Lord Jesus Christ, that all of you be in agreement and that there be no divisions among you, but that you be united in the same mind and the same purpose.

For it has been reported to me by Chloe's people that there are quarrels among you, my brothers and sisters. What I mean is that each of you says, "I belong to Paul," or "I belong to Apollos," or "I belong to Cephas," or "I belong to Christ."

Has Christ been divided? Was Paul crucified for you? Or were you baptized in the name of Paul?

For Christ did not send me to baptize but to proclaim the Gospel, and not with eloquent wisdom so that the Cross of Christ might not be emptied of its power.

For the message about the Cross is foolishness to those who are perishing, but to us who are being saved it is the power of God.

The word of the Lord. **Thanks be to God.**

A reading from the holy Gospel according to Matthew (4.12-23)

The shorter version ends at the asterisks.

When Jesus heard that John had been arrested, he withdrew to Galilee. He left Nazareth and made his home in Capernaum by the sea, in the territory of Zebulun and Naphtali, so that what had been spoken through the Prophet Isaiah might be fulfilled: "Land of Zebulun, land of Naphtali, on the road by the sea, across the Jordan, Galilee of the Gentiles — the people who sat in darkness have seen a great light, and for those who sat in the region and shadow of death light has dawned."

From that time Jesus began to proclaim, "**Repent**, for the **kingdom of heaven** has come near."

* * *

As he walked by the Sea of Galilee, he saw two brothers, Simon, who is called Peter, and Andrew his brother, casting a net into the sea, for they were fishermen. And he said to them, "Come, follow me, and I will make you fishers of people." Immediately they left their nets and followed him.

As he went from there, he saw two other brothers, James son of Zebedee and his brother John, in the boat with their father Zebedee, mending their nets, and he called them. Immediately they left the boat and their father, and followed him.

Jesus went throughout Galilee, teaching in their synagogues and proclaiming the good news of the kingdom and curing every disease and every sickness among the people.

The Gospel of the Lord. **Praise to you, Lord Jesus Christ.**

Key Words

When Isaiah mentions **Zebulun** and **Naphtali**, his listeners remember towns where God had shown his anger because the people did not heed his words. God promises to send the Messiah who will bring freedom and joy to God's people.

People, families or even nations can **walk in darkness** when they feel lost and do not know where to turn. They need God's light to show them the way.

Saul was a man who bullied and terrorized the first Christians. One day, he had a vision of the risen Jesus and the experience changed his whole life. When he was baptized he changed his name to **Paul** and became a great apostle, travelling to cities all around the Mediterranean Sea to tell people about the love of Jesus. Several letters he wrote are now in the Bible.

The holy Gospel according to Matthew is the first book in the New Testament. This Gospel tells us about the life of Jesus. It points out that he is the promised Messiah, and that the Church is the chosen people, the new Israel.

To **repent** means to be sorry for doing something wrong, and to change your way of thinking and living for the better.

In the **kingdom of heaven**, all people will be brought together in God. We will all live like brothers and sisters, sharing in God's abundant love and mercy.

January 29

4th Sunday in Ordinary Time

A reading from the book of the Prophet Zephaniah (2.3; 3.12-13)

Seek the Lord, all you humble of the land,
who do his commands;
seek righteousness, seek **humility**;
perhaps you may be hidden on the day of the Lord's wrath.

For I will leave in the midst of you
a people humble and lowly.
They shall seek refuge in the name of the Lord —
the **remnant of Israel**;
they shall do no wrong and utter no lies,
nor shall a deceitful tongue be found in their mouths.
Then they will pasture and lie down,
and no one shall make them afraid.

The word of the Lord. **Thanks be to God.**

Psalm 146

R. **Blessed are the poor in spirit;
the kingdom of heaven is theirs!**

or **Alleluia!**

It is the Lord who keeps faith forever,
who executes justice for the oppressed;
who gives food to the hungry.
The Lord sets the prisoners free. R.

The Lord opens the eyes of the blind
and lifts up those who are bowed down;
the Lord loves the righteous
and watches over the strangers. R.

The Lord upholds the orphan and the widow,
but the way of the wicked he brings to ruin.
The Lord will reign forever,
your God, O Zion, for all generations. R.

A reading from the first Letter of Saint Paul to the Corinthians (1.26-31)

Consider your own call, brothers and sisters: not many of you were wise by human standards, not many were powerful, not many were of noble birth. But God chose what is foolish in the world to shame the wise; God chose what is weak in the world to shame the strong; God chose what is low and despised in the world, things that are not, to reduce to nothing things that are, so that no one might boast in the presence of God.

God is the **source** of your life in Christ Jesus, who became for us wisdom from God, and righteousness and sanctification and redemption, in order that, as it is written, "Let the one who boasts, boast in the Lord."

The word of the Lord. **Thanks be to God.**

A reading from the holy Gospel according to Matthew (5.1-12)

When Jesus saw the crowds, he went up the mountain; and after he sat down, his disciples came to him. Then he began to speak, and taught them, saying:

"Blessed are the **poor in spirit**,
for theirs is the kingdom of heaven.
Blessed are those who mourn,
for they will be comforted.
Blessed are the meek,
for they will inherit the earth.
Blessed are those who hunger and thirst for righteousness,
for they will be filled.

"Blessed are the **merciful**,
for they will receive mercy.
Blessed are the pure in heart,
for they will see God.
Blessed are the peacemakers,
for they will be called children of God.
Blessed are those who are persecuted for righteousness' sake,
for theirs is the kingdom of heaven.

"Blessed are you when people revile you and persecute you and utter all kinds of evil against you falsely on my account. Rejoice and be glad, for your reward is great in heaven, for in the same way they persecuted the Prophets who were before you."

The Gospel of the Lord. **Praise to you, Lord Jesus Christ.**

Key Words

The prophet **Zephaniah** lived about 700 years before Jesus was born. The people of Israel had fallen away from their faith. Zephaniah tried to help them return to God.

People who have **humility** do not show off or boast. They don't worry about how much money they have, but try in their hearts to do the will of God and think of others before they think of themselves.

In times when many of the Israelites had turned away from God, the few who remained faithful to God's covenant were called the **remnant of Israel**.

The **Corinthians** were a community of Christians who lived in Corinth, a city in Greece. Saint Paul wrote them several letters, two of which are in the Bible.

The **source** is the spot where a river or a stream begins — where life-giving water originates. God is the source of our life — we are united with Jesus by the waters of baptism.

The **poor in spirit** are people who put their confidence in God and do not worry about material things. The poor in spirit are in fact rich in God's spirit.

Those who are **merciful** share in God's loving concern for everyone, but most especially for the poor and the weak. They are always ready to forgive and show mercy. Jesus asks us to be merciful.

February 5
5th Sunday in Ordinary Time

A reading from the book of the Prophet Isaiah
(58.6-10)

Thus says the Lord:
Is this not the **fast** that I choose:
to loose the bonds of injustice,
to undo the thongs of the **yoke**,
to let the oppressed go free,
and to break every yoke?
Is it not to share your bread with the hungry,
and bring the homeless poor into your house;
when you see the naked, to cover them,
and not to hide yourself from your own kin?

Then your light shall break forth like the dawn,
and your healing shall spring up quickly;
your **vindicator** shall go before you,
the glory of the Lord shall be your rear guard.
Then you shall call, and the Lord will answer;
you shall cry for help, and he will say, Here I am.

If you remove the yoke from among you,
the pointing of the finger, the speaking of evil,
if you offer your food to the hungry
and satisfy the needs of the afflicted,
then your light shall rise in the darkness
and your gloom be like the noonday.

The word of the Lord. **Thanks be to God.**

Psalm 112

R. **Light rises in the darkness for the upright.**

or **Alleluia!**

Light rises in the darkness for the upright:
gracious, merciful and righteous.
It is well with the person who deals generously and lends,
who conducts their affairs with justice. R.

R̺. **Light rises in the darkness for the upright.**

For the righteous person will never be moved;
they will be remembered forever.
Unafraid of evil tidings;
their heart is firm, secure in the Lord. R̺.

That person's heart is steady and will not be afraid.
One who has distributed freely, who has given to the poor,
their righteousness endures forever:
their name is exalted in honour. R̺.

A reading from the first Letter of Saint Paul to the Corinthians (2.1-5)

When I came to you, brothers and sisters, I did not come proclaiming the mystery of God to you in lofty words or wisdom. For I decided to know nothing among you except Jesus Christ, and him crucified.

And I came to you in weakness and in fear and in much trembling. My speech and my proclamation were not with **plausible** words of wisdom, but with a demonstration of the Spirit and of power, so that your faith might rest not on human wisdom but on the power of God.

The word of the Lord. **Thanks be to God.**

A reading from the holy Gospel according to Matthew (5.13-16)

Jesus said to his disciples: "You are the **salt** of the earth; but if salt has lost its taste, how can its saltiness be restored? It is no longer good for anything, but is thrown out and trampled under foot.

"You are the light of the world. A city built on a hill cannot be hidden. No one after lighting a lamp puts it under the bushel basket, but on the lampstand, and it gives light to all in the house. In the same way, let your light shine before human beings, so that they may see your good works and give glory to your Father in heaven."

The Gospel of the Lord. **Praise to you, Lord Jesus Christ.**

Key Words

When we **fast**, we eat less than usual in order to focus more closely on God. It is also a way of sympathizing with the poor, since the poor often don't have enough to eat. In this reading from Isaiah, God tells us that when we fast, we must also work to ease the burdens of the poor; otherwise, our fasting is without purpose.

A **yoke** is a heavy wooden frame that fits over a person's shoulders so they can carry buckets of water or pull a plough. Imagine how good it feels, after a long day working in the hot sun, to remove the yoke! God wants us to help one another to remove any burdens we might be carrying.

A **vindicator** is a person who proves that something is true or right. When we obey God and defend what is right, God is our vindicator; God shows that our work is good and right.

Saint Paul tells the people of Corinth that our lives are not based on **plausible** or believable words of wisdom, but rather on the work of the Spirit. We do not rely on our own power but on the power of God.

Salt brings out the flavours of the foods we eat. In ancient times, salt was an essential preservative for meat, fish and vegetables, since refrigerators did not exist. Because of its long-lasting, preserving nature, salt became a symbol of enduring friendships and a sign of a contract between persons or groups. As "salt of the earth," Jesus' followers bring out the best flavours in life, preserve the Good News of Jesus' loving presence, and are faithful friends of God.

A reading from the book of Sirach (15.15-20)

If you choose, you can keep the commandments, and they will save you. If you trust in God, you too shall live, and to act faithfully is a matter of your own choice.

The Lord has placed before you fire and water; stretch out your hand for whichever you choose. Before each person are life and death, good and evil and whichever one chooses, that shall be given.

For great is the wisdom of the Lord; he is mighty in power and sees everything; his eyes are on those who fear him, and he knows every human action. He has not commanded anyone to be wicked, and he has not given anyone permission to sin.

The word of the Lord. **Thanks be to God.**

Psalm 119

R. **Blessed are those who walk in the law of the Lord!**

Blessed are those whose way is blameless,
who walk in the **law** of the Lord.
Blessed are those who keep his **decrees**,
who seek him with their whole heart. R.

You have commanded your **precepts**
to be kept diligently.
O that my ways may be steadfast
in keeping your **statutes!** R.

Deal bountifully with your servant,
so that I may live and observe your word.
Open my eyes, so that I may behold
wondrous things out of your law. R.

Teach me, O Lord, the way of your statutes,
and I will observe it to the end.
Give me understanding, that I may keep your law
and observe it with my whole heart. R.

A reading from the first Letter of Saint Paul to the Corinthians (2.6-10)

Brothers and sisters: Among the mature we do speak wisdom, though it is not a wisdom of this age or of the rulers of this age, who are doomed to perish. But we speak God's wisdom, **secret and hidden**, which God decreed before the ages for our glory. None of the rulers of this age understood this; for if they had, they would not have crucified the Lord of glory.

As it is written, "What no eye has seen, nor ear heard, nor the human heart conceived, what God has prepared for those who love him." These things God has revealed to us through the Spirit; for the Spirit searches everything, even the depths of God.

The word of the Lord. **Thanks be to God.**

A reading from the holy Gospel according to Matthew (5.17-37)

For the shorter version, omit the indented parts.

Jesus said to his disciples: "Do not think that I have come to abolish the Law or the Prophets; I have come not to abolish but to **fulfill**.

> For truly I tell you, until heaven and earth pass away, not one letter, not one stroke of a letter, will pass from the Law until all is accomplished. Therefore, whoever breaks one of the least of these commandments, and teaches others to do the same, will be called least in the kingdom of heaven; but whoever does them and teaches them will be called great in the kingdom of heaven.

"For I tell you, unless your righteousness exceeds that of the scribes and Pharisees, you will never enter the kingdom of heaven.

"You have heard that it was said to those of ancient times, 'You shall not murder'; and 'whoever murders shall be liable to judgment.' But I say to you that the one who is angry with their brother or sister, will be liable to judgment; and whoever insults their brother or sister, will be liable to the council; and whoever says, 'You fool,' will be liable to the hell of fire.

"So when you are offering your gift at the altar, if you remember that your brother or sister has something against you, leave your gift there before the altar and go; first be reconciled to your brother or sister, and then come and offer your gift.

"Come to terms quickly with your accuser while the two of you are on the way to court, or your accuser may hand you over to the judge, and the judge to the guard, and you will be thrown into prison. Truly I tell you, you will never get out until you have paid the last penny.

"You have heard that it was said, 'You shall not commit adultery.' But I say to you that everyone who looks at a woman with lust has already committed adultery with her in his heart.

"If your right eye causes you to sin, tear it out and throw it away; it is better for you to lose one of your members than for your whole body to be thrown into hell. And if your right hand causes you to sin, cut it off and throw it away; it is better for you to lose one of your members than for your whole body to go into hell.

"It was also said, 'Whoever divorces his wife, let him give her a certificate of divorce.' But I say to you that anyone who divorces his wife, except on the ground of unchastity, causes her to commit adultery; and whoever marries a divorced woman commits adultery.

"Again, you have heard that it was said to those of ancient times, 'You shall not **swear falsely**, but carry out the vows you have made to the Lord.' But I say to you: Do not swear at all.

either by heaven, for it is the throne of God, or by the earth, for it is his footstool, or by Jerusalem, for it is the city of the great King. And do not swear by your head, for you cannot make one hair white or black.

"Let your word be 'Yes,' if 'Yes,' or 'No,' if 'No'; anything more than this comes from the evil one."

The Gospel of the Lord. **Praise to you, Lord Jesus Christ.**

Key Words

The book of **Sirach** in the Bible was written 200 years before Jesus was born. In some Bibles, it is called the book of Ecclesiasticus. It tells us that wisdom is respecting God and obeying God's plans for us.

In the Psalm, the writer uses legal terms when he speaks about following God: **law, decrees, precepts and statutes**. We might think it is hard to follow all these rules, but the psalmist sees these laws as blessings and life-giving. Jesus says in the Gospel that he has come not to abolish the law but to **fulfill** it.

Saint Paul speaks of God's wisdom as **secret and hidden**: it cannot be known by logic or reason. God reveals his wisdom to us through the Spirit. Those who rely on worldly wisdom will not have eternal life.

To swear is to make a promise relying on something or someone else, and to **swear falsely** is to break a promise, or to lie when we are making that promise. Because we are not perfect as God is, Jesus says that it is better if we do not make any promises that we cannot keep.

A reading from the book of Leviticus
(19.1-2, 17-18)

The Lord spoke to Moses:
"Speak to all the congregation of the children of Israel
and say to them:
'You shall be holy, for I the Lord your God am holy.
You shall not hate in your heart anyone of your kin;
you shall **reprove** your neighbour,
or you will incur guilt yourself.
You shall not take vengeance
or bear a grudge against any of your people,
but you shall love your neighbour as yourself:
I am the Lord.'"

The word of the Lord. **Thanks be to God.**

Psalm 103

R. **The Lord is merciful and gracious.**

Bless the Lord, O my soul,
and all that is within me, bless his holy name.
Bless the Lord, O my soul,
and do not forget all his benefits. R.

It is the Lord who forgives all your iniquity,
who heals all your diseases,
who redeems your life from the Pit,
who crowns you with steadfast love and mercy. R.

The Lord is merciful and gracious,
slow to anger and abounding in steadfast love.
He does not deal with us according to our sins,
nor repay us according to our iniquities. R.

As far as the east is from the west,
so far he removes our transgressions from us.
As a father has compassion for his children,
so the Lord has compassion for those who fear him. R.

A reading from the first Letter of Saint Paul to the Corinthians (3.16-23)

Brothers and sisters: Do you not know that you are God's **temple** and that God's Spirit dwells in you? If anyone destroys God's temple, God will destroy that person. For God's temple is holy, and you are that temple.

Do not deceive yourselves. If you think that you are wise in this age, you should become fools so that you may become wise. For the wisdom of this world is foolishness with God. For it is written, "He catches the wise in their craftiness," and again, "The Lord knows the thoughts of the wise, that they are futile."

So let no one boast about human beings. For all things are yours — whether Paul or Apollos or Cephas, or the world or life or death, or the present or the future — all belong to you, and you belong to Christ, and Christ belongs to God.

The word of the Lord. **Thanks be to God.**

A reading from the holy Gospel according to Matthew (5.38-48)

Jesus said to his disciples, "You have heard that it was said, '**An eye for an eye** and a tooth for a tooth.' But I say to you, Do not resist an evildoer. But if anyone strikes you on the right cheek, turn the other also; and if anyone wants to sue you and take your **coat**, give your **cloak** as well; and if anyone forces you to go one mile, go with them also the second mile. Give to everyone who begs from you, and do not refuse anyone who wants to borrow from you.

"You have heard that it was said, 'You shall love your neighbour and hate your enemy.' But I say to you, Love your enemies and pray for those who persecute you, so that you may be children of your Father in heaven; for he makes his sun rise on the evil and on the good, and sends rain on the righteous and on the unrighteous.

"For if you love those who love you, what reward do you have? Do not even the tax collectors do the same? And if you greet only your brothers and sisters, what more are you doing than others? Do not even the Gentiles do the same? Be perfect, therefore, as your heavenly Father is perfect."

The Gospel of the Lord. **Praise to you, Lord Jesus Christ.**

Key Words

To **reprove** is to correct someone or show them where they have done something wrong. The Lord tells Moses that we have a duty to do this, but we must do it in a loving way — loving our neighbour as ourselves.

A **temple** is a place where God dwells — a synagogue or a church, for example. It is startling when Saint Paul reminds us that our bodies and souls are God's temple! We must take good care of our bodies as well as live lives of justice and mercy.

It seems harsh to us when Jesus mentions the saying, "**An eye for an eye**." But this saying was seen as just and fair, for it meant that compensation for an injury was limited to the value of what had been harmed or taken. What Jesus proposes is radical and surprising, going beyond what was ordinarily seen as acceptable.

In the time of Jesus, most people owned two garments — a **coat** for daytime use, and a **cloak** to provide warmth night and day. When Jesus says to offer not only your coat but your cloak as well, he is saying to let go of everything you have!

February 26
8th Sunday in Ordinary Time

A reading from the book of the Prophet Isaiah
(49.14-15)

Zion said, "The Lord has forsaken me,
my Lord has forgotten me."
Can a woman forget her nursing child,
or show no compassion for the child of her womb?
Even these may forget,
yet I will not forget you.

The word of the Lord. **Thanks be to God.**

Psalm 62

R̰. **For God alone my soul waits in silence.**

For God alone my soul waits in silence;
from him comes my salvation.
He alone is my rock and my salvation, my fortress;
I shall never be shaken. R̰.

For God alone my soul waits in silence,
for my hope is from him.
He alone is my rock and my salvation, my fortress;
I shall not be shaken. R̰.

On God rests my deliverance and my honour;
my mighty rock, my refuge is in God.
Trust in him at all times, O people;
pour out your heart before him. R̰.

A reading from the first Letter of Saint Paul to the Corinthians (4.1-5)

Brothers and sisters: Think of us in this way, as servants of Christ and **stewards** of God's mysteries. Moreover, it is required of stewards that they be found trustworthy.

But with me it is a very small thing that I should be judged by you or by any human court. I do not even judge myself. I am not aware of anything against myself, but I am not thereby acquitted. It is the Lord who judges me.

Therefore do not pronounce judgment before the time, before the Lord comes, who will bring to light the things now hidden in darkness and will disclose the purposes of the heart. Then each one will receive commendation from God.

The word of the Lord. **Thanks be to God.**

A reading from the holy Gospel according to Matthew (6.24-34)

Jesus taught his disciples, saying. "No one can serve two masters; for a slave will either hate the one and love the other, or be devoted to the one and despise the other. You cannot serve God and wealth.

"Therefore I tell you, do not worry about your life, what you will eat or what you will drink, or about your body, what you will wear. Is not life more than food, and the body more than clothing?

"Look at the birds of the air; they neither sow nor reap nor gather into barns, and yet your heavenly Father feeds them. Are you not of more value than they? And can any one of you by worrying add a single hour to their span of life?

"And why do you worry about clothing? Consider the lilies of the field, how they grow; they neither toil nor spin, yet I tell you, even **Solomon** in all his glory was not clothed like one of these. But if God so clothes the grass of the field, which is **alive today** and tomorrow is thrown into the oven, will he not much more clothe you — you of little faith?

"Therefore do not worry, saying, 'What will we eat?' or 'What will we drink?' or 'What will we wear?' For it is the Gentiles who strive for all these things; and indeed your heavenly Father knows that you need all these things. But strive first for the kingdom of God and his righteousness, and all these things will be given to you as well.

"So do not worry about tomorrow, for tomorrow will bring worries of its own. Today's trouble is enough for today."

The Gospel of the Lord. **Praise to you, Lord Jesus Christ.**

Key Words

Zion was the name of a hill in Jerusalem, where the temple was built, but the city and the people living within it were often called Zion as well. Zion is another way of naming the entire nation, the whole people of God.

Stewards are people who are given the responsibility to care for and manage things that belong to someone else. They are given this task because they are honest and trustworthy. Saint Paul tells us that as Christians we are stewards of God's mysteries.

Solomon became king of Israel after his father David. Solomon was famous for his wisdom and for the beauty and magnificence of his royal court.

The land around Israel is naturally dry and brown most of the year. When wild grasses and flowers bloom, they live a short time and then wither — they are **alive today** and gone shortly after. Jesus uses the example of these plants to show us how insignificant are the things we worry so much about.

March 1
Ash Wednesday

A reading from the book of the Prophet Joel
(2.12-18)

Even now, says the Lord, return to me with all your heart, with fasting, with weeping, and with mourning; **rend** your hearts and not your clothing.

Return to the Lord, your God, for he is gracious and merciful, slow to anger, and abounding in steadfast love, and relents from punishing.

Who knows whether the Lord will not turn and relent, and leave a blessing behind him: a grain offering and a drink offering to be presented to the Lord, your God?

Blow the trumpet in Zion; sanctify a fast; call a solemn assembly; gather the people. Sanctify the **congregation**; assemble the aged; gather the children, even infants at the breast. Let the bridegroom leave his room, and the bride her canopy.

Between the vestibule and the altar let the priests, the ministers of the Lord, weep. Let them say, "Spare your people, O Lord, and do not make your heritage a mockery, a byword among the nations. Why should it be said among the peoples, 'Where is their God?'"

Then the Lord became jealous for his land, and had pity on his people.

The word of the Lord. **Thanks be to God.**

Psalm 51

R. **Have mercy, O Lord, for we have sinned.**

Have mercy on me, O God,
according to your steadfast love;
according to your abundant mercy
blot out my transgressions.
Wash me thoroughly from my iniquity,
and cleanse me from my sin. R.

For I know my transgressions,
and my sin is ever before me.
Against you, you alone, have I sinned,
and done what is evil in your sight. R.

Create in me a clean heart, O God,
and put a new and right spirit within me.
Do not cast me away from your presence,
and do not take your holy spirit from me. R.

Restore to me the joy of your salvation,
and sustain in me a willing spirit.
O Lord, open my lips,
and my mouth will declare your praise. R.

A reading from the second Letter of Saint Paul to the Corinthians (5.20 – 6.2)

Brothers and sisters: We are **ambassadors** for Christ, since God is making his appeal through us; we entreat you on behalf of Christ, be **reconciled** to God. For our sake God made Christ to be sin who knew no sin, so that in Christ we might become the righteousness of God. As we work together with him, we urge you also not to accept the grace of God in vain. For the Lord says, "At an acceptable time I have listened to you, and on a day of salvation I have helped you." See, now is the acceptable time; see, now is the day of salvation!

The word of the Lord. **Thanks be to God.**

A reading from the holy Gospel according to Matthew (6.1-6, 16-18)

Jesus said to the disciples: "Beware of practising your piety before people in order to be seen by them; for then you have no reward from your Father in heaven.

"So whenever you give **alms**, do not sound a trumpet before you, as the **hypocrites** do in the synagogues and in the streets, so that they may be praised by others. Truly I tell you, they have received their reward. But when you give alms, do not let your left hand know what your right hand is doing, so that your alms may be done in secret; and your Father who sees in secret will reward you.

"And whenever you pray, do not be like the hypocrites; for they love to stand and pray in the synagogues and at the street corners, so that they may be seen by others. Truly I tell you, they have received their reward. But whenever you pray, go into your room and shut the door and pray to your Father who is in secret; and your Father who sees in secret will reward you.

"And whenever you fast, do not look dismal, like the hypocrites, for they disfigure their faces so as to show others that they are fasting. Truly I tell you, they have received their reward. But when you fast, put oil on your head and wash your face, so that your fasting may be seen not by others but by your Father who is in secret; and your Father who sees in secret will reward you."

The Gospel of the Lord. **Praise to you, Lord Jesus Christ.**

Key Words

Ash Wednesday marks the beginning of Lent. Ashes are used as a sign of our sorrow for having turned away from God; they are placed on our forehead in the sign of the cross and we keep them until they wear off. The ashes are often produced by burning palms from the previous year's Passion (Palm) Sunday celebration.

To **rend** something is to tear it apart forcefully. In biblical times, people would tear their clothing and cover themselves with ashes as signs of their repentance or sorrow. The Prophet Joel is saying that God would rather we rend or open our hearts as a sign of our willingness to return to God.

A **congregation** is a gathering of people, usually for worship. In the Hebrew Scriptures, it can also mean the whole people of God.

Ambassadors are messengers who have special authority to deliver a message or speak on someone else's behalf. Saint Paul is telling us that we have a role to play as followers of Christ: we are chosen to spread the Good News. If we are to be faithful messengers, then we must open our hearts and be reconciled to God.

To be **reconciled** means to be 'at-one' with someone, by making up for something wrong we may have done. Through his death, Jesus makes up for our sins and we are reconciled with God.

The three traditional Lenten practices are prayer, fasting and almsgiving. To give **alms** is to give money to the poor. The word comes from the Greek word for compassion or pity. During Lent, we not only focus on our own spiritual life, we also make a special effort to help those around us who are in need.

Hypocrites are people whose actions don't match their words. They may say they love God, but they don't act in a loving way. Such behaviour hurts that person, those around them and God.

March 5
1st Sunday of Lent

A reading from the book of Genesis
(2.7-9, 16-18, 25; 3.1-7)

The Lord God formed man from the dust of the ground, and **breathed** into his nostrils the breath of life; and the man became a living being. And the Lord God planted a garden in Eden, in the east; and there he put the man whom he had formed. Out of the ground the Lord God made to grow every tree that is pleasant to the sight and good for food, the tree of life also in the midst of the garden, and the tree of the knowledge of **good and evil**.

And the Lord God commanded the man, "You may freely eat of every tree of the garden; but of the tree of the knowledge of good and evil you shall not eat, for in the day that you eat of it you shall die."

Then the Lord God said, "It is not good that the man should be alone; I will make him a helper as his partner." And the man and his wife were both naked, and were not ashamed.

Now the serpent was more crafty than any other wild animal that the Lord God had made. He said to the woman, "Did God say, 'You shall not eat from any tree in the garden'?" The woman said to the serpent, "We may eat of the fruit of the trees in the garden; but God said, 'You shall not eat of the fruit of the tree that is in the middle of the garden, nor shall you touch it, or you shall die.'" But the serpent said to the woman, "You will not die; for God knows that when you eat of it your eyes will be opened, and you will be like God, knowing good and evil." So when the woman saw that the tree was good for food, and that it was a delight to the eyes, and that the tree was to be desired to make one wise, she took of its fruit and ate; and she also gave some to her husband, who was with her, and he ate.

Then the eyes of both were opened, and they knew that they were naked; and they sewed fig leaves together and made loincloths for themselves.

The word of the Lord. **Thanks be to God.**

Psalm 51

R. **Have mercy, O Lord, for we have sinned.**

Have mercy on me, O God,
according to your steadfast love;
according to your abundant mercy
blot out my transgressions.
Wash me thoroughly from my iniquity,
and cleanse me from my sin. R.

For I know my transgressions,
and my sin is ever before me.
Against you, you alone, have I sinned,
and done what is evil in your sight. R.

Create in me a clean heart, O God,
and put a new and right spirit within me.
Do not cast me away from your presence,
and do not take your holy spirit from me. R.

Restore to me the joy of your salvation,
and sustain in me a willing spirit.
O Lord, open my lips,
and my mouth will declare your praise. R.

A reading from the Letter of Saint Paul to the Romans (5.12-19)

For the shorter version, omit the indented parts.

Brothers and sisters: Just as sin came into the world through one man, and death came through sin, so death spread to all people, because all have sinned.

Sin was indeed in the world before the law, but sin is not reckoned when there is no law. Yet death exercised dominion from Adam to Moses, even over those whose sins were not like the transgression of Adam, who is a type of the one who was to come.

But the free gift is not like the trespass. For if the many died through the one man's trespass, much more surely have the grace of God and the free gift in the grace of the one man,

Jesus Christ, abounded for the many. And the free gift is not like the effect of the one man's sin. For the judgment following one trespass brought condemnation, but the free gift following many trespasses brings justification.

If, because of the one man's trespass, death exercised dominion through that one, much more surely will those who receive the abundance of grace and the free gift of righteousness exercise dominion in life through the one man, Jesus Christ.

Therefore just as one man's trespass led to condemnation for all people, so one man's act of righteousness leads to justification and life for all people. For just as by the one man's disobedience the many were made sinners, so by the one man's obedience the many will be made righteous.

The word of the Lord. **Thanks be to God.**

A reading from the holy Gospel according to Matthew (4.1-11)

Jesus was led up by the Spirit into the wilderness to be **tempted** by the devil. He fasted forty days and forty nights, and afterwards he was famished. The tempter came and said to him, "If you are the Son of God, command these stones to become loaves of bread." But he answered, "It is written, 'Man does not live by bread alone, but by every word that comes from the mouth of God.'"

Then the devil took him to the holy city and placed him on the **pinnacle** of the temple, saying to him, "If you are the Son of God, throw yourself down; for it is written, 'He will command his Angels concerning you,' and 'On their hands they will bear you up, so that you will not dash your foot against a stone.'" Jesus said to him, "Again it is written, 'Do not put the Lord your God to the test.'"

Again, the devil took him to a very high mountain and showed him all the kingdoms of the world and their splendour; and he said to him, "All these I will give you, if you will fall down and **worship** me." Jesus said to him, "Away with you, Satan! for it is written, 'Worship the Lord your God, and serve only him.'"

Then the devil left him, and suddenly Angels came and waited on him.

The Gospel of the Lord. **Praise to you, Lord Jesus Christ.**

Key Words

Genesis is the first book of the Bible. It tells many stories, including the stories of creation, Adam and Eve, the Flood, Abraham, and the people's faith in God. These stories help us understand that God loves us and wants us to love him too.

God **breathed** life into the first human being. This is a way of showing us how we share God's life. One meaning of "inspiration" is "breathing in."

It is hard to understand fully the notions of **good and evil**. In this story from Genesis, we see evil as an enemy of God's, an enemy who tempts us to turn away from our Creator who is all-good.

The letter of Saint Paul to the Romans was written to the small community of Christians who lived in Rome. Saint Paul wanted to visit them, so he sent them this letter ahead of him, to encourage them and to remind them of the teachings of Jesus.

When we are **tempted**, we think about doing something we know to be wrong. The Spirit of God within us gives us the strength to say no to temptation. Every time we pray the Our Father, we ask God to give us this strength.

The **pinnacle** of the temple was its highest point. From here, Jesus could see a great distance. It was also dangerously high.

When we **worship** God, we praise him for his love and mercy.

March 12

2nd Sunday of Lent

A reading from the book of Genesis (12.1-4)

The Lord said to **Abram**, "Go from your country and your kindred and your father's house to the land that I will show you. I will make of you a **great nation**, and I will bless you, and make your name great, so that you will be a blessing. I will bless those who bless you, and the one who curses you I will curse; and in you all the families of the earth shall be blessed."

So Abram went, as the Lord had told him.

The word of the Lord. **Thanks be to God.**

Psalm 33

R. **Let your love be upon us, Lord,
even as we hope in you.**

The word of the Lord is upright,
and all his work is done in faithfulness.
He loves righteousness and justice;
the earth is full of the steadfast love of the Lord. R.

Truly the eye of the Lord is on those who fear him,
on those who hope in his steadfast love,
to deliver their soul from death,
and to keep them alive in famine. R.

Our soul waits for the Lord;
he is our help and shield.
Let your steadfast love, O Lord, be upon us,
even as we hope in you. R.

A reading from the second Letter of Saint Paul to Timothy (1.8-10)

Brothers and sisters: Join with me in suffering for the Gospel, relying on the power of God, who saved us and called us with a holy **calling**, not according to our works but according to his own purpose and grace.

This grace was given to us in Christ Jesus before the ages began, but it has now been revealed through the appearing of our Saviour Christ Jesus, who abolished death and brought life and **immortality** to light through the Gospel.

The word of the Lord. **Thanks be to God.**

A reading from the holy Gospel according to Matthew (17.1-9)

Jesus took with him Peter and James and his brother John and led them up a high mountain, by themselves. And he was **transfigured** before them, and his face shone like the sun, and his clothes became dazzling white. Suddenly there appeared to them Moses and Elijah, talking with him.

Then Peter said to Jesus, "Lord, it is good for us to be here; if you wish, I will make three dwellings here, one for you, one for Moses, and one for **Elijah**."

While he was still speaking, suddenly a bright cloud overshadowed them, and from the cloud a voice said, "This is my Son, the Beloved; with him I am well pleased; listen to him!"

When the disciples heard this, they fell to the ground and were overcome by fear. But Jesus came and touched them, saying, "Get up and do not be afraid." And when they looked up, they saw no one except Jesus himself alone.

As they were coming down the mountain, Jesus ordered them, "Tell no one about the vision until after the Son of Man has been raised from the dead."

The Gospel of the Lord. **Praise to you, Lord Jesus Christ.**

Key Words

Abram means "noble father." Abram had true faith in God. God promised that if Abram was faithful to God, he would become the head of a huge family. When he proved his faithfulness, God then gave him a new name: Abraham, which means "father of many."

Abraham's descendants (including us) became a **great nation**, as God had promised. The people of God all over the world are also a great nation, brothers and sisters in Christ.

Timothy was a friend of Saint Paul's. He helped Paul to spread the Gospel and was in charge of the Church in Ephesus, Greece. In the New Testament there are two letters to Timothy.

When we live the life Jesus has planned for us, we are responding to his **calling**. Little by little, God opens our ears so that we will hear this call and follow Jesus.

Because Jesus died and rose again, and because we are united with Jesus, we share in his **immortality** (life without death).

When Jesus was **transfigured**, he looked different somehow. His friends saw Jesus as he really is: the Son of God.

The prophet **Elijah** lived about 900 years before Jesus. He is one of the great prophets in the Hebrew Scriptures or Old Testament. He taught the people to believe in God alone.

March 19

3rd Sunday of Lent

A reading from the book of Exodus (17.3-7)

In the wilderness the people thirsted for water; and the people complained against Moses and said, "Why did you bring us out of Egypt, to kill us and our children and livestock with thirst?" So Moses cried out to the Lord, "What shall I do with this people? They are almost ready to stone me."

The Lord said to Moses, "Go on ahead of the people, and take some of the elders of Israel with you; take in your hand the **staff** with which you struck the Nile, and go. I will be standing there in front of you on the rock at Horeb. Strike the rock, and water will come out of it, so that the people may drink." Moses did so, in the sight of the elders of Israel.

He called the place Massah and Meribah, because the children of Israel quarrelled and tested the Lord, saying, "Is the Lord among us or not?"

The word of the Lord. **Thanks be to God.**

Psalm 95

R. **O that today you would listen to the voice of the Lord. Do not harden your hearts!**

O come, let us sing to the Lord;
let us make a joyful noise to the rock of our salvation!
Let us come into his presence with thanksgiving;
let us make a joyful noise to him with songs of praise! R.

O come, let us worship and bow down,
let us kneel before the Lord, our Maker!
For he is our God, and we are the people of his pasture,
and the sheep of his hand. R.

O that today you would listen to his voice!
Do not harden your hearts, as at Meribah,
as on the day at Massah in the wilderness,
when your ancestors tested me,
and put me to the proof,
though they had seen my work. R.

A reading from the Letter of Saint Paul to the Romans (5.1-2, 5-8)

Brothers and sisters: Since we are **justified** by faith, we have peace with God through our Lord Jesus Christ, through whom we have obtained access to this grace in which we stand; and we boast in our **hope** of sharing the glory of God.

And hope does not disappoint us, because God's love has been poured into our hearts through the Holy Spirit that has been given to us. For while we were still weak, at the right time Christ died for the ungodly. Indeed, rarely will anyone die for a righteous person — though perhaps for a good person someone might actually dare to die. But God proves his love for us in that while we still were sinners Christ died for us.

The word of the Lord. **Thanks be to God.**

A reading from the holy Gospel according to John (4.5-42)

For the shorter reading, omit the indented parts.

Jesus came to a Samaritan city called Sychar, near the plot of ground that **Jacob** had given to his son Joseph. Jacob's well was there, and Jesus, tired out by his journey, was sitting by the well. It was about noon.

A Samaritan woman came to draw water, and Jesus said to her, "Give me a drink." (His disciples had gone to the city to buy food.)

The Samaritan woman said to him, "How is it that you, a Jew, ask a drink of me, a woman of Samaria?" (Jews do not share things in common with Samaritans.) Jesus answered her, "If you knew the gift of God, and who it is that is saying to you, 'Give me a drink,' you would have asked him, and he would have given you living water."

The woman said to him, "Sir, you have no bucket, and the well is deep. Where do you get that living water? Are you greater than our father Jacob, who gave us the well, and with his children and his flocks drank from it?" Jesus said to her, "Everyone who drinks of this water will be thirsty again, but the one who drinks of the water that I will give will never be thirsty. The water that I will give him will become in him a

113

spring of water gushing up to eternal life." The woman said to him, "Sir, give me this water, so that I may never be thirsty or have to keep coming here to draw water."

Jesus said to her, "Go, call your husband, and come back." The woman answered him, "I have no husband." Jesus said to her, "You are right in saying, 'I have no husband'; for you have had five husbands, and the one you have now is not your husband. What you have said is true!" The woman said to him, "Sir,

"I see that you are a Prophet. Our ancestors worshipped on this mountain, but you say that the place where people must worship is in Jerusalem."

Jesus said to her, "Woman, believe me, the hour is coming when you will worship the Father neither on this mountain nor in Jerusalem. You worship what you do not know; we worship what we know, for salvation is from the Jews. But the hour is coming, and is now here, when the true worshippers will **worship the Father in spirit and truth**, for the Father seeks such as these to worship him. God is spirit, and those who worship him must worship in spirit and truth."

The woman said to him, "I know that the **Messiah** is coming" (who is called the Christ). "When he comes, he will proclaim all things to us." Jesus said to her, "I am he, the one who is speaking to you."

Just then his disciples came. They were astonished that he was speaking with a woman, but no one said, "What do you want?" or, "Why are you speaking with her?" Then the woman left her water jar and went back to the city. She said to the people, "Come and see a man who told me everything I have ever done! He cannot be the Messiah, can he?" They left the city and were on their way to him. Meanwhile the disciples were urging him, "Rabbi, eat something." But he said to them, "I have food to eat that you do not know about." So the disciples said to one another, "Surely no one has brought him something to eat?"

Jesus said to them, "My food is to do the will of him who sent me and to complete his work. Do you not say, 'Four months more, then comes the harvest'? But I tell you, look around you, and see how the fields are ripe for harvesting. The reaper is already receiving wages and is gathering fruit for eternal life, so that sower and reaper may rejoice together. For here the saying holds true, 'One sows and another reaps.' I sent you to reap that for which you did not labour. Others have laboured, and you have entered into their labour."

Many Samaritans from that city believed in Jesus.

because of the woman's testimony, "He told me everything I have ever done."

So when they [the Samaritans] came to him, they asked him to stay with them; and he stayed there two days. And many more believed because of his word. They said to the woman, "It is no longer because of what you said that we believe, for we have heard for ourselves, and we know that this is truly the Saviour of the world."

The Gospel of the Lord. **Praise to you, Lord Jesus Christ.**

Key Words

The book of **Exodus** is the second book of the Bible. It tells the story of how God freed his people from slavery in Egypt. God made a promise or covenant with his people and gave them the Ten Commandments to show them how to live well.

A **staff** is large stick or cane used by a shepherd and other herdsmen. It can also be used as a walking stick. It is a symbol of authority carried by a leader.

When we hurt others, we break our friendship with God. Jesus came to restore our friendship with God, and we are **justified** or brought back to God by our faith in Jesus.

We have **hope** or confidence that God will fulfill his promises. Hope is one of the three great Christian virtues. The other two are faith and love.

The holy Gospel according to John tells us about the life, death and resurrection of Jesus. It was written about 60 years after Jesus died. John's Gospel includes some stories and sayings that are not in the other three Gospels (Matthew, Mark and Luke).

Jacob, also called Israel, was the son of Isaac and the grandson of Abraham. The twelve tribes of Israel are all descended from Jacob.

When Jesus says to **worship the Father in spirit and truth**, he is reminding us that God does not want us to bring a sacrifice or gift when we worship. God would rather we bring him our hearts full of love.

Jesus and his disciples spoke Aramaic. **Messiah** is an Aramaic word meaning 'anointed.' The chosen person was anointed or blessed with holy oil and given a special mission. The Greek word for 'anointed' is 'Christ.'

March 26

4th Sunday of Lent

A reading from the first book of Samuel
(16.1, 6-7, 10-13)

The Lord said to Samuel, "Fill your horn with oil and set out; I will send you to Jesse of Bethlehem, for I have provided for myself a king among his sons."

When the sons of Jesse came, Samuel looked on Eliab and thought, "Surely the Lord's anointed is now before the Lord." But the Lord said to Samuel, "Do not look on his appearance or on the height of his stature, because I have rejected him; for the Lord does not see as the human sees; the human looks on the outward appearance, but the Lord looks on the heart."

Jesse made seven of his sons pass before Samuel, and Samuel said to Jesse, "The Lord has not chosen any of these." Samuel said to Jesse, "Are all your sons here?" And he said, "There remains yet the youngest, but he is keeping the sheep." And Samuel said to Jesse, "Send and bring him; for we will not sit down until he comes here." Jesse sent and brought David in. Now he was ruddy, and had beautiful eyes, and was handsome. The Lord said, "Rise and **anoint** him; for this is the one."

Then Samuel took the horn of oil, and anointed him in the presence of his brothers; and the spirit of the Lord came mightily upon David from that day forward.

The word of the Lord. **Thanks be to God.**

Psalm 23

R. **The Lord is my shepherd; I shall not want.**

The Lord is my shepherd, I shall not want.
He makes me lie down in green pastures;
he leads me beside still waters;
he restores my soul. R.

He leads me in right paths for his name's sake.
Even though I walk through the darkest valley,
    I fear no evil;
for you are with me;
your rod and your staff — they comfort me. R.

You prepare a table before me
in the presence of my enemies;
you anoint my head with oil;
my cup overflows. R.

Surely goodness and mercy shall follow me
all the days of my life,
and I shall dwell in the house of the Lord
my whole life long. R.

A reading from the Letter of Saint Paul to the Ephesians (5.8-14)

Brothers and sisters: Once you were darkness, but now in the Lord you are light. Live as children of light — for the fruit of the light is found in all that is good and right and true.

Try to find out what is pleasing to the Lord. Take no part in the unfruitful works of darkness, but instead expose them. For it is shameful even to mention what such people do secretly; but everything exposed by the light becomes visible, for everything that becomes visible is light. Therefore it is said, "Sleeper, awake! Rise from the dead, and Christ will shine on you."

The word of the Lord. **Thanks be to God.**

A reading from the holy Gospel according to John (9.1-41)

For the shorter version, omit the indented parts.

As Jesus walked along, he saw a man **blind** from birth.

His disciples asked him, "Rabbi, who sinned, this man or his parents, that he was born blind?"

Jesus answered, "Neither this man nor his parents sinned; he was born blind so that God's works might be revealed in him. We must work the works of him who sent me while it is day; night is coming when no one can work. As long as I am in the world, I am the light of the world." When he had said this,

He spat on the ground and made mud with the saliva and spread the mud on the man's eyes, saying to him, "Go, wash in the pool of Siloam" (which means Sent).

Then the man who was blind went and washed, and came back able to see. The neighbours and those who had seen him before as a beggar began to ask, "Is this not the man who used to sit and beg?" Some were saying, "It is he." Others were saying, "No, but it is someone like him." He kept saying, "I am the man."

But they kept asking him, "Then how were your eyes opened?" He answered, "The man called Jesus made mud, spread it on my eyes, and said to me, 'Go to Siloam and wash.' Then I went and washed and received my sight." They said to him, "Where is he?" He said, "I do not know."

They brought to the **Pharisees** the man who had formerly been blind. Now it was a Sabbath day when Jesus made the mud and opened his eyes. Then the Pharisees also began to ask him how he had received his sight. He said to them, "He put mud on my eyes. Then I washed, and now I see." Some of the Pharisees said, "This man is not from God, for he does not observe the **Sabbath**." But others said, "How can a man who is a sinner perform such signs?" And they were divided. So they said again to the blind man, "What do you say about him? It was your eyes he opened." He said, "He is a Prophet."

They did not believe that he had been blind and had received his sight until they called the parents of the man who had received his sight and asked them, "Is this your son, who you say was born blind? How then does he now see?" His parents answered, "We know that this is our son, and that he was born blind; but we do not know how it is that now he sees, nor do we know who opened his eyes. Ask him; he is of age. He will speak for himself." His parents said this because they were afraid of the Jewish authorities, who had already agreed that anyone who confessed Jesus to be the Messiah would be put out of the synagogue. Therefore his parents said, "He is of age; ask him."

So for the second time they called the man who had been blind, and they said to him, "Give glory to God! We know that this man is a sinner." He answered, "I do not know whether he is a sinner. One thing I do know, that though I was blind, now I see." They said to him, "What did he do to you? How did he open your eyes?" He answered them, "I have told you already, and you would not listen. Why do you want to hear it again? Do you also want to become his disciples?" Then they reviled him, saying, "You are his disciple, but we are disciples of Moses. We know that God has spoken to Moses, but as for this man, we do not know where he comes from."

The man answered, "Here is an astonishing thing! You do not know where he comes from, and yet he opened my eyes. We know that God does not listen to sinners, but he does listen to one who worships him and obeys his will. Never since the world began has it been heard that anyone opened the eyes of a person born blind. If this man were not from God, he could do nothing."

They answered him, "You were born entirely in sins, and are you trying to teach us?" And they drove him out.

Jesus heard that they had driven him out, and when he found him, he said, "Do you believe in the Son of Man?" He answered, "And who is he, sir? Tell me, so that I may believe in him." Jesus said to him, "You have seen him, and the one speaking with you is he." He said, "Lord, I believe." And he worshipped him.

Jesus said, "I came into this world for judgment so that those who do not see may see, and those who do see may become blind." Some of the Pharisees near him heard this and said to him, "Surely we are not blind, are we?" Jesus said to them, "If you were blind, you would have no sin. But now that you say, 'We see,' your sin remains."

The Gospel of the Lord. **Praise to you, Lord Jesus Christ.**

Key Words

Samuel, a prophet and judge in Israel, was born over 1,000 years before Jesus. The Lord chose Samuel to **anoint** Saul, the first king of Israel. Samuel also anointed David, who was king after Saul. The Bible contains two books in his name: 1 Samuel and 2 Samuel.

To **anoint** means to bless with oil. In the Bible it can also mean to give someone a mission, an important job. Christians are anointed at baptism and confirmation: our mission is to love people as God loves them.

The **Ephesians** were a group of Christians in the city of Ephesus. A letter Saint Paul wrote to them is now part of the Bible. Ephesus is located in modern-day Turkey.

In the time of Jesus, if someone was born **blind**, people assumed this was because God was punishing the parents for something they had done wrong. Jesus says this is not true and then heals the man born blind to show that Jesus has power over evil.

The **Pharisees** were Jewish leaders who tried to follow the letter of the law, but sometimes forgot to live by love. Jesus pointed out this lack of love.

The **Sabbath** is the day of the week when human beings rest as God did on the seventh day of creation. It is a chance for us to spend time praising God and enjoying creation. One of the Ten Commandments instructs us to keep the Sabbath holy.

April 2
5th Sunday of Lent

A reading from the book of the Prophet Ezekiel (37.12-14)

Thus says the Lord God: "I am going to **open your graves**, and bring you up from your graves, O my people; and I will bring you back to the land of Israel. And you shall know that I am the **Lord**, when I open your graves, and bring you up from your graves, O my people.

"I will put my spirit within you, and you shall live, and I will place you on your own soil; then you shall know that I, the Lord, have spoken and will act," says the Lord.

The word of the Lord. **Thanks be to God.**

Psalm 130

R̬. **With the Lord there is steadfast love and great power to redeem.**

Out of the depths I cry to you, O Lord.
Lord, hear my voice!
Let your ears be attentive
to the voice of my supplications! R̬.

If you, O Lord, should mark iniquities,
Lord, who could stand?
But there is forgiveness with you,
so that you may be revered. R̬.

I wait for the Lord,
my soul waits, and in his word I hope;
my soul waits for the Lord
more than watchmen for the morning. R̬.

For with the Lord there is steadfast love,
and with him is great power to **redeem**.
It is he who will redeem Israel
from all its iniquities. R̬.

A reading from the Letter of Saint Paul to the Romans (8.8-11)

Brothers and sisters: Those who are in the flesh cannot please God. But you are not in the flesh; you are in the Spirit, since the Spirit of God dwells in you. Anyone who does not have the Spirit of Christ does not belong to him.

But if Christ is in you, though the body is dead because of sin, the Spirit is life because of righteousness.

If the **Spirit of God** who raised Jesus from the dead dwells in you, he who raised Christ from the dead will give life to your mortal bodies also through his Spirit that dwells in you.

The word of the Lord. **Thanks be to God.**

A reading from the holy Gospel according to John (11.1-45)

For the shorter version, omit the indented parts.

> Now a certain man, Lazarus, was ill. He was from Bethany, the village of Mary and her sister Martha. Mary was the one who anointed the Lord with perfume and wiped his feet with her hair; her brother Lazarus was ill. So

The **sisters of Lazarus** sent a message to Jesus, "Lord, he whom you love is ill." But when Jesus heard this, he said, "This illness does not lead to death; rather it is for God's glory, so that the Son of God may be glorified through it." Accordingly, though Jesus loved Martha and her sister and Lazarus, after having heard that Lazarus was ill, he stayed two days longer in the place where he was. Then after this he said to the disciples, "Let us go to Judea again."

> The disciples said to him, "Rabbi, the people there were just now trying to stone you, and are you going there again?" Jesus answered, "Are there not twelve hours of daylight? Those who walk during the day do not stumble, because they see the light of this world. But those who walk at night stumble, because the light is not in them."

> After saying this, he told them, "Our friend Lazarus has fallen asleep, but I am going there to awaken him." The

disciples said to him, "Lord, if he has fallen asleep, he will be all right." Jesus, however, had been speaking about his death, but they thought that he was referring merely to sleep. Then Jesus told them plainly, "Lazarus is dead. For your sake I am glad I was not there, so that you may believe. But let us go to him." Thomas, who was called the Twin, said to his fellow disciples, "Let us also go, that we may die with him."

When Jesus arrived, he found that Lazarus had already been in the tomb four days.

Now Bethany was near Jerusalem, some two miles away, and many Jews had come to Martha and Mary to console them about their brother.

When Martha heard that Jesus was coming, she went and met him, while Mary stayed at home. Martha said to Jesus, "Lord, if you had been here, my brother would not have died. But even now I know that God will give you whatever you ask of him." Jesus said to her, "Your brother **will rise** again." Martha said to him, "I know that he will rise again in the resurrection on the last day." Jesus said to her, "I am the resurrection and the life. Whoever believes in me, even though they die, will live, and everyone who lives and believes in me will never die. Do you believe this?" She said to him, "Yes, Lord, I believe that you are the Christ, the Son of God, the one coming into the world."

When she had said this, she went back and called her sister Mary, and told her privately, "The Teacher is here and is calling for you." And when Mary heard it, she got up quickly and went to him. Now Jesus had not yet come to the village, but was still at the place where Martha had met him. The Jews who were with her in the house, consoling her, saw Mary get up quickly and go out. They followed her because they thought that she was going to the tomb to weep there.

When Mary came where Jesus was and saw him, she knelt at his feet and said to him, "Lord, if you had been here, my brother would not have died." When Jesus saw her weeping, and the Jews who came with her also weeping,

Jesus was greatly disturbed in spirit and deeply moved. He said, "Where have you laid him?" They said to him, "Lord, come and see." Jesus began to weep. So the Jews said, "See how he loved him!" But some of them said, "Could not he who opened the eyes of the blind man have kept this man from dying?"

Then Jesus, again greatly disturbed, came to the tomb. It was a cave, and a stone was lying against it. Jesus said, "Take away the stone." Martha, the sister of the dead man, said to him, "Lord, already there is a stench because he has been dead four days." Jesus said to her, "Did I not tell you that if you believed, you would see the glory of God?" So they took away the stone. And Jesus looked upward and said, "Father, I thank you for having heard me. I knew that you always hear me, but I have said this for the sake of the crowd standing here, so that they may believe that you sent me."

When he had said this, he cried with a loud voice, "Lazarus, come out!" The dead man came out, his hands and feet bound with strips of cloth, and his face wrapped in a cloth. Jesus said to them, "Unbind him, and let him go."

Many of the Jews therefore, who had come with Mary and had seen what Jesus did, believed in him.

The Gospel of the Lord. **Praise to you, Lord Jesus Christ.**

Key Words

Ezekiel was one of the most important prophets in Israel. He lived during a time when many of the people of Jerusalem were taken prisoner and forced to live in exile in Babylon. The king and Ezekiel were taken away, too. Ezekiel helped the people follow God's ways even though they were far from home.

The people of Israel lived in exile in Babylon and were very unhappy. Through the prophet Ezekiel, God promised to bring the people back to Israel. God said, "I am going to **open your graves**" and bring new life to the dry, dead bones of the people of Israel.

In the Bible, God is called the **Lord** because God is more powerful than all human power.

To **redeem** is to buy something back or to pay to free someone. God is called our Redeemer because God freed Israel from slavery in Egypt. Christ is our Redeemer, for by his resurrection he freed us from the power of death.

The **Spirit of God**, or the Holy Spirit, is the third person of the Holy Trinity. The Spirit of God is always present in our hearts and in the Church, helping us to live like brothers and sisters.

The **sisters of Lazarus** were Martha and Mary, and all three were Jesus' friends. They lived in Bethany, just a few kilometres from Jerusalem. When Jesus had visited them before, he had reminded the sisters that it was more important to listen to the word of God than to worry about daily chores.

When Jesus says that Lazarus **will rise** again, he is speaking of the resurrection of the dead when Jesus comes again at the end of time.

April 9

Passion Sunday

A reading from the holy Gospel according to Matthew (21.1-11)

When they had come near Jerusalem and had reached Bethphage, at the Mount of Olives, Jesus sent two disciples, saying to them, "Go into the village ahead of you, and immediately you will find a donkey tied, and a colt with her; untie them and bring them to me. If anyone says anything to you, just say this, 'The Lord needs them.' And he will send them immediately."

This took place to fulfill what had been spoken through the Prophet, saying, "Tell the **daughter of Zion**, Look, your king is coming to you, humble, and mounted on a donkey, and on a colt, the foal of a donkey."

The disciples went and did as Jesus had directed them; they brought the donkey and the colt, and put their cloaks on them, and he sat on them. A very large crowd spread their cloaks on the road, and others cut branches from the trees and spread them on the road. The crowds that went ahead of him and that followed were shouting, "**Hosanna** to the **Son of David!** Blessed is the one who comes in the name of the Lord! Hosanna in the highest heaven!"

When Jesus entered Jerusalem, the whole city was in turmoil, asking, "Who is this?" The crowds were saying, "This is the Prophet Jesus from Nazareth in Galilee."

The Gospel of the Lord. **Praise to you, Lord Jesus Christ.**

A reading from the book of the Prophet Isaiah (50.4-7)

The servant of the Lord said:
"The Lord God has given me the tongue of a teacher,
that I may know how to **sustain the weary** with a word.
Morning by morning he wakens —
wakens my ear to listen as those who are taught.
The Lord God has opened my ear,
and I was not rebellious,
I did not turn backward.

I gave my back to those who struck me,
and my cheeks to those who pulled out the beard;
I did not hide my face
from insult and spitting.

The Lord God helps me;
therefore I have not been disgraced;
therefore I have set my face like flint,
and I know that I shall not be put to shame."

The word of the Lord. **Thanks be to God.**

Psalm 22

R. **My God, my God, why have you forsaken me?**

All who see me mock at me;
they make mouths at me, they shake their heads;
"Commit your cause to the Lord; let him deliver;
let him rescue the one in whom he delights!" R.

For dogs are all around me;
a company of evildoers encircles me.
My hands and feet have shrivelled;
I can count all my bones. R.

They divide my clothes among themselves,
and for my clothing they cast lots.
But you, O Lord, do not be far away!
O my help, come quickly to my aid! R.

I will tell of your name to my brothers and sisters;
in the midst of the congregation I will praise you:
You who fear the Lord, praise him!
All you offspring of Jacob, glorify him;
stand in awe of him, all you offspring of Israel! R.

A reading from the Letter of Saint Paul to the Philippians (2.6-11)

Christ Jesus, though he was in the form of God, did not regard equality with God as something to be exploited, but emptied himself, taking the form of a slave, being born in human likeness. And being found in human form, he humbled himself and became obedient to the point of death — even death on a cross.

Therefore God highly exalted him and gave him the name that is above every name, so that at the name of Jesus every knee should bend, in heaven and on earth and under the earth, and every tongue should confess that Jesus Christ is Lord, to the glory of God the Father.

The word of the Lord. **Thanks be to God.**

A reading from the holy Gospel according to Matthew (26.14 – 27.66)

Several readers may proclaim the passion narrative today. N indicates the narrator, J the words of Jesus, and S the words of other speakers.

N The **Passion** of our Lord Jesus Christ according to Matthew.

One of the twelve, who was called Judas Iscariot, went to the chief priests and said,

S *What will you give me if I betray him to you?*

N They paid him thirty pieces of silver. And from that moment he began to look for an opportunity to betray him.

On the first day of Unleavened Bread the disciples came to Jesus, saying,

S *Where do you want us to make the preparations for you to eat the Passover?*

J **Go into the city to a certain man, and say to him, "The Teacher says, My time is near; I will keep the Passover at your house with my disciples."**

N So the disciples did as Jesus had directed them, and they prepared the Passover meal.

When it was evening, he took his place with the twelve; and while they were eating, he said,

J Truly I tell you, one of you will betray me.

N And they became greatly distressed and began to say to him one after another,

S *Surely not I, Lord?*

J The one who has dipped his hand into the bowl with me will betray me. The Son of Man goes as it is written of him, but woe to that one by whom the Son of Man is betrayed! It would have been better for that one not to have been born.

N Judas, who betrayed him, said,

S *Surely not I, Rabbi?*

J You have said so.

N While they were eating, Jesus took a loaf of bread, and after blessing it he broke it, gave it to the disciples, and said,

J Take, eat; this is my Body.

N Then he took a cup, and after giving thanks he gave it to them, saying,

J Drink from it, all of you; for this is my Blood of the covenant, which is poured out for many for the forgiveness of sins. I tell you, I will never again drink of this fruit of the vine until that day when I drink it new with you in my Father's kingdom.

N When they had sung the hymn, they went out to the Mount of Olives. Then Jesus said to them,

J You will all become deserters because of me this night; for it is written, "I will strike the shepherd, and the sheep of the flock will be scattered." But after I am raised up, I will go ahead of you to Galilee.

N Peter said to him,

S *Though all become deserters because of you, I will never desert you.*

J Truly I tell you, this very night, before the cock crows, you will deny me three times.

N Peter said to him,

S *Even though I must die with you, I will not deny you.*

N And so said all the disciples.

Then Jesus went with them to a place called Gethsemane; and he said to his disciples,

J **Sit here while I go over there and pray.**

N He took with him Peter and the two sons of Zebedee, and began to be grieved and agitated. Then he said to them,

J **I am deeply grieved, even to death; remain here, and stay awake with me.**

N And going a little farther, he threw himself on the ground and prayed,

J **My Father, if it is possible, let this cup pass from me; yet not what I want, but what you want.**

N Then he came to the disciples and found them sleeping; and he said to Peter,

J **So, could you not stay awake with me one hour? Stay awake and pray that you may not come into temptation; for the spirit indeed is willing, but the flesh is weak.**

N Again he went away for the second time and prayed,

J **My Father, if this cannot pass unless I drink it, your will be done.**

N Again he came and found them sleeping, for their eyes were heavy. So leaving them again, he went away and prayed for the third time, saying the same words. Then he came to the disciples and said to them,

J **Are you still sleeping and taking your rest? See, the hour is at hand, and the Son of Man is betrayed into the hands of sinners. Get up, let us be going. See, my betrayer is at hand.**

N While he was still speaking, Judas, one of the twelve, arrived; with him was a large crowd with swords and clubs, from the chief priests and the elders of the people. Now the betrayer had given them a sign, saying,

S *The one I will kiss is the man; arrest him.*

N At once he came up to Jesus and said,

S *Greetings, Rabbi!*

N and kissed him. Jesus said to him,

J **Friend, do what you are here to do.**

N Then they came and laid hands on Jesus and arrested him.

Suddenly, one of those with Jesus put his hand on his sword, drew it, and struck the slave of the high priest, cutting off his ear. Then Jesus said to him,

J **Put your sword back into its place; for all who take the sword will perish by the sword. Do you think that I cannot appeal to my Father, and he will at once send me more than twelve legions of Angels? But how then would the Scriptures be fulfilled, which say it must happen in this way?**

N At that hour Jesus said to the crowds,

J **Have you come out with swords and clubs to arrest me as though I were a bandit? Day after day I sat in the temple teaching, and you did not arrest me. But all this has taken place so that the Scriptures of the Prophets may be fulfilled.**

N Then all the disciples deserted him and fled.

Those who had arrested Jesus took him to Caiaphas the high priest, in whose house the scribes and the elders had gathered.

But Peter was following him at a distance, as far as the courtyard of the high priest; and going inside, he sat with the guards in order to see how this would end.

Now the chief priests and the whole council were looking for false testimony against Jesus so that they might put him to death, but they found none, though many false witnesses came forward. At last two came forward and said,

S *This fellow said, "I am able to destroy the temple of God and to build it in three days."*

N The high priest stood up and said,

S *Have you no answer? What is it that they testify against you?*

N But Jesus was silent.

Then the high priest said to him,

S *I put you under oath before the living God, tell us if you are the Christ, the Son of God.*

N Jesus said to him,

J **You have said so. But I tell you, from now on you will see the Son of Man seated at the right hand of Power and coming on the clouds of heaven.**

N Then the high priest tore his clothes and said,

S *He has blasphemed! Why do we still need witnesses? You have now heard his blasphemy. What is your verdict?*

N They answered,

S *He deserves death.*

N Then they spat in his face and struck him; and some slapped him, saying,

S *Prophesy to us, Christ! Who is it that struck you?*

N Now Peter was sitting outside in the courtyard. A servant girl came to him and said,

S *You also were with Jesus the Galilean.*

N But he denied it before all of them, saying,

S *I do not know what you are talking about.*

N When Peter went out to the porch, another servant girl saw him, and she said to the bystanders,

S *This man was with Jesus of Nazareth.*

N Again he denied it with an oath,

S *I do not know the man.*

N After a little while the bystanders came up and said to Peter,

S *Certainly you are also one of them, for your accent betrays you.*

N Then he began to curse, and he swore an oath,

S *I do not know the man!*

N At that moment the cock crowed. Then Peter remembered what Jesus had said: "Before the cock crows, you will deny me three times." And he went out and wept bitterly.

When morning came, all the chief priests and the elders of the people conferred together against Jesus in order to bring about his death. They bound him, led him away, and handed him over to Pilate the governor.

When Judas, his betrayer, saw that Jesus was condemned, he repented and brought back the thirty pieces of silver to the chief priests and the elders.

S *I have sinned by betraying innocent blood.*

N But they said,

S *What is that to us? See to it yourself.*

N Throwing down the pieces of silver in the temple, he departed; and he went and hanged himself.

But the chief priests, taking the pieces of silver, said,

S *It is not lawful to put them into the treasury, since they are blood money.*

N After conferring together, they used them to buy the potter's field as a place to bury foreigners. For this reason that field has been called the Field of Blood to this day. Then was fulfilled what had been spoken through the Prophet Jeremiah, "And they took the thirty pieces of silver, the price of the one on whom a price had been set, on whom some of the people of Israel had set a price, and they gave them for the potter's field, as the Lord commanded me."

Now Jesus stood before the governor; and the governor asked him,

S *Are you the King of the Jews?*

J You say so.

N But when he was accused by the chief priests and elders, he did not answer. Then Pilate said to him,

S *Do you not hear how many accusations they make against you?*

N But Jesus gave him no answer, not even to a single charge, so that the governor was greatly amazed.

Now at the festival the governor was accustomed to release a prisoner for the crowd, anyone they wanted. At that time they had a notorious prisoner, called Barabbas. So after they had gathered, Pilate said to them,

S *Whom do you want me to release for you, Barabbas or Jesus who is called the Christ?*

N For he realized that it was out of jealousy that they had handed him over.

While he was sitting on the judgment seat, his wife sent word to him,

S *Have nothing to do with that innocent man, for today I have suffered a great deal because of a dream about him.*

N Now the chief priests and the elders persuaded the crowds to ask for Barabbas and to have Jesus killed. The governor again said to them,

S *Which of the two do you want me to release for you?*

N And they said,

S *Barabbas.*

N Pilate said to them,

S *Then what should I do with Jesus who is called the Christ?*

N All of them said,

S *Let him be crucified!*

N Then he asked,

S *Why, what evil has he done?*

N But they shouted all the more,

S *Let him be crucified!*

N So when Pilate saw that he could do nothing, but rather that a riot was beginning, he took some water and washed his hands before the crowd, saying,

S *I am innocent of this man's blood; see to it yourselves.*

N Then the people as a whole answered,

S *"His blood be on us and on our children!"*

N So he released Barabbas for them; and after flogging Jesus, he handed him over to be crucified.

Then the soldiers of the governor took Jesus into the governor's headquarters, and they gathered the whole cohort around him. They stripped him and put a scarlet robe on him, and after twisting some thorns into a crown, they put it on his head. They put a reed in his right hand and knelt before him and mocked him, saying,

S *Hail, King of the Jews!*

N They spat on him, and took the reed and struck him on the head. After mocking him, they stripped him of the robe and put his own clothes on him. Then they led him away to crucify him.

As they went out, they came upon a man from Cyrene named Simon; they compelled this man to carry his Cross.

And when they came to a place called Golgotha which means Place of a Skull, they offered him wine to drink, mixed with gall; but when he tasted it, he would not drink it.

And when they had crucified him, they divided his clothes among themselves by casting lots; then they sat down there and kept watch over him.

Over his head they put the charge against him, which read, "This is Jesus, the King of the Jews."

Then two bandits were crucified with him, one on his right and one on his left. Those who passed by derided him, shaking their heads and saying,

S *You who would destroy the temple and build it in three days, save yourself! If you are the Son of God, come down from the Cross.*

N In the same way the chief priests also, along with the scribes and elders, were mocking him, saying,

S *He saved others; he cannot save himself. He is the King of Israel; let him come down from the Cross now, and we will believe in him. He trusts in God; let God deliver him now, if he wants to; for he said, "I am God's Son."*

N The bandits who were crucified with him also taunted him in the same way.

From noon on, darkness came over the whole land until three in the afternoon. And about three o'clock Jesus cried with a loud voice,

J Eli, Eli, lema sabachthani?

N that is, "My God, my God, why have you forsaken me?" When some of the bystanders heard it, they said,

S *This man is calling for Elijah.*

N At once one of them ran and got a sponge, filled it with sour wine, put it on a stick, and gave it to him to drink. But the others said,

S *Wait, let us see whether Elijah will come to save him.*

N Then Jesus cried again with a loud voice and breathed his last.

Here all kneel and pause for a short time.

N At that moment the curtain of the temple was torn in two, from top to bottom. The earth shook, and the rocks were split. The tombs also were opened, and many bodies of the saints who had fallen asleep were raised. After his resurrection they came out of the tombs and entered the holy city and appeared to many.

Now when the centurion and those with him, who were keeping watch over Jesus, saw the earthquake and what took place, they were terrified and said,

S *Truly this man was God's Son!*

N Many women were also there, looking on from a distance; they had followed Jesus from Galilee and had provided for him. Among them were Mary Magdalene, and Mary the mother of James and Joseph, and the mother of the sons of Zebedee.

When it was evening, there came a rich man from Arimathea, named Joseph, who was also a disciple of Jesus. He went to Pilate and asked for the body of Jesus; then Pilate ordered it to be given to him. So Joseph took the body and wrapped it in a clean linen cloth and laid it in his own new tomb, which he had hewn in the rock. He then rolled a great stone to the door of the tomb and went away.

Mary Magdalene and the other Mary were there, sitting opposite the tomb. The next day, that is, after the day of Preparation, the chief priests and the Pharisees gathered before Pilate and said,

S *Sir, we remember what that impostor said while he was still alive, "After three days I will rise again." Therefore command the tomb to be made secure until the third day; otherwise his disciples may go and steal him away, and tell the people, "He has been raised from the dead," and the last deception would be worse than the first.*

N Pilate said to them,

S *You have a guard of soldiers; go, make it as secure as you can.*

N So they went with the guard and made the tomb secure by sealing the stone.

Key Words

Holy Week begins on **Passion Sunday**, which is also called Palm Sunday. On this day we recall Jesus' arrival in Jerusalem, where people greeted him in the streets like a hero, shouting and waving palm branches. During the Gospel, we listen to the whole story of Jesus' last days on earth.

Zion was the name of a hill in Jerusalem where the temple was built, but the city itself was often called Zion. **Daughter of Zion** is another way of naming the entire nation, the whole People of God.

Hosanna is a Hebrew word that means "save us." When the people in Jerusalem shout it as Jesus approaches, they are saying that they know he is the Messiah who has come to save them.

Son of David (or descendant of King David) is a name people used to describe the Messiah who was to come. It is one of the many names given to Jesus in the Bible.

An important task of a prophet (and also of the Church and all Christians) is to **sustain the weary** — to give strength to those who have fallen or who are weak, to offer hope to the hopeless and comfort to the lonely, and to bring consolation to those who mourn.

The **Passion** of Jesus is the story of the last hours of his life. It begins with the Last Supper and ends when his body is placed in the tomb. When we speak of the "passion" of Jesus, we mean his suffering.

April 16

Resurrection of the Lord
Easter Sunday

A reading from the Acts of the Apostles
(10.34, 37-43)

Peter began to speak: "You know the message that spread throughout Judea, beginning in Galilee after the baptism that John announced: how God **anointed** Jesus of Nazareth with the Holy Spirit and with power; how he went about doing good and healing all who were oppressed by the devil, for God was with him.

"We are witnesses to all that he did both in Judea and in Jerusalem. They put him to death by hanging him on a tree; but **God raised him** on the third day and allowed him to appear, not to all the people but to us who were chosen by God as witnesses, and who ate and drank with him after he rose from the dead.

"He commanded us to preach to the people and to testify that he is the one ordained by God as judge of the living and the dead. All the **Prophets** testify about him that everyone who believes in him receives forgiveness of sins through his name."

The word of the Lord. **Thanks be to God.**

Psalm 118

R. **This is the day the Lord has made;
let us rejoice and be glad.**

or **Alleluia! Alleluia! Alleluia!**

O give thanks to the Lord, for he is good;
his steadfast love endures forever.
Let Israel say,
"His steadfast love endures forever." R.

"The right hand of the Lord is exalted;
the right hand of the Lord does valiantly."
I shall not die, but I shall live,
and recount the deeds of the Lord. R.

The stone that the builders rejected
has become the chief cornerstone.
This is the Lord's doing;
it is marvellous in our eyes. R.

An alternate reading follows.

A reading from the Letter of Saint Paul to the Colossians (3.1-4)

Brothers and sisters: If you have been raised with Christ, seek the **things that are above**, where Christ is, seated at the right hand of God. Set your minds on things that are above, not on things that are on earth, for you have died, and your life is hidden with Christ in God. When Christ who is your life is revealed, then you also will be revealed with him in glory.

The word of the Lord. **Thanks be to God.**

or

A reading from the first Letter of Saint Paul to the Corinthians (5.6-8)

Do you not know that a little yeast leavens the whole batch of dough? Clean out the old yeast so that you may be a new batch, as you really are unleavened. For our paschal lamb, Christ, has been sacrificed. Therefore, let us celebrate the festival, not with the old yeast, the yeast of malice and evil, but with the unleavened bread of sincerity and truth.

The word of the Lord. **Thanks be to God.**

A reading from the holy Gospel according to John (20.1-18)

The shorter version ends at the asterisks.

Early on the first day of the week, while it was still dark, Mary Magdalene came to the tomb and saw that the stone had been removed from the tomb. So she ran and went to Simon Peter and the other disciple, the one whom Jesus loved, and said to them, "They have taken the Lord out of the tomb, and we do not know where they have laid him."

Then Peter and the other disciple set out and went toward the tomb. The two were running together, but the other disciple outran Peter and reached the tomb first. He bent down to look in and saw the **linen wrappings** lying there, but he did not go in.

Then Simon Peter came, following him, and went into the tomb. He saw the linen wrappings lying there, and the cloth that had been on Jesus' head, not lying with the linen wrappings but rolled up in a place by itself. Then the other disciple, who reached the tomb first, also went in, and he saw and believed; for as yet they did not understand the Scripture, that he must rise from the dead.

* * *

Then the disciples returned to their homes. But Mary Magdalene stood weeping outside the tomb. As she wept, she bent over to look into the tomb; and she saw two Angels in white, sitting where the body of Jesus had been lying, one at the head and the other at the feet. They said to her, "Woman, why are you weeping?" She said to them, "They have taken away my Lord, and I do not know where they have laid him."

When she had said this, she turned around and saw Jesus standing there, but she did not know that it was Jesus. Jesus said to her, "Woman, why are you weeping? Whom are you looking for?" Supposing him to be the gardener, she said to him, "Sir, if you have carried him away, tell me where you have laid him, and I will take him away."

Jesus said to her, "Mary!" She turned and said to him in Hebrew, "Rabbouni!" which means Teacher. Jesus said to her, "Do not hold on to me, because I have not yet ascended to the Father. But go to my brothers and say to them, 'I am ascending to my Father and your Father, to my God and your God.'"

Mary Magdalene went and announced to the disciples, "I have seen the Lord," and she told them that he had said these things to her.

The Gospel of the Lord. **Praise to you, Lord Jesus Christ.**

Key Words

The **Acts of the Apostles** is a book in the New Testament or Christian Scriptures that describes how the Church grew after Jesus rose from the dead. It was written by Saint Luke, who also wrote a Gospel.

To **anoint** means to bless with oil. In the Bible it can also mean to give someone a mission, an important job. God anoints Jesus with the Holy Spirit to show that God was giving Jesus his mission. Christians are anointed at baptism and confirmation: our mission is to live as Jesus taught us.

God raised him: Jesus' resurrection, his passing through death to eternal life, is the most important element of the Christian faith. We believe that Jesus did not remain dead in the tomb, but overcame death, suffering and sin. We want to live as he taught, in order to be united with him now and in the next life.

The **Prophets** were good men and women who spoke for God. Sometimes their message was harsh: they asked people to make big changes in their lives and attitudes in order to grow closer to God. At other times, they brought words of comfort.

Saint Paul wrote to the **Colossians**, a Christian community at Colossae in modern-day Turkey, to help them understand that Jesus Christ is above everything. No powers are greater than he is.

The **things that are above**, that is, in heaven, are those that Jesus teaches: finding the truth, living simply, trusting in God, and caring for those in need. The things of earth distract us from Jesus: being selfish, hurting others and ignoring the poor.

The **linen wrappings** were the fabric that covered the body of a dead person in the tomb. Joseph of Arimathea and Nicodemus made sure that Jesus' body was treated with dignity and buried properly: they covered his face and then wrapped his body with linen wrappings.

April 23
2nd Sunday of Easter

A reading from the Acts of the Apostles (2.42-47)

They devoted themselves to the Apostles' teaching and fellowship, to the **breaking of bread** and the prayers. Awe came upon everyone, because many wonders and signs were being done by the Apostles.

All who believed were together and had all things **in common**; they would sell their possessions and goods and distribute the proceeds to all, as any had need. Day by day, as they spent much time together in the temple, they broke bread in various houses and ate their food with glad and generous hearts, praising God and having the goodwill of all the people. And day by day the Lord added to their number those who were being saved.

The word of the Lord. **Thanks be to God.**

Psalm 118

R. **Give thanks to the Lord, for he is good;**
his steadfast love endures forever.

or **Alleluia!**

Let Israel say,
"His steadfast love endures forever."
Let the house of Aaron say,
"His steadfast love endures forever."
Let those who fear the Lord say,
"His steadfast love endures forever." R.

I was pushed hard, so that I was falling,
but the Lord helped me.
The Lord is my strength and my might;
he has become my salvation.
There are glad songs of victory
in the tents of the righteous. R.

The stone that the builders rejected
has become the chief cornerstone.
This is the Lord's doing;
it is marvellous in our eyes.
This is the day that the Lord has made;
let us rejoice and be glad in it. R.

A reading from the first Letter of Saint Peter
(1.3-9)

Blessed be the God and Father of our Lord Jesus Christ! By his great mercy he has given us a new birth into a living hope through the resurrection of Jesus Christ from the dead: a birth into an inheritance that is imperishable, undefiled, and unfading, kept in heaven for you, who are being protected by the power of God through faith for a salvation ready to be revealed in the last time.

In this you **rejoice**, even if now for a little while you have had to suffer various trials, so that the genuineness of your faith — being more precious than gold that, though perishable, is tested by fire — may be found to result in praise and glory and honour when Jesus Christ is revealed.

Although you have not seen him, you love him; and even though you do not see him now, you believe in him and rejoice with an indescribable and glorious joy, for you are receiving the outcome of your faith, the salvation of your souls.

The word of the Lord. **Thanks be to God.**

A reading from the holy Gospel according to John (20.19-31)

It was evening on the day Jesus rose from the dead, the first day of the week, and the doors of the house where the disciples had met were locked for fear of the Jews. Jesus came and stood among them and said, "Peace be with you." After he said this, he showed them **his hands and his side**. Then the disciples rejoiced when they saw the Lord.

Jesus said to them again, "Peace be with you. As the Father has sent me, so I send you."

When he had said this, he **breathed** on them and said to them, "Receive the Holy Spirit. If you forgive the sins of any, they are forgiven them; if you retain the sins of any, they are retained."

But Thomas, who was called the Twin, one of the twelve, was not with them when Jesus came. So the other disciples told him, "We have seen the Lord." But he said to them, "Unless I see the mark of the nails in his hands, and put my finger in the mark of the nails and my hand in his side, I will not believe."

After eight days his disciples were again in the house, and Thomas was with them. Although the doors were shut, Jesus came and stood among them and said, "Peace be with you." Then he said to Thomas, "Put your finger here and see my hands. Reach out your hand and put it in my side. Do not doubt but believe." Thomas answered him, "My Lord and my God!"

Jesus said to him, "Have you believed because you have seen me? Blessed are those who have not seen and yet have come to believe."

Now Jesus did many other signs in the presence of his disciples, which are not written in this book. But these are written so that you may come to believe that Jesus is the Christ, the Son of God, and that through believing you may have life in his name.

The Gospel of the Lord. **Praise to you, Lord Jesus Christ.**

Key Words

The apostles gathered in the **breaking of bread**, which means they celebrated the Lord's supper, as we do at every Eucharist or Mass.

In the early Christian community, those who believed in Jesus shared all their belongings **in common**. This way, everyone had all they needed. Today, we can do the same by making sure that no one in our community is in need.

The first Letter of Saint Peter is found in the New Testament. It is a summary of the Good News of Jesus and was written to help the early Christians lead faithful lives.

We **rejoice** in our salvation, even when life seems difficult. Jesus conquered death by rising from the dead and we know we will see him when he comes again.

The holy Gospel according to John tells us about the life, death and resurrection of Jesus. It was written about 90 years after Jesus died. John's Gospel includes some stories and sayings that are not in the other three Gospels (Matthew, Mark and Luke).

By showing **his hands and his side**, Jesus presents the scars left by the nails and the lance that pierced him. It is a way of saying, "It's really me. I was dead, but now I am alive."

When God created the first humans, he **breathed** life into them. Our life comes from the depths of God's being. When Jesus appeared to his disciples after his death, he also breathed on them, filling them with his Spirit.

April 30

3rd Sunday of Easter

A reading from the Acts of the Apostles
(2.14, 22-28)

When the day of **Pentecost** had come, Peter, standing with the eleven, raised his voice and addressed the crowd, "Men of Judea and all who live in Jerusalem, let this be known to you, and listen to what I say. Jesus of Nazareth, a man attested to you by God with deeds of power, wonders, and signs that God did through him among you, as you yourselves know — this man, handed over to you according to the definite plan and foreknowledge of God, you crucified and killed by the hands of those outside the law.

"But God raised him up, having freed him from death, because it was impossible for him to be held in its power. For **David** says concerning him, 'I saw the Lord always before me, for he is at my right hand so that I will not be shaken; therefore my heart was glad, and my tongue rejoiced; moreover my flesh will live in hope. For you will not abandon my soul to Hades, or let your Holy One experience corruption. You have made known to me the ways of life; you will make me full of gladness with your presence.'"

The word of the Lord. **Thanks be to God.**

Psalm 16

℟. **Lord, you will show me the path of life.**

or **Alleluia!**

Protect me, O God, for in you I take refuge.
I say to the Lord, "You are my Lord;
I have no good apart from you."
The Lord is my chosen portion and my cup;
    you hold my lot. ℟.

I bless the Lord who gives me counsel;
in the night also my heart instructs me.
I keep the Lord always before me;
because he is at my right hand, I shall not be moved. ℟.

Therefore my heart is glad, and my soul rejoices;
my body also rests secure.
For you do not give me up to Sheol,
or let your faithful one see the Pit. R.

You show me the path of life.
In your presence there is fullness of joy;
In your right hand are pleasures forevermore. R.

A reading from the first Letter of Saint Peter
(1.17-21)

Beloved: If you invoke as Father the one who judges each person impartially according to each one's deeds, live in **reverent fear** during the time of your exile.

You know that you were ransomed from the futile ways inherited from your ancestors, not with perishable things like silver or gold, but with the precious blood of Christ, like that of a **lamb** without defect or blemish.

Christ was destined before the foundation of the world, but was revealed at the end of the ages for your sake. Through him you have come to trust in God, who raised him from the dead and gave him glory, so that your faith and hope are set on God.

The word of the Lord. **Thanks be to God.**

A reading from the holy Gospel according to Luke (24.13-35)

On the first day of the week, two of the disciples were going to a village called Emmaus, about eleven kilometres from Jerusalem, and talking with each other about all these things that had happened. While they were talking and discussing, Jesus himself came near and went with them, but their eyes were kept from recognizing him.

And he said to them, "What are you discussing with each other while you walk along?" They stood still, looking sad. Then one of them, whose name was Cleopas, answered him, "Are you the only stranger in Jerusalem who does not know the things that have taken place there in these days?"

He asked them, "What things?" They replied, "The things about Jesus of Nazareth, who was a Prophet mighty in deed and word before God and all the people, and how our chief priests and leaders handed him over to be condemned to death and crucified him. But we had hoped that he was the one to redeem Israel. Yes, and besides all this, it is now the third day since these things took place. Moreover, some women of our group astounded us. They were at the tomb early this morning, and when they did not find his body there, they came back and told us that they had indeed seen a vision of Angels who said that he was alive. Some of those who were with us went to the tomb and found it just as the women had said; but they did not see him."

Then he said to them, "Oh, how foolish you are, and how slow of heart to believe all that the Prophets have declared! Was it not necessary that the Christ should suffer these things and then enter into his glory?"

Then beginning with Moses and all the Prophets, he interpreted to them the things about himself in all the **Scriptures**. As they came near the village to which they were going, he walked ahead as if he were going on. But they urged him strongly, saying, "Stay with us, because it is almost evening and the day is now nearly over." So he went in to stay with them.

When he was at the table with them, he took bread, blessed and broke it, and gave it to them. Then their eyes were opened, and they recognized him; and he vanished from their sight.

They said to each other, "Were not our hearts burning within us while he was talking to us on the road, while he was opening the Scriptures to us?"

That same hour they got up and returned to Jerusalem; and they found the eleven and their companions gathered together. These were saying, "The Lord has risen indeed, and he has appeared to Simon!"

Then they told what had happened on the road, and how he had been made known to them in the **breaking of the bread**.

The Gospel of the Lord. **Praise to you, Lord Jesus Christ.**

Key Words

Pentecost is the Greek word for a Jewish festival that takes place on the fiftieth day after Passover. Fifty days after Jesus' resurrection, the Holy Spirit descended upon all those present in the house. For Christians, Pentecost is the feast of the coming of the Holy Spirit (see page 177).

David was the second king of Israel. He lived about 1,000 years before Christ. David is considered to be the author of the 150 psalms. In this passage from the Acts of the Apostles, Peter is quoting from Psalm 16.

If we have **reverent fear** for someone, we are not afraid because they are frightening. Instead, we are filled with awe because of their greatness and we try to honour them with our lives.

Jewish people made sacrifices of animals to God. Because Jesus' sacrifice brought us back to God, the Bible compares Jesus to a **lamb**, one without any stain.

The holy Gospel according to Luke is one of the four Gospels in the New Testament or Christian Scriptures. It was written for people who, like Luke, weren't Jewish before becoming Christian.

The **Scriptures** are the written word of God. We read them in the Bible, both the Hebrew Scriptures (Old Testament) and the Christian Scriptures (New Testament).

Jesus' disciples recognized him in the **breaking of the bread**, because Jesus had done the same thing at many meals, especially the Last Supper. Jesus said to do this in his memory, and we remember Jesus as our living bread when we celebrate the Eucharist.

May 7
4th Sunday of Easter

A reading from the Acts of the Apostles
(2.14, 36-41)

When the day of Pentecost had come, Peter, standing with **the eleven**, raised his voice and addressed the crowd. "Let the entire house of Israel know with certainty that God has made him both Lord and Christ, this Jesus whom you crucified."

Now when the people heard this, they were cut to the heart and said to Peter and to the other Apostles, "Brothers, what should we do?" Peter said to them, "**Repent**, and be baptized every one of you in the name of Jesus Christ so that your sins may be forgiven; and you will receive the gift of the Holy Spirit. For the promise is for you, for your children, and for all who are far away, **everyone** whom the Lord our God calls to him."

And he testified with many other arguments and exhorted them, saying, "Save yourselves from this corrupt generation." So those who welcomed his message were baptized, and that day were added about three thousand souls.

The word of the Lord. **Thanks be to God.**

Psalm 23

℟. **The Lord is my shepherd; I shall not want.**

or **Alleluia!**

The Lord is my **shepherd**, I shall not want.
He makes me lie down in green pastures;
he leads me beside still waters;
he restores my soul. ℟.

He leads me in right paths for his name's sake.
Even though I walk through the darkest valley,
    I fear no evil;
for you are with me;
your rod and your staff — they comfort me. ℟.

R. **The Lord is my shepherd; I shall not want.**

You prepare a table before me
in the presence of my enemies;
you anoint my head with oil;
my cup overflows. R.

Surely goodness and mercy shall follow me
all the days of my life,
and I shall dwell in the house of the Lord
my whole life long. R.

A reading from the first Letter of Saint Peter (2.20-25)

Beloved: If you endure when you do right and suffer for it, you have God's approval. For to this you have been called, because Christ also suffered for you, leaving you an example, so that you should follow in his steps. "He committed no sin, and no deceit was found in his mouth." When he was abused, he did not return abuse; when he suffered, he did not threaten; but he entrusted himself to the one who judges justly.

Christ himself bore our sins in his body on the Cross, so that, free from sins, we might live for righteousness; by his wounds you have been healed. For you were going astray like sheep, but now you have returned to the shepherd and guardian of your souls.

The word of the Lord. **Thanks be to God.**

A reading from the holy Gospel according to John (10.1-10)

Jesus said: "Very truly, I tell you, anyone who does not enter the **sheepfold** by the gate but climbs in by another way is a thief and a bandit. The one who enters by the gate is the shepherd of the sheep. The gatekeeper opens the gate for him, and the sheep hear his voice. He calls his own sheep by name and leads them out. When he has brought out all his own, he goes ahead of them, and the sheep follow him because they know his voice. They will not follow a stranger, but they will run from him because they do not know the voice of strangers."

Jesus used this figure of speech with them, but they did not understand what he was saying to them. So again Jesus said to them, "Very truly, I tell you, I am the gate for the sheep. All who came before me are thieves and bandits; but the sheep did not listen to them. I am the gate. Whoever enters by me will be saved, and will come in and go out and find pasture. The thief comes only to steal and kill and destroy. I came that they may have life, and have it **abundantly**."

The Gospel of the Lord. **Praise to you, Lord Jesus Christ.**

Key Words

The eleven mentioned in the Acts of the Apostles are the disciples of Jesus. They were twelve at first, but Judas Iscariot, who betrayed Jesus, left before Jesus died.

To **repent** means to be sorry for doing something wrong and to change our behaviour for the better.

When Peter says that God's promises are for **everyone**, he is saying something new. He means that God's promises are not just for the People of Israel, but for all people everywhere. This is the New Covenant.

A **shepherd** is someone who takes care of a flock of sheep. He would spend days or weeks with his flock, sleeping with them and making sure they were always safe. God loves us with the same constant care.

The **sheepfold** is a fenced-in area for sheep. It helps keep the sheep safe from other animals that might attack them.

When we have life **abundantly**, it means our hearts are full of joy and peace. We live our lives wanting to help others because of our friendship with Jesus.

A reading from the Acts of the Apostles (6.1-7)

Now during those days, when the disciples were increasing in number, the Hellenists complained against the Hebrews because their widows were being neglected in the daily distribution of food. And the twelve called together the whole community of the disciples and said, "It is not right that we should neglect the **word of God** in order to wait on tables. Therefore, brothers, select from among yourselves seven men of good standing, full of the Spirit and of wisdom, whom we may appoint to this task, while we, for our part, will devote ourselves to prayer and to serving the word."

What they said pleased the whole community, and they chose **Stephen**, a man full of faith and the Holy Spirit, together with Philip, Prochorus, Nicanor, Timon, Parmenas, and Nicolaus, a convert of Antioch. They had these men stand before the Apostles, who prayed and **laid their hands** on them.

The word of God continued to spread; the number of the disciples increased greatly in Jerusalem, and a great many of the priests became obedient to the faith.

The word of the Lord. **Thanks be to God.**

Psalm 33

R. **Let your love be upon us, Lord, even as we hope in you.**

or **Alleluia!**

Rejoice in the Lord, O you righteous.
Praise befits the upright.
Praise the Lord with the lyre;
make melody to him with the harp of ten strings. R.

For the word of the Lord is upright,
and all his work is done in faithfulness.
He loves righteousness and justice;
the earth is full of the steadfast love of the Lord. R.

Truly the eye of the Lord is on those who fear him,
on those who hope in his steadfast love,
to deliver their soul from death,
and to keep them alive in famine. R.

A reading from the first Letter of Saint Peter
(2.4-9)

Beloved: Come to the Lord, a living stone, though rejected by human beings yet chosen and precious in God's sight. Like **living stones**, let yourselves be built into a spiritual house, to be a **holy priesthood**, to offer spiritual sacrifices acceptable to God through Jesus Christ.

For it stands in Scripture: "See, I am laying in Zion a stone, a cornerstone chosen and precious; and whoever believes in him will not be put to shame." To you then who believe, he is precious; but for those who do not believe, "The stone that the builders rejected has become the very head of the corner," and "A stone that makes them stumble, and a rock that makes them fall." They stumble because they disobey the word, as they were destined to do.

But you are a chosen race, a royal priesthood, a holy nation, God's own people, in order that you may proclaim the mighty acts of him who called you out of darkness into his marvellous light.

The word of the Lord. **Thanks be to God.**

A reading from the holy Gospel according to John (14.1-12)

Jesus said to his disciples: "Do not let your hearts be troubled. Believe in God, believe also in me. In my Father's house there are many dwelling places. If it were not so, would I have told you that I go to prepare a place for you? And if I go and prepare a place for you, I will come again and will **take you to myself**, so that where I am, there you may be also. And you know the way to the place where I am going."

Thomas said to him, "Lord, we do not know where you are going. How can we know the way?"

Jesus said to him, "I am the way, and the truth, and the life. No one comes to the Father except through me. If you know me, you will know my Father also. From now on you do know him and have seen him."

Philip said to him, "Lord, show us the Father, and we will be satisfied." Jesus said to him, "Have I been with you all this time, Philip, and you still do not know me? Whoever has seen me has seen the Father. How can you say, 'Show us the Father'? Do you not believe that I am in the Father and the Father is in me? The words that I say to you I do not speak on my own; but the Father who dwells in me does his works. Believe me that I am in the Father and the Father is in me; but if you do not, then believe me because of the works themselves. Very truly, I tell you, the one who believes in me will also do the works that I do and, in fact, will do greater works than these, because I am going to the Father."

The Gospel of the Lord. **Praise to you, Lord Jesus Christ.**

Key Words

The **word of God** is the Good News — that Jesus is the Saviour of the world! The disciples were worried that people were getting too busy and were not spending time praying and sharing this Good News. So they named some people to devote themselves especially to the word of God.

Stephen was one of the first ministers in the early Church. He did much good work. Stephen was killed because of his faith in Jesus and was the first martyr. The feast of Stephen is December 26.

The disciples **laid their hands** on the heads of others as a form of prayer. It was also a way of sending someone off to do a task. This gesture is now part of certain sacraments, such as confirmation and holy orders (priesthood). It is a sign that the power of God, the Holy Spirit, is being given to the person.

When Peter calls us **living stones**, he is telling us that we are a very important part of the Church. If we do not all stand together, the Church will lose its strength.

Through our baptism, all Christians share in the **holy priesthood** of Jesus: we offer our lives to God and rejoice in his love. Some Christians are specially anointed as priests to preside at Eucharist and be leaders of the community.

When Jesus says that he will **"take you to myself,"** he is making a beautiful promise. Jesus will take us into his heart.

May 21
6th Sunday of Easter

A reading from the Acts of the Apostles
(8.5-8, 14-17)

In those days: **Philip** went down to the city of Samaria and proclaimed the Christ to them. The crowds with one accord listened eagerly to what was said by Philip, hearing and seeing the signs that he did, for unclean spirits, crying with loud shrieks, came out of many who were possessed; and many others who were paralysed or lame were cured. So there was great joy in that city.

Now when the Apostles at Jerusalem heard that Samaria had accepted the word of God, they sent Peter and John to them. The two went down and prayed for them that they might receive the **Holy Spirit**; (for as yet the Spirit had not come upon any of them; they had only been baptized in the name of the Lord Jesus). Then Peter and John laid their hands on them, and they received the Holy Spirit.

The word of the Lord. **Thanks be to God.**

Psalm 66

R. **Make a joyful noise to God, all the earth!**

or **Alleluia!**

Make a joyful noise to God, all the earth!
sing the glory of his name;
give to him glorious praise.
Say to God, "How awesome are your deeds!" R.

"All the earth worships you;
they sing praises to you, sing praises to your name."
Come and see what God has done:
he is awesome in his deeds among the children
of Adam. R.

He turned the sea into dry land;
they passed through the river on foot.
There we rejoiced in him,
who rules by his might forever. R.

℟. **Make a joyful noise to God, all the earth!**

Come and hear, all you who fear God,
and I will tell what he has done for me.
Blessed be God, because he has not rejected my prayer
or removed his steadfast love from me. ℟.

A reading from the first Letter of Saint Peter (3.15-18)

Beloved: In your hearts **sanctify** Christ as Lord. Always be ready to make your defence to anyone who demands from you an accounting for the hope that is in you; yet do it with gentleness and reverence. Keep your conscience clear, so that, when you are maligned, those who abuse you for your good conduct in Christ may be put to shame. For it is better to suffer for doing good, if suffering should be God's will, than to suffer for doing evil.

For **Christ** also suffered for sins once for all, the righteous for the unrighteous, in order to bring you to God. He was put to death in the flesh, but made alive in the spirit.

The word of the Lord. **Thanks be to God.**

A reading from the holy Gospel according to John (14.15-21)

Jesus said to his disciples: "If you love me, you will keep my commandments. And I will ask the Father, and he will give you another **Advocate**, to be with you forever. This is the Spirit of truth, whom the world cannot receive, because it neither sees him nor knows him. You know him, because he **abides** with you, and he will be in you.

"I will not leave you orphaned; I am coming to you. In a little while the world will no longer see me, but you will see me; because I live, you also will live. On that day you will know that I am in my Father, and you in me, and I in you.

"The one who has my commandments and keeps them is **the one who loves me**; and the one who loves me will be loved by my Father, and I will love them and reveal myself to them."

The Gospel of the Lord. **Praise to you, Lord Jesus Christ.**

Key Words

Philip in today's reading from the Acts of the Apostles is not Philip the apostle, but one of the seven deacons named by the apostles to care for widows and the poor. He was mentioned last Sunday, along with Stephen, the first martyr.

Before Jesus went to heaven, he said not to be afraid, because he would send the **Holy Spirit** to help us remember all that Jesus taught. The Holy Spirit came upon the early Church at Pentecost.

To **sanctify** something is to make it holy. When we carry the Holy Spirit in our hearts, and try to love each other, we proclaim that Jesus is holy and sanctify Jesus.

Christ is a Greek word that means 'anointed.' The chosen person was blessed with holy oil and given a special mission. The Aramaic word for 'anointed' is 'Messiah.'

The **Advocate** is another name for the Holy Spirit, sent by Jesus to be our helper and guide until the end of time.

The Holy Spirit **abides** or lives in us. The Spirit encourages us and gives us the words we need to speak about our faith in Jesus Christ.

When Jesus speaks of "**the one who loves me**," he means those who show their love of God by their loving actions. Love is more than a good feeling — it is a way of life.

May 28

Ascension of the Lord

A reading from the Acts of the Apostles (1.1-11)

In the first book, **Theophilus**, I wrote about all that Jesus did and taught from the beginning until the day when he was taken up to heaven, after giving instructions through the Holy Spirit to the Apostles whom he had chosen. After his suffering he presented himself alive to them by many convincing proofs, appearing to them during forty days and speaking about the kingdom of God.

While staying with them, he ordered them not to leave Jerusalem, but to wait there for the promise of the Father. "This," he said, "is what you have heard from me; for John baptized with water, but you will be baptized with the Holy Spirit not many days from now."

So when they had come together, they asked him, "Lord, is this the time when you will restore the **kingdom** to Israel?" He replied, "It is not for you to know the times or periods that the Father has set by his own authority. But you will receive power when the Holy Spirit has come upon you; and you will be my witnesses in Jerusalem, in all Judea and Samaria, and to the ends of the earth."

When he had said this, as they were watching, he was lifted up, and a cloud took him out of their sight. While he was going and they were gazing up toward heaven, suddenly two men in white robes stood by them. They said, "Men of **Galilee**, why do you stand looking up toward heaven? This Jesus, who has been taken up from you into heaven, will come in the same way as you saw him go into heaven."

The word of the Lord. **Thanks be to God.**

Psalm 47

R. **God has gone up with a shout,**
the Lord with the sound of a trumpet.

or   **Alleluia!**

Clap your hands, all you peoples;
shout to God with loud songs of joy.
For the Lord, the Most High, is awesome,
a great king over all the earth.   R.

God has gone up with a shout,
the Lord with the sound of a trumpet.
Sing praises to God, sing praises;
sing praises to our King, sing praises.   R.

For God is the king of all the earth;
sing praises with a Psalm.
God is king over the nations;
God sits on his holy throne.   R.

A reading from the Letter of Saint Paul to the Ephesians (1.17-23)

Brothers and sisters: I pray that the God of our Lord Jesus Christ, the Father of glory, may give you a spirit of wisdom and revelation as you come to know him, so that, with the eyes of your heart enlightened, you may know what is the hope to which he has called you, what are the riches of his glorious inheritance among the saints, and what is the immeasurable greatness of his power for us who believe, according to the working of his great power.

God put this power to work in Christ when he raised him from the dead and seated him at his **right hand** in the heavenly places, far above all **rule and authority and power and dominion**, and above every name that is named, not only in this age but also in the age to come.

And he has put all things under his feet and has made him the head over all things for the Church, which is his body, the fullness of him who fills all in all.

The word of the Lord. **Thanks be to God.**

A reading from the holy Gospel according to Matthew (28.16-20)

The eleven disciples went to Galilee, to the mountain to which Jesus had directed them. When they saw him, they worshipped him; but some doubted.

And Jesus came and said to them, "All authority in heaven and on earth has been given to me. Go therefore and make disciples of all nations, baptizing them in the name of the Father and of the Son and of the Holy Spirit, and teaching them to obey everything that I have commanded you. And remember, **I am with you** always, to the end of the age."

The Gospel of the Lord. **Praise to you, Lord Jesus Christ.**

Key Words

On the feast of the **Ascension**, we remember the moment when Jesus returned to the house of his Father, forty days after rising from the dead. Jesus no longer appeared to his disciples, but he sent the Holy Spirit at Pentecost.

Theophilus (a Greek name that means 'friend of God') lived in Antioch. He was a leader of the Christian communities of Greece. Luke sent his Gospel as well as the Acts of the Apostles to him.

In the days of Jesus, Israel was part of the Roman Empire and was not free to govern itself. Some of the disciples hoped that Jesus would free Israel from Rome's bitter rule and bring back the ancient **kingdom** of Israel.

Galilee is a province in the north of Israel. Nazareth, the town where Jesus lived with his parents, is in Galilee. So is the Sea of Tiberias, where some of Jesus' disciples worked as fishermen. In Jerusalem, to the south, Jesus and his followers were recognized as Galileans because of their accent.

When Saint Paul says that Jesus sits at the **right hand** of God, he is saying that Jesus is as close as possible to God the Father. There is no place closer to God.

When Saint Paul speaks of all **rule and authority and power and dominion**, he is not talking about earthly governments. Instead, he means different kinds of angels in heaven. Jesus sits so close to the Father in heaven that he is above all the angels.

"**I am with you**" is the promise Jesus made to the disciples and to us. He is with us when we gather in his name as a community, when we listen to God's word, when we celebrate the Eucharist, and when we share his love with others.

June 4
Pentecost Sunday

A reading from the Acts of the Apostles (2.1-11)

When the day of Pentecost had come, they were all together in one place. And suddenly from heaven there came a sound like the rush of a violent wind, and it filled the entire house where they were sitting. Divided tongues, as of fire, appeared among them, and a tongue rested on each of them. All of them were filled with the Holy Spirit and began to speak in other languages, as the Spirit gave them ability.

Now there were devout Jews from every nation under heaven living in Jerusalem. And at this sound the crowd gathered and was bewildered, because each one heard them speaking in their own language. Amazed and astonished, they asked, "Are not all these who are speaking Galileans? And how is it that we hear, each of us, in our own language? Parthians, Medes, Elamites, and residents of Mesopotamia, Judea and Cappadocia, Pontus and Asia, Phrygia and Pamphylia, Egypt and the parts of Libya belonging to Cyrene, and visitors from Rome, both Jews and converts, Cretans and Arabs — in our own languages we hear them speaking about God's **deeds of power**."

The word of the Lord. **Thanks be to God.**

Psalm 104

R. **Lord, send forth your Spirit,**
and renew the face of the earth.

or **Alleluia!**

Bless the Lord, O my soul.
O Lord my God, you are very great.
O Lord, how manifold are your works!
The earth is full of your creatures. R.

When you take away their breath,
they die and return to their dust.
When you send forth your spirit, they are created;
and you renew the face of the earth. R.

May the glory of the Lord endure forever;
may the Lord rejoice in his works.
May my meditation be pleasing to him,
for I rejoice in the Lord. R.

A reading from the first Letter of Saint Paul to the Corinthians (12.3-7, 12-13)

Brothers and sisters: No one can say "Jesus is Lord" except by the Holy Spirit.

Now there are varieties of gifts, but the same Spirit; and there are varieties of services, but the same Lord; and there are varieties of activities, but it is the same God who activates all of them in everyone. To each is given the manifestation of the Spirit for the **common good**.

For just as the **body** is one and has many members, and all the members of the body, though many, are one body, so it is with Christ. For in the one Spirit we were all baptized into one body — Jews or Greeks, slaves or free — and we were all made to drink of one Spirit.

The word of the Lord. **Thanks be to God.**

A reading from the holy Gospel according to John (20.19-23)

It was evening on the day Jesus rose from the dead, the first day of the week, and the doors of the house where the disciples had met were locked for fear of the Jews. Jesus came and stood among them and said, "**Peace** be with you." After he said this, he showed them his hands and his side. Then the disciples rejoiced when they saw the Lord.

Jesus said to them again, "Peace be with you. As the Father has sent me, so I send you."

When he had said this, he breathed on them and said to them, "Receive the Holy Spirit. If you **forgive the sins** of any, they are forgiven them; if you retain the sins of any, they are retained."

The Gospel of the Lord. **Praise to you, Lord Jesus Christ.**

Key Words

God's **deeds of power** are so great that they cannot be counted, but the greatest of these is that he sent his Son to save us. The disciples proclaimed the Good News of God's marvellous deed — the death and resurrection of Jesus.

The **Corinthians** were a community of Christians who lived in Corinth, a city in Greece. Saint Paul wrote them several letters, two of which are in the Bible.

Each of us is unique and has received our own gifts through the Holy Spirit. But we must not keep these gifts to ourselves: they are for the **common good**, for the good of everyone in the community.

Saint Paul compares the Church to a human **body**. Although all the parts are different, each is important and all the parts together make one complete body.

Each time Jesus appears to his disciples after the resurrection, he says "**Peace** be with you." The disciples are afraid and confused, and Jesus tells them not to worry and to be at peace. We can turn to Jesus when we are frightened and confused and we will know his peace in our hearts.

Jesus gives his disciples an important power — to **forgive the sins** of others. We promise to do the same each time we pray the Our Father ("as we forgive those who trespass against us").

June 11

Solemnity of the
Most Holy Trinity

A reading from the book of Exodus (34.4-6, 8-9)

Moses rose early in the morning and went up on **Mount Sinai**, as the Lord had commanded him, and took in his hand the **two tablets of stone**. The Lord descended in the cloud and stood with him there, and proclaimed the name, "The Lord."

The Lord passed before Moses, and proclaimed, "The Lord, the Lord, a God merciful and gracious, slow to anger, and abounding in steadfast love and faithfulness."

And Moses quickly bowed his head toward the earth, and worshipped. He said, "If now I have found favour in your sight, O Lord, I pray, let the Lord go with us. Although this is a stiff-necked people, pardon our iniquity and our sin, and take us for your inheritance."

The word of the Lord. **Thanks be to God.**

Daniel 3

R. **Glory and praise for ever!**

Blessed are you, O Lord, God of our fathers
and blessed is your glorious and holy name. R.

Blessed are you in the temple of your holy glory,
and to be extolled and highly glorified forever. R.

Blessed are you on the throne of your kingdom,
and to be extolled and highly exalted forever. R.

Blessed are you who look into the depths
from your throne on the cherubim. R.

Blessed are you in the firmament of heaven,
to be sung and glorified forever. R.

A reading from the second Letter of Saint Paul to the Corinthians (13.11-13)

Brothers and sisters, put things in order, listen to my appeal, agree with one another, live in peace; and the God of love and peace will be with you. Greet one another with a holy kiss. All the saints greet you.

The grace of the Lord Jesus Christ, the love of God, and the communion of the Holy Spirit be with all of you.

The word of the Lord. **Thanks be to God.**

A reading from the holy Gospel according to John (3.16-18)

Jesus said to Nicodemus: "God so loved the world that he gave his only-begotten Son, so that everyone who believes in him may not **perish** but may have eternal life.

"Indeed, God did not send the Son into the world to condemn the world, but in order that the world might be saved through him. The one who believes in him is not condemned; but the one who does not believe is condemned already, for not having believed in the name of the only-begotten Son of God."

The Gospel of the Lord. **Praise to you, Lord Jesus Christ.**

Key Words

The **Trinity** is the idea of three persons in one God: the Father, the Son and the Holy Spirit. Today, on Trinity Sunday, we celebrate this mystery.

The second book of the Bible is called **Exodus**. It is an important book because it tells us how God liberated his people from slavery in Egypt, made a covenant with them and gave them the Ten Commandments, which taught them how to live correctly.

Mount Sinai is a place where God often visited his people. God spoke to Moses on Mount Sinai and gave him the Ten Commandments. Mount Sinai was also called Mount Horeb.

Even today we might inscribe important things in stone. We do this so that the words will not be erased or forgotten. When God spoke to Moses on Mount Sinai, God ordered him to write the Ten Commandments on **two tablets of stone**.

Saying "**Blessed** are you, O Lord" is a way of praising God. We are saying, "Let the whole world know how great and wonderful God is!"

The phrase **brothers and sisters** is used often in the New Testament and in the Church today. Jesus called the apostles his brothers and the early Christians also called each other brother and sister. This shows that we are members of one family because we share the same Father.

To **perish** is to die. Jesus promises that those who believe in him will not perish forever. Jesus promises us eternal life with God, and even though we will die, we already enjoy our new life with God.

June 18

Solemnity of the Most Holy Body and Blood of Christ

A reading from the book of Deuteronomy
(8.2-3, 14-16)

Moses spoke to the people: "Remember the long way that the Lord your God has led you these forty years in the wilderness, in order to humble you, testing you to know what was in your heart, whether or not you would keep his **commandments**. He humbled you by letting you hunger, then by feeding you with **manna**, with which neither you nor your ancestors were acquainted, in order to make you understand that man does not live by bread alone, but by every word that comes from the mouth of the Lord.

"Do not exalt yourself, forgetting the Lord your God, who brought you out of the land of Egypt, out of the house of slavery, who led you through the great and terrible wilderness, an arid wasteland with poisonous snakes and scorpions. He made water flow for you from flint rock, and fed you in the wilderness with manna that your ancestors did not know, to humble you and to test you, and in the end to do you good."

The word of the Lord. **Thanks be to God.**

Psalm 147

R. **Praise the Lord, Jerusalem.**

or **Alleluia!**

Praise the Lord, O Jerusalem!
Praise your God, O Zion!
For he strengthens the bars of your gates;
he blesses your children within you. R.

He grants peace within your borders;
he fills you with the finest of wheat.
He sends out his command to the earth;
his word runs swiftly. R.

He declares his word to Jacob,
his statutes and ordinances to Israel.
He has not dealt thus with any other nation;
they do not know his ordinances. R.

A reading from the first Letter of Saint Paul to the Corinthians (10.16-17)

Brothers and sisters: The cup of blessing that we bless, is it not a sharing in the Blood of Christ? The bread that we break, is it not a sharing in the Body of Christ?

Because there is one bread, we who are many are one body, for we all partake of the one bread.

The word of the Lord. **Thanks be to God.**

A reading from the holy Gospel according to John (6.51-59)

Jesus said to the people: "I am the living bread that came down from heaven. Whoever eats of this bread will live forever; and the bread that I will give for the life of the world is my flesh."

The people then disputed among themselves, saying, "How can this man give us his flesh to eat?"

So Jesus said to them, "Very truly, I tell you, unless you eat the flesh of the Son of Man and drink his blood, you have no life in you. Whoever eats my flesh and drinks my blood has eternal life, and I will raise them up on the last day; for my flesh is true food and my blood is true drink. Whoever eats my flesh and drinks my blood abides in me, and I in them.

"Just as the living Father sent me, and I live because of the Father, so whoever eats me will live because of me. This is the bread that came down from heaven, not like that which your **ancestors** ate, and they died. But the one who eats this bread will live forever."

Jesus said these things while he was teaching in the synagogue at Capernaum.

The Gospel of the Lord. **Praise to you, Lord Jesus Christ.**

Key Words

God gave his **commandments** to Moses and God's people on Mount Sinai. They help us to love God and all the people we meet along the road of life.

Manna is a food that God sent to the Israelites when they fled from Egypt. They were crossing the desert and had nothing to eat. After Moses asked God for help, the people woke up the next morning and found manna on the ground. Manna was like bread falling from heaven.

The holy Gospel according to John tells us about the life, death and resurrection of Jesus. It was written about 90 years after Jesus died. John's Gospel includes some stories and sayings that are not in the other three Gospels (Matthew, Mark and Luke).

The people who lived before us, our **ancestors**, left slavery in Egypt 1,000 years before Christ was born. They wandered in the desert for forty years before coming to the Promised Land. When they were hungry, God sent them manna from heaven. God sent his son, Jesus, to be *our* living bread. God always takes care of his people!

June 25

12th Sunday in Ordinary Time

A reading from the book of the Prophet Jeremiah (20.10-13)

Jeremiah cried out: I hear many whispering: "Terror is all around! Denounce him! Let us denounce him!" All my close friends are watching for me to stumble. "Perhaps he can be enticed, and we can prevail against him, and take our revenge on him."

But the Lord is with me like a dread warrior; therefore my persecutors will stumble, and they will not prevail. They will be greatly shamed, for they will not succeed. Their eternal dishonour will never be forgotten.

O Lord of hosts, you test the righteous, you see the heart and the mind; let me see your retribution upon them, for to you I have committed my cause.

Sing to the Lord; praise the Lord! For he has delivered the life of the needy from the hands of evildoers.

The word of the Lord. **Thanks be to God.**

Psalm 69

R. **Lord, in your steadfast love, answer me.**

It is for your sake that I have borne reproach,
that shame has covered my face.
I have become a stranger to my kindred,
an alien to my mother's children.
It is zeal for your house that has consumed me;
the insults of those who insult you have fallen on me. R.

But as for me, my prayer is to you, O Lord.
At an acceptable time, O God,
in the abundance of your steadfast love, answer me.
With your steadfast help, rescue me.
Answer me, O Lord, for your steadfast love is good;
according to your abundant mercy, turn to me. R.

Let the oppressed see it and be glad;
you who seek God, let your hearts revive.
For the Lord hears the needy,
and does not despise his own that are in bonds.
Let heaven and earth praise him,
the seas and everything that moves in them. R.

A reading from the Letter of Saint Paul to the Romans (5.12-15)

Brothers and sisters: Just as **sin came into the world** through one man, and death came through sin, so death spread to all people because all have sinned. Sin was indeed in the world before the **law**, but sin is not reckoned when there is no law. Yet death exercised dominion from Adam to Moses, even over those whose sins were not like the **transgression** of Adam, who is a **type** of the one who was to come.

But the free gift is not like the **trespass**. For if the many died through the one man's trespass, much more surely have the grace of God and the free gift in the grace of the one man, Jesus Christ, abounded for the many.

The word of the Lord. **Thanks be to God.**

A reading from the holy Gospel according to Matthew (10.26-33)

Jesus said to his Apostles: "Fear no one; for nothing is covered up that will not be uncovered, and nothing secret that will not become known. What I say to you in the dark, tell in the light; and what you hear whispered, proclaim from the housetops.

"Do not fear those who kill the body but cannot kill the soul; rather fear him who can destroy both soul and body in hell. Are not two sparrows sold for a penny? Yet not one of them will fall to the ground apart from your Father. And even the hairs of your head are all counted. So do not be afraid; you are of more value than many sparrows.

"Everyone therefore who acknowledges me before humans, I also will acknowledge before my Father in heaven; but whoever denies me before humans, I also will deny before my Father in heaven."

The Gospel of the Lord. **Praise to you, Lord Jesus Christ.**

Key Words

A **Prophet** was a holy man or woman who spoke publicly against poverty and injustice, and criticized the people whenever they refused to listen to God's word. Many of the books of the Old Testament were written by prophets (Isaiah, Jeremiah, Amos, and Micah, for example).

Jeremiah lived about 600 years before Jesus. When Jeremiah was still a young boy, God called him to guide the people of Israel back to God. Many people ignored Jeremiah at first and sent him away. But when they faced serious problems and feared that God had stopped loving them, Jeremiah gave them hope that God would not abandon them.

In the Letter to the Romans, Saint Paul reminds us that **sin came into the world** by Adam (and Eve) in the Garden of Eden, and with sin came death. New life also came into the world by one man — Jesus Christ, the Son of God.

The **law** refers to the Ten Commandments that God gave to Moses at Mount Sinai. Saint Paul tells us that even though there was no 'law' in the time between Adam and Moses, there were still sin and death in the world.

Transgression and **trespass** are other ways to talk of sin. We use the word 'trespasses' to mean 'sin' when we pray the Our Father.

A **type** is a model or example. Saint Paul shows us how Adam as the first human being brought sin and death into the world, and then Jesus, the son of God and first-born from the dead, brought grace and eternal life for all.

July 2
13th Sunday in Ordinary Time

A reading from the second book of Kings
(4.8-12, 14-16)

One day Elisha was passing through Shunem, where a wealthy woman lived, who urged him to have a meal. So whenever he passed that way, he would stop there for a meal. She said to her husband, "Look, I am sure that this man who regularly passes our way is a holy man of God. Let us make a small roof chamber with walls, and put there for him a bed, a table, a chair, and a lamp, so that he can stay there whenever he comes to us."

One day when Elisha came there, he went up to the chamber and lay down there. He said to his servant Gehazi, "What then may be done for the woman?" Gehazi answered, "Well, she has no **son**, and her husband is old." Elisha said, "Call her." When the servant had called her, she stood at the door. Elisha said, "At this season, in due time, you shall embrace a son."

The word of the Lord. **Thanks be to God.**

Psalm 89

> R̰. **Forever I will sing of your steadfast love, O Lord.**
>
> I will sing of your steadfast love, O Lord, forever;
> with my mouth I will proclaim your faithfulness
>   to all generations.
> I declare that your steadfast love is established forever;
> your faithfulness is as firm as the heavens. R̰.
>
> Blessed are the people who know the **festal** shout,
> who walk, O Lord, in the light of your countenance;
> they exult in your name all day long,
> and extol your righteousness. R̰.
>
> For you are the glory of their strength;
> by your favour our horn is exalted.
> For our shield belongs to the Lord,
> our king to the Holy One of Israel. R̰.

A reading from the Letter of Saint Paul to the Romans (6.3-4, 8-11)

Brothers and sisters: All of us who have been baptized into Christ Jesus were baptized into his death. Therefore we have been buried with him by baptism into death, so that, just as Christ was raised from the dead by the glory of the Father, so we too might walk in newness of life.

But if we have died with Christ, we believe that we will also live with him. We know that Christ, being raised from the dead, will never die again; death no longer has **dominion** over him. The death he died, he died to sin, once for all; but the life he lives, he lives to God.

So you also must consider yourselves dead to sin and alive to God in Christ Jesus.

The word of the Lord. **Thanks be to God.**

A reading from the holy Gospel according to Matthew (10.37-42)

Jesus said to his Apostles: "Whoever loves father or mother more than me is not worthy of me; and whoever loves son or daughter more than me is not worthy of me; and whoever does not take up their cross and follow me is not worthy of me. Whoever finds their life will lose it, and whoever loses their life for my sake will find it.

"Whoever welcomes you welcomes me, and whoever welcomes me welcomes the one who sent me. Whoever welcomes a prophet in the name of a prophet will receive a prophet's reward; and whoever welcomes a righteous person in the name of a righteous person will receive the reward of the righteous; and whoever gives even a cup of cold water to one of these little ones in the name of a disciple — truly I tell you — that person will not lose their reward."

The Gospel of the Lord. **Praise to you, Lord Jesus Christ.**

Key Words

In the Bible, the two books of **Kings** tell the story of a time when Israel was ruled by kings. The books begin with the death of King David, nearly 1,000 years before Jesus was born, and end when the Babylonians capture Jerusalem, nearly 600 years before Jesus. The writer wants us to see how God helps his people throughout history.

In the ancient world, children were important for a family's future. Daughters would marry into neighbouring families, and **sons** would inherit family possessions and position in the community. If the father died, the son would be responsible for caring for his mother and siblings. Elisha is blessing the wealthy woman's family for their hospitality by promising them a son.

Festal means having to do with a feast or celebration. The psalmist uses this word to celebrate God's great love and faithfulness.

Dominion is a word meaning the authority to govern. Before Jesus rose from the dead, death had dominion or power over all people. Jesus broke death's power when he rose from the dead, bringing eternal life to all who believe.

July 9
14th Sunday in Ordinary Time

A reading from the book of the Prophet Zechariah (9.9-10)

Thus says the Lord:
Rejoice greatly, O **daughter Zion!**
Shout aloud, O daughter Jerusalem!
Lo, your king comes to you;
triumphant and victorious is he,
humble and riding on a donkey,
on a colt, the foal of a donkey.

He will cut off the chariot from **Ephraim**
and the war horse from Jerusalem;
and the warrior's bow shall be cut off,
and he shall command peace to the nations;
his dominion shall be from sea to sea,
and from the River to the ends of the earth.

The word of the Lord. **Thanks be to God.**

Psalm 145

R. **I will bless your name for ever, my King and my God.**

or **Alleluia!**

I will extol you, my God and King,
and bless your name forever and ever.
Every day I will bless you,
and praise your name forever and ever. R.

The Lord is gracious and merciful,
slow to anger and abounding in steadfast love.
The Lord is good to all,
and his compassion is over all that he has made. R.

All your works shall give thanks to you, O Lord,
and all your faithful shall bless you.
They shall speak of the glory of your kingdom,
and tell of your power. R.

The Lord is faithful in all his words,
and gracious in all his deeds.
The Lord upholds all who are falling,
and raises up all who are bowed down. R.

A reading from the Letter of Saint Paul to the Romans (8.9, 11-13)

Brothers and sisters: You are not in the flesh; you are in the Spirit, since the **Spirit of God** dwells in you. Anyone who does not have the Spirit of Christ does not belong to him.

If the Spirit of God who raised Jesus from the dead dwells in you, he who raised Christ from the dead will give life to your mortal bodies also through his Spirit that dwells in you.

So then, brothers and sisters, we are debtors, not to the flesh, to live according to the flesh — for if you live according to the flesh, you will die; but if by the Spirit you put to death the deeds of the body, you will live.

The word of the Lord. **Thanks be to God.**

A reading from the holy Gospel according to Matthew (11.25-30)

At that time Jesus said, "I thank you, Father, Lord of heaven and earth, because you have hidden these things from the wise and the intelligent and have revealed them to infants; yes, Father, for such was your gracious will."

He continued: "All things have been handed over to me by my Father; and no one knows the Son except the Father, and no one knows the Father except the Son and anyone to whom the Son chooses to reveal him.

"Come to me, all you that are weary and are carrying heavy **burdens**, and I will give you rest. Take my yoke upon you, and learn from me; for I am gentle and humble in heart, and you will find rest for your souls. For my yoke is easy, and my burden is light."

The Gospel of the Lord. **Praise to you, Lord Jesus Christ.**

Key Words

Zechariah was a prophet who lived 520 years before Christ. The temple in Jerusalem had been destroyed by Nebuchadnezzar, and Zechariah was trying to lift the spirits of the people of Israel. A good part of the book of Zechariah is dedicated to announcing the coming of the Messiah. He will come like a king, like a shepherd, or like the servant of the Lord.

Zion was the name of a hill in Jerusalem where the temple was built, but the city itself was often called Zion. **Daughter Zion** is another way of naming the entire nation, the whole People of God.

Ephraim is the name of one of Jacob's sons and one of the twelve tribes of Israel. The Bible sometimes uses this name for the whole people of Israel.

The **Spirit of God** dwells in us by speaking in our hearts and leading us to follow Jesus by our words and actions. If we listen to the Spirit and follow where it leads, we are living according to the Spirit.

The **Gospel** is the message of Jesus. It comes from an old English word *godspel* that means 'good news.'

Everyone has **burdens** to carry in life — times of pain or suffering. But if we live as Jesus taught us, we will also have great joy and the hard times will be easier to bear. Jesus brings us true consolation and comfort.

July 16

15th Sunday in Ordinary Time

A reading from the book of the Prophet Isaiah
(55.10-11)

Thus says the Lord: "As the rain and the snow come down from heaven, and do not return there until they have watered the earth, making it bring forth and sprout, giving seed to the sower and bread to the one who eats, so shall my word be that goes out from my mouth; it shall not return to me empty, but it shall accomplish that which I purpose, and succeed in the thing for which I sent it."

The word of the Lord. **Thanks be to God.**

Psalm 65

R. **The seed that fell on good soil produced a hundredfold.**

You visit the earth and water it,
you greatly enrich it;
the river of God is full of water;
you provide the people with grain. R.

For so you have prepared the earth:
you water its furrows abundantly,
settling its ridges, softening it with showers,
and blessing its growth. R.

You crown the year with your bounty;
your pathways overflow with richness.
The pastures of the wilderness overflow,
the hills gird themselves with joy. R.

The meadows clothe themselves with flocks,
the valleys deck themselves with grain,
they shout and sing together for joy. R.

A reading from the Letter of Saint Paul to the Romans (8.18-23)

Brothers and sisters: I consider that the sufferings of this present time are not worth comparing with the **glory** about to be revealed to us. For the creation waits with eager longing for the revealing of the children of God; for the creation was subjected to **futility**, not of its own will but by the will of the one who subjected it, in hope that the creation itself will be set free from its bondage to decay and will obtain the freedom of the glory of the children of God.

We know that the whole creation has been groaning in labour pains until now; and not only the creation, but we ourselves, who have the first fruits of the Spirit, groan inwardly while we wait for adoption to sonship, the redemption of our bodies.

The word of the Lord. **Thanks be to God.**

A reading from the holy Gospel according to Matthew (13.1-23)

The shorter reading ends at the asterisks.

Jesus went out of the house and sat beside the sea. Such great crowds gathered around him that he got into a boat and sat there, while the whole crowd stood on the beach. And he told them many things in **parables**.

"Listen! A **sower** went out to sow. And as he sowed, some seeds fell on the path, and the birds came and ate them up. Other seeds fell on rocky ground, where they did not have much soil, and they sprang up quickly, since they had no depth of soil. But when the sun rose, they were scorched; and since they had no **root**, they withered away. Other seeds fell among thorns, and the thorns grew up and choked them. Other seeds fell on good soil and brought forth grain, some a hundredfold, some sixty, some thirty. Let anyone with ears listen!"

* * *

Then the disciples came and asked Jesus, "Why do you speak to them in parables?" He answered, "To you it has been given to know the secrets of the kingdom of heaven, but to them it has not been given. For to those who have, more will be given, and

203

they will have an abundance; but from those who have nothing, even what they have will be taken away.

"The reason I speak to them in parables is that 'seeing they do not perceive, and hearing they do not listen, nor do they understand.' With them indeed is fulfilled the prophecy of Isaiah that says: 'You will indeed listen, but never understand, and you will indeed look, but never perceive. For this people's heart has grown dull, and their ears are hard of hearing, and they have shut their eyes; so that they might not look with their eyes, and listen with their ears, and understand with their heart and turn — and I would heal them.'

"But blessed are your eyes, for they see, and your ears, for they hear. Truly I tell you, many Prophets and righteous people longed to see what you see, but did not see it, and to hear what you hear, but did not hear it.

"Hear then the parable of the sower. When anyone hears the word of the kingdom and does not understand it, the evil one comes and snatches away what is sown in the heart; this is what was sown on the path. As for what was sown on rocky ground, this is the one who hears the word and immediately receives it with joy; yet such a person has no root, but endures only for a while, and when trouble or persecution arises on account of the word, that person immediately falls away. As for what was sown among thorns, this is the one who hears the word, but the cares of the world and the lure of wealth choke the word, and it yields nothing.

"But as for what was sown on good soil, this is the one who hears the word and understands it, who indeed bears fruit and yields, in one case a hundredfold, in another sixty, and in another thirty."

The Gospel of the Lord. **Praise to you, Lord Jesus Christ.**

Key Words

Saul was a man who bullied and terrorized the first Christians. One day, he had a vision of the risen Jesus and the experience changed his whole life. When he was baptized he changed his name to **Paul** and became a great apostle, travelling to cities all around the Mediterranean Sea to tell people about the love of Jesus. His letters found in the Bible are the earliest books of the New Testament or Christian Scriptures.

When we speak of God's **glory**, we are talking about God's power, importance and splendour.

When we are distracted from our friendship with God, our lives are ones of **futility** or aimlessness — they have no meaning. God wants us to direct our lives to following the Spirit.

Parables are brief stories or wise sayings that Jesus used when he was teaching. Jesus used everyday situations to help his listeners understand what he meant. The parables invite us to change our lives and turn to God.

A **sower** is a farmer who is planting seeds by hand. In this parable, the seeds represent the word of God. Sometimes it bears fruit and sometimes it does not. We must try to be fertile ground for the word of God.

A plant needs a good **root** system, deep and strong, in order to survive times of stress. We also need a solid and secure faith, rooted deep in the Spirit of God, dwelling in our hearts.

July 23
16th Sunday in Ordinary Time

A reading from the book of Wisdom
(12.13, 16-19)

There is no god besides you, Lord,
whose care is for all people,
to whom you should prove that you have not judged unjustly.

For your strength is the source of righteousness,
and your sovereignty over all causes you to **spare** all.
For you show your strength
when people doubt the completeness of your power,
and you rebuke any insolence among those who know it.
Although you are sovereign in strength,
you **judge** with mildness,
and with great forbearance you govern us;
for you have power to act whenever you choose.

Through such works you have taught your people
that the righteous must be kind,
and you have filled your children with good hope,
because you give repentance for sins.

The word of the Lord. **Thanks be to God.**

Psalm 86

R̶. **Lord, you are good and forgiving.**

You, O Lord, are good and forgiving,
abounding in steadfast love to all who call on you.
Give ear, O Lord, to my prayer;
listen to my cry of supplication. R̶.

All the nations you have made shall come
and bow down before you, O Lord,
and shall glorify your name.
For you are great and do wondrous things;
you alone are God. R̶.

But you, O Lord, are a God merciful and gracious,
slow to anger and abounding in steadfast love and
    faithfulness.
Turn to me and be gracious to me.
Give your strength to your servant. R̶.

A reading from the Letter of Saint Paul to the Romans (8.26-27)

Brothers and sisters: The Spirit helps us in our weakness; for we do not know how to pray as we ought, but that very Spirit **intercedes** with sighs too deep for words.

And God, who searches the heart, knows what is the mind of the Spirit, because the Spirit intercedes for the saints according to the will of God.

The word of the Lord. **Thanks be to God.**

A reading from the holy Gospel according to Matthew (13.24-43)

The shorter reading ends at the asterisks.

Jesus put before the crowds a parable: "The kingdom of heaven may be compared to someone who sowed good seed in his field; but while everybody was asleep, an enemy came and sowed **weeds** among the wheat, and then went away.

"So when the plants came up and bore grain, then the weeds appeared as well. And the slaves of the householder came and said to him, 'Master, did you not sow good seed in your field? Where, then, did these weeds come from?' He answered, 'An enemy has done this.' The slaves said to him, 'Then do you want us to go and gather them?' But he replied, 'No; for in gathering the weeds you would uproot the wheat along with them. Let both of them grow together until the harvest; and at harvest time I will tell the reapers, Collect the weeds first and bind them in **bundles** to be burned, but gather the wheat into my barn.'"

Jesus put before them another parable: "The kingdom of heaven is like a mustard seed that someone took and sowed in his field; it is the smallest of all the seeds, but when it has grown it is the greatest of shrubs and becomes a tree, so that the birds of the air come and make nests in its branches."

He told them another parable: "The kingdom of heaven is like **yeast** that a woman took and mixed in with three measures of flour until all of it was leavened."

* * *

Jesus told the crowds all these things in parables; without a parable he told them nothing. This was to fulfill what had been spoken through the Prophet: "I will open my mouth to speak in parables; I will proclaim what has been hidden from the foundation of the world."

Then Jesus left the crowds and went into the house. And his disciples approached him, saying, "Explain to us the parable of the weeds of the field." He answered, "The one who sows the good seed is the Son of Man; the field is the world, and the good seed are the children of the kingdom; the weeds are the children of the evil one, and the enemy who sowed them is the devil; the harvest is the end of the age, and the reapers are Angels.

"Just as the weeds are **collected** and **burned** up with fire, so will it be at the end of the age. The Son of Man will send his Angels, and they will collect out of his kingdom all causes of sin and all evildoers, and they will throw them into the furnace of fire, where there will be weeping and gnashing of teeth. Then the righteous will shine like the sun in the kingdom of their Father. Let anyone with ears listen!"

The Gospel of the Lord. **Praise to you, Lord Jesus Christ.**

Key Words

The book of **Wisdom** was written not long before Jesus was born. It urges us to make good decisions in life. It teaches about justice and fairness.

To **spare** someone is to decide not to punish them or to relieve them of trouble — to show them mercy.

To **judge** is to decide a question based on the evidence. For example, in court a judge may decide whether someone is innocent or guilty of a crime. God is a loving judge who shows great patience and mercy.

To **intercede** is to ask for something on behalf of another person. After Jesus rose from the dead, he sent the Holy Spirit to speak on our behalf and to dwell in our hearts.

When **weeds** grow alongside a crop, they take water and nutrition away from the good plants. A weed-free field will produce a better harvest.

At the time of harvest, both the weeds and the wheat are tied into their own **bundles**, to make them easier to handle by the fieldworkers. This separates the good plants from the bad.

A small amount of **yeast** is added to bread dough to make it rise. The bread is then light and easy to eat. A very small amount of yeast can leaven a large amount of bread — just as our kind words or good deeds can make a difference to others.

The weeds are **collected** and **burned** by the farmer in order to prevent the weeds and their seeds from spreading. The crops will grow better if the field is weed-free.

A reading from the first book of Kings (3.5-12)

At Gibeon the Lord appeared to **Solomon** in a dream by night; and God said, "Ask what I should give you." And Solomon said, "You have shown great and steadfast love to your servant my father David, because he walked before you in faithfulness, in righteousness, and in uprightness of heart toward you; and you have kept for him this great and steadfast love, and have given him a son to sit on his throne today.

"And now, O Lord my God, you have made your servant king in place of my father David, although I am only a little child; I do not know how to go out or come in. And your servant is in the midst of the people whom you have chosen, a great people, so numerous they cannot be numbered or counted. Give your servant therefore an **understanding mind** to govern your people, able to discern between good and evil; for who can govern this, your great people?"

It pleased the Lord that Solomon had asked this. God said to him, "Because you have asked this, and have not asked for yourself long life or riches, or for the life of your enemies, but have asked for yourself understanding to discern what is right, I now do according to your word. Indeed I give you a wise and discerning mind; no one like you has been before you and no one like you shall arise after you."

The word of the Lord. **Thanks be to God.**

Psalm 119

R. **Lord, how I love your law!**

The Lord is my portion;
I promise to keep your words.
The law of your mouth is better to me
than thousands of gold and silver pieces. R.

Let your steadfast love become my comfort
according to your promise to your servant.
Let your mercy come to me, that I may live;
for your law is my delight. R.

Truly I love your commandments more than gold,
more than fine gold.
Truly I direct my steps by all your precepts;
I hate every false way. R.

Your decrees are wonderful;
therefore my soul keeps them.
The unfolding of your words gives light;
it imparts understanding to the simple. R.

A reading from the Letter of Saint Paul to the Romans (8.28-30)

Brothers and sisters: We know that all things work together for good for those who love God, who are called according to his **purpose**.

For those whom God foreknew he also **predestined** to be conformed to the image of his Son, in order that he might be the firstborn among many brothers and sisters.

And those whom God predestined he also called; and those whom he called he also **justified**; and those whom he justified he also glorified.

The word of the Lord. **Thanks be to God.**

A reading from the holy Gospel according to Matthew (13.44-52)

The shorter reading ends at the asterisks.

Jesus spoke to the crowds: "The kingdom of heaven is like **treasure** hidden in a field, which someone found and hid; then in his joy he goes and sells all that he has and buys that field.

"Again, the kingdom of heaven is like a merchant in search of fine pearls; on finding one pearl of great value, he went and sold all that he had and bought it.

"Again, the kingdom of heaven is like a net that was thrown into the sea and caught fish of every kind; when it was full, they drew it ashore, sat down, and put the good into baskets but threw out the bad.

* * *

"So it will be at the end of the age. The Angels will come out and separate the evil from the righteous and throw them into the furnace of fire, where there will be weeping and gnashing of teeth.

"Have you understood all this?" They answered, "Yes." And he said to them, "Therefore every scribe who has been trained for the kingdom of heaven is like the master of a household who brings out of his treasure what is new and what is old."

The Gospel of the Lord. **Praise to you, Lord Jesus Christ.**

Key Words

Solomon was the king of Israel after his father, David. He lived 1,000 years before Christ. Solomon was a wise and prudent king.

An **understanding mind** is one that relies not only on what the brain knows, but also on the wisdom of the heart. Solomon knew God as the Creator of all and made his decisions based on this deep knowledge.

God's **purpose** from the beginning has been the salvation of all creation. God wants all humankind to live in friendship with him.

God knows us before we are born, and we are **predestined** or meant to be God's children. We should live like Jesus did, loving the Father and taking care of others, especially those who are weaker or in need. This is the destiny God has for us.

When we hurt others, we break our friendship with God. But Jesus came to restore our friendship with God, and we are **justified** or brought back to friendship with God by our faith in Jesus.

By comparing the kingdom of heaven to **treasure**, Jesus is saying that life with God is more valuable than anything we can find or buy on earth. It is priceless.

August 6
Transfiguration of the Lord

A reading from the book of the Prophet Daniel
(7.9-10, 13-14)

As I watched, thrones were set in place, and the **One who is Ancient of Days** took his throne. His clothing was white as snow, and the hair of his head like pure wool. His throne was fiery flames, and its wheels were burning fire. A stream of fire issued and flowed out from his presence. A thousand thousands served him, and ten thousand times ten thousand stood attending him. The court sat in judgment, and the books were opened.

As I watched in the night visions, I saw one like a son of man coming with the clouds of heaven. And he came to the One who is Ancient of Days and was presented before him.

To him was given **dominion** and glory and kingship, that all peoples, nations, and languages should serve him. His dominion is an everlasting dominion that shall not pass away, and his kingship is one that shall never be destroyed.

The word of the Lord. **Thanks be to God.**

Psalm 97

R. **The Lord is king, the most high over all the earth.**

The Lord is king! Let the earth rejoice;
let the many coastlands be glad!
Clouds and thick darkness are all around him;
righteousness and justice are the foundation
of his throne. R.

The mountains melt like wax before the Lord,
before the Lord of all the earth.
The heavens proclaim his righteousness;
and all the peoples behold his glory. R.

For you, O Lord, are most high over all the earth;
you are exalted far above all gods. R.

A reading from the second Letter of Saint Peter (1.16-19)

We did not follow cleverly devised myths when we made known to you the power and coming of our Lord Jesus Christ, but we had been **eyewitnesses** of his majesty. For he received honour and glory from God the Father when that voice was conveyed to him by the Majestic Glory, saying, "This is my Son, the Beloved. With him I am well pleased."

We ourselves heard this voice come from heaven, while we were with him on the holy mountain. So we have the prophetic message more fully confirmed. You will do well to be attentive to this as to a lamp shining in a dark place, until the day dawns and the morning star rises in your hearts.

The word of the Lord. **Thanks be to God.**

A reading from the holy Gospel according to Matthew (17.1-9)

Jesus took with him Peter and James and his brother John and led them up a high mountain, by themselves. And he was **transfigured** before them, and his face shone like the sun, and his clothes became dazzling white. Suddenly there appeared to them Moses and Elijah, talking with him.

Then Peter said to Jesus, "Lord, it is good for us to be here; if you wish, I will make three dwellings here, one for you, one for Moses, and one for **Elijah**."

While he was still speaking, suddenly a bright cloud overshadowed them, and from the cloud a voice said, "This is my Son, the Beloved; with him I am well pleased; listen to him!"

When the disciples heard this, they fell to the ground and were overcome by fear. But Jesus came and touched them, saying, "Get up and do not be afraid." And when they looked up, they saw no one except Jesus himself alone.

As they were coming down the mountain, Jesus ordered them, "Tell no one about the vision until after the Son of Man has been raised from the dead."

The Gospel of the Lord. **Praise to you, Lord Jesus Christ.**

Key Words

The **book of Daniel** gave the Hebrew people comfort and hope in hard times. It was written about 160 years before Jesus was born, and is the first book of the Bible to talk about the resurrection of the dead.

Daniel calls God the **One who is Ancient of Days** as a way to show how God is eternal — his kingdom will have no end.

Dominion is a word meaning the authority to govern. To the Hebrew people, God's dominion extended to all peoples, all creation, heaven and hell. God is ruler over all.

Saint Peter was fortunate in that he actually knew Jesus — he and the other disciples were **eyewitnesses** to Jesus' teachings, his miracles, and his death and resurrection. While we cannot say the same, we do have their eyewitness accounts to guide us and strengthen us in our faith.

When Jesus was **transfigured**, he was changed and looked different somehow. His friends saw who Jesus really is: the Son of God.

The prophet **Elijah** lived about 900 years before Jesus. He taught the people about God. He is one of the great prophets in the Old Testament or Hebrew Scriptures.

August 13
19th Sunday in Ordinary Time

A reading from the first book of Kings
(19.9, 11-13)

When Elijah reached **Horeb**, the mountain of God, he came to a cave, and spent the night there. Then the word of the Lord came to him, saying, "Go out and stand on the mountain before the Lord, for the Lord is about to pass by."

Now there was a great wind, so strong that it was splitting mountains and breaking rocks in pieces before the Lord, but the Lord was not in the wind; and after the wind an earthquake, but the Lord was not in the earthquake; and after the earthquake a fire, but the Lord was not in the fire; and after the fire a sound of sheer silence.

When Elijah heard it, he wrapped his face in his mantle and went out and stood at the entrance of the cave.

The word of the Lord. **Thanks be to God.**

Psalm 85

R. **Show us your steadfast love, O Lord,
and grant us your salvation.**

Let me hear what God the Lord will speak,
for he will speak peace to his people.
Surely his salvation is at hand for those who fear him,
that his glory may dwell in our land. R.

Steadfast love and faithfulness will meet;
righteousness and peace will kiss each other.
Faithfulness will spring up from the ground,
and righteousness will look down from the sky. R.

The Lord will give what is good,
and our land will yield its increase.
Righteousness will go before him,
and will make a path for his steps. R.

A reading from the Letter of Saint Paul to the Romans (9.1-5)

Brothers and sisters: I am speaking the truth in Christ. I am not lying; my conscience confirms it by the Holy Spirit. I have great sorrow and unceasing anguish in my heart.

For I could wish that I myself were accursed and cut off from Christ for the sake of my own people, my kindred according to the flesh. They are children of Israel, and to them belong the adoption, the glory, the covenants, the giving of the law, the worship, and the promises; to them belong the **patriarchs**, and from them, according to the flesh, comes the Christ, who is over all, God be blessed forever. **Amen**.

The word of the Lord. **Thanks be to God.**

A reading from the holy Gospel according to Matthew (14.22-33)

Immediately after feeding the crowd with the five loaves and two fish, Jesus made the disciples get into the boat and go on ahead to the other side, while he dismissed the crowds. And after he had dismissed the crowds, he went up the mountain by himself to pray.

When evening came, he was there alone, but by this time the boat, battered by the waves, was far from the land, for the wind was against them.

And early in the morning Jesus came walking toward them on the sea. But when the disciples saw him walking on the sea, they were terrified, saying, "It is a ghost!" And they cried out in fear. But immediately Jesus spoke to them and said, "Take heart, it is I; do not be afraid."

Peter answered him, "Lord, if it is you, command me to come to you on the water." Jesus said, "Come." So Peter got out of the boat, started walking on the water, and came toward Jesus. But when he noticed the strong wind, he became frightened, and beginning to sink, he cried out, "Lord, save me!"

Jesus immediately reached out his hand and caught him, saying to him, "You of little faith, why did you doubt?" When they got into the boat, the wind ceased. And those in the boat **worshipped** him, saying, "Truly you are the Son of God."

The Gospel of the Lord. **Praise to you, Lord Jesus Christ.**

Key Words

Mount **Horeb** (or Mount Sinai, as it is also called) is a place where God often visited his people. God spoke to Moses there and gave him the Ten Commandments.

The **patriarchs** were the ancestors of the people of Israel. Abraham, Isaac and Jacob were all known as patriarchs. God promised them that this people would become a great nation.

Amen is a Hebrew word that means 'so be it' or 'I know this is true.' By saying Amen after hearing or saying a prayer, we are agreeing with what it says. We say 'Amen' many times during Mass, especially after the Eucharistic Prayer when we sing the Great Amen, showing that we join with the priest in this great hymn of praise.

The apostles **worshipped** Jesus because they recognized that he was more than a man. Jesus is true God and true man. Worship is a gesture that recognizes the greatness of the one being worshipped.

August 20

20th Sunday in Ordinary Time

A reading from the book of the Prophet Isaiah
(56.1, 6-7)

Thus says the Lord: "**Maintain justice**, and do what is right, for soon my salvation will come, and my deliverance be revealed.

"And the foreigners who join themselves to the Lord, to minister to him, to love the name of the Lord, and to be his servants, all who **keep the Sabbath**, and do not profane it, and hold fast my covenant — these I will bring to my holy mountain, and make them joyful in my house of prayer; their **burnt offerings** and their sacrifices will be accepted on my altar; for my house shall be called a house of prayer for all peoples."

The word of the Lord. **Thanks be to God.**

Psalm 67

R. **Let the peoples praise you, O God,
let all the peoples praise you!**

May God be gracious to us and bless us
and make his face to shine upon us,
that your way may be known upon earth,
your saving power among all nations. R.

Let the nations be glad and sing for joy,
for you judge the peoples with equity
and guide the nations upon earth.
Let the peoples praise you, O God;
let all the peoples praise you. R.

The earth has yielded its increase;
God, our God, has blessed us.
May God continue to bless us;
let all the ends of the earth revere him. R.

A reading from the Letter of Saint Paul to the Romans (11.13-15, 29-32)

Brothers and sisters: Now I am speaking to you Gentiles. Inasmuch then as I am an **Apostle to the Gentiles**, I glorify my ministry in order to make my own flesh and blood jealous, and thus save some of them. For if their rejection is the reconciliation of the world, what will their acceptance be but life from the dead!

The gifts and the calling of God are irrevocable. Just as you were once disobedient to God but have now received mercy because of their disobedience, so they have now been disobedient in order that, by the mercy shown to you, they too may now receive mercy. For God has imprisoned all in disobedience so that he may be merciful to all.

The word of the Lord. **Thanks be to God.**

A reading from the holy Gospel according to Matthew (15.21-28)

Jesus went away to the district of Tyre and Sidon. A **Canaanite** woman from that region came out, and started shouting, "Have mercy on me, Lord, Son of David; my daughter is tormented by a demon." But he did not answer her at all.

And his disciples came and urged him, saying, "Send her away, for she keeps shouting after us." He answered, "I was sent only to the lost sheep of the **house of Israel**."

But the woman came and knelt before him, saying, "Lord, help me." He answered, "It is not fair to take the children's food and throw it to the dogs." She said, "Yes, Lord, yet even the dogs eat the crumbs that fall from their masters' table."

Then Jesus answered her, "Woman, **great is your faith!** Let it be done for you as you wish." And her daughter was healed instantly.

The Gospel of the Lord. **Praise to you, Lord Jesus Christ.**

Key Words

Our faith in God requires us to **maintain justice** — to take care of the rights of others. Working for the dignity and freedom of others is one way of obeying God's commandments.

The Sabbath is the day of the week when human beings rest as God did on the seventh day of creation. It is a chance for us to spend time praising God and enjoying creation. One of the Ten Commandments instructs us to **keep the Sabbath** holy.

Burnt offerings are a type of sacrifice to God where a dead animal (such as a lamb or calf) is put on a fire. Another type of offering is a libation or drink-offering that is poured out.

Saint Paul calls himself an **Apostle to the Gentiles**, meaning a messenger to people who were not Jewish. He wants all people, Jews and Gentiles, to be saved from death by faith in Jesus.

Canaanites were people from Canaan. After forty years in the desert, Moses brought the people to the land of Canaan, the promised land. In the time of Jesus, people from Canaan were considered foreigners.

House of Israel is one of the many names for the Israelites. Other names include House of David and House of Judah.

When Jesus says, "**great is your faith**," he is pointing to the confidence the Canaanite woman has. She asks Jesus to heal her daughter's illness and her own pain, believing that he will help them, even though they are strangers in the Jewish society.

August 27
21st Sunday in Ordinary Time

A reading from the book of the Prophet Isaiah
(22.15, 19-23)

Thus says the Lord God of hosts: Go to the steward, to **Shebna**, who is master of the household, and say to him:

"I will thrust you from your office, and you will be pulled down from your post. On that day I will call my servant Eliakim son of Hilkiah, and will clothe him with your robe and bind your sash on him. I will commit your authority to his hand, and he shall be a father to the inhabitants of Jerusalem and to the **house of Judah**.

"I will place on his shoulder the key of the house of David; he shall open, and no one shall shut; he shall shut, and no one shall open. I will fasten him like a peg in a secure place, and he will become a throne of honour to the house of his ancestors."

The word of the Lord. **Thanks be to God.**

Psalm 138

R. **Your steadfast love, O Lord, endures forever.
Do not forsake the work of your hands.**

I give you thanks, O Lord, with my whole heart;
before the Angels I sing your praise;
I bow down toward your holy temple, and give thanks
    to your name
for your steadfast love and your faithfulness. R.

For you have exalted your name
and your word above everything.
On the day I called, you answered me,
you increased my strength of soul. R.

For though the Lord is high, he regards the lowly;
but the haughty he perceives from far away.
Your steadfast love, O Lord, endures forever.
Do not forsake the work of your hands. R.

A reading from the Letter of Saint Paul to the Romans (11.33-36)

O the depth of the riches and wisdom and knowledge of God! How unsearchable are his judgments and how inscrutable his ways! "For who has known the mind of the Lord? Or who has been his counsellor?" "Or who has given a gift to him, to receive a gift in return?" For from him and through him and to him are all things. To him be the glory forever. Amen.

The word of the Lord. **Thanks be to God.**

A reading from the holy Gospel according to Matthew (16.13-20)

When Jesus came into the district of Caesarea Philippi, he asked his disciples, "Who do people say that the **Son of Man** is?" And they said, "Some say John the Baptist, but others Elijah, and still others Jeremiah or one of the Prophets."

He said to them, "But who do you say that I am?" Simon Peter answered, "You are the **Christ**, the Son of the living God."

And Jesus answered him, "Blessed are you, Simon son of Jonah! For flesh and blood has not revealed this to you, but my Father in heaven. And I tell you, you are **Peter**, and on this **rock** I will build my Church, and the gates of Hades will not prevail against it. I will give you the **keys** of the kingdom of heaven, and whatever you **bind** on earth will be bound in heaven, and whatever you loose on earth will be loosed in heaven."

Then Jesus sternly ordered the disciples not to tell anyone that he was the Christ.

The Gospel of the Lord. **Praise to you, Lord Jesus Christ.**

Key Words

Shebna's error was to construct a luxurious tomb at a time when many people were in great need. He should have used his wealth in a just way to take care of the needs of others, rather than to glorify himself.

House of Judah is one of the many names for the Israelites. Other names include House of David and House of Israel.

When Jesus began to preach, he called himself the **Son of Man**. This is another way of telling us that he was sent by God.

The Greek word for 'anointed' is **Christ**. The chosen person was anointed or blessed with holy oil and given a special mission. The Aramaic word meaning 'anointed' is Messiah (Jesus and his disciples spoke Aramaic).

When Simon shows both his understanding and faith in Jesus as the Messiah, Jesus gives him a new name — **Peter** (from the Greek word *petra* for **rock** or stone). In many other languages, the name Peter is also related to rock or stone (such as *pierre* in French). Jesus is saying that Peter's faith will be the foundation for the Church's future.

Keys are a symbol of power. Whoever has the keys can enter and leave at will; they can also allow or deny entry to others. Jesus uses this symbol to show that Peter is the person with this power in the early Church.

When Jesus promises Peter, "Whatever you **bind** on earth will be bound in heaven," he is letting Peter know that Jesus will be with him always, guiding his thoughts and actions through the presence of the Holy Spirit.

September 3
22nd Sunday in Ordinary Time

A reading from the book of the Prophet Jeremiah (20.7-9)

O Lord, you have enticed me, and I was enticed; you have overpowered me, and you have prevailed. I have become a laughingstock all day long; everyone mocks me. For whenever I speak, I must cry out, I must shout, "Violence and destruction!" For the word of the Lord has become for me a reproach and derision all day long.

If I say, "I will not mention him, or speak any more in his name," then within me there is something like a burning **fire** shut up in my bones; I am weary with holding it in, and I cannot.

The word of the Lord. **Thanks be to God.**

Psalm 63

R. **My soul thirsts for you, O Lord my God.**

O God, you are my God, I seek you,
my soul thirsts for you;
my flesh faints for you,
as in a dry and weary land where there is no water. R.

So I have looked upon you in the sanctuary,
beholding your power and glory.
Because your steadfast love is better than life,
my lips will praise you. R.

So I will bless you as long as I live;
I will lift up my hands and call on your name.
My soul is satisfied as with a rich feast,
and my mouth praises you with joyful lips. R.

For you have been my help,
and in the shadow of your wings I sing for joy.
My soul clings to you;
your right hand upholds me. R.

A reading from the Letter of Saint Paul to the Romans (12.1-2)

I appeal to you, brothers and sisters, by the mercies of God, to present your bodies as a living sacrifice, holy and acceptable to God, which is your **spiritual worship**. Do not be conformed to this world, but be transformed by the renewing of your minds, so that you may discern what is the will of God — what is good and acceptable and perfect.

The word of the Lord. **Thanks be to God.**

A reading from the holy Gospel according to Matthew (16.21-27)

Jesus began to show his disciples that he must go to Jerusalem and undergo great suffering at the hands of the elders and chief priests and scribes, and be killed, and on the third day be raised.

And Peter took Jesus aside and began to rebuke him, saying, "God forbid it, Lord! This must never happen to you." But he turned and said to Peter, "Get behind me, **Satan!** You are a stumbling block to me; for you are thinking not as God does, but as humans do."

Then Jesus told his disciples, "If anyone wants to become my follower, let him deny himself and take up his **cross** and follow me. For whoever wants to save their life will lose it, and whoever loses their life for my sake will find it. For what will it profit anyone to gain the whole world but forfeit their life? Or what will anyone give in return for their life?

"For the Son of Man is to come with his Angels in the glory of his Father, and then he will repay each according to their work."

The Gospel of the Lord. **Praise to you, Lord Jesus Christ.**

Key Words

Jeremiah lived about 600 years before Jesus. When Jeremiah was still a young boy, God called him to guide the people of Israel back to God. Many people ignored Jeremiah at first and sent him away. But when they faced serious problems and feared that God had stopped loving them, Jeremiah gave them hope that God would not abandon them.

Jeremiah found being a prophet very hard work and he wanted to give it up. But he found he couldn't because the voice of God within him was like an intense **fire** that he could not ignore.

Saint Paul reminds us that God does not want elaborate or expensive sacrifices when we worship. God wants us to offer ourselves and our lives. Paul calls this our **spiritual worship**.

Satan is one of the names given to the enemy of God and our strongest enemy. Satan works against God and tries to lead people away from God's love. Other names for Satan are the Evil One, Lucifer or the Devil.

To take up our **cross** means to accept all that comes with being human, the good and the bad alike, because we are called to follow the path taken by Jesus.

September 10

23rd Sunday in Ordinary Time

A reading from the book of the Prophet Ezekiel (33.7-9)

Thus says the Lord: "So you, O son of man, I have made a **watchman** for the house of Israel; whenever you hear a word from my mouth, you shall give them warning from me.

"If I say to the wicked, 'O wicked one, you shall surely die,' and you do not speak to warn the wicked to turn from their ways, the wicked person shall die in their iniquity, but their blood I will require at your hand.

"But if you warn the wicked person to turn from their ways, and they do not turn from their ways, they shall die in their iniquity, but you will have saved your life."

The word of the Lord. **Thanks be to God.**

Psalm 95

R. **O that today you would listen to the voice of the Lord. Do not harden your hearts!**

O come, let us sing to the Lord;
let us make a joyful noise to the rock of our salvation!
Let us come into his presence with thanksgiving;
let us make a joyful noise to him with songs of praise! R.

O come, let us worship and bow down,
let us kneel before the Lord, our Maker!
For he is our God, and we are the people of his pasture,
and the sheep of his hand. R.

O that today you would listen to his voice!
Do not harden your hearts, as at Meribah,
as on the day at Massah in the wilderness,
when your ancestors tested me,
and put me to the proof,
though they had seen my work. R.

A reading from the Letter of Saint Paul to the Romans (13.8-10)

Brothers and sisters: Owe no one anything, except to **love one another**; for the one who loves another has fulfilled the law.

The commandments, "You shall not commit adultery; You shall not murder; You shall not steal; You shall not covet"; and any other commandment, are summed up in this word, "Love your neighbour as yourself."

Love does no wrong to a neighbour; therefore, love is the fulfilling of the law.

The word of the Lord. **Thanks be to God.**

A reading from the holy Gospel according to Matthew (18.15-20)

Jesus spoke to his disciples. "If your brother or sister sins against you, go and **point out** the fault when the two of you are alone. If he or she listens to you, you have regained your brother or sister. But if the person does not listen, take one or two others along with you, so that every word may be confirmed by the evidence of two or three witnesses. If the person refuses to listen to them, tell it to the Church; and if that person refuses to listen even to the Church, let such a one be to you as a **Gentile** and a **tax collector**.

"Truly I tell you, whatever you bind on earth will be bound in heaven, and whatever you loose on earth will be loosed in heaven. Again, truly I tell you, if two of you agree on earth about anything you ask, it will be done for you by my Father in heaven. For **where two or three are gathered in my name**, I am there among them."

The Gospel of the Lord. **Praise to you, Lord Jesus Christ.**

Key Words

Ezekiel was the **watchman** or look-out for Israel because it was his mission to teach the people how to live as God wants and to warn them away from error and danger.

Love one another — these words sum up what every Christian must do. All the commandments and all that Jesus said and did have their foundation in this simple phrase.

Jesus tells us to **point out** to our friends anything we see them doing that we feel is wrong. But Jesus also tells us to do this with love in our hearts, with respect for the other person.

Gentiles are people who are not Jewish. At the time of Jesus, Gentiles could not participate fully in Jewish society because they were excluded from temple life.

The Jews didn't like **tax collectors** because they worked for the Romans who were enemies of Israel. Also, many tax collectors cheated people and took more money than they needed for taxes.

Jesus shows us that God listens to our prayers. It is especially important to pray with others — "**where two or three are gathered in my name**" — with all people who believe in God.

September 17
24th Sunday in Ordinary Time

A reading from the book of Sirach (27.30 – 28.7)

Anger and wrath, these are **abominations**, yet a sinner holds on to them. The vengeful person will face the Lord's vengeance, for he keeps a strict account of their sins. **Forgive** your neighbour the wrong that is done, and then your sins will be pardoned when you pray.

Does anyone harbour anger against another, and expect healing from the Lord? If one has no mercy toward another like oneself, can one then seek pardon for one's own sins? If one who is but flesh harbours wrath, who will make an atoning sacrifice for that person's sins?

Remember the end of your life, and set enmity aside; remember corruption and death, and be true to the commandments. Remember the commandments, and do not be angry with your neighbour; remember the covenant of the Most High, and overlook faults.

The word of the Lord. **Thanks be to God.**

Psalm 103

R. **The Lord is merciful and gracious;
slow to anger, and abounding in steadfast love.**

Bless the Lord, O my soul,
and all that is within me, bless his holy name.
Bless the Lord, O my soul,
and do not forget all his benefits. R.

It is the Lord who forgives all your iniquity,
who heals all your diseases,
who redeems your life from the Pit,
who crowns you with steadfast love and mercy. R.

He will not always accuse,
nor will he keep his anger forever.
He does not deal with us according to our sins,
nor repay us according to our **iniquities**. R.

For as the heavens are high above the earth,
so great is his steadfast love toward those who fear him;
as far as the east is from the west,
so far he removes our **transgressions** from us. R.

A reading from the Letter of Saint Paul to the Romans (14.7-9)

Brothers and sisters: We do not live to ourselves, and we do not die to ourselves. If we live, we live to the Lord, and if we die, we die to the Lord; so then, whether we live or whether we die, we are the Lord's. For to this end Christ died and lived again, so that he might be Lord of both the dead and the living.

The word of the Lord. **Thanks be to God.**

A reading from the holy Gospel according to Matthew (18.21-35)

Peter came and said to Jesus, "Lord, how often should I forgive my brother or sister if they sin against me? As many as **seven** times?" Jesus said to him, "Not seven times, but, I tell you, **seventy-seven** times.

"For this reason the kingdom of heaven may be compared to a king who wished to settle accounts with his slaves. When he began the reckoning, one who owed him **ten thousand talents** was brought to him; and, as he could not pay, his lord ordered him to be sold, together with his wife and children and all his possessions, and payment to be made. So the slave fell on his knees before him, saying, 'Have patience with me, and I will pay you everything.' The lord of that slave released him and forgave him the debt.

"But that same slave, as he went out, came upon one of his fellow slaves who owed him **a hundred denarii**; and seizing him by the throat, he said, 'Pay what you owe.' Then his fellow slave fell down and pleaded with him, 'Have patience with me, and I will pay you.' But he refused; then he went and threw him into prison until he would pay the debt.

"When his fellow slaves saw what had happened, they were greatly distressed, and they went and reported to their lord all that had taken place. Then his lord summoned him and said to him, 'You wicked slave! I forgave you all that debt because you pleaded with me. Should you not have had mercy on your fellow slave, as I had mercy on you?' And in anger his lord handed him over to be tortured until he would pay his entire debt.

"So my heavenly Father will also do to every one of you, if you do not forgive your brother or sister from your heart."

The Gospel of the Lord. **Praise to you, Lord Jesus Christ.**

Key Words

Abominations are hateful things, things that even make us feel sick. In this reading, Sirach is reminding us that when we hold onto our anger and wish evil on another person, we are offending God in the strongest possible way.

This verse in the reading, telling us to **forgive** our neighbour, sounds just like part of the Our Father: Forgive us our trespasses, as we forgive those who trespass against us. From the very beginning, God has called his people to be a forgiving people.

Iniquities and **transgressions** are other words for sins or trespasses — things we do to other people that are wrong, unjust or unkind.

The number **seven** indicates something complete, like seven days in a week — so Peter is suggesting that forgiving seven times would be enough. But Jesus replies with **seventy-seven** — a super-seven — to show that we must never stop forgiving others.

Jesus uses sums of money in this parable to show how extravagant God is in his mercy, and how stingy we can be in ours. **Ten thousand talents** is a huge debt — one that no person could ever hope to repay. **A hundred denarii** is a much smaller amount — a denarius represented a day's pay for a labourer.

September 24
25th Sunday in Ordinary Time

A reading from the book of the Prophet Isaiah
(55.6-9)

Seek the Lord while he may be found,
call upon him while he is near;
let the wicked person **forsake** their way,
and the unrighteous person their thoughts;
let that person return to the Lord that he may have mercy on them,
and to our God, for he will abundantly pardon.

For my **thoughts** are not your thoughts,
nor are your ways my ways, says the Lord.
For as the heavens are higher than the earth,
so are my ways higher than your ways
and my thoughts than your thoughts.

The word of the Lord. **Thanks be to God.**

Psalm 145

R. **The Lord is near to all who call on him.**

Every day I will bless you,
and praise your name forever and ever.
Great is the Lord, and greatly to be praised;
his greatness is unsearchable. R.

The Lord is gracious and merciful,
slow to anger and abounding in steadfast love.
The Lord is good to all,
and his compassion is over all that he has made. R.

The Lord is just in all his ways,
and kind in all his doings.
The Lord is near to all who call on him,
to all who call on him in truth. R.

A reading from the Letter of Saint Paul to the Philippians (1.20-24, 27)

Brothers and sisters: Christ will be **exalted** now as always in my body, whether by life or by death. For to me, living is Christ and dying is gain. If I am to live in the flesh, that means fruitful labour for me; and I do not know which I prefer. I am hard pressed between the two: my desire is to depart and be with Christ, for that is far better; but to remain in the flesh is more necessary for you. Live your life in a manner worthy of the Gospel of Christ.

The word of the Lord. **Thanks be to God.**

A reading from the holy Gospel according to Matthew (20.1-16)

Jesus spoke this parable to his disciples: "The **kingdom of heaven** is like a landowner who went out early in the morning to hire labourers for his **vineyard**. After agreeing with the labourers for the usual daily wage, he sent them into his vineyard. When he went out about nine o'clock, he saw others standing idle in the marketplace; and he said to them, 'You also go into the vineyard, and I will pay you whatever is right.' So they went.

"When he went out again about noon and about three o'clock, he did the same. And about five o'clock he went out and found others standing around; and he said to them, 'Why are you standing here idle all day?' They said to him, 'Because no one has hired us.' He said to them, 'You also go into the vineyard.'

"When evening came, the owner of the vineyard said to his manager, 'Call the labourers and give them their pay, beginning with the last and then going to the first.' When those hired about five o'clock came, each of them received the usual daily wage.

"Now when the first came, they thought they would receive more; but each of them also received the usual daily wage. And when they received it, they grumbled against the landowner, saying, 'These last worked only one hour, and you have made them equal to us who have borne the burden of the day and the scorching heat.' But he replied to one of them, 'Friend, I am doing you no wrong; did you not agree with me for the usual daily wage? Take what belongs to you and go; I choose to give to this last the same as I give to you. Am I not allowed to do what I choose with what belongs to me? Or are you envious because I am generous?'

"So the last will be first, and the first will be last."

The Gospel of the Lord. **Praise to you, Lord Jesus Christ.**

Key Words

To **forsake** means to abandon or give up something. Isaiah was telling the people of Israel that they had fallen away from God and needed to journey back to the Lord their God, giving up their wicked ways.

God's **thoughts** are wise and loving, full of compassion and mercy. We can trust in God, even though we cannot understand the greatness of God.

When he was in prison Saint Paul wrote to the **Philippians**, a community of Christians living in Philippi in Greece. He thanked them for their help and encouraged them to strengthen their faith in Jesus.

Saint Paul reminds us that when we hear the word of God and act on it, Jesus is **exalted** or praised through our actions.

In the **kingdom of heaven**, all people will be brought together in Jesus. We will all live like brothers and sisters, sharing in God's abundant love and mercy.

A **vineyard** is a farm where grapevines are grown. At the time of Jesus, there were many vineyards in Israel. Grapes are an important crop because wine is made from the grapes.

October 1

26th Sunday in Ordinary Time

A reading from the book of the Prophet Ezekiel (18.25-28)

Thus says the Lord: "You object, O House of Israel! You say, 'The way of the Lord is unfair.' Hear now, O house of Israel: Is my way unfair? Is it not your ways that are unfair?

"When the **righteous** person turns away from their righteousness and commits iniquity, they shall die for it; for the **iniquity** that they have committed they shall die.

"Again, when the wicked person turns away from the wickedness they have committed and does what is lawful and right, they shall save their life. Because that person **considered** and turned away from all the transgressions that they had committed, they shall surely live; they shall not die."

The word of the Lord. **Thanks be to God.**

Psalm 25

R. **Lord, be mindful of your mercy.**

Make me to know your ways, O Lord;
teach me your paths.
Lead me in your truth, and teach me,
for you are the God of my salvation. R.

Be mindful of your mercy, O Lord, and of your
steadfast love,
for they have been from of old.
According to your steadfast love remember me,
for the sake of your goodness, O Lord! R.

Good and upright is the Lord;
therefore he instructs sinners in the way.
He leads the humble in what is right,
and teaches the humble his way. R.

A reading from the Letter of Saint Paul to the Philippians (2.1-11)

The shorter version ends at the asterisks.

Brothers and sisters: If there is any encouragement in Christ, any consolation from love, any sharing in the Spirit, any compassion and sympathy, then make my joy complete: be of the same mind, having the same love, being in full accord and of one mind. Do nothing from selfish ambition or conceit, but in **humility** regard others as better than yourselves. Let each of you look not to your own interests, but to the interests of others.

Let the same mind be in you that was in Christ Jesus.

* * *

who, though he was in the form of God,
did not regard equality with God as something to be exploited,
but emptied himself, taking the form of a slave,
being born in human likeness.
And being found in human form,
he humbled himself
and became obedient to the point of death —
even death on a cross.

Therefore God highly exalted him
and gave him the name that is above every name,
so that at the name of Jesus every knee should bend,
in heaven and on earth and under the earth,
and every tongue should confess that Jesus Christ is Lord,
to the glory of God the Father.

The word of the Lord. **Thanks be to God.**

A reading from the holy Gospel according to Matthew (21.28-32)

Jesus said to the chief priests and the elders of the people: "What do you think? A man had two sons; he went to the first and said, 'Son, go and work in the vineyard today.' He answered, 'I will not'; but later he **changed his mind** and went. The father went to the second and said the same; and he answered, 'I am going, sir'; but he did not go. Which of the two did the will of his father?" They said, "The first."

Jesus said to them, "Truly I tell you, the tax collectors and the prostitutes are going into the kingdom of God ahead of you. For John came to you in the way of righteousness and you did not believe him, but the tax collectors and the prostitutes believed him; and even after you saw it, you did not change your minds and believe him."

The Gospel of the Lord. **Praise to you, Lord Jesus Christ.**

Key Words

Ezekiel was one of the most important prophets in Israel. He lived during a time when many of the people of Jerusalem were taken prisoner and forced to live in exile, in Babylon. The king and Ezekiel were taken away, too. Ezekiel helped the people follow God's ways even though they were far from home.

In the Old Testament, to be **righteous** means to follow the laws Moses gave to the people of Israel. This is the way to life in God; a life of sin is the way to death.

Iniquity is another word for sin. It is related to the word 'unequal' and means something that is very unjust or unfair — something that is wicked.

When we follow God's commandments, we show that we have **considered** or thought deeply about our way of life and are determined to live as children of God.

Humility means knowing we are children of God without feeling too important. We accept all the qualities God gave us — the ones we think are not so good as well as our talents or the things we do well.

When the son in the parable **changed his mind**, he regretted his earlier decision. He wanted to be an obedient child and show by his actions that he loved his father. In our lives, our actions should show that we are followers of Jesus.

A reading from the book of the Prophet Isaiah
(5.1-7)

Let me sing for **my beloved** my love song concerning his vineyard:

"My beloved had a vineyard on a very fertile hill. He dug it and cleared it of stones, and planted it with choice vines; he built a watchtower in the midst of it, and hewed out a wine vat in it; he expected it to yield grapes, but it yielded wild grapes.

"And now, inhabitants of Jerusalem and people of Judah, judge between me and my vineyard. What more was there to do for my vineyard that I have not done in it? When I expected it to yield grapes, why did it yield wild grapes?

"And now I will tell you what I will do to my vineyard. I will remove its hedge, and it shall be devoured; I will break down its wall, and it shall be trampled down. I will make it a **waste**; it shall not be pruned or hoed, and it shall be overgrown with **briers** and thorns; I will also command the clouds that they rain no rain upon it. For the vineyard of the Lord of hosts is the house of Israel, and the people of Judah are his pleasant planting; he expected justice, but saw **bloodshed**; righteousness, but heard a cry!"

The word of the Lord. **Thanks be to God.**

Psalm 80

R. **The vineyard of the Lord is the house of Israel.**

You brought a vine out of Egypt;
you drove out the nations and planted it.
It sent out its branches to the sea,
and its shoots to the River. R.

Why then have you broken down its walls,
so that all who pass along the way pluck its fruit?
The boar from the forest ravages it,
and all that move in the field feed on it. R.

Turn again, O God of hosts;
look down from heaven, and see;
have regard for this vine,
the stock that your right hand planted. R.

Then we will never turn back from you;
give us life, and we will call on your name.
Restore us, O Lord God of hosts;
let your face shine, that we may be saved. R.

A reading from the Letter of Saint Paul to the Philippians (4.6-9)

Brothers and sisters: Do not worry about anything, but in everything by prayer and supplication with thanksgiving let your requests be made known to God. And the peace of God, which surpasses all understanding, will guard your hearts and your minds in Christ Jesus.

Finally, brothers and sisters, whatever is true, whatever is honourable, whatever is just, whatever is pure, whatever is pleasing, whatever is commendable, if there is any excellence and if there is anything worthy of praise, think about these things. Keep on doing the things that you have learned and received and heard and seen in me, and the **God of peace** will be with you.

The word of the Lord. **Thanks be to God.**

A reading from the holy Gospel according to Matthew (21.33-43)

Jesus said to the chief priests and the **elders** of the people: "Listen to another parable. There was a landowner who planted a vineyard, put a fence around it, dug a **wine press** in it, and built a watchtower. Then he leased it to tenants and went to another country.

"When the harvest time had come, he sent his slaves to the tenants to collect his produce. But the tenants seized his slaves and beat one, killed another, and stoned another. Again he sent other slaves, more than the first; and they treated them in the same way.

"Finally he sent his son to them, saying, 'They will respect my son.' But when the tenants saw the son, they said to themselves, 'This is the heir; come, let us kill him and get his inheritance.' So they seized him, threw him out of the vineyard, and killed him.

"Now when the owner of the vineyard comes, what will he do to those tenants?" They said to him, "He will put those wretches to a miserable death, and lease the vineyard to other tenants who will give him the produce at the harvest time."

Jesus said to them, "Have you never read in the Scriptures:
'The stone that the builders rejected
has become the cornerstone;
this was the Lord's doing,
and it is amazing in our eyes'?
Therefore I tell you, the kingdom of God will be taken away from you and given to a people that produces the fruits of the kingdom."

The Gospel of the Lord. **Praise to you, Lord Jesus Christ.**

Key Words

My beloved is another way of saying 'the person I love.' Israel is God's vineyard and God cares for his vineyard with great love and attention. In fact, God sings a love song for his beloved!

A **waste** is a dry, lifeless place where nothing grows. It is ignored and brings nothing good to the community.

Briers are wild thorny plants that grow in untended fields. They discourage both people and animals from entering the field.

Justice promotes peace. But injustice brings about **bloodshed** and destruction. We must work for justice in our world.

God of peace is a name for God. When we follow what God teaches, peace becomes possible — not only peace between enemies, but peace in our hearts as well.

Elders are older people who have a great deal of life experience and wisdom. They hold a position of respect in society and they help us make wise choices.

A **wine press** is used to squeeze the juice from grapes, so that wine can be made from the juice. Presses are also used to make cider from apples and olive oil from olives.

October 15

28th Sunday in Ordinary Time

A reading from the book of the Prophet Isaiah
(25.6-10)

On this **mountain** the Lord of hosts will make for all peoples a **feast** of rich food, a feast of well-aged wines, of rich food filled with marrow, of well-aged wines strained clear.

And he will destroy on this mountain the shroud that is cast over all peoples, the sheet that is spread over all nations; he will swallow up death forever. Then the Lord God will wipe away the tears from all faces, and the disgrace of his people he will take away from all the earth, for the Lord has spoken.

It will be said on that day, "Lo, this is our God; we have waited for him, so that he might save us. This is the Lord for whom we have waited; let us be glad and rejoice in his salvation. For the hand of the Lord will rest on this mountain."

The word of the Lord. **Thanks be to God.**

Psalm 23

R. **I shall dwell in the house of the Lord my whole life long.**

The Lord is my shepherd, I shall not want.
He makes me lie down in green pastures;
he leads me beside still waters;
he restores my soul. R.

He leads me in right paths for his name's sake.
Even though I walk through the darkest valley,
    I fear no evil;
for you are with me;
your rod and your staff — they comfort me. R.

You prepare a table before me
in the presence of my enemies;
you anoint my head with oil;
my cup overflows. R.

R̠. **I shall dwell in the house of the Lord my whole life long.**

Surely goodness and mercy shall follow me
all the days of my life,
and I shall dwell in the house of the Lord
my whole life long. R̠.

A reading from the Letter of Saint Paul to the Philippians (4.12-14, 19-20)

Brothers and sisters: I know what it is to have little, and I know what it is to have plenty. In any and all circumstances I have learned the secret of being well-fed and of going hungry, of having plenty and of being in need. I can do all things through him who strengthens me. In any case, it was kind of you to share my distress.

My God will fully satisfy every need of yours according to his riches in glory in Christ Jesus. To our God and Father be glory forever and ever. **Amen**.

The word of the Lord. **Thanks be to God.**

A reading from the holy Gospel according to Matthew (22.1-14)

The shorter version ends with the asterisks.

Once more Jesus spoke to the chief priests and Pharisees in **parables**: "The **kingdom of heaven** may be compared to a king who gave a wedding banquet for his son. He sent his slaves to call those who had been invited to the wedding banquet, but they would not come.

"Again he sent other slaves, saying, 'Tell those who have been invited: "Look, I have prepared my dinner, my oxen and my fat calves have been slaughtered, and everything is ready; come to the wedding banquet."' But they made light of it and went away, one to his farm, another to his business, while the rest seized his slaves, mistreated them, and killed them. The king was enraged. He sent his troops, destroyed those murderers, and burned their city.

"Then he said to his slaves, 'The wedding is ready, but those invited were not worthy. Go therefore into the main streets, and invite everyone you find to the wedding banquet.' Those slaves went out into the streets and gathered all whom they found, both good and bad; so the wedding hall was filled with **guests**.

* * *

"But when the king came in to see the guests, he noticed a man there who was not wearing a wedding robe, and he said to him, 'Friend, how did you get in here without a wedding robe?' And he was speechless. Then the king said to the attendants, 'Bind him hand and foot, and throw him into the outer darkness, where there will be weeping and gnashing of teeth.' For many are called, but few are chosen."

The Gospel of the Lord. **Praise to you, Lord Jesus Christ.**

261

Key Words

In the Bible, the people of God often encounter God up a **mountain**. The mountain is a place that is close to God. It is where God gave Moses the Ten Commandments. Sometimes Jesus also went up the mountain to meet God, such as when he was transfigured.

A **feast** or banquet with delicious foods and fine wines represents the joyful celebration that God prepares for us. The Eucharist gives us a taste of this final celebration.

Amen is a Hebrew word that means 'so be it' or 'I know this is true.' By saying Amen after hearing or saying a prayer, we are agreeing with what it says.

Parables are brief stories or wise sayings that Jesus used when he was teaching. Jesus used everyday situations to help his listeners understand what he meant. The parables invite us to change our lives and turn to God.

Jesus came to tell us about the **kingdom of heaven**, where people will live peacefully, respecting others and recognizing God as the source of all our joys.

When we are **guests** at a celebration, we wear our best clothes and often bring a gift. This shows that the host and the occasion are important to us. It is the same when we come to Sunday Mass. We come prepared to celebrate, to be attentive, and to share our gifts with God and the community.

October 22

29th Sunday in Ordinary Time

A reading from the book of the Prophet Isaiah
(45.1, 4-6)

Thus says the Lord to his **anointed**, to Cyrus, whose right hand I have grasped to subdue nations before him and strip kings of their robes, to open doors before him — and the gates shall not be closed:

"For the sake of my servant Jacob, and Israel my chosen, I call you by your name, I surname you, though you do not know me. I am the Lord, and **there is no other**; besides me there is no god. I arm you, though you do not know me, so that all may know, from the rising of the sun and from the west, that there is no one besides me; I am the Lord, and there is no other."

The word of the Lord. **Thanks be to God.**

Psalm 96

R. **Ascribe to the Lord glory and strength.**

O sing to the Lord a new song;
sing to the Lord, all the earth.
Declare his glory among the nations,
his marvellous works among all the peoples. R.

For great is the Lord, and greatly to be praised;
he is to be revered above all gods.
For all the gods of the peoples are idols,
but the Lord made the heavens. R.

Ascribe to the Lord, O families of the peoples,
ascribe to the Lord glory and strength.
Ascribe to the Lord the glory due his name;
bring an offering, and come into his courts. R.

Worship the Lord in holy splendour;
tremble before him, all the earth.
Say among the nations, "The Lord is king!
He will judge the peoples with **equity**." R.

A reading from the first Letter of Saint Paul to the Thessalonians (1.1-5)

From Paul, Silvanus, and Timothy, to the Church of the Thessalonians in God the Father and the Lord Jesus Christ: Grace to you and peace.

We always give thanks to God for all of you and mention you in our prayers, constantly remembering before our God and Father your work of faith and labour of love and steadfastness of hope in our Lord Jesus Christ. For we know, brothers and sisters beloved by God, that he has chosen you, because our message of the Gospel came to you not in word only, but also in power and in the Holy Spirit and with full conviction.

The word of the Lord. **Thanks be to God.**

A reading from the holy Gospel according to Matthew (22.15-21)

The Pharisees went and plotted to entrap Jesus in what he said. So they sent their disciples to him, along with the Herodians, saying, "Teacher, we know that you are sincere, and teach the way of God in accordance with truth, and show deference to no one; for you do not regard people with partiality. Tell us, then, what you think. Is it lawful to pay taxes to the emperor, or not?"

But Jesus, aware of their malice, said, "Why are you putting me to the test, you **hypocrites?** Show me the coin used for the tax." And they brought him a **denarius**.

Then he said to them, "Whose head is this, and whose title?" They answered, "Caesar's." Then he said to them, "Give therefore to Caesar the things that are Caesar's, and to God the things that are God's."

The Gospel of the Lord. **Praise to you, Lord Jesus Christ.**

Key Words

To anoint means to bless with oil. In the Bible it can also mean to give someone a mission, an important job. Christians are **anointed** at baptism and confirmation: our mission is to live as Jesus taught us.

At the time of Isaiah, neighbouring peoples worshipped different gods. But through Isaiah the Lord told Israel that God wasn't just better than the other gods — God is the only God, and **there is no other** at all.

To judge with **equity** is to be fair to everyone. The psalmist praises God for his fairness to all people on earth.

Saint Paul wrote two letters to the **Thessalonians**, Christians who lived in Thessalonica, in Greece. In this letter Paul praises them and encourages them to continue to love one another.

Hypocrites are people who say one thing but do another. They may say they love God, but they don't act in a loving way. Such behaviour demeans the person, hurts others and insults God.

A **denarius** was a coin worth one day's pay. It had the profile of the Roman emperor stamped on one side of it.

October 29
30th Sunday in Ordinary Time

A reading from the book of Exodus (22.21-27)

Thus says the Lord: "You shall not wrong or **oppress** a resident alien, for you were aliens in the land of Egypt. You shall not **abuse** any widow or orphan. If you do abuse them, when they cry out to me, I will surely heed their cry; my wrath will burn, and I will kill you with the sword, and your wives shall become widows and your children orphans.

"If you lend money to my people, to the poor one among you, you shall not deal with them as a **creditor**; you shall not exact interest from them. If you take your neighbour's cloak in pawn, you shall restore it to that person before the sun goes down; for it may be their only clothing to use as cover; in what else shall that person sleep? And if that person cries out to me, I will listen, for I am compassionate."

The word of the Lord. **Thanks be to God.**

Psalm 18

R. **I love you, O Lord, my strength.**

I love you, O Lord, my strength.
The Lord is my rock, my fortress, and my deliverer.
My God, my rock in whom I take refuge,
my shield, and the source of my salvation,
    my stronghold. R.

I call upon the Lord, who is worthy to be praised,
so I shall be saved from my enemies.
From his temple he heard my voice,
and my cry to him reached his ears. R.

The Lord lives! Blessed be my rock,
and exalted be the God of my salvation.
Great triumphs he gives to his king,
and shows steadfast love to his anointed. R.

A reading from the first Letter of Saint Paul to the Thessalonians (1.5-10)

Brothers and sisters: You know what kind of persons we proved to be among you for your sake. And you became imitators of us and of the Lord, for in spite of persecution you received the word with **joy** inspired by the Holy Spirit, so that you became an example to all the believers in Macedonia and in Achaia. For the word of the Lord has sounded forth from you not only in Macedonia and Achaia, but in every place your faith in God has become known, so that we have no need to speak about it. For the people of those regions report about us what kind of welcome we had among you, and how you turned to God from idols, to serve a living and true God, and to wait for his Son from heaven, whom he raised from the dead — Jesus, who rescues us from the wrath that is coming.

The word of the Lord. **Thanks be to God.**

A reading from the holy Gospel according to Matthew (22.34-40)

When the **Pharisees** heard that Jesus had silenced the **Sadducees**, they gathered together, and one of them, a lawyer, asked him a question to test him. "Teacher, which commandment in the Law is the greatest?"

Jesus said to him, "'You shall love the Lord your God with all your heart, and with all your soul, and with all your mind.' This is the greatest and first commandment.

"And a second is like it: 'You shall love your **neighbour** as yourself.' On these two commandments hang all the Law and the Prophets."

The Gospel of the Lord. **Praise to you, Lord Jesus Christ.**

Key Words

To **oppress** or **abuse** someone is to take advantage of their work for personal benefit. The result is workers who are poorly paid and cannot provide the necessities of life for their families, while the oppressor grows richer and stronger.

A **creditor** is someone who lends money and charges interest on the loan. Repaying the loan can be a hardship for someone already living in poverty, such as the widows and orphans in the Bible, and can leave them in even greater need than before.

True **joy** is a gift of the Holy Spirit. It is a feeling that stays with us even if we have problems or troubles. Saint Paul tells us the source of this joy is knowing that we are God's beloved children.

The **Pharisees** and the **Sadducees** were people who belonged to two Jewish religious sects. Pharisees were very strict and believed religion consisted in obeying the rules, sometimes forgetting that love is the greatest rule. The Sadducees did not believe in the resurrection of the dead.

The word **neighbour** is related to the word 'nigh' which means 'near.' When Jesus says to love our neighbour, though, he doesn't mean just the people who are close to us — Jesus commands us to think of everyone as our neighbour and to love everyone as we love ourselves.

November 5

31st Sunday in
Ordinary Time

A reading from the book of the Prophet Malachi (1.14 – 2.2, 8-10)

"I am a great King," says the Lord of hosts, "and my name is reverenced among the nations.

"And now, O priests, this command is for you. If you will not listen, if you will not lay it to heart to give glory to my name," says the Lord of hosts, "then I will send the curse on you and I will curse your blessings; indeed I have already cursed them, because you do not lay it to heart.

"You have turned aside from the way; you have caused many to stumble by your instruction; you have corrupted the covenant of **Levi**," says the Lord of hosts, "and so I make you despised and abased before all the people, inasmuch as you have not kept my ways but have shown partiality in your instruction."

Have we not all one father? Has not one God created us? Why then are we faithless to one another, profaning the covenant of our ancestors?

The word of the Lord. **Thanks be to God.**

Psalm 131

R. **In you, Lord, I have found my peace.**

O Lord, my heart is not lifted up,
my eyes are not raised too high;
I do not occupy myself with things
too great and too marvellous for me. R.

But I have calmed and quieted my soul,
like a weaned child with its mother;
my soul is like the weaned child
that is with me. R.

O Israel, hope in the Lord
from this time on and forevermore. R.

A reading from the first Letter of Saint Paul to the Thessalonians (2.7-9, 13)

Brothers and sisters: Though we might have made demands as Apostles of Christ, we were gentle among you, like a nurse tenderly caring for her own children. So deeply do we care for you that we are determined to share with you not only the Gospel of God but also our own selves, because you have become very dear to us. You remember our labour and toil, brothers and sisters; we worked night and day, so that we might not burden any of you while we proclaimed to you the Gospel of God.

We also constantly give thanks to God for this, that when you received the word of God that you heard from us, you accepted it not as a human word but as what it really is, the word of God, which is also at work in you believers.

The word of the Lord. **Thanks be to God.**

A reading from the holy Gospel according to Matthew (23.1-12)

Then Jesus said to the crowds and to his disciples, "The scribes and the Pharisees sit **in Moses' chair**; therefore, do whatever they teach you and follow it; but do not do as they do, for they do not practise what they teach. They tie up heavy burdens, hard to bear, and lay them on the shoulders of others; but they themselves are unwilling to lift a finger to move them. They do all their deeds to be seen by others; for they make their **phylacteries** broad and their fringes long. They love to have the place of honour at banquets and the best seats in the synagogues, and to be greeted with respect in the marketplaces, and to have people call them rabbi.

"But you are not to be called rabbi, for you have one teacher, and you are all brothers and sisters. And call no one your father on earth, for you have one Father — the one in heaven. Nor are you to be called instructors, for you have one instructor, the Christ. The greatest among you will be your servant. Whoever exalts himself will be humbled, and whoever humbles himself will be exalted."

The Gospel of the Lord. **Praise to you, Lord Jesus Christ.**

Key Words

The book of the Prophet **Malachi** was written to try to awaken hope in the people of Israel at a time when religious practice had deteriorated. It was written 515 years before Christ.

Levi was one of Jacob's twelve sons and head of one of the twelve tribes of Israel. Levites were of the priestly class and therefore represented the covenant between God and Israel.

When Jesus says that the scribes and Pharisees sit **in Moses' chair**, he is recognizing that their authority to teach goes back to Moses who received the Ten Commandments from God.

Phylacteries are small boxes worn by Jewish men on the left wrist and on the forehead. The boxes contain Biblical texts; they are worn to help the wearer keep God's word always at hand and in mind. Jesus wants us to see that what counts is what is in our heart, and not what we wear on the outside.

November 12
32nd Sunday in Ordinary Time

A reading from the book of Wisdom (6.12-16)

Wisdom is radiant and unfading,
and she is easily discerned by those who love her,
and is found by those who seek her.
She hastens to make herself known to those who desire her.
One who rises early to seek her will have no difficulty,
for she will be found sitting at the gate.

To fix one's thought on her is perfect understanding,
and one who is vigilant on her account will soon be free
    from care,
because she goes about seeking those worthy of her,
and she graciously appears to them in their paths,
and meets them in every thought.
The word of the Lord. **Thanks be to God.**

Psalm 63

R. **My soul thirsts for you, O Lord my God.**

O God, you are my God, I seek you,
my soul thirsts for you;
my flesh faints for you,
as in a dry and weary land where there is no water. R.

So I have looked upon you in the **sanctuary**,
beholding your power and glory.
Because your steadfast love is better than life,
my lips will praise you. R.

So I will bless you as long as I live;
I will lift up my hands and call on your name.
My soul is satisfied as with a rich feast,
and my mouth praises you with joyful lips. R.

I think of you on my bed,
and meditate on you in the watches of the night;
for you have been my help,
and in the shadow of your wings I sing for joy. R.

A reading from the first Letter of Saint Paul to the Thessalonians (4.13-18)

We do not want you to be uninformed, brothers and sisters, about those who have died, so that you may not grieve as others do who have no hope. For since we believe that Jesus died and rose again, even so, through Jesus, God will bring with him those who have died. For this we declare to you by the word of the Lord, that we who are alive, who are left until the coming of the Lord, will by no means precede those who have died.

For the Lord himself, with a cry of command, with the Archangel's call and with the sound of God's trumpet, will descend from heaven, and the dead in Christ will rise first. Then we who are alive, who are left, will be caught up in the clouds together with them to meet the Lord in the air; and so we will be with the Lord forever. Therefore encourage one another with these words.

The word of the Lord. **Thanks be to God.**

A reading from the holy Gospel according to Matthew (25.1-13)

Jesus spoke this parable to the disciples: "The kingdom of heaven will be like this. Ten bridesmaids took their **lamps** and went to meet the bridegroom. Five of them were foolish, and five were wise. When the foolish took their lamps, they took no oil with them; but the wise took flasks of oil with their lamps. As the bridegroom was delayed, all of them became drowsy and slept.

"But at midnight there was a shout, 'Look! Here is the bridegroom! Come out to meet him.' Then all those bridesmaids got up and **trimmed** their lamps. The foolish said to the wise, 'Give us some of your oil, for our lamps are going out.' But the wise replied, 'No! There will not be enough for you and for us; you had better go to the dealers and buy some for yourselves.' And while they went to buy it, the bridegroom came, and those who were ready went with him into the wedding banquet; and the door was shut.

"Later the other bridesmaids came also, saying, 'Lord, lord, open to us.' But he replied, 'Truly I tell you, I do not know you.' Keep awake therefore, for you know neither the day nor the hour."

The Gospel of the Lord. **Praise to you, Lord Jesus Christ.**

Key Words

The **book of Wisdom** was written not long before Jesus was born. It urges us to make good decisions in life. It teaches about justice and fairness.

The **sanctuary** is the holiest part of the Jewish temple (from the same Latin word for 'holy' that gives us 'saint'). In a church, the sanctuary is the place where the word of God is proclaimed and the Eucharist is celebrated.

In the time of Jesus, wedding ceremonies were held at night. Therefore, the bridesmaids needed to have **lamps** ready to light the way when they went to meet the bridegroom. If their lamps went out, there was no other source of light until morning.

The bridesmaids used oil lamps with wicks. The wicks needed to be **trimmed** properly before lighting so that the lamps would burn brightly, cleanly and not too quickly.

November 19
33rd Sunday in Ordinary Time

A reading from the book of Proverbs
(31.10-13, 16-18, 20, 26, 28-31)

A capable wife, who can find her?
She is far more precious than jewels.
The heart of her husband trusts in her,
and he will have no lack of gain.
She does him good, and not harm,
all the days of her life.
She seeks **wool and flax**,
and works with willing hands.

She considers a field and buys it;
with the fruit of her hands she plants a vineyard.
She girds herself with strength,
and makes her arms strong.
She perceives that her merchandise is profitable.
Her lamp does not go out at night.

She opens her hand to the poor,
and reaches out her hands to the needy.
She opens her mouth with wisdom,
and the teaching of kindness is on her tongue.

Her children rise up and call her happy;
her husband too, and he praises her:
"Many women have done excellently,
but you surpass them all."
Charm is deceitful, and beauty is vain,
but a woman who fears the Lord is to be praised.
Give her a share in the fruit of her hands,
and let her works praise her in the city gates.

The word of the Lord. **Thanks be to God.**

Psalm 128

R̥. **Blessed is everyone who fears the Lord.**

Blessed is everyone who fears the Lord,
who walks in his ways.
You shall eat the fruit of the labour of your hands;
you shall be happy, and it shall go well with you. R̥.

Your wife will be like a fruitful vine
within your house;
your children will be like olive shoots
around your table. R.

Thus shall the man be blessed who fears the Lord.
The Lord bless you from Zion.
May you see the prosperity of Jerusalem
all the days of your life. R.

A reading from the first Letter of Saint Paul to the Thessalonians (5.1-6)

Now concerning the times and the seasons, brothers and sisters, you do not need to have anything written to you. For you yourselves know very well that the day of the Lord will come like a thief in the night. When they say, "There is peace and security," then sudden destruction will come upon them, as labour pains come upon a pregnant woman, and there will be no escape!

But you, beloved, are not in **darkness** for that day to surprise you like a thief. You are all children of **light** and children of the day; we are not of the night or of darkness. So then let us not fall asleep as others do, but let us keep awake and be **sober**.

The word of the Lord. **Thanks be to God.**

A reading from the holy Gospel according to Matthew (25.14-30)

For the shorter version, omit the indented parts.

Jesus spoke this parable to his disciples: "For it is as if a man, going on a journey, summoned his slaves and entrusted his property to them; to one he gave five **talents**, to another two, to another one, to each according to his ability. Then he went away.

"The one who had received the five talents went off at once and traded with them, and made five more talents. In the same way, the one who had the two talents made two more talents. But the one who had received the one talent went off and dug a hole in the ground and hid his master's money.

"After a long time the master of those slaves came and settled accounts with them. Then the one who had received the five talents came forward, bringing five more talents, saying, 'Master, you handed over to me five talents; see, I have made five more talents.' His master said to him, 'Well done, good and **trustworthy** slave; you have been trustworthy in a few things, I will put you in charge of many things; enter into the joy of your master.'

"And the one with the two talents also came forward, saying, 'Master, you handed over to me two talents; see, I have made two more talents. His master said to him, 'Well done, good and trustworthy slave; you have been trustworthy in a few things, I will put you in charge of many things; enter into the joy of your master.'

"Then the one who had received the one talent also came forward, saying, 'Master, I knew that you were a harsh man, reaping where you did not sow, and gathering where you did not scatter seed; so I was afraid, and I went and hid your talent in the ground. Here you have what is yours.'

"But his master replied, 'You wicked and lazy slave! You knew, did you, that I reap where I did not sow, and gather where I did not scatter? Then you ought to have invested my money with the bankers, and on my return I would have received what was my own with interest. So take the talent from him, and give it to the one with the ten talents. For to all those who have, more will be given, and they will have an abundance; but from those who have nothing, even what they have will be taken away. As for this worthless slave, throw him into the outer darkness, where there will be weeping and gnashing of teeth.'"

The Gospel of the Lord. **Praise to you, Lord Jesus Christ.**

Key Words

The book of Proverbs is a collection of popular sayings and parables filled with advice and wisdom.

Wool and flax are two natural materials that are used in making cloth and ropes, both of which were very important in ancient households. It was the woman's responsibility to spin the yarn and weave the cloth needed in a home.

Light is a symbol of everything good and especially of Jesus, who is the Light of the World. **Darkness** represents evil, especially turning away from God.

To live a **sober** life means to do things in moderation, without excess. If we do not live soberly, then we may be too caught up in our own pleasure and will not pay attention to the needs of others or to the Holy Spirit living within us.

The **talents** in the parable are coins that represent the gifts God has given to each one of us: our intelligence, our memory, our capacity for generosity and kindness. These gifts must be used for the good of all.

To be **trustworthy** is to be honest and dependable. When someone gives us a task or asks us to keep a secret and we keep our promises, we show that we value that person's friendship.

November 26

Our Lord Jesus Christ, King of the Universe

A reading from the book of the Prophet Ezekiel (34.11-12, 15-17)

Thus says the Lord God:
"I myself will search for **my sheep**,
and will seek them out.
As a **shepherd** seeks out his flock
when he is among his scattered sheep,
so I will seek out my sheep.
I will rescue them from all the places
to which they have been scattered
on a day of clouds and thick darkness.

"I myself will be the shepherd of my sheep,
and I will make them lie down,"
says the Lord God.
"I will seek the lost,
and I will bring back the strayed,
and I will bind up the injured,
and I will strengthen the weak,
but the fat and the strong I will destroy.
I will feed my sheep with justice.

"As for you, my flock," thus says the Lord God:
"I shall judge between one sheep and another,
between rams and goats."

The word of the Lord. **Thanks be to God.**

Psalm 23

R. **The Lord is my shepherd; I shall not want.**

The Lord is my shepherd, I shall not want.
He makes me lie down in green pastures;
he leads me beside still waters;
he restores my soul. R.

He leads me in right paths for his name's sake.
Even though I walk through the darkest valley,
    I fear no evil;
for you are with me;
your rod and your staff — they comfort me. R.

R̷. **The Lord is my shepherd; I shall not want.**

You prepare a table before me
in the presence of my enemies;
you anoint my head with oil;
my cup overflows. R̷.

Surely goodness and mercy shall follow me
all the days of my life,
and I shall dwell in the house of the Lord
my whole life long. R̷.

A reading from the first Letter of Saint Paul to the Corinthians (15.20-26, 28)

Brothers and sisters: Christ has been raised from the dead, the **first fruits** of those who have fallen asleep. For since death came through a man, the resurrection of the dead has also come through a man; for as all die in Adam, so all will be made alive in Christ. But each in his own order: Christ the first fruits, then at his **coming** those who belong to Christ.

Then comes the end, when he hands over the kingdom to God the Father, after he has destroyed every ruler and every authority and power. For he must reign until he has put all his enemies under his feet. The last enemy to be destroyed is death.

When all things are subjected to him, then the Son himself will also be subjected to the one who put all things in subjection under him, so that God may be all in all.

The word of the Lord. **Thanks be to God.**

A reading from the holy Gospel according to Matthew (25.31-46)

Jesus said to his **disciples**: "When the Son of Man comes in his glory, and all the Angels with him, then he will sit on the throne of his glory. All the nations will be gathered before him, and he will separate people one from another as a shepherd separates the sheep from the goats, and he will put the sheep at his right hand and the goats at the left.

"Then the king will say to those at his right hand, 'Come, you that are blessed by my Father, inherit the kingdom prepared for you from the foundation of the world; for I was hungry and you gave me food, I was thirsty and you gave me something to drink, I was a stranger and you welcomed me, I was naked and you gave me clothing, I was sick and you took care of me, I was in prison and you visited me.'

"Then the righteous will answer him, 'Lord, when was it that we saw you hungry and gave you food, or thirsty and gave you something to drink? And when was it that we saw you a stranger and welcomed you, or naked and gave you clothing? And when was it that we saw you sick or in prison and visited you?' And the king will answer them, 'Truly I tell you, just as you did it to one of the least of these brothers and sisters of mine, you did it to me.'

"Then he will say to those at his left hand, 'You that are accursed, depart from me into the eternal fire prepared for the devil and his angels; for I was hungry and you gave me no food, I was thirsty and you gave me nothing to drink, I was a stranger and you did not welcome me, naked and you did not give me clothing, sick and in prison and you did not visit me.'

"Then they also will answer, 'Lord, when was it that we saw you hungry or thirsty or a stranger or naked or sick or in prison, and did not take care of you?' Then he will answer them, 'Truly I tell you, just as you did not do it to one of the least of these, you did not do it to me.' And these will go away into eternal punishment, but the righteous into eternal life."

The Gospel of the Lord. **Praise to you, Lord Jesus Christ.**

Key Words

Ezekiel was one of the most important prophets in Israel. He lived during a time when many of the people of Jerusalem were taken prisoner and forced to live in exile, in Babylon. The king and Ezekiel were taken away, too. Ezekiel helped the people follow God's ways even though they were far from home.

God calls his people **my sheep** to show how valuable we are to God. Because they provide wool for clothing as well as meat for food, sheep are very important animals. A community's survival could depend on the safety and health of its sheep.

A **shepherd** is someone who takes care of a flock of sheep. He would spend days or weeks with his flock, sleeping with them and making sure they were always safe. God loves us with the same constant care.

The **Corinthians** were a community of Christians who lived in Corinth, a city in Greece. Saint Paul wrote them several letters, two of which are in the Bible.

First fruits were the first crops collected at harvest time. These were offered to God. Saint Paul tells us that Jesus is the first fruits of salvation, the first to die and rise again.

Christ's **coming** or advent is his return at the end of time. All history is longing for Christ's return, when God's plan of salvation will be complete.

A **disciple** is a person who follows the teachings of a master and helps to spread these teachings. Jesus was such a master; he had many disciples, including us.

Mealtime Prayers

Grace before Meals

Bless us, O Lord,
and these your gifts
which we are about to receive
from your bounty.
Through Christ our Lord. Amen.

* * *

For food in a world where many walk in hunger,
for friends in a world where many walk alone,
for faith in a world where many walk in fear,
we give you thanks, O God. Amen.

* * *

God is great, God is good!
Let us thank God for our food. Amen.

* * *

Be present at our table, Lord.
Be here and everywhere adored.
Your creatures bless
and grant that we may feast
in paradise with you. Amen.

Grace after Meals

We give you thanks, Almighty God, for these and all the benefits
we receive from your bounty. Through Christ our Lord. Amen.

* * *

Blessed be the name of the Lord.
Now and forever. Amen.

Morning Prayers

A Child's Prayer for Morning

Now, before I run to play,
let me not forget to pray
to God who kept me through the night
and waked me with the morning light.

Help me, Lord, to love you more
than I have ever loved before.
In my work and in my play
please be with me through the day.
Amen.

Morning Prayer

Dear God, we thank you for this day.
We thank you for our families and friends.
We thank you for our classmates.
Be with us as we work and play today.
Help us always to be kind to each other.
We pray in the name of the Father,
and of the Son and of the Holy Spirit. Amen.

Heather Reid, *Let's Pray! Prayers for the Elementary Classroom* (Ottawa: Novalis, 2006).

Angel of God

Angel of God, my guardian dear,
to whom God's love entrusts me here,
ever this day be at my side,
to light and guard, to rule and guide.
Amen.

Evening Prayers

Children's Bedtime Prayer

Now I lay me down to sleep,
I pray you, Lord, your child to keep.
Your love will guard me through the night
and wake me with the morning light. Amen.

Child's Evening Prayer

I hear no voice, I feel no touch,
I see no glory bright;
but yet I know that God is near,
in darkness as in light.

He watches ever by my side,
and hears my whispered prayer:
the Father for his little child
both night and day does care.

God Hear My Prayer

God in heaven hear my prayer,
keep me in your loving care.
Be my guide in all I do,
bless all those who love me too.
Amen.

Prayers for Family

Family Prayer

Father, what love you have given us.
May we love as you would have us love.
Teach us to be kind to each other,
patient and gentle with one another.
Help us to bear all things together,
to see in our love, your love,
through Christ our Lord. Amen.

World Meeting of Families Prayer

God and Father of us all,
in Jesus, your Son and our Saviour,
you have made us
your sons and daughters
in the family of the Church.

May your grace and love
help our families
in every part of the world
be united to one another
in fidelity to the Gospel.

May the example of the Holy Family,
with the aid of your Holy Spirit,
guide all families, especially those most troubled,
to be homes of communion and prayer
and to always seek your truth and live in your love.

Through Christ our Lord. Amen.

Jesus, Mary and Joseph,
Pray for us!

Prayer of Gratitude for a Family

Loving God,

Thank you for the gift of my family.
(Pause to name each person in the family.)

Thank you for the times we have
to be together.
(Pause to name a particular way of being together.)

Thank you for the ways in which we care
for each other.
(Pause to name a specific act of kindness.)

May the joy and affection we share increase
each and every day.

With gratitude for your bountiful love, I pray. Amen.

Kathy Hendricks, *Pocket Prayers for Parents* (Toronto: Novalis, 2014), p. 31.

More Prayers

Prayer for Friends

Loving God, you are the best friend we can have.
We ask today that you help us to be good friends to each other.
Help us to be fair, kind and unselfish.
Keep our friends safe and happy.
Bless us and bless all friends in this community.
We pray in the name of Jesus,
who was always the friend of children. Amen.

Heather Reid, *Let's Pray! Prayers for the Elementary Classroom* (Ottawa: Novalis, 2006).

In the Silence

If we really want to pray,
we must first learn to listen,
for in the silence of the heart,
God speaks.

Saint Teresa of Calcutta

Prayer for the Birthday Child

May God bless you with every good gift
and surround you with love and happiness.
May Jesus be your friend and guide
all the days of your life.
May the Spirit of God guide your footsteps
in the path of truth. Amen.

Prayer for Pets

Dear Father, hear and bless
your beasts and singing birds,
and guard with care and tenderness
small things that have no words. Amen.

When Someone Has Died

Lord God, hear our cries.
Grant us comfort in our sadness,
gently wipe away our tears,
and give us courage in the days ahead.
We ask this through Christ our Lord. Amen.

Prayer for Student / Teacher Who Is Sick

Gracious God, _____ is sick right now. We pray for
(him/her/them) and ask that they get better quickly and be able
to return to us. Bless all nurses, doctors and everyone who cares
for people who are ill. May all sick people find comfort through
their families and friends. We ask this in the name of Jesus, who
healed many people. Amen.

Heather Reid, *Let's Pray: Prayers for the Elementary Classroom*
(Ottawa: Novalis, 2007), p. 61.

Daily Prayers for School

Prayer for the Beginning of the School Day

God of wisdom,
you call us to grow in your grace
with hearts to love you,
with souls open to you,
with minds to learn from you.
Help us to see beyond distractions
and keep our vision clear –
a vision of your reign.
Amen.

Prayer at the Closing of the School Day

Loving God,
our creator, our friend, our companion,
bless our journey of learning.
Refresh our souls and renew our spirits.
Lead us in paths of wisdom,
compassion and understanding.
Bless us with an enduring love of learning.
May the Holy Spirit flow freely
through the classrooms and halls of our school,
through the rooms and gardens of our home,
through our churches and our nation.
We make this prayer in the name of Jesus.
Amen.

Lisa Freemantle and Les Miller, *Words for the Journey: Ten-Minute Prayer Services for Teachers and Administrators* (Toronto: Novalis, 2009), p. 19.

Sacraments: A Gift from God

Sacraments are rituals through which we receive God's grace. Grace is the gift of God's love and strength, given freely to us to help us lead good and just lives. Sacraments always involve signs appealing to our senses that point to God's saving presence in our lives. Baptism requires water, for example, and when we are confirmed, we are anointed with a special oil called chrism.

The seven sacraments of the Catholic Church are **Baptism, Reconciliation, Eucharist, Confirmation, Marriage, Holy Orders** and the **Anointing of the Sick**.

Sometimes you will hear people refer to **Sacraments of Initiation, Sacraments of Healing**, and **Sacraments of Service**.

The **Sacraments of Initiation** — Baptism, Eucharist and Confirmation — help welcome us into a life of faith.

The **Sacraments of Healing** are Reconciliation and the Anointing of the Sick. Reconciliation helps us when our actions have injured our relationship with God, while the Anointing of the Sick helps us physically, mentally and spiritually when we face illness and suffering.

The **Sacraments of Service** — Marriage and Holy Orders (priesthood) — are linked to our call to serve others.

The sacraments of Baptism, Confirmation and Holy Orders can only be received once. As Catholics, we believe that when these sacraments are received, they leave a lasting mark — or seal — on the soul.

The Rosary

In the Rosary we focus on 20 events or mysteries in the life and death of Jesus and meditate on how we share with Mary in the saving work of Christ. Reading a relevant passage from the Bible can help us to understand better a particular mystery of the Rosary. The Bible references below are suggestions; other biblical texts can also be used for meditation.

- Begin the Rosary at the crucifix by praying the Apostles' Creed
- At each large bead, pray the Lord's Prayer
- At each small bead, pray the Hail Mary
- At the first three beads it is customary to pray a Hail Mary for each of the gifts of faith, hope, and love
- For each mystery, begin with the Lord's Prayer, then recite the Hail Mary ten times, and end with Glory Be to the Father.

The Five Joyful Mysteries:

The Annunciation (Luke 1.26-38)
The Visitation (Luke 1.39-56)
The Nativity (Luke 2.1-20)
The Presentation (Luke 2.22-38)
The Finding in the Temple (Luke 2.41-52)

The Five Mysteries of Light:

The Baptism in the Jordan (Matthew 3.13-17)
The Wedding at Cana (John 2.1-12)
The Proclamation of the Kingdom (Mark 1.15)
The Transfiguration (Luke 9.28-36)
The First Eucharist (Matthew 26.26-29)

The Five Sorrowful Mysteries:

The Agony in the Garden (Matthew 26.36-56)
The Scourging at the Pillar (Matthew 27.20-26)
The Crowning with Thorns (Matthew 27.27-30)
The Carrying of the Cross (Matthew 27.31-33)
The Crucifixion (Matthew 27.34-60)

The Five Glorious Mysteries:

The Resurrection (John 20.1-18)
The Ascension (Acts 1.9-11)
The Descent of the Holy Spirit (John 20.19-23)
The Assumption of Mary (John 11.26)
The Crowning of Mary (Philippians 2.1-11)

A Young Person's Examination of Conscience

For use in preparing for the Sacrament of Reconciliation, based on The Ten Commandments

1. **God Comes First**
   - *Did I pray each day?*
   - *Did I act with respect in church?*
   - *Did I participate at Mass?*

2. **God's Name Is Holy**
   - *Did I always use God's name in the right way?*
   - *Did I treat and talk about holy things with respect?*

3. **God's Day Is Holy**
   - *Did I go to Mass on Sundays and Holy Days?*
   - *Did I miss Mass through my own fault?*

4. **Honour Mom & Dad**
   - *Did I obey my parents?*
   - *Did I treat them with respect?*
   - *Was I obedient and respectful to my teachers?*

5. **Do Not Kill**
   - *Have I been kind to my siblings and friends?*
   - *Did I hit or hurt anyone?*
   - *Did I harm anyone with mean or cruel words?*

6. **Be pure**
   - *Were my thoughts and actions good and pure?*
   - *Have I been careful to watch good movies and TV shows?*

7. **Do Not Steal**
   - *Have I always been honest?*
   - *Did I take anything that doesn't belong to me?*

8. **Do Not Lie**
   - *Have I always told the truth?*
   - *Have I spread rumours?*
   - *Have I been quiet about something when I should have spoken up?*

9. **Do Not Want Other People** and
10. **Do Not Want Their Things**
    - *Have I been satisfied with what I have?*
    - *Have I been jealous of another's things, toys or belongings?*
    - *Am I thankful for what I have?*

Year A and the Gospel of Matthew

The Gospels of Matthew, Mark and Luke are known as the synoptic gospels, a name which refers to the fact that these three books of the New Testament contain similar material, offering synopsis – or summary – of the life and ministry of Jesus.

Each year, the gospel we hear on the majority of the Sundays in Ordinary Time that year rotates through these three books. This year (2016-2017) is what is known as Year A, the year which focuses on the Gospel of Matthew.

The Gospel of Matthew is the first book of the New Testament. It was written around 85 CE in one of the cities of Syria or Palestine. We do not know who the author was, but our tradition associates him with Matthew the tax collector in Matthew 9.9.

This Gospel tells us how Jesus, who had been rejected by Israel, sends his disciples to preach his Gospel to the whole world. The Gospel tells us about the Kingdom of God which God gives us, and teaches us how to live our lives.

The Liturgical Year

The readings for Sunday Mass and feast days change according to the liturgical calendar.

What is the liturgical year?

Throughout the year, Christians celebrate together important moments in Jesus' life. This is the liturgical year. There are five seasons: Advent, Christmas, Lent, Easter and Ordinary Time.

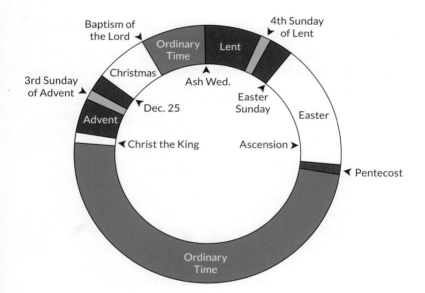

Advent is a time of waiting. It begins 4 weeks before Christmas. We prepare to welcome Jesus.

Christmas time celebrates the life of Jesus from his birth to his baptism. It includes Epiphany: Jesus welcomes the whole world.

During the 40 days of **Lent** we prepare for the great feast of Easter, the most important moment of the year.

Easter time is a season to celebrate Jesus' victory over death. It lasts from Easter Sunday to Pentecost, when the Holy Spirit comes upon the disciples.

The season in green above is called **Ordinary Time** because the Sundays are arranged using 'ordinal numbers.' It recounts many of the things Jesus did and said during his lifetime.

Celebrating Our Faith throughout the Week

As Mass ends, the priest dismisses us with one of several prayers: "Go forth, the Mass is ended," for example, or "Go and announce the Gospel of the Lord." As people of faith, we are called to carry all that we have celebrated at Mass out into our daily lives.

There are several ways to do this:

- Prepare for Mass by reading the coming Sunday's first and second readings, the Psalm and the gospel in advance, so that you are familiar with what you will hear at Mass. Try imagining yourself in the gospel story, witnessing first-hand the story you will hear. Who might you be? What would your reaction be if you were to hear Jesus tell a parable? How would you feel if you were to witness Jesus perform a miracle? What must it have been like to travel with Jesus and listen to him teach and preach?

- After you have heard the gospel proclaimed at Mass, ask yourself what message or idea really made an impression on you. Think about that throughout the week. If there is a phrase or passage that particularly appealed to you, try reciting it to yourself throughout the week. Think of ways it relates to you and to the world today.

- Listen closely to the priest's homily and ask yourself what you have learned from it. Reflect on that point throughout the week.

- Listen to the Prayer of the Faithful and remember who and what were being prayed for at Mass. Keep these petitions in mind as you say your prayers during the week. As you leave Mass, say to yourself, "This week I will pray for _____."

ORDER TODAY!

Sunday Missal for Young Catholics 2017-2018 and Living with Christ Sunday Missal 2017-2018

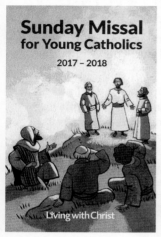

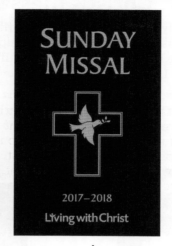

ONLY $10.95
Call for quantity prices.

ONLY $6.00
Call for quantity prices.

QTY	ITEM NO.	Title	Unit Price	Total
	196771	Sunday Missal for Young Catholics 2017-2018	$10.95	
	196772	Living with Christ Sunday Missal 2017-2018	$6.00	

*All orders must be prepaid. Price is subject to change without notice.

Shipping:

Shipping and Handling:
$1.00 to $60.00 . . . . $7.00
$61.00 to $99.00 . . .$8.00
$100.00 and up . . . . .Free

Order Total:

Name:

Address:

City: Prov.:   Postal Code:

Email: Telephone:

Payment enclosed (please do not send cash) *or* Charge my: ☐ Visa ☐ Mastercard

Name on Card:

Card Number: Exp.: /   Signature:

TO ORDER Call: 1-800-387-7164 Fax: 1-855-393-1555 E-mail: resources@novalis.ca

Living with Christ — Subscription Order Form

Receive Christ's message every day!

This monthly missalette provides a fitting way to enter more fully into the Mass and is designed to accompany you in your prayer life. Add the PLUS and receive a beautiful daily devotional for Advent and Lent.

☑ **YES!** Please send me *Living with Christ* for 1 year – that's 14 issues (1 per month plus a special issue for Christmas 2016 and Easter 2017) or 14 issues PLUS *Word Made Flesh* and *Sacred Journey* as specified below:

☐ **PLUS Edition**
$43.50/ yr (+tax)

☐ **Essential Edition**
$38.50/yr (+tax)

PLUS Edition: With tax, in QC, NS: $50.01, ON, NB, NL, MB: $49.16 Rest of Canada: $45.68
Essential Edition: With tax, in QC, NS: $44.26, ON, NB, NL, MB: $43.51 Rest of Canada: $40.43

Payment Methods: Cheque (Made out to Bayard Presse Canada), Visa or Mastercard

Name: _____ Client # _____

Apt: _____ Address: _____

City: _____ Prov.: _____ Postal Code: _____

Email: _____ Telephone: _____

☐ Enclosed is my cheque/money order (do not send cash) *or* Charge my: ☐ Visa ☐ Mastercard

Card Number: _____ Exp.: ___ / ___

Signature: _____

Subscription to be paid in CDN $ in Canada. Outside of Canada please call for prices. Special offer expires June 30, 2017.
On occasion, we make our customer list available to carefully screened companies or organizations for mailing. Do you wish to be excluded from these mailings? ☐ Yes.

P.O Box 11050, Centre-Ville Stn, Montreal, QC, H3C 4Y6
Tel: 1-800-387-7164 (US & Canada)
Email: living@novalis.ca